Level Up!
The Guide to Great
Video Game Design

2nd Edition

Scott Rogers

WILEY

This edition first published 2014

© 2014 John Wiley and Sons, Ltd.

Registered office

John Wiley & Sons Ltd, The Atrium, Southern Gate, Chichester, West Sussex, PO19 8SQ, United Kingdom

For details of our global editorial offices, for customer services and for information about how to apply for permission to reuse the copyright material in this book please see our website at www.wiley.com.

A catalogue record for this book is available from the British Library.

ISBN 978-1-118-87716-6 (paperback); ISBN 978-1-118-87719-7 (ePub); 978-1-118-87721-0 (ePDF)

Set in 10/12 Chaparral Pro-Light by SPS/TCS

Printed in the U.S. by Bind-Rite

Copyright Information

Please note that the following characters and works are copyrighted to the following corporations:

Publisher's Acknowledgements

Some of the people who helped bring this book to market include the following:

Editorial and Production

VP Consumer and Technology Publishing Director: Michelle Leete

Associate Director–Book Content Management: Martin Tribe

Associate Publisher: Chris Webb

Associate Commissioning Editor: Ellie Scott

Senior Project Editor: Sara Shlaer

Copy Editor: Chuck Hutchinson

Technical Editor: Noah Stein

Editorial Managers: Jodi Jensen, Rev Mengle

Editorial Assistant: Annie Sullivan

Marketing

Marketing Manager: Lorna Mein

Marketing Executive: Polly Thomas

Contents

Foreword

LIKE A MAGICIAN laying bare the means with which he amazes his audience, Scott Rogers in this, the second edition of *Level Up!* reveals the tricks of the trade for creating compelling video games.

A number of game designers have attempted this feat in the past, but Scott's great book provides something rare and important: a breaking down of and then a deep dive into the specific elements that must come together to create engaging interactive entertainment.

The fact that this book does that important work with a breezy, fun writing style and silly cartoons is a testament to Scott's abilities as a game designer; for the best designers are always aware that no matter how complicated the section of gameplay, the most important rule is to keep things engaging! This book—like Scott's games—does that in spades!

Readers across the spectrum of experience will find much to love and learn in this fun, giant, and necessary book. Folks new to the medium will be amazed at just how much thought goes into creating 'fun.' And experienced game designers who, like myself, have been doing this stuff by gut for decades will be stunned as they discover that there is indeed a method to the madness. Many times reading this book I caught myself thinking, "Oh, THAT'S why that works!"

As you turn the page, know that you are in for a treat! I look forward to playing the games you create after having taken in the great knowledge this book contains!

Best of luck—and enjoy!

David Jaffe, Creative director of the *Twisted Metal* series and *God of War* San Diego, CA
December 2013

Press Start!

If You Are Anything Like Me . . .

. . . **YOU READ THE** first page of a book before you buy it. I find that if I like the first page, I'll probably like the whole thing. I have noticed that many books have an exciting excerpt on the first page in order to grab the reader's interest, such as:

> *The skeleton dragon grabbed the helicopter with bony talons and shook it so hard that Jack's teeth rattled. Evelyn fought at the controls, attempting any maneuver that would free the copter from beast's unyielding clutches. "Hang on!" she screamed over the engine's tortured whine. "We're going down!" The world whirled around and around as the copter and dragon performed a death waltz. Jack didn't remember the copter slamming hard into the skyscraper or the crash or the dragon's bones raining down or being thrown from the wreckage—until Evelyn shook him into consciousness. "Jack! Jack!" she said. "We need to move. Now!" "What's the hurry, Sis? That dragon's toast." Then his eyes finally focused. On the cemetery gate. On the crooked gravestones. On the zombies pulling themselves from the dirt. Jack thought, "Nuts. I should have never opened that book."*

Not that I would ever resort to such cheap tactics in *this* book. I have also noticed that some books try to gain respectability by publishing a positive quote from an industry professional or famous person on their first page:

> *I learned more from reading the first page of the second edition of* Level Up! The Book of Great Video Game Design *than I learned from working for 25 years in the video game industry!*
>
> *–A very famous game designer*[1]

---

[1] No doubt you are smart enough to have realized that this isn't a real quote, because there isn't a very famous game designer. Unless you count Shigeru Miyamoto, the creator of Mario. Drat! I should have translated the quote into Japanese!

You obviously don't need someone else to tell you how to make up your mind. Just by picking up this book, I can tell you are a discriminating reader. I can also tell you are seeking the straight truth on the creation of video games. This book will teach you the who, what, where and, most importantly, how to design video games. If you have an interest in arcade games, boss fights, chili, deadly traps, ergonomics, fun, giant hydras, haunted mansions, islands and alleys, jumps, killer bunnies, leitmotifs, Mexican pizza, non-player characters, one-sheet designs, pitch sessions, quests, robotic chickens, smart bombs, the triangle of weirdness, unfun, violence, whack-a-mole, XXX, Y-axis and zombies, then this is the book for you.

Before we start, keep in mind that there are many ways to approach game design. All of them are valid, as long as they can communicate the designer's ideas. The tricks and techniques found in this second edition of *Level Up!* are MY WAYS of creating game design.

Another quick reminder: when I say "I designed a game," this is an oversimplification. Video games are created by many, many, many talented people (you'll be introduced to them shortly) and to give the impression that I did all the work myself is not only incorrect but egotistical.[2] There is no "I" in team.[3]

The majority of the games I've helped design were single player action games, so many of the examples found in this edition of *Level Up!* are skewed towards that perspective. It's just the way I think. But I have also found that most of the gameplay concepts are transferable to many different genres of games. It won't be too hard for you to translate my advice to your own game, no matter what the genre.

Another thing before we get started. If you are looking for a single chapter about gameplay, don't bother. Because EVERY chapter in this book is about gameplay. You should be thinking about gameplay all the time and how things affect the player, even when designing passive elements like cutscenes, monetization models, and pause screens.

Since you have made it this far, I may as well start by actually telling you the bad news first. Making video games is very hard work.[4] I have worked in video games for over 20 years and on games that have sold millions of copies.

But in that time, I have learned that making video games is also the best job in the world. It can be thrilling, frustrating, rewarding, nerve-wracking, hectic, boring, vomit-inducing, and just plain fun.

---

[2] It's a small industry. No one can afford to make enemies! Be a nice, hardworking person and you'll go far.

[3] Ironically, there is a "me."

[4] I once had an employer who would walk the halls of our office muttering how "video games are a haaaard business." I used to laugh at him back then, but I don't any more. He was right.

No, You Can't Have My Job

Over the course of my career, I came up with some **Clever Ideas** and learned some **Universal Truths.** For your convenience, I have added these at the end of each "level."

I also learned a couple of **very important things.** You can tell they are **very important** because they are written in all uppercase letters. The first **very important thing** I learned was:

GAME DESIGNERS HAVE MORE FUN

I know this, because my first job in the video game industry was as an artist.[5] Back in those 16-bit days, video game artists drew images with pixels. There are several great 16-bit artists, like Paul Robertson and the teams that made the Metal Slug and classic Capcom fighting games; but for me, drawing pictures out of pixels is like drawing with bathroom tiles. Here is what a drawing I made out of pixels looks like:

Anyway, as I was "pushing pixels" I heard the sound of raucous laughter coming from the group of cubicles next to mine. I peered over the wall to see a bunch of video game designers yukking it up and have a good ol' time. For the record, I was not having a good ol' time pushing pixels. I realized, "Those game designers are having more fun than I am! Making video games should be fun! I want to have fun! I want to become a game designer too!" And so I did. I eventually worked my way up the ladder to become a game designer. After I became a real game designer, I learned the second **very important thing:**

NO ONE ON YOUR TEAM WANTS TO READ
YOUR DESIGN DOCUMENT

This is a horrible thing to discover, but it is something every game designer needs to hear. Here I was, a brand new game designer with brand new game designs ready to go, and no one wanted to read any of them! What was I to do? In order to solve this problem and get my

---

[5] Actually we were called "pixel pushers" and "sprite monkeys," neither of which, despite how cute those terms sound, were ever meant as a compliment.

colleagues to read my design documents, I started drawing them as cartoons. And guess what? It worked. They conveyed the ideas I wanted to get across to my teammates. And I've been designing games this way ever since, many of which have gone on to become top-selling titles. That is why you will find many cartoons, so you will continue reading and understand the ideas presented. If you do, then you can apply them to your own design and become a great designer, too.

Who Is This Book For?

Why *you*, of course. Provided you are one of the following people.

A working video games professional. There are lots of books about video game design, but most of them are full of THEORY, which I have never found very helpful while making a game. Don't get me wrong, theory is great when you are at a game developers conference or one of those wine and cheese affairs we game designers always find ourselves at. But when I am working on a game, with my sleeves rolled up and blood splattered all over the walls,[6] I need practical nuts n' bolts advice on how to solve any problems I may encounter.

---

[6] Figurative blood. To my knowledge, no one has died from making a video game.

I mention this because I assume that some of you reading this second edition of *Level Up!* will be experienced video game professionals. I hope you find the techniques and tips in this book useful in your day-to-day work. Not that this book doesn't have uses for beginners.

I'm talking about you, **future video game designers.** Remember, one page ago when I told you I was a pixel pusher? There was a point to that story, which is *I was just like you.* Maybe you're also an artist who is tired of hearing the game designers laughing it up over in the other office. Or a programmer who knows he can design a better enemy encounter than the knucklehead currently doing it on your game. Or maybe you are a tester who wants to move up in the world, but you don't know how to do it. When I wanted to become a video game designer, there weren't any books on the subject. We had to learn everything from other game designers. I was lucky to have a mentor and an opportunity to work as a game designer. If you don't have either of these things, don't fret. Read this book; I will be your mentor. All *you* need to do is follow my advice, be prepared, and take advantage of the opportunity when it finally arrives.

This book is also great for **students of video game design.** Back when I started making games, I didn't take any classes on video game design—because they didn't exist! I just made stuff up as I went along! And I made a lot of mistakes. This is why I wrote this book: so you can learn from all **my** mistakes before they become **your** mistakes too.

Finally, this book is for **anyone who loves video games.** I love video games. I love to play them. I love to make them and I love to read about making them. If you want to make video games, then you must love them too. Ironically, I know several people who work in video games that freely admit they do not like to play video games. That does not make any sense to me. Why would you work in video games if you do not love video games? They are fools. They should just step aside and let someone who loves video games make video games. Someone like you.

Why a Second Edition?

When I first wrote *Level Up! The Guide to Great Level Design* back in 2009, the gaming industry was a different place. Consoles were the undisputed kings, motion controls had just hit the scene, social gaming on Facebook was still becoming a thing, and the app store had just launched the year before.

Things move very fast in the gaming industry. No one was anticipating the popularity of mobile gaming, the importance of monetizaton, or the explosion of the indy gaming market. Looking over the first edition, I realized many topics needed to added, content needed to be updated, references modified, concepts re-explored. I hope that you find that this updated edition provides enough new information to warrant a second purchase for returning readers or a first for new ones.

At the very least, make sure to try the new chili recipe.

Level 1

Welcome, N00bs!

THIS CHAPTER IS written especially for people who are new to video games and how they are made. I talk about what is a game, who makes them, and what kinds of games there are. It's pretty basic stuff and if you already know it all and are not a n00b,[1] feel free to skip it. However, you are going to be missing out on a lot of great stuff. Don't say I didn't warn you.

Within the academic gaming community, there are many different definitions for what qualifies as a game. Some scholars insist that "a game needs to be a closed formal system that subjectively represents a subset of reality."[2] Others say that games need to have "players in conflict with each other."[3] I think those definitions are trying too hard to sound smart.

Game definitions are often simpler than that. Bernard Suits wrote that "playing a game is a voluntary effort to overcome unnecessary obstacles."[4] This is a pretty amusing definition, but still a bit too scholarly for my taste. Let's keep things simple. Let's consider hand ball. You need only one player for hand ball. Where are the other players to be in conflict with? Bouncing a ball against a wall without missing it is hardly a metaphor for reality—unless you lead a very boring life. Let's face it, sometimes a ball bouncing against a wall is just a ball bouncing against a wall.

---

[1] The term "n00b" is short for "newbie," or someone who is new to a game or other venture. While the term predates the Internet, it became popular with MMORPG communities. Not a particularly flattering term, as it implies inexperience and/or ignorance. For example, only a real n00b would read a footnote defining what a n00b is!

[2] "What Is a Game?" Chris Crawford in *The Art of Computer Game Design*, McGraw-Hill/Osborne Media, 1984.

[3] "What Is a Game?" Roger Lewis in *The New Thesaurus*, Putnam Pub Group, 1979.

[4] *The Grasshopper: Games, Life and Utopia*, Bernard Suits, University of Toronto Press, 1978.

Playing hand ball may therefore seem like a time-waster, but a time-waster becomes a game when you add rules and an objective. A rule may be to throw the ball with your right hand and catch it with your left, or to not drop the ball. A victory condition could be that you have to catch the ball ten times in a row. A failure state would be if you violated any of the rules or victory conditions. When those criteria have been met, you have created a game. Ironically, while simple, hand ball was enough of a game to inspire the creators of one of the earliest video games: *Tennis for Two*.

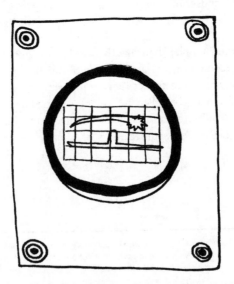

Tennis for Two

So, let's ask this basic question:

Q: What is a game?

A: A game is an activity that

- Requires at least one player

- Has rules

- Has a win and/or lose condition

That's pretty much it.[5]

Now that you know what a game is, let's ask:

Q: What is a video game?

A: A video game is a game that is played on a video screen.

Sure, you can start complicating the definition and add requirements about devices, peripherals, control schemes, player metrics, boss fights, and zombies (and don't worry; we'll tackle these things soon enough). But by my reckoning, that is pretty much as simple as it gets.

Oh, there's one other thing to consider at this early stage. A game needs a clear **objective** so the player knows what the goal is. You should be able to sum up a game's objectives quickly and clearly. If you can't, you've got a problem.

Danny Bilson, THQ's former EVP of Core Games, has a great rule of thumb about a game's objective. He says that you should be able to sum up the game's objectives as easily as those old Milton Bradley board games did on the front of their box. Check out these examples taken from real game boxes:

- *Battleship*: Sink all of your opponent's ships.

- *Operation*: Successful operations earn "Money." Failures set off alarms.

- *Mouse Trap*: Player turns the crank, which rotates gears, causing lever to move and push the stop sign against shoe. Shoe tips bucket holding metal ball. Ball rolls down rickety stairs and into rain pipe, which leads it to hit helping hand rod. This causes bowling ball to fall from top of helping hand rod through thing-a-ma-jig and bathtub to land on diving board. Weight of bowling ball catapults diver through the air and right into wash tub, causing cage to fall from top of post and trap unsuspecting mouse.

---

[5] A game should also be fun, although it's not mandatory . . . but we'll talk about that later.

Okay, let's just ignore that last one. The lesson is, you need to keep your game objectives simple. Speaking of simple games, let's take a moment to travel back to the dawn of video games. They had to start somewhere, right?

A Brief History of Video Games

The 1950s. The dawn of television, 3-D movies, and rock 'n' roll. Video games were invented in the 1950s too, only they were played by very few people, on very large computers. The first video game programmers were students in the computer labs of large universities like MIT and employees of military facilities at Brookhaven National Laboratories. Early games like *OXO* (1952), *Spacewar!* (1962), and *Colossal Cave* (1976) had very simple or even no graphics at all. They were displayed on very small black-and-white oscilloscope screens.

After playing *Spacewar!* at the University of Utah's computer lab, future Atari founders Ted Dabney and Nolan Bushnell were inspired to create *Computer Space*, the first **arcade** video game, in 1971. While (despite the name) the first arcade games could be found in bars, arcades dedicated to video games began appearing by the late 1970s.

Early arcade games were rendered using either **vector graphics** (images constructed from lines) or **raster graphics** (images constructed from a grid of dots called pixels). Vector graphics allowed for bright, striking images like those seen in *Battlezone* (Atari, 1980), *Tempest* (Atari, 1981) and *Star Wars* (Atari, 1983) while raster graphics spawned cartoon-inspired characters like Pac-Man (Namco, 1980) and Donkey Kong (Nintendo, 1982). These early characters became pop culture icons overnight; appearing in everything from cartoons and t-shirts to pop-music and breakfast cereals.

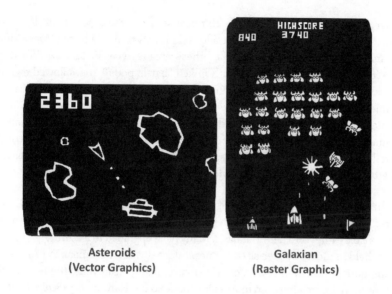

**Asteroids
(Vector Graphics)**

**Galaxian
(Raster Graphics)**

During the early 1980s, three styles of game machines dominated arcades: **uprights** (cabinets which the player stood in front of while playing), **cocktail tables** (arcade games set into the top of a small table, allowing the player to sit down while playing), and **cockpits** (elaborate game cabinets that allowed the player to lean or sit down to further enhance the gaming experience).

Upright Cabinet   Cocktail Table   Arcade Cockpit

In the mid-1980s, arcades began springing up everywhere, and video games took the world by storm. Game genres and themes became more varied, while gaming controls and cabinets became more elaborate with realistic controllers and beautiful graphics decorating uniquely designed cabinets. You could sit back to back in a two-player spaceship cockpit while playing *Tail Gunner* (Vectorbeam, 1979), battle Klingons from a replica of Captain Kirk's command chair in *Star Trek* (Sega, 1982), or "drive" in a miniature Ferrari Testarossa that moved and shook in *Out Run* (Sega, 1986). By the late 1990s, many arcade games started to resemble single-rider theme-park rides complete with rideable race horses, gyroscopically moving virtual simulators, and fighting booths that allowed players to battle virtual foes using actual punches and kicks. The most elaborate of these arcades was Virtual World's BattleTech Centers—steampunk-themed arcades with linked "battle pods"[6] that allowed eight players to fight each other while stomping around in giant virtual "mechs." But these elaborate arcade games required lots of floor space and were very expensive to maintain. In the late 1990s, home systems began to rival and eventually surpassed the graphics seen in most arcade games. Arcades went out of business by the dozens. The video games were replaced with more lucrative redemption machines[7] and games of skill like skeeball, whack-a-mole, and basketball hoops. The golden age of video game arcades was over.

But you can't keep a good idea down. Since the late 90s arcades have become social and virtual experiences. **LAN gaming centers** combine retail and social space to allow players to play computer and console games on a per-hour basis. Many have upgraded to feature large-scale gaming experiences held in movie theater-sized venues. Internet cafes are similar to LAN centers but with an emphasis on cultivating a café-style environment. Meanwhile, the few arcade game manufacturers left are creating even more epic experiences—Namco's *Deadstorm Pirates (2009)* and *Dark Escape 4D* (2013) are more like theme-park dark rides[8] than arcade games.

If arcades are becoming more like theme-park rides, theme parks are becoming arcades. Theme park creators are gamifying their attractions, turning dark rides into full sensory arcade games. Theme parks around the world such as Futuroscope and Warner Brother's Movie World offer several virtual games and interactive dark rides. For example, *Toy Story Midway Mania!* at Disney's California Adventure (2008) whisks a four-player cart past a succession of giant video screens where players compete in a variety of carnival-style shooting games. Players use cart-mounted pop-guns to shoot virtual projectiles at on-screen targets. When some targets are hit, players are sprayed with air or water mist effects, creating an immersive "four-D" effect. The cycle of modern arcade gaming and home gaming has come full circle with the release of a Wii version of the *Toy Story Midway Mania!* attraction for home use (minus the air and water effects).

---

[6] In the mid-1990s, I had the pleasure of going to a BattleTech Center on several occasions. The battle pods were a video gamer's dream come true. The player sat in a photo booth-sized cockpit. Dual control joysticks and foot pedals operated the mech's movement. Triggers and thumb switches fired the arsenal of weapons. Surrounding the pod's video monitor were banks of dipswitches—each one actually having a function within the game from activating tracking devices to venting overheating weapons. It took at least one gaming session (about a half hour) just to learn what all the switches did! It was as realistic a gaming experience as I've ever had.

[7] Redemption machines are those claw catcher "games" you see in American toy stores and supermarkets. Personally, I would rather play the lottery than try my luck with one of these vending machines, which are rigged to (almost) guarantee you to lose. However, if you are ever in Japan, I recommend playing them as they are winnable and are usually stocked with some very cool toys and prizes.

[8] A "dark ride" is an indoor amusement park attraction where riders travel in vehicles past scenes containing animation, sound, music, and effects. Famous examples of dark rides include Disneyland's *Pirates of the Caribbean* and *Haunted Mansion* and Universal Studio's *Men in Black: Alien Attack* and *Revenge of the Mummy*.

Happily, historians and academics have realized the impact and importance of video gaming. Museums have sprung up around the world, such as the Computerspielemuseum Berlin and New York's Museum of the Moving Image. Retro 80s arcades are making a comeback, complete with glo-in-the-dark carpet and tokens, offering players another chance to play their favorite vintage arcade games and revisit their old-school home system favorites.

A **console** is a gaming platform that can be used in the home. A microprocessor runs the electronic device, which sends a video display signal to the user's TV set or monitor.[9] Unlike the dedicated controllers of an arcade machine, a home console controller has enough buttons, triggers, and analog controls to allow for a variety of games to be played. And unlike the dedicated motherboards in early arcade games, which could hold only one game, console games use cartridge, CD, and DVD media to allow players to quickly change games. The first commercial home console was the Magnavox Odyssey (1972) created by gaming pioneer Ralph Baer. Technologically, the Odyssey was pretty far ahead of its time. It featured an analog controller, games on removable ROM cartridges, and a light gun—the first gaming peripheral. From the late 1970s onwards, there have been many home consoles. Some of the more popular and/or well-known previous generation ones include the Atari 2600 and Jaguar, the Mattel Intellivision, the ColecoVision, the Nintendo Entertainment System and Super Nintendo, the Sega Genesis and Dreamcast, the 3DO interactive player, PlayStation 3, Xbox 360, and the Nintendo Wii. Current consoles such as the PlayStation 4, Xbox One, Nintendo Wii U, and the Ouya continue to bring gaming into the homes of millions of gamers worldwide.

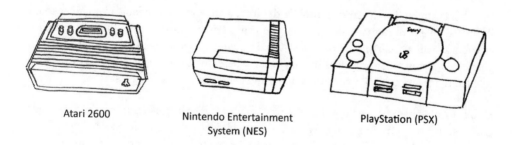

Atari 2600   Nintendo Entertainment   PlayStation (PSX)
                        System (NES)

Like arcade games, **handheld games** have a visual display, a processor, and a controller, but are small enough to fit in the hands of the player. The first handheld titles were dedicated to only one game per unit. *Auto Race* (Mattel Electronics, 1976) used a digital display while the Game & Watch series (Nintendo, 1980) featured a more appealing liquid crystal display. Microvision (Milton Bradley, 1979) was one of the earliest handheld systems to have switchable cartridges.

---

[9] One console exception is the wonderful Vectrex portable game system (Smith Engineering, 1982). The Vectrex's processor, screen, controller, and even one game were all in a self-contained, portable system.

Handheld gaming took off when Tetris became a phenomenon on the Game Boy (Nintendo, 1989), the forerunner of the Nintendo DS.[10] Recent handheld systems have become quite powerful. The processor on the Sony PlayStation Portable (PSP) can run the equivalent of a PlayStation 1 game. That's quite a jump since the digital blips of Mattel Football! Recent systems like the Sony Vita and Nintendo 2DS and 3DS offer a wide variety of games and control schemes, combining more traditional controls and games with second screens, touch controls, and digital content.

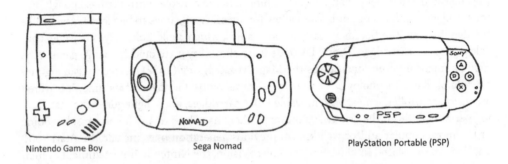

Nintendo Game Boy   Sega Nomad   PlayStation Portable (PSP)

The Brave New World of Gaming: Mobiles, Online Distribution, and Touchscreens

Handheld gaming, particularly on **mobile devices,** is the main way people play games today. With the advent of digital-only content, you can carry an entire gaming library around in your pocket on a smartphone or tablet. Gaming, which used to require a monitor, a computer, and a controller, can now be played anywhere and at any time. Touchscreens have enabled the creation of new control systems and genres of games.

Mobile gaming has changed not only the way we play games but also the way they are made. Games that used to require large teams and large budgets to create are now being made by small teams and even individuals. The games can be created quicker and for less money than their console and computer counterparts. Gameplay is built around short play sessions and repeated play. Sounds familiar, doesn't it? Mobile game production resembles the early days of game development, when games where the product of small teams or even one person. And even the way a game can earn money has changed. Monetized game design has changed the way revenue can be generated, giving the developer and publisher more opportunities to earn money. It is fair to say that mobile gaming has changed the way we game forever.

---

[10] Not ironically, the Nintendo DS bears several design semblances to the original Game & Watch series devices.

Another impact to gaming is the advent of **digital distribution.** Games can be purchased and downloaded at any time through the Internet. Digital gaming platforms such as Steam, Ouya, XBLA, the PlayStation Store, the Nintendo Store, GameStop App (formerly Stardock), and Origin's Client have enhanced or even replaced the need for a console. iTunes and the Android store allow gamers to download games for mobile and tablet devices. Physical storage space is no longer an issue because gamers can have as many games as their hard drives can hold. Of course, digital distribution has caused retailers to react with incentives for gamers who want to buy games the traditional way—sweetening the offer with season passes of exclusive content and collectable merchandise.

As **personal computers** (or **PCs**) became popular in the late 1970s, both video game programming and video game playing became more common. An entire generation of game developers started off in their bedrooms, programming games on their PCs. These early games were stored on cassette tapes that would be placed in tape drives or later on floppy disks that were placed in floppy drives. While early video game consoles attempted to emulate games found in arcades, early computers like the Apple II took advantage of the keyboard. The keyboard allowed greater user input and created unique genres including the text adventure game, like 1976's *Colossal Cave Adventure.* Since computer players could spend more time gaming (and would be more comfortable sitting down!) computer games necessitated a different gaming experience. Story-based adventure games, construction and management games and strategy games provided longer play experiences than their arcade counterparts and gave the consumer more perceived value for their money. I distinctly remember determining how much play time I was getting for my money: let's see, an average arcade game costs a quarter and *Temple of Apshai* cost $30, so I should be able to play it for how long . . . ?

As the computer hardware, memory, and storage evolved to CD and DVD media, computer games became more detailed, more involved, and more complex. The rise of the **first person shooter** (or **FPS**) can be attributed to the popularity of the mouse controller. By the mid-1990s, the computer was the ultimate gaming platform. Several gaming genres, particularly strategy, FPSs, and **massively multiplayer online** games (or **MMOs**) remain very strong on the computer platform. Touchscreen games, which were found only on handheld devices, are even more popular now that touchscreens are becoming the standard on desktop and laptop computers.

Commodore 64 (C64)   Macintosh Plus   Personal Computer (PC)

Game Genres

The term **genre** is used to describe a category of something—often the categories used to describe books, movies or music. Music can be rock and roll, gospel, or country. Movies can be action, romance, or comedies. Books can be dramas, biographies, or horror; you get the idea.

Video games can be classified into genres too, but here's where it gets a little tricky. Games have *two* types of genres: **story genre** and **game genre.** Just like the preceding examples, *story genre* describes the type of story-fantasy, historical, sports, and so on. *Game genre* describes the type of *gameplay*—much in the way that a movie can be a documentary or an art film. The difference is in the game's format and the player's interaction. The game genre describes the play, not the art or story. Simple enough, right? While I talk about story genre later, let's look now at the different kinds of game genres:

- **Action**—Action games rely on eye/hand coordination and skill to play. There are lots of stylistic variations available, making it one of the most diverse genres. Many of the earliest arcade games were action games.

- **Adventure**—Adventure games focus on characters (like in a role playing game), inventory management, story, and sometimes puzzle solving.

- **Augmented Reality**—Augmented Reality (or AR games) incorporate peripheral devices like cameras and global positioning (GPS) into gameplay.

- **Educational**—An educational game's primary intention is to educate while entertaining. These games are often aimed at a younger audience.

- **Party**—A party game is specifically designed for several players to compete in a variety of different styles of gameplay from quizzes to games of skill.

- **Puzzle**—Puzzle games are based on logic, observation, and pattern completion. Sometimes they are slow and methodical. Other times they require quick eye/hand coordination like an action game.

- **Rhythm**—In a rhythm game, a player tries to match a rhythm or beat to score points.

- **Serious**—At first glance, serious games seem similar to educational games but with a focus on social issues. But the genre is more diverse than that. Serious games are used to provide training, for advertising, or just exist as art!

- **Shooter**—Shooters primarily focus on players firing projectiles at each other. It's one of the most popular genres (at least here in the West) and there are many variations.

- **Simulation**—Simulations focus on creating and managing a world. Or a theme park. Or a farm. Or the life of an adorable monster. Many simulations cross over into the realm of "**toy games**"—games that provide tools for creativity but have no win or lose conditions.

- **Sports**—These games are based on athletic competitions from traditional sports to extreme ones. Like action games, there are many stylistic forms with this genre ranging from realistic simulations to fantasy variants.

- **Strategy**—Thinking and planning are the hallmarks of strategy games. This is one of the oldest genres of games; strategy games' roots are in ancient games like Senet, Chess, Go, and Mancala games.

- **Traditional**—Speaking of board games, traditional games are usually (but not always) based on games that existed in other, often physical, formats. Card games, board games, and casino games fall into this genre.

- **Vehicle simulation**—Players simulate piloting or driving a vehicle, from a race car to a star fighter. There are a variety of stylistic and control options for the player making the experience arcade-like or like a realistic simulation.

This list is just the tip of the iceberg! In addition to the genres in this list, you'll find a big list in **Bonus Level 5** describing all sorts of sub-genres and hybrids genres with lots of examples.

As games combine several genres and subgenres, new ones are constantly being created. For example, the *Grand Theft Auto* series combines action-adventure, third person shooter, driving, life simulation, and action-arcade genres into one game! *Tuper Tario Tros.*[11] seamlessly combines *Super Mario Bros.* and *Tetris*! What's next? What will be the most popular game genre in the future? Who knows? Perhaps you will create it!

Who Makes This Stuff?

Just as there are many genres of games, there are many types of people who make them. Video game teams that create games are known as **developers** or **development teams.** They are similar to a production team that makes a movie or TV show—several creative people all working together to create entertainment.

In the early days of video game development, games were created by individuals; one example is the original *Prince of Persia,* created by one person[12] who programmed, designed, and animated the entire game. He even composed the game's music!

---

[11] You can play *Tuper Tario Tros.* by Swing Swing Submarine at www.newgrounds.com/portal/view/522276.

[12] The one-man development team in question is Jordan Mechner.

Game creation eventually evolved into teams as commercial video game development became more technologically complex, and games that originally required two or three programmers to make now needed people with a wider range of skills. As graphics capabilities improved, many game creators lacked the artistic skills to fully utilize the new computing power. Since audiences demand better-looking games, teams added art specialists.

Games were initially designed by whichever team member had the best idea for a game. When game content became too involved to design by the programmers and artists, a dedicated design position was created. Both *Mario* creator Shiguru Miyamoto and I started as artists who moved into the area of game design. Although team members can still wear many hats, specialization is common place on larger production teams.

With the rise of mobile and independent gaming, the production cycle has swung away from the larger development teams. More and more games are being created by small teams and even individuals. *Minecraft, Spelunky,* and *Tiny Wings* were each created by one person! Now that creative teams are no longer reliant on huge budgets and publishers, the power is back in the hands of the developers! So who has this power? Here's a rundown of the different members of a development team.

Programmer

Using programming languages such as C++ and Unity, a **programmer** writes the code that draws the game's graphics and on-screen text, develops the control systems that allow players to interact with the game, creates the camera system that allows the players to view the game world, programs the physics system that affects the players and game world, writes the artificial intelligence (AI) system that controls enemies and object scripting . . . you get the idea.

One programmer may work exclusively on tools to help team members build the game more efficiently. Another programmer may write code to simulate real-world physics making water look realistic or develop inverse kinematics for characters. A programmer may even work solely on sound tools to play music and effects.

Like many of the jobs in the game industry, programming jobs are becoming more specialized. Regardless of the position, a programmer needs to have an excellent understanding of mathematics, 2-D and 3-D graphics, physics, particle systems, user interface, artificial intelligence, input devices, and computer networking. These skills are always in high demand, and some programmers make a good living as contractors, moving from project to project as "hired guns," writing code and providing temporary solutions to beleaguered teams.

Artist

In the early days of video games, programmers created all of a game's art. Because that early art was so blocky and crude, we now call placeholder game art "programmer art."[13] Thank goodness real artists came along. One of the first artists working in video games was Shigeru Miyamoto, who created Mario and Donkey Kong. He was able to create memorable cartoon characters with an 8-bit CPU using only 2-bit pixels—that means background elements have four colors and sprites only have three. That's a lot of personality per pixel! There were a few exceptions in the early days, such as *Dragon's Lair* (Cinematronics, 1983) and *Space Ace* (Cinematronics, 1984), beautifully animated games created by ex-Disney animators like Don Bluth, but those games were rare exceptions because they employed laser discs to play the video footage. Eventually, new, better hardware with more memory, color depth, and the ability to display larger graphics meant artists could create more detailed images, backgrounds, and characters like those seen in beautifully

hand-drawn and animated games such as *Darkstalkers* (Capcom, 1994) and *Metal Slug* (SNK, 1996).

As high-end computer software became more affordable to developers, 3-D graphics, which had been limited to movies like *Tron* (Disney, 1982) and Pixar's animated shorts like *Luxo Jr.* (1986), began appearing in games. True 3-D graphics had been in arcade games as early as *Battlezone* (Atari, 1980), but the move to bring 3-D into homes started on the 3DO with *Crash and Burn* and *Total Eclipse* (both by *Crystal Dynamics, 1993)*. The popularity of real-time 3-D games like *Wolfenstein 3D* and *Doom* (both by *id software, 1993)* and the use of pre-rendered 3-D graphics *Myst* (Broderbund, 1993) and *Donkey Kong Country* (Nintendo, 1994) made sure that 3-D was here to stay.

Just as with programming, video game art has become a specialized job. A **concept artist** uses both traditional medium and computers to draw what game characters, worlds, and enemies will look like in the game. Concept art is never used in the final game, only as reference for other artists. **Storyboard artists** illustrate the game's cinematics and sometimes elements of gameplay design to be passed along to other artists and animators. **3-D Modelers** and **environmental artists** build characters and environments using programs such as Maya and 3D Studio Max. **Texture artists** literally paint surfaces onto 3-D models and locations. **Visual effects artists** create spectacular visual effects using a combination of 2-D and 3-D art. A **user interface (UI) artist** designs icons and elements that are used in the game's interface and heads-up display (HUD). **Animators** animate the player character and create cutscenes exactly

---

[13] I apologize to any programmers reading this, but I didn't make up this term.

as they do in big-budget animated movies. **Technical artists** help every artist on the team by doing a variety of tasks, including rigging models to allow animators to move them and teaching fellow artists the latest tools and technology. The **art director** supervises the work of all the artists while maintaining the artistic vision for the entire project. Regardless of what kind of art position you are interested in, make sure you study the basics and keep drawing!

Designer

Director, planner, lead designer, or senior game designer—no matter what the job title is, the designer's role is the same: create the ideas and rules that comprise a game. A **game designer** needs to possess many, many skills,[14] and must love to play games. As a game designer, you should be able to tell the difference between a good and bad game and, more importantly, communicate why. Remember, "because it sucks" is *never* an acceptable answer.

Just as with programmers and artists, design is becoming a specialized profession. **Level designers** create paper maps, build "gray box"[15] worlds using 3-D programs, and populate the levels with everything from enemies to treasure. **System designers** develop how the game elements relate to one another, whether it is the game's economy or technology tree. **Scripters** use tools to write code that allow things to happen within the game, from springing a trap to choreographing a camera movement. **Combat designers** specialize in the player's combat experience, whether against an AI or human opponent, and "balancing" the player's experience. The **creative director** maintains the vision of the game while supervising the other designers, often offering suggestions for improving their work.

There is one other task that a designer is responsible for: ensuring that the game is "fun." However, I will leave this can of worms unopened until later in the book. I hope you can stand the suspense.

Producer

Overseeing the entire game development team is a **producer.** Originally, producers were members of the development team who also managed the work of their team members and had the authority to make all decisions, including creative ones. A producer's role has expanded

---

[14] According to Jesse Schell in his book *The Art of Game Design* (Morgan Kaufmann, 2008), a "well-rounded" game designer understands animation, anthropology, architecture, brainstorming, business, cinematography, communication, creative writing, economics, engineering, history, management, mathematics, music, psychology, public speaking, sound design, technical writing, and visual arts. I think it's a pretty accurate list.

[15] A "gray box" level is a preliminary version of a game level that contains gameplay but lacks visual detail.

dramatically over the years in some cases requiring several producer roles on one game including **executive producers** who oversee all the other producers!

The producer's responsibilities include hiring and building teams; writing contracts; contributing to the game's design; managing the team's work schedule; balancing the game's budget; resolving disputes between creative and programming leads; acting as the team representative to upper management and publishers; coordinating the creation of outside resources such as art, music, and cutscenes; and arranging testing and localization. Producers are usually the first team member on and the last team member off a game's production. More often than not, you will find producers acting as the public face of the game, talking to the press and public about the game they are managing.[16]

Because a producer has many things to do, often you will find **assistant** and **associate producers** helping out with day-to-day tasks. Sometimes the task can be as "trivial" as ordering dinner for a team that is working late. Believe it or not, some of those "menial" chores are some of the most important that a producer can provide to a team.

Regardless of how helpful producers can be, some development studios consider producers to be an unnecessary part of development. Others feel that producers should not have any creative control, just manage the game's production and schedule. As with designers, the role and influence of producers varies wildly across the industry.

Tester

Do you like to play games? Do you like to play games over and over? Do you like to play the same level over and over and over and over and over and over and over and over and over and over and over again? Then testing is for you!

While **testers** work long hours, work in cramped environments, and have to play games to a degree that many would classify as mind-numbingly boring, being a tester requires more skills than you may think. Good testers have patience, persistence, and great communication skills to report back any problems (or **bugs**) they find in the game. It's not a glamorous job,

---

[16] Producers often end up as the "face of the game" because they are the one team member who can keep all the moving parts straight!

but without testers, we would be plagued with games that crash upon loading and have crappy cameras, broken combat systems, and unfair difficulty balances.

Quality assurance (or **QA**)[17] is crucial to the successful completion of a game. Publishers hold games to a rigorous standard of quality so the game that you buy is (mostly) bug free. That standard can be met only by thoroughly testing a game for weeks, if not months. Only after it has passed muster with the QA department can it be offered for **submission** to the game manufacturer. Then only after the submitted version of the game is approved is it truly ready to be released to the public. Sometimes several submissions are needed before a game is ready for release.

Testing is a great gateway job position for newcomers to the game industry. I have seen testers go on to become designers, artists, producers, and even heads of studios. You can find out a lot about games in a short time by working as a tester. Testers prevent games from sucking. Remember that the next time you think about making fun of a tester.

Composer

In the earliest days of video games, music was nothing more than crude beeps and bloops to accompany the game's action. But how many of you can still hum the music to *The Legend of Zelda* or the *Super Mario Bros.* theme?

Music is extremely important to the gaming experience, and a **composer** creates that music. Most modern composers create their music on a keyboard or synthesizer because it can be used to simulate any musical instrument. As sound technology has improved, many composers have created actual "live" and orchestral pieces; this requires a whole new set of skills, including conducting an orchestra, waving a baton and all.

Home versions of modern audio software are powerful enough to mix and master professional-sounding samples. If you want to become a composer, you should write some music, record it, and get your samples into the hands of a game producer. As someone who has reviewed lots and lots of composers' audio resumes, I can tell you it goes something like this: the designer has a specific idea for the style or feel of music in his mind. If your music sample matches what the designer wants, she will contact you for the job. What matters most is that your music is unique and fits the needs of the game. Look at the success of a movie score composer such as Danny Elfman. He composed very distinct music for *Beetlejuice* and *Pee*

---

[17] "Quality assurance" is just a fancy way of saying "test department."

Wee's Big Adventure, and soon all the producers in Hollywood wanted his style of music in their own movies.

Writing music for games is somewhat different than writing music for movies. Most game themes are either very short or have to repeat over and over again. Being able to compose powerful and exciting music with these limitations in mind will make your music more appealing than someone who just writes "songs."[18] Don't worry; I cover more about music in Level 16.

Sound Designer

Unlike a composer who creates the music for a game, the **sound designer** creates all the sound effects that are used in a game. Go ahead and fire up a game, turn off the sound, and try playing it. Do you notice that the game just isn't the same without sound effects? Often, a lot of information is delivered to the player via sound. These audio cues are the sound designer's responsibility to create.

Personally, I think sound design is a lot of fun. Games tend to come to life when sound is added to them. That is why it is important to even have placeholder sound effects while creating your game. Sound design requires a lot of creativity. Mixing and blending sounds to create something no one has ever heard before is pretty cool. However, a good sound designer needs to understand the game he is working on and how to create sounds that help the player with the game. Some sound effects need to sound "positive" to encourage players that they are doing something right or collecting something good. Other sounds warn players of danger or possible bad choices. A sound designer can make a sound effect sound happy, deadly, scary, or like a big pile of treasure. Or sometimes all the above!

If you want to be a sound designer, you also need to take direction from people who may or may not know what they want. For example, see whether you can create a sound effect based on the following description: "I need this creature to sound like a phlegmy cougar from hell . . . but make it sound more shriek-ey than growl-y."[19] Did you do it? Congratulations! You are now ready to be a sound designer.

Writer

Unlike in Hollywood, where **writers** come up with the initial ideas for a movie, in the video game world, writers are usually hired pretty late in the game's production process. If you want to be the "idea guy," I suggest sticking to game design.

---

[18] Don't let that comment cause you despair, songwriters. Plenty of games still use traditional songs—in particular, sport and rhythm games.

[19] Sadly, yes: this was an actual direction to a sound designer. And yet, he still delivered a great sound effect.

That's not to say that writers don't contribute to games. However, writer is not usually a full-time team position. Typically, writers are freelancers brought into the game's production for one of the following reasons:

- To rewrite the design team's story into something that makes sense after everyone on the team realizes that it is drivel.

- To write dialogue for the game characters and cutscenes after everyone on the team realizes that writing good dialogue is actually hard to do.

- To make elements in the game clearer to understand, as in the case of instructional or directional prompts.

- To write content for heads-up displays that must meet manufacturer's submission requirements.

Lately, game developers have begun to understand the importance of bringing a writer into the game development process earlier. The writer can help direct the flow of the game's content. In this era of story-driven games, a lot of content needs to be created. Some games have scripts that run as long as hundreds of pages! Sometimes it can be difficult to find steady work as a writer at a single company, which is why most game writers work freelance.

Once upon a time, development teams hired **technical writers** to create game manuals—little books that came with the game to explain how to play them. However, physical manuals have mostly become a thing of the past; the content is either included in the in-game tutorial system or made available digitally.

The upside of being a writer in the game industry is that there is usually plenty of work, as long as you don't mind doing different writing jobs and working for different companies. If you want to be a game writer, you obviously need to know how to write, use proper grammar, and write in screenplay format. But the most important thing to know is how to write for video games. Writing for video games can be very different from writing a novel or a screenplay. Fortunately, this book has a whole chapter on how to do this.[20] Good thing you are reading it!

Well, now you know all the different employment possibilities in video games, right? Wrong! People don't generally know this, but there is a second career path in video games: publishing.

---

[20] Level 3, to be exact.

Have You Thought about Publishing?

Publishers provide the funding for game development teams, manage the game's production, handle any legal issues, manufacture the game, and provide public relations and marketing for the game. They even handle distribution of the finished product. The following sections describe some of the more common positions found in publishing.

Product Manager

Much like game producers, **product managers** work with the development team and manage them based on the agreed production schedule. They help determine production priorities for the game's production, act as an intermediary between the studio and the publisher's legal department, review and approve milestones, and make payments to the studio. They talk to licensors to ensure they approve of how the development is turning out. They also work with the ESRB[21] to secure a rating for the game. Needless to say, they're pretty busy people.

At some publishers, the product manager has extensive say in the game's content. At others, the product manager is there to make sure the game's development goes smoothly. All I know is, I'm glad I'm not the one making the schedule.

Creative Manager

When people ask me what I did as a **creative manager** for THQ, I tell them "I had the job that people think of when they think of working in video games." To be honest, working as a creative manager isn't just "thinking up and playing games all day." But sometimes it is.

Creative managers are usually game designers or writers who are working in publishing. Like a product manager's involvement, a creative manager's involvement on a game can vary from publisher to publisher. In my own experience, I have worked with teams to create and develop games, written game pitches, and worked with licensors to create game concepts. One of my most common responsibilities is to play game builds[22] and make sure that they remain true to the core idea and are "fun" (there's that word again).

The best benefit a creative manager can provide is what I call the **"thousand foot view"** (as in looking down on the game from a thousand feet in the air, not looking at thousands of feet!)—an unbiased viewpoint on a game that can help root out weaknesses in the game's

---

[21] ESRB stands for the Entertainment Software Ratings Board, an organization that determines a game's rating (in the United States, at least).

[22] A "build" (or a "burn") is an in-progress version of the game that can be played either on a computer or a special console.

design and construction. When games aren't solid, I need to provide the team clear feedback on how gameplay can be improved or give advice on how the team can explore another creative direction.

Creative managers also work with marketing and public relation departments to provide press materials to make sure a game is shown in the very best light.

Art Director

An **art director** is similar to a creative manager, but deals only with the game's art. Art directors can help a team create a visual style for their game and take their game in directions that the team hadn't previously considered. An art director can help the team globalize the visual language of their game to make it clear to the player. Art directors also work with the marketing teams to create packaging materials (such as the cover of a game's box) or wrangle assets such a screen shots and concept art that are used to publicize the game.

Technical Director

Technical directors come from a programming background. They review and recommend tools and software to teams to help them work more efficiently. They provide technical support and advice when there are deficiencies in a team's programming staff. They also help perform **due diligence** on a new team to help assess whether they can actually make the game they are being hired to make.

Marketing Team

The marketing team promotes the game to the world. They work with magazines, websites, and TV shows to promote the game. They help design packaging materials and write copy for the back of the box. They work with advertising firms to create promotional materials for the games. When working with a marketing team, make sure they play your game (something, sadly, I have found many marketing teams do not do). They should understand what's great about your game so they can sell it as best they can.

And the Rest . . .

Other publishing positions aren't directly involved in making games but are important in creating and selling a game nonetheless. **Business development** staff build relationships with studios, hold game pitch meetings, and review prospective game demos. They make deals with external studios and find emerging studios to acquire. If you ever own a gaming studio, odds are you'll meet a lot of business developers. A **lawyer** negotiates all the contracts and makes sure the production team isn't creating content that will get the publisher into any legal trouble. A **brand manager** creates the marketing strategy to promote and advertise a game. This person develops print material such as manuals and box covers. A **public relations manager** talks to gaming magazines and organizes press events to show off the game in the best possible light. A **quality assurance manager** runs the test department, organizing and relaying the bug sheets back to the developer.

In addition to production and publishing staff, many others interact with development teams and publishers. A **talent recruiter** searches for new talent and helps get them employment with developers and publishers, **game reviewers** play the games before they come out and write reviews and interviews for magazines and online sites, and **licensors** work for major entertainment companies to make sure their brands are properly represented in games based on their properties.

As you can see, there are plenty of options if you want a career in games. But I say forget all those other jobs. You want to find out how to make great game designs, right? Trust me, game design is where the real fun is!

But to make great games, you need great ideas. Where do you get great ideas? Let's find out!

Level 1's Universal Truths and Clever Ideas

- A game is an activity with rules and a victory condition.
- Your game objective should be simple, like that of a 1950s board game.
- Game genres come in all shapes and sizes. Don't be afraid to mix and match.
- Gaming technology is always improving. Adapt, or get left behind.
- It takes all kinds of people with all kinds of skills to make video games.

Level 2
Ideas

LET'S TALK ABOUT *making* video games. To most people, making a video game is a mystery. The average party conversation goes like this:

So, you program video games? Is it hard to write all of that code?

No, I said I *design* games.

Oh, so you draw the characters? That must be fun.

No, I don't draw them. That's what an artist does.

I don't get it. If you don't code the games or draw the games what *do* you do?

Apparently nothing.

At this point in the conversation, I tell the person that games are made by elves. (Sometimes it's just easier to tell someone a fantasy answer than explain what I do for a living.) However, a question people ask that *is* easier to answer is: "Where do your **ideas** for games come from?"

Ideas: Where to Get Them and Where to Stick Them

Every good idea borders on the stupid.
—Michel Gondry[1]

I like this quote because many game ideas often sound stupid. Try these on for size:

- A yellow creature eats dots while being chased by ghost monsters.
- A plumber jumps on the heads of mushrooms to find his girlfriend.
- A prince rebuilds stars by rolling balls of junk into bigger balls of junk.

All those stupid-sounding ideas ended up being games that made lots and lots of money. I guess they aren't so stupid after all. To me, the lesson is, never dismiss a game idea, even if it does sound stupid.

So, where do I get my own stupid ideas to turn into video games? The traditional way to get an idea is to get inspired. The good news is that a good game idea can come from anywhere. Here is a list of things I do to get inspired. I suggest you try them yourself the next time you need to come up with an idea.

1. **Cram your head.** I find the process of creation goes something like this: watch/read/ listen to a lot of stuff. Consume as much as you can. Then, let all those images, stories, sounds, ideas, and thoughts percolate in your head. Apply your own perspective on life to them. With any luck, a new idea will form. Make sure you have a pencil and paper (or a voice recorder, if you're so inclined) handy to catch those ideas when they pop out.

2. **Read something you normally wouldn't read.** Don't just cram your head with the same old stuff. For example, I once attended a roundtable discussion with the famous game designer Will Wright. Mr. Wright said he got his inspiration for his games from Japanese gardening, architectural design, and biology. I replied that was great, as long as you were into Japanese gardening, architectural design, and biology; but what about "normal folks" who were into comic books, sci-fi movies, and video games? But to tell the truth, I realized that I knew what the answer to my question was even as I asked it.

---

[1] While Michel Gondry doesn't make video games, he does make excellent movies like *Eternal Sunshine of the Spotless Mind*, *The Science of Sleep*, and *Be Kind, Rewind*. I suggest you add them all to your Netflix list immediately.

One of the reasons why many video games sometimes feel the same is that many game developers love the same stuff. There's nothing wrong with liking video games, comics, and movies; however, when developers all get their inspiration from the same things, games start to feel the same. When popular movies come out, their themes start to show up in games. When popular games come out, you find their mechanics being used in other games. Games start to feel derivative. You also get that creepy synchronicity when developers put out similar games at the same time.[2] Take the time to expand your educational horizons, even just a little. You don't have to get a degree in the subject; just thumb through a magazine or two, spend an afternoon at the library, or research something new on the Internet. In other words, stop reading so much crap and break the cycle, fanboy!

3. **Take a walk, drive, or shower.** When the active part of your brain is being occupied by a familiar activity like walking or driving, your subconscious is free to start wandering and making connections it would normally never make. These connections often lead to great ideas. Besides, many game designers could stand an occasional shower. Please make sure, though, that if you drive to get ideas, you invest in a hands-free recording device or stop your car before you jot down your thoughts.

4. **Attend a lecture.** I love the Game Developer's Conference because I get inspired by the game design lectures and discussions. I often end up with a notebook full of ideas. Make sure you share some of your ideas with your fellow game designers, too. It's always good to "stretch your idea's legs" to find out where it bends and where it breaks. Just be prepared to be told your ideas are stupid.[3]

5. **Play a game, preferably a bad one.** Playing a good[4] video game has its benefits, but I find it more educational to play a bad game. As you play a bad game, look at the things in the game that were done poorly. Then think about what **you** would do to improve them. Consider how many people "invented" the airplane before the Wright Brothers built and flew their plane. Sometimes it takes several iterations on an idea before it works successfully.

6. **Play a different game.** Your mom was right when she told you not to play video games all day, so how about playing a tabletop game instead? Many video games have been inspired by board and card games: *Colossal Cave Adventure* was inspired by *Dungeons and Dragons* and *Sid Meir's Civilization* was inspired by Avalon Hill's *Civilization* board game. Not into board games? How about Tag or Capture the Flag or Cops and Robbers? It might inspire you to create the next *Pac-Man, Team Fortress 2,* or *Grand Theft Auto.*

---

[2] This is the same phenomenon that gave us two Snow White-themed movies in one year, *Mirror Mirror* and *Snow White and the Huntsman,* in 2012.

[3] And then when someone tells you your idea is stupid, you can retort with Michel Gondry's quote!

[4] I realize that "good" is extremely subjective. Good could mean highly rated, best-selling, competently made, or even just super cool.

7. **Regardless of the preceding tips, follow your passion.** You never know when you'll get a chance to use something you love in a game design. Even if you do read comics and play video games, if you really love something, that love will shine through in your game. Satoshi Tajiri designed *Pokémon* as a game version of his love for collecting insects. Dave Jaffe turned his love for Ray Harryhausen movies into *God of War*. Shigeru Miyamoto often turns his real-world hobbies into game designs. If you follow your passions, designing your game won't even feel like work.

It's one thing to have a good idea; it's another thing to have a *marketable* one. During the course of my career, I have been told many times (usually by my colleagues in the marketing department) that my idea is a "designer's idea," which means that they think my idea is one that I would love to play, but it isn't marketable to the general gaming public. Personally, I am torn with this assessment. On the one hand, I can understand their desire to make a game that will sell. If your game sells, that means you can make more games.

But on the other hand, before I am ready to give in to "the suits," I am reminded of all the innovative games that have been created over the years. I am sure that at one point the designers of these games were told by their marketing colleagues that their ideas were too weird, too unmarketable, or too stupid. If that were the case, innovative games like *PaRappa the Rapper*, *The Sims*, or *Braid* would never have been made.

Getting Ahead of the Game

However, let me tell you a little secret. Come a little closer . . . a little closer . . . too close!

If you think something is innovative, it just means you haven't been paying enough attention.
—Scott Rogers

Although I am sure there is probably still a completely original idea out there in the galaxy of ideas, the majority of gameplay design works by each game building on its predecessors. I truly believe that this strategy is one of the keys to creating great game design. Even the most innovative games like the aforementioned *PaRappa*, *Sims*, and *Braid* had their predecessors in *Simon*, *Sim City*[5] and *blinx: the Time Sweeper*.

---

[5] Will Wright, the creator/designer of *The Sims*, is one of if not *the* smartest guy in video games. His genius is that his entire video game career appears to be dedicated to the iteration of a single idea. His creations, *Sim City*, *Sim Ant*, *Sim Earth*, *Sim City 2000*, *The Sims*, and *Spore*, showcase the natural evolution of a single idea (the world-building simulation) to literally galactic proportions. That he has been able to develop and polish this idea over the years is a luxury of which any game designer would be envious.

Here's another secret. My idea isn't even original. Raph Koster charted the evolution of the shoot 'em up genre in his book *A Theory of Fun for Game Design* (Paraglyph, 2004). Taking Raph's chart as inspiration, I will show you the evolution of gameplay design within the platformer game genre:

- *Space Panic*'s (Universal, 1980) walking character climbed ladders and dug holes to temporarily stun enemies.

- *Donkey Kong* (Nintendo, 1981) added jumping and a power-up that could defeat enemies.

- *Popeye* (Nintendo, 1982) introduced moving collectables and environmental mechanics that the player could interact with.

- *Pitfall!* (Activision, 1982) added alternative moves including vine swinging and hopping on alligators' heads.

- *Mario Bros.* (Nintendo, 1983) added a second player and enemies that could be defeated by the player's skill rather than just a power-up.

- *Pac-Land* (Namco, 1984) featured a world map, a variety of themed levels, and dynamic hazards.

- *Ghosts 'N' Goblins* (Capcom, 1985) featured multiple weapons including projectiles, health (in the form of armor that shattered off), and combatable "boss" monsters.

- *Super Mario Bros.* (Nintendo, 1985) launched a wave of imitators who were inspired by its tight controls, whimsical environments, and creative level design.

- *Dark Castle*'s (Silicon Beach Software, 1986) hero, Duncan, could "hide" from enemies. It was also the first game where players didn't immediately die from falling but rather ended up in the dungeon.

- *Mega Man* (Capcom, 1987) introduced themed stages ending with similarly themed bosses who possessed powers that could be gained by the player once they were defeated.

- *Crash Bandicoot* (Universal, 1996) used 3-D models and environments to create the camera view called "2 and a half D."

- *Mario 64* (Nintendo, 1996) brought all the gameplay of the *Mario* platform games into true 3-D.

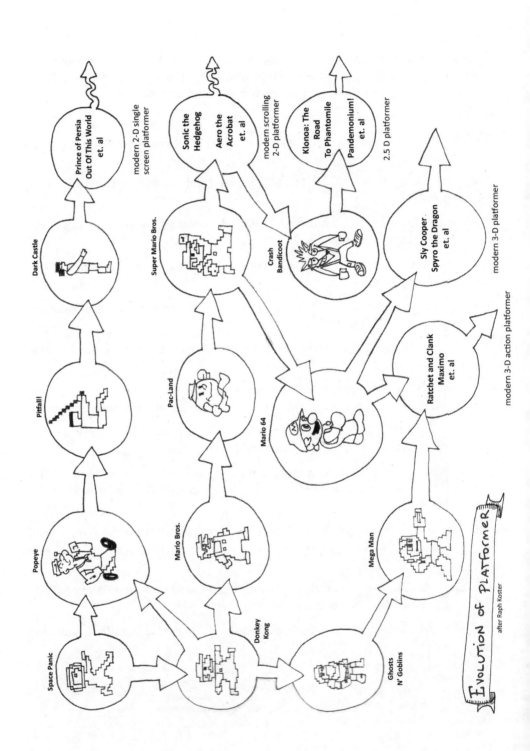

Prince of Persia
Out Of This World
et. al

modern 2-D single
screen platformer

Dark Castle

Pitfall!

Popeye

Space Panic

Sonic the
Hedgehog

Aero the
Acrobat
et. al

modern scrolling
2-D platformer

Klonoa: The
Road
To Phantomile

Pandemonium!
et. al

2.5 D platformer

Super Mario Bros.

Pac-Land

Crash
Bandicoot

Mario 64

Mario Bros.

Donkey
Kong

Ghosts
N' Goblins

Sly Cooper
Spyro the Dragon
et. al

modern 3-D platformer

Ratchet and Clank
Maximo
et. al

modern 3-D action platformer

Mega Man

Evolution of Platformer

after Raph Koster

As you can see, each idea builds on the next. Each game designer inspires the one who comes after him. Or as Pablo Picasso once said, "Bad artists copy. Good artists steal."

Now that you have a great game idea to start with, you have to ask yourself the question posed in the following heading.

What Do Gamers Want?

Automobile inventor Henry Ford once said "If I had asked people what they wanted, they would have said faster horses." The same is true with video games. I believe that most gamers don't know what they want until it is shown to them. That is why it is important for game designers to have ideas born from passion. To have a vision of what their game is supposed to be. Gamers can feel when developers are passionate about their games. They can smell it like a dog smells fear. Don't be afraid to hold onto your unique vision: just be aware that it may not turn out exactly how you envisioned.

But that didn't really answer the question did it? Okay, here's a simple answer:

GAMERS WANT GOOD GAMES[6]

Of course, there is no guarantee that your game will be good. Although no one sets out to make bad games, bad games still get made. You can lay the blame for a bad game at the feet of a multitude of reasons, which we cover later.

Tim Schafer, the designer of *Psychonauts* and *Brütal Legend*, says that all good games provide **wish fulfillment.** Playing as characters they wish they could be gives players a chance to be something they aren't in the real world. I think the same is true about games *in general*. Regardless of the genre, games should *make players feel something that they aren't in the real world*: powerful, smart, sneaky, skillful, successful, rich, bad, or heroic.

As you are developing your idea, you need to know "What audience is my game for?" The rise of casual gaming has created renewed interest in shorter play sessions for players don't have the time for long-form games. You need to decide who your game idea is for: the casual or the hardcore player. You can rule out certain design decisions early on by setting the audience in stone near the beginning of the idea development process.

Don't forget to ask this important question: "What is the age of my audience?" Having made dozens of "kids'" games, I have observed a useful fact about kids and games. Kids always want what is made for an audience older than their own age group. For example, an 8-year-old kid

---

[6] Yes, this is in ALL CAPS and **bold** because it is a **VERY IMPORTANT THING.**

wants to play a game that is made for a 10-year-old kid. A 10-year-old kid wants to play a game that is made for a 13-year-old kid. A 13-year-old kid wants to play a game that is made for an 18-year-old. Many kids aren't interested in playing games directly targeting their age range. If asked, they will tell you "that's a game for my little brother." Believe me, in kid language, there is no greater put-down!

Developers, especially ones who have never made a game for kids before, tend to oversimplify and talk down to younger audiences. They say, "We don't want this game to be too challenging because it is for kids." Don't make that mistake! Kids are far smarter and way better gamers than we give them credit for. Often, they pick up on concepts faster than many adults. There are some limitations you have to consider when making games for kids though. It's true that their little hands can't perform overly complex control schemes. A first grader or younger (6 to 7 years old) may not be able to read many complex words or long amounts of text. And please watch the swearing.

Brainstorming

When coming up with ideas, I like to brainstorm. To brainstorm properly, you need the following five things:

1. A working brain

2. Something to write with

3. Something to write on

4. A place to work

5. Collaborators, preferably ones who also have working brains

Before you start brainstorming, you need to set some ground rules. First, there is no such thing as a stupid or bad idea. Say yes to everything at this stage. Make sure you collaborate with people from other disciplines than game design— programmers, artists, testers, writers. The more diverse your brainstorming group is, the better.[7] People always surprise me with what they bring to the idea creation process.

---

[7] Keep in mind that everyone you invite to your brainstorming session should understand how to make a game, though; otherwise, you might waste a lot of time on unrealistic ideas.

Think about all the things you want your game to be. Then write them down. Your goal is to free associate an idea as far as it can go. Milk the idea completely. When you have reached the ridiculous, squeeze it once more and let it go. Here are some of the notes from one of my brainstorming sessions:

KART RACING BRAINSTORM

SPEED RELATED:

GO SO FAST THAT YOU CAN SKIM WATER
LEAP LONG GAPS/ VIBRATE THROUGH
WALLS/ LEAVE TRAIL OF FIRE/ DODGE
BULLETS/ CREATE A SONIC BOOM/
GET BULLET-TIME (TIME SLOWS)/
AVOID DETECTION OF NON-HUMAN
DEVICE/ DRAG OTHER CHARACTERS
IN YOUR WAKE (SLIP STREAM)
DRIVE DONUTS TO CREATE TORNADO
ROCKET BOOST/ TEAM SPEED BOOST

DAMAGE RELATED:

FLAME BLAST (FROM EXHAUST OR
GOUT FROM FRONT)
BACKWARDS ATTACK = STICKY
BOMBS - BOUNCING BETTY BOMB
FORWARD ATTACK = BULLET /
HEAT-SEEK
WHANGING ON CAR - KNOCK PARTS
LOOSE/ HEALTH LEECH/
SHIELD LEECH/ WEAPON/POWER
UP STEAL
POWERFUL BOMB THAT YOU MUST
SHOOT BEFORE IT EXPLODES
ATOM BOMB FORCE FIELD
(CHARGES UP THEN HURTS
ALL NEARBY)

As you can see, the topics didn't really relate exactly to each other. Sure, they are all features you may find a combat/driving game to have. The ideas don't have to be original at this stage either; you are merely cataloging ideas and concepts. As you design them further, you can start thinking of things such as originality or even fun.

When I am brainstorming, I like to write on a very big whiteboard. You may prefer to use lots of sticky notes. Index cards work pretty well too. It doesn't matter. What matters is that these ideas get recorded. Even if they don't work out, you can always use them for some other game.

An excellent exercise you can use to brainstorm your game idea is to create the box and the manual. What would the cover image be? How would the bullet points on the back of the box read? How would you communicate the game in a black-and-white, 16-page manual? By placing these limitations on your idea, you can streamline your idea to the bare essentials. Here's an example of the back of a game box that you can use as a template:

Breaking Writer's Block

What do you do when the ideas won't come? You don't need to be ashamed. Everyone gets creatively stopped up from time to time. Here are a few tricks to try when you are dealing with writer's block:

1. **Narrow your focus.** Maybe you are trying to think of too many things at once. Tackle your problems one by one by making an outline or breaking things down to a minute level if you have to. Give yourself a timeline to complete each of these tasks, but don't take days. Try to get them done in hours.

2. **Take a walk or exercise.** Everyone knows the brain is fueled by blood. Don't let that blood coagulate in your butt; get outside and move around. When your blood starts circulating again, the new ideas will be coming back in no time.

3. **Deal with something else that may be distracting you.** Sometimes when I am stuck, the reason is that I am worrying about something else. It may be an unfiled expense report or a floor that needs vacuuming. Take a break and deal with whatever is bothering you. When it is done, it won't be a concern anymore!

4. **Jump ahead to the good stuff.** Sometimes you have to come up with ideas for game features that may not excite you as much as other parts of the game. If these are bogging you down, go ahead and jump to the good parts. Take some time to design a

boss fight rather than worrying about the UI design. However, I recommend this trick ONLY as a last resort because it can be very dangerous! The truth is that games are built around schedules, deadlines, and budgets. If you don't get your work done on time and choose fun over the drudge work, the game, the whole team, and even the company can suffer. Don't procrastinate. Time management is very important, so be responsible.

5. **Change your environment.** I find that my office is full of distractions. E-mail beckons, video games call out to be played, and game design documents flutter their little pages at me, begging to be read. When this happens, I get out of my office and go to the nearest conference room to work. Or sometimes I go outside to sit in the sun and get some "vitamin Duh."

6. **Learn from others.** Sometimes when you are trying to think of an answer to a problem, it's a good idea to look at other games and see how they solved it. Maybe you'll solve your problem the same way, or maybe their solutions will provide inspiration for a new, unique solution!

When you have your list of ideas, it is time to get critical. Start narrowing down your list. Some items will immediately jump out as keepers, whereas others are clear losers. Be merciless. It is better to have more good ideas than you can use than to have a game be full of lots of bad ideas.

Present these ideas to another party. Miyamoto has his "wife-o-meter:" He presents his ideas to his wife; if she hates them, they get thrown away. I used to have the executive assistants in my office take a look at game ideas. Someone who has no vested creative interest in your ideas will often give you the clearest and most honest insight.

Why I Hate "Fun"

"Is it fun?" is the question I dread the most when coming up with new game ideas. Many gaming academics have attempted to define what fun is. Designer Marc LeBlanc breaks down fun into eight categories: Sensation, Fellowship, Fantasy, Discovery, Narrative, Expression, Challenge, and Submission.[8] Although the classification of fun is an interesting exercise, I don't find it that helpful "in the field." There are always problems. For example, a game idea (or mechanic or boss fight or whatever) can sound fun on paper but may not be fun when you get it working in the game. Or it may work, but only be fun to you.

The problem with fun is, like humor, it is completely subjective. You can try to skew the odds in your favor by basing your game on existing, proven gameplay style, but more often than not, you end up with a "clone" game. Look at how many lousy first person shooters and survival horror games have been made.

Even if I find something fun the first time I play it, it will almost certainly not be fun on the hundredth go. This ultimately happens to all game developers while working on a game. You will play the same level hundreds of times over the course of the production. Then you will start to lose all objectivity. I distinctly remember several times when a producer would come in and ask:

---

[8] Taken from Marc's GDC lecture and corresponding website: www.8kindsoffun.com/.

When it comes to fun and games, I have found there is only one truth:

YOU HAVE NO GUARANTEE THAT YOUR GAME IDEA IS GOING TO BE FUN

Because developers always lose their objectivity during the course of production, I have created the **Theory of Un-Fun.** The Theory of Un-Fun states:

> Start with a "fun" idea. As you develop the game, if you find something in the game that is not fun (or un-fun), remove it. After you have removed all the un-fun, all that should be left is the fun.

Seems like common sense, right? And yet I have encountered many developers who have left bad gameplay mechanics and ugly art and broken cameras in their games because they got used to them or couldn't recognize them as problems. They just didn't possess the objectivity to see that something in their game was not fun. (Of course, you need to start with a game idea that is fun to begin with. Otherwise, after you have removed all the un-fun, you'll be left with nothing!)

The theory of un-fun must be applied several times during the game's development. Stop what you are doing and take a look at the game. Make a list to determine what is making the game "un-fun." How do you recognize un-fun? Usually, something that is un-fun is pretty obvious. It could be a crappy camera that makes it impossible to see where you are going. It could be laggy controls that make the players feel as if they are moving too "floaty." It could be an animation that takes so long that it impacts the timing of an attack. The puzzles may be too hard. The enemies may be too easy to defeat. The list goes on and on.

While removing un-fun from your game might seem obvious, you are going to have to remove some things that you might have gotten used to, or you might have to change something that took a fair amount of work to make. A producer I once worked with gave me a great piece of advice when it came to ideas: "Don't be too dear." And what he meant was "Don't become so attached to your ideas that you lose objectivity." Don't be afraid to kill bad ideas. If un-fun is ruining your game, kill the un-fun. That's the priority. Don't worry; there are plenty more ideas where those came from.

Now that you have your ideas, you can put them to good use!

Level 2's Universal Truths and Clever Ideas

- All gamers want are good games.
- You have no guarantee that your game is going to be fun.
- Start with a "fun" idea. As you develop the game, remove the "un-fun." All that should be left is the fun.
- Be willing to throw out bad ideas. Throw out some good ideas along with the bad if they don't fit or you have more than you need.
- Ideas are cheap; it's how you use them that matters.
- If you're stuck, take a break—but don't procrastinate.

Level 3

Writing the Story

ALMOST SINCE THE dawn of gaming, designers have debated which is more important: story or gameplay? Some designers believe games require a story to engage the players. Other designers think a story is what people use to describe play when it is finished. Pro-story designers reply that games are an artistic medium used to tell a story. Anti-story designers counter that a story is what you watch while the game loads. Designers at Game Developer Conferences all around the world face off against each other—one group yelling "*BioShock*!" while the other side shouts back "*Doom*!" Silly designers. They are both right and wrong. A game doesn't need to have a story, and yet it always has a story. Perplexing? While you are chewing over that concept, let's look at the classical definition of "story" as taught by everyone from Aristotle to famous screenwriters.

Once Upon a Time . . .

Here's the most basic structure of a story:

1. First, there is a **hero** who has a **desire**.

2. Our hero encounters an **event** that throws his life into disarray and interferes with obtaining the desire. This event causes a **problem** for the hero.

3. The hero tries to **overcome the problem** . . .

4. . . . but **his method fails.**

5. There is a **reversal of fortune,** which causes more trouble for the hero.

6. An **even greater problem** is created for the hero that puts the hero at greater risk.

7. Finally, there is **one last problem** that threatens the hero with the **most risk of all.**

8. The hero must **resolve the final problem . . .**

9. . . . in order to gain his **object of desire.** And everyone lives happily ever after. Well, until the sequel anyway.

Remember that no matter what your story is about, a story ALWAYS has a beginning, a middle, and an end. Hollywood has spent many years analyzing and deconstructing the story. Don't feel that you have to reinvent the wheel; learn what those in Hollywood have. Read screenwriting books, take classes, visit screenwriting websites. But you don't have to feel chained to a standard story structure like Joseph Campbell's "Hero's Journey" or Syd Field's "Three Act Structure." Try using another medium's structures to tell your story. How is a story told in a song? In a TV news report? In a Homeric poem? Try looking at other forms of storytelling for inspiration, like "Kishōtenketsu," which contains four acts: introduction, development, twist, and reconciliation, or "Repetition-Break Structure," which is the format used in fairy-tales like *The Three Little Pigs* and *Goldilocks and the Three Bears*.

Just remember that video games are an interactive medium, and as William Shakespeare reminds us, "The play's the thing." That was one guy who knew story, and he was pretty smart for someone who never played a video game. If gameplay is the meat of the game, then story should be the salt: just enough will add flavor, but too much can ruin everything and kill you.

Some games don't even have stories. Games like *Tetris* or *Bejeweled* or even *Pac-Man* don't need them to be engaging for the player. However, they still generate a **narrative,** which literally means "an order of events."

Because we humans perceive time as linear, we express our experiences linearly as well—even if they aren't presented in a traditional story structure. Let's look at it this way: every time someone plays a game, he creates a narrative. The player can create an infinite number of narratives. As a designer, you need to look at all[1] the narratives possible and find out how to make them ALL fun. The goal is to create multiple narratives that the player will enjoy playing.

In a narrative, the player is the "hero" of the game. The designer needs to look at the game from the player's perspective and be aware of the ordering of the events and experiences that will eventually help the play create the narrative. As each experience builds on the next, the goal is to create rising emotional states for the player. Then the designer can design systems to choreograph these interesting experiences, which in turn create emotions. Savvy? How about an example instead?

Left 4 Dead uses an **artificial intelligence** called the "Director" to control the game's pacing. Depending on the player's "stress level," which is calculated using many variables including health, skill, and location, the Director then adjusts the number of zombies that attack, what items such as ammo and health are generated, and even the music. In the end, the game itself generates a unique and dynamic play experience for the player. However, because most developers don't yet have technology like *Left 4 Dead*'s Director, it is up to designers to create these situations as best they can within their own games.

When you are designing a game, it is extremely important to know the narrative that the player will experience. You'll find that the player's narrative can end up quite different from the game's story. **Remember to never mistake story for gameplay and similarly never mistake gameplay for story.**

I am also a firm believer that almost ANYTHING can be made into gameplay. Don't feel as though you are limited by subject matter. Look at games like *Mr. Mosquito* (the player is a mosquito who drinks the blood of a family), *SimCity* (the player builds and manages a city),

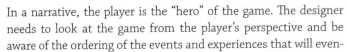

---

[1] Or as many as you can guess will happen. It's like playing a massive session of "what if." However, because these possibilities can stretch on to infinity, predicting everything might not be worth the time investment. That's why when something happens that the designer didn't expect and doesn't break the game, we're more than happy to call it a "feature" and move on!

Diner Dash (a woman serves restaurant guests their meals), or *PaRappa the Rapper* (a dog raps to win the love of his flower girlfriend).

Still don't believe me? Let's look at the classic and simple story *Little Red Riding Hood*. This children's story has all the elements you need to make a great video game:

1. Little Red Riding Hood walks through the forest to Grandma's house = classic player exploration. Give Red some goodies to collect to fill up her picnic basket (inventory system) and have her jump over a fallen log or two on her way.

2. Red meets the Big Bad Wolf = the player has her first enemy encounter. Of course, you can't kill off the wolf yet . . . (unless the enemies are "wolf minions").

3. Carrying a full basic set of goodies (gating mechanism), Red reaches Grandma's house (next level), where she finds "Grandma" waiting in bed.

4. Red questions "Grandma's" true identity ("what big eyes you have"). This can take the form of a quiz, a puzzle, or even a rhythm game.

5. "Grandma" is revealed as the Big Bad Wolf, and Red and the wolf battle to the death = boss fight! [2]

See? Even a "simple" classic story can still offer all the elements to make an exciting and varied video game! [3]

---

[2] We all know that Little Red Riding Hood ends with Red nearly being eaten by the wolf and having the woodcutter save her, but where is the fun in that? Why watch a cutscene when you can have a boss fight? It's not my fault boss fights weren't invented when they wrote this story. Personally, I think my ending is better.

[3] Okay, the story of Little Red Riding Hood might not make for a very LONG video game, but it can be made into a game nonetheless.

The Triangle of Weirdness

I am sure you have heard of the famous production triangle, shown here:

The production triangle

One of the best things about video games is that, technical restraints of your chosen platform aside, you are limited only by your imagination.

Developers can craft virtual worlds that feature unrealistic physics, bizarre characters, and absurd quests. However, it is possible to go crazy with creativity, especially when writing the game story. This is why I created the **"Triangle of Weirdness."** Notice the difference in the choices on the triangle of weirdness: characters, activities, and world.

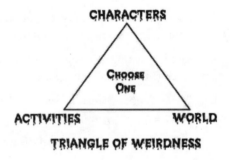

TRIANGLE OF WEIRDNESS

Unlike the production triangle where you can have any two points, you can choose only **one** corner on the triangle of weirdness. Choose any more than that and you risk alienating your audience.

Let's look at three examples of how to apply the Triangle of Weirdness to your story and world.

While the *Wizard of Oz* features weird characters such as a Tin Man, a Lion, and a Scarecrow, the land of Oz was a pretty typical fairy tale location when it was created in the 1900s. The characters of the *Wizard of Oz* have desires readers can relate to: courage, love, and the wish to return home.

While the main characters of *Star Wars* are familiar (the young hero, the princess in distress, the charming rogue), and their desires are familiar (join the war effort, defeat the villains, get the girl), it is the world of *Star Wars* that is weird with its Jawas, Wookies, Jedis, and a cantina populated by the craziest-looking scum in the galaxy.

Monty Python and the Holy Grail features typical (if not archetypical) characters: King Arthur and his knights of the round table. These stalwart knights travel through medieval England on their quest for the Holy Grail. However, that quest is filled with weird activities like designing shrubs for the knights who say "Ni!" or being slaughtered by the killer rabbit of Caerbannog.

It is possible to go too far. Movies like *Dune* (1984) and *The City of Lost Children* (1995), or video games like *SkullMonkeys* or *Muscle Man March,* while incredibly unique and creative, just left many audiences feeling that they "didn't get it." And nobody likes to feel stupid.

What do these games and movies have in common? They all violate the Triangle of Weirdness. Do so at your own peril . . .

A Likely Story

When developing a game story, you will find you have three different types of people in your audience:

1. Players who are into your story as it happens

2. Players who want to get into your story in depth

3. Players who don't care what the story is at all[4]

Making your story appealing to all three types of players can be a challenge. The best rule of thumb is to always make the story be in service of the gameplay and not the other way around. Here are some tips on involving story into the game:

- To satisfy players who are looking for a deeper experience, provide details but make sure they don't get in the way of the story. For example, *BioShock* and *Batman: Arkham Asylum* both have non-mandatory collectable audiotapes that reveal deeper story details to players without intruding on the main story.

---

[4] I can't take credit for this observation. This statement was made by Ken Levine, the director of *BioShock,* during his excellent 2009 GDC speech.

- Because players who are just along for the ride will indiscriminately press the "A" button to get through audio cues and cutscenes that reveal story points, make sure your game's story is also revealed through gameplay and level design to prevent players from skipping it entirely. Otherwise, they will get lost and confused.[5] You can also introduce story as gameplay by making stories playable flashbacks or puzzles.

- Another option is to start your story as late into the action as possible. This can be in the middle of a boss fight, at the end of a level, or during a car chase. Keep in mind that your story will still have a beginning; you are just choosing not to start the game by showing it. You can flash back or tell the story in a non-chronological order. This change in structure works better in story-based games. I'm not sure it's such a good idea to start a puzzle game of *Tetris* with dozens of tiles raining down on the players.

- Always keep your stories lively and moving. Professional screenwriters may introduce a change in the plot or action every 15 minutes. Even with non-story games, play sessions are becoming "bite-sized" so they're short enough for players to enjoy in short bursts.

Speaking of surprises, there is a trend in game stories that I blame squarely on Hollywood: the twist/surprise ending. "It was all a dream." "He was really a dead the whole time." "He wasn't really my friend after all." These kind of O. Henry endings have become more and more common as video game creators try to tell what they consider a "mature" story. While audiences like to be taken by surprise, more and more often these twist endings wind up feeling like a predicable cliché. There is merit to a predictable ending. Why? Because people also like it when the good guys win and the bad guys lose, even though that's the oldest story in the book. While you want to have some surprises to keep things interesting, don't sacrifice consistency. If everything in your story (or game for that matter) is a surprise, the player won't have anything to latch onto and will constantly be thrown off-balance.

Take, for example, the James Bond movies of the 1980s. When I was growing up, I loved to go see those films. Even before I saw them, I knew that Bond was going to use a cool new gadget and drive an awesome car, defeat the villain's scheme, save the world, and end up with the hot girl. So, if I knew all of these things, why did I bother watching the movie? For me, the fun was the twists and turns the story took. I knew the WHO, the WHAT, and the WHY, but I didn't know the HOW.

There is a delight in predicting how things will turn out. It makes the players feel smart, as if they "called it" in an election or solved a mystery. Besides, life is unpredictable enough as it is; why not give your audience a little predictability? The point I am making is you don't have to be especially clever when writing your story, just entertaining.

---

[5] Yeah, I know. It's their own darn fault if they get confused for skipping the cutscenes in the first place, but remember the first rule of responsible game design: love thy player.

Conversely, something that I don't find very clever is a video game story in which the main character has amnesia. Amnesia ranks as the number one video game cliché of all time, but I understand why game writers use it. It's an attempt to approximate the lack of information about the characters and the world as a player begins the game. However, it ultimately becomes an excuse for the writer to construct an "unreliable narrative" and intentionally omit information to the player to be able to create a "shock ending." It just feels forced and, frankly, isn't fair to the player.

Instead, here is a great theory about the value of surprise versus suspense from classic director Alfred Hitchcock. Imagine that two men are sitting at a table talking about baseball. The conversation lasts about five minutes, when suddenly there is a huge explosion! This shocks the audience, but that surprise lasts only about 15 seconds.

However, here is how you can get a greater impact from your audience. Start the scene by showing the bomb under the table. The bomb is set to explode in five minutes. The two men discuss baseball while the audience members are squirming in their seats thinking, "Don't just sit there talking about baseball! There's a bomb under the table! Get out of there!" When you make the audience aware of the danger the characters are in, they get emotionally involved. By the time your scene reaches its climax, you have created more excitement with your audience than just the surprise of the bomb exploding.[6]

Some people believe that **theme** is even more important than story to a game. Why is that? Because theme is the central topic of the game. A theme can often be summed up in a statement like "love conquers all" or "order is better than chaos" or "with great power comes great responsibility." Your game can have a theme without even having a story. *Pac-Man's* theme? "Eat or be eaten." *Plants vs. Zombies'* theme? "Good vs. evil." *Journey's* theme? "Life is a journey

---

[6] Hitchcock also recommends that you don't actually kill the characters in this scenario. In the case of video games, the game would be over!

that is better with others." Gameplay should be centered around the game's theme. If the gameplay doesn't support the game's theme, maybe it doesn't belong in the game.

Another question to consider when developing your story is "what is at stake?" Many video games are about saving the world from evil or destruction. But just like every movie doesn't have to be a slam-bang blockbuster, not every video game has to be about saving the world. Small themes can be just as important as big ones. In my opinion, using a theme for your story other than "violence solves all problems" is a worthwhile pursuit. It worked for games like *Frogger*, *Zoo Tycoon*, and *Braid*.

Time to Wrap It Up

Ending games can be just as hard as starting them. In the good old days, there wasn't an end to a game, just a kill screen.[7] Or games just ran forever, frequently wrapping their scores around like your car's odometer. Then along came *Dragon's Lair*, and everyone wanted to know whether or not Dirk rescued the Princess—and players spent lots of money to find out.[8]

How long should a game be? In the old days, the average was 20 hours. In the really old days, it was 40. For modern story-based console games, playtime averages 8–12 hours. Contrast that with mobile games with play sessions that can last minutes but still offer dozens of hours of gameplay for a single title. Multiplayer games can offer years of gameplay. Even after logging more than 400 hours on *Team Fortress 2* (Valve, 2007), I still enjoy playing it.

I recommend ending the game when you feel that you have left the players feeling satisfied. If you leave plot points dangling open up storylines for sequels, your players will feel like they are missing something or not getting the whole story. I always suggest that you play fair with the players. Let them feel as though they accomplished everything they needed to do during the game.

Some games even offer extra experiences so the players can continue playing after the story has ended. Multiple endings, minigames, unlockable and downloadable content, or "deleted levels" (akin to deleted scenes on a DVD) will let your players experience new stories in your established world.

---

[7] A *kill screen* originally wasn't the "game over" screen, but rather a screen that appeared due to a programming error or design oversight. The most famous kill screen from classic gaming is the 256th level of *Pac-Man*. At this point, due to a bug, half the screen becomes garbled data, which keeps the player from collecting all the dots and clearing the board to move on. Arcade owners had to unplug or "kill" the game to start it back up again.

[8] Since *Dragon's Lair* cost twice the amount of money than an average arcade game to play (a whopping 50 cents!), my brother and I would observe the other players at our local arcade and write down the patterns required to get through each of the game's trap- and monster-laden rooms. When it was our turn to play, one of us would man the joystick while the other called out which way to go. We managed to save the princess without spending more than five dollars. The world's first cooperative gaming experience!

This advice is particularly true with the living world of an MMORPG, which needs long-term, evolving storylines to keep players engaged (and paying monthly subscription fees). Blizzard's *World of Warcraft* has been continuously running since 2004 thanks to the addition of quests and even new worlds that add more content for the players.

Or you can just throw away all the previous advice and write your story at the last minute. Some development teams concentrate solely on the gameplay and create the storyline last. They claim this approach works. Personally, I think it would make me nervous.

A Game by Any Other Name

Oh, I almost forgot to address one of the most important things about your game's story: the title! There are several ways to approach naming your game.

- A **literal title** makes it easy to figure out where the title came from. It can be the name of your main character, like *Sonic the Hedgehog* or *Voodoo Vince*. It can be the main location of your game, like *Castle Wolfenstein* or *Saint's Row*. Or you can name your game after a gameplay activity or component like *Command and Conquer* or *Boom Blocks*.

- The **action/cool title** is one that captures the spirit of the game without mentioning any of the game characters or locations. I think games like *Darksiders*, *Brütal Legend*, and *Gears of War* all have cool titles.

- The **punny title** is one that makes you appreciate its cleverness. *System Shock*, *Half Life*, and *Dead Space* are all good examples of punny titles. As puns are word play, you have to be careful because your audience may not get the reference or think the pun is funny. As columnist Doug Larson said "A pun is the lowest form of humor, unless you thought of it yourself."

- A **purple cow title** is one that makes your audience stop in their tracks and wonder why the title was chosen.[9] It is a title that captures your curiosity and begs your attention. Purple cow titles include *LittleBigPlanet*, *Resident Evil*, and *Naughty Bear*. The advantage to a purple cow title is that it becomes strongly associated with the game because the title is so unique.

- The **dramatic title** is one that sounds more like a movie than a game. Typically it's a phrase that sounds dramatic rather than a title. It often refers to the theme of the game or tries to connote the feeling of the game. Examples include *The Sum of All Fears*, *The Suffering of Isaac*, and *The Last of Us*.

---

[9] The term "purple cow" comes from the poem by Gelett Burgess, who wrote: "I never saw a purple cow, I never hope to see one. But I can tell you anyhow, I'd rather see than be one."

- The **referential title** refers to something in the game that you have no idea what it is about unless you have played the game. After players have played the game, they understand the significance of the title. For example, if you were to hear the word "halo" before playing *Halo*, you might have thought of that glowing circular band over an angel's head. Now that everyone has played the game, it's going to be a long time before anyone thinks of using the word halo in a game title; it's just too strongly associated with that game. Other examples include *Unreal, Portal,* and *Spore.*

No matter what naming convention you use, I think that shorter titles are better than longer ones. First of all, they are easier to remember and say. I like to keep them to two or three syllables like *Star Wars, Don-kee Kong, Pac-Man,* or *Hey-lo.* I think this started because of marquee sizes on arcade cabinets: they needed to attract the players' attention, create some mystery, and describe the gameplay. "Defender" is still one of the best names ever: it perfectly sums up the game in one three-syllable word.

Second, shorter titles are easier to make into logos for your game's start screen and read on the cover of a game's box. Don't forget to consider marketing aspects when you are creating your game's title. If you have to use a longer title or a subtitle, still try to keep it short. *Uncharted 3: Drake's Deception* combines a couple of purple cows to make a pretty good title. *Uncharted* gives you the image of exploring or sailing into unknown and dangerous territory. Players will want to know who Drake is and what his deception is. *Batman: Arkham City* lets you know who you are playing (Batman) and where the action takes place (Arkham City). This title is especially good because it adds a bit of the "what the ?" factor, since most Batman fans know that Batman lives in Gotham City and Arkham is the asylum home of his greatest villains! The title alone compels you to play the game!

Try to name your game sooner than later. I have always preferred the titles created by the game's developers over those made up by someone else such as the marketing team. And publishers have a bad habit of vetoing developers' suggested names or outright name the game themselves. The larger the budget, the more power the publisher will have over the name. However, I believe that the developer knows what is important about the game and often know best who they are making the game for. Trust their instincts.

I once worked on a game that was pitched with a great purple cow title: *Mr. Hong's Violent Orchestra.* The title drew our attention and really made people sit up and take notice. Folks wanted to know who Mr. Hong was. They were delightfully confused to what a "violent orchestra" could be. What kind of music did a violent orchestra play? Because it was a silly musical fighting game, the title was very appropriate. Sadly, management didn't agree. As the game was transformed into a music-centric rhythm game (rather than a musical combat game), the title was changed to the more forgettable *Battle of the Bands.* Needless to say, the game didn't do very well, and I feel the lackluster title was part of the reason why.

When you have finally named your game, you may discover that your great title is already in use or trademarked by someone else. In the U.S., you can check for patents on U.S. Patent and Trademark Office web site: `http://uspto.gov`. Be sure you check with your publisher's legal department to make sure you can use your title before you become too attached to it. Even a quick word search on the Internet will help get you started.

Creating Characters Your Players Care About

My friend and fellow designer Andy Ashcraft believes that video game developers don't care about telling the second act of their story. He points out that developers love telling the setup and background of their game, and they love getting to the big finish of the game. What they neglect to concentrate on is the middle of the story—the second act—where character and story development happens. I tend to agree with Andy. However, games that skip the second art are missing an important part of the storytelling process.[10] In games, the first act is this is usually told with a cutscene or, even worse, the game's manual—which no one ever reads![11] The second act is the grind that moves the player toward the third act, which is the completion of the story, usually the last level and a boss fight. This is a mistake. In the first act, the player should be given an opportunity to find out about and care about the character. You need that first act to bond with the character, even if you kill off that character repeatedly (common in video games) or radically change him into a killing machine. Case in point, you don't need to look any further than the 1986 movie *Robocop*.

---

[10] Remember, all stories have what? A beginning, a middle, and an end.

[11] Maybe I am exaggerating a little, but c'mon. When was the last time you really read a game manual? Then again, when was a game manual worth reading?

In the film *Robocop*, the audience is introduced to police officer Alex Murphy. He's an honest cop and a decent guy fighting crime in futuristic Detroit. By page 25 of the script, you actually care about the guy and feel bad when he's gunned down by criminal scumbags. The second act kicks off when Murphy is rebuilt as the cyborg Robocop. Several video game adaptations of this movie have been made, and in all of them, Murphy's death is shown only as a cutscene. Players start the game as Robocop, and the killing of bad guys commences immediately.[12] But in our hypothetical Robocop game, why not start with Murphy as a cop? The first level of the game would have Murphy tracking down the bad guys and end with his death. The players should have time to bond with him, making his death and resurrection have much more of an impact.

Death should mean something to the players, especially when it isn't the main character dying. When was the last time you cried when a game character died? (Other than when you accidently deleted your save file?) Writers forget that you have to care about a character first if it is going to mean anything when you kill him. And the solution isn't to make the character a relative or part of a meaningful relationship, especially if that character is killed off in the first cutscene. I remember playing a game that opened with the player's relative getting murdered after interacting with him for one level. I didn't feel the righteous anger that the player felt for the rest of the game because I knew the character for such a short time. Invest the time in these characters, even if the ultimate goal is to kill them off.

A tried-and-true way to get players to care about a video game character is to use what I call the **Yorda Effect.** Named after the non-player character (NPC) from *Ico* (SCEA, 2001), Yorda is a young girl that Ico has to protect from enemies and help traverse the environment as the pair attempt to escape a mysterious castle. Yorda is portrayed as a (mostly) helpless character, and her survival is critical to the player's success. If Yorda dies, so do you. But your Yorda character cannot be completely helpless. The character needs to offer limited assistance to the player in the form of healing, assisting in combat, providing extra ammo, or solving puzzles. If designed correctly, this co-dependency between characters creates a protective relationship in which the player comes to genuinely care about the welfare of the NPC. This allows the storyteller to solicit stronger emotions between the characters over the course of the game. One particularly brilliant mechanic from *Ico* is that the ever-distracted Yorda runs only when Ico holds her hand. It might seem like a small detail, but it is a lovely way of illustrating the relationship between the two characters.

---

[12] Just so you realize that I'm not a complete idiot, I do know why the developers of Robocop began the player as Robocop. (1) It's more appealing to play as a criminal-blasting cyborg than as a fragile human; (2) game carts in 1988 didn't have the memory to store two completely different player character models, and why would you go through all the work to create them, especially if you were only going to be the human player character for one level; and (3) the game is called *Robocop*, not "Guy who gets shot and eventually becomes *Robocop*."

If you want to get players to care about a character, make sure that the players spend some time with that character, even if it's only for a little while. *Heavy Rain's* (Quantic Dream, 2010) protagonist Ethan spends a (playable) day with his son Shaun before the boy is kidnapped by the Origami Killer. By the time you get to the scene where you are trying to find Shaun in a crowd, you have built up a relationship and genuinely care about his welfare.

The *Uncharted* series' Victor "Sully" Sullivan, *BioShock Infinite's* Elizabeth, Shadow the dog from *Dead to Rights*, and Ellie from *The Last of Us* all offer examples of the Yorda Effect because the respective games attempt to make you care about these NPCs . . . with varying degrees of success.

Creating a Yorda-type character for your game takes a lot of design time and effort . . . that you just might not have. The point is, you have to make the characters in your game important somehow to the players. A character can provide information on how to play the game, be the economy system (like the proprietor of the game's store), or provide health power-ups to the player on a regular basis. When that character is taken out of the game, the player will feel the impact.

Spoiler alert, but in my humble opinion, the only game character whose death felt impactful in *Final Fantasy VII* was Aeris. Aeris filled many roles for the player: she was a damsel in distress, one part of the hero's love triangle, a character who contributed solutions to the problems in the plot, and a "playable" part of the gaming party. When she died, her loss to the player was felt on many levels. The point is to build up your game characters before you tear them down. Make their loss count.

Your party members don't have to be human: the deaths of Agro the horse in *Shadow of the Colossus* and Dogmeat the dog in *Fallout 3* have similar effects on players. All that matters is that your players have a bond with these characters to feel the loss when it happens.

All this talk about death has bummed me out. So, what about humor in games? Most writers agree that comedy is harder than drama. However, I believe that the secret to humor is character. My favorite first person shooter is *Team Fortress 2*, and I believe it is one of the funniest games I have ever played. The game doesn't feature humor like other games have; you won't find physical gags, "hilarious" jokes, or burping and farting. What makes the game so funny is how true the characters are to themselves. From the wry Australian sniper who has to defend his occupation to his parents, to the Russian heavy gunner who is overly fond of "sanviches." All the game characters' appearances, animations, and vocal barks reinforce their personalities, raising them from stereotypes to truly original (and funny) characters.

Your game character's actions should be defined by his personality. When we were creating *Maximo*, we decided that he was an impatient guy, always in a hurry to rescue the princess or get into a fight. He didn't even stop to open a treasure chest; he just kicked it open, collected the treasure, and kept moving. If you start with your character's personality, you will end up with some interesting animations and gameplay. Characters can have many motivations: the desire for success or revenge, they could be seeking love or acceptance. Many characters have more than one and often conflicting motivations. Knowing their motivations will help you determine what your characters will do and say. The result will be much richer characters.

Speaking of characters, just like giving your game the right title is important, it is equally important to name your characters correctly. Would you name a strapping barbarian hero Mortimer? Only if your hero is a parody or it's a comedy game. Names carry great weight. It is important to give your characters the right name. Baby books are a great place to start. I like names that have some significance to a character's personality or what her occupation is. *Star Wars* has some of the best names. What does the name Luke Skywalker tell you about the character? Luke feels like a simple, homespun name fitting for a farm boy who yearns to "walk among the stars."[13]

It's also fun to have characters' names juxtapose each other. Two of my favorite character names are from *When Harry Met Sally*. Billy Crystal's character is named Harry Burns—a curmudgeonly, burned-out name if ever there was one. Meg Ryan's character is Sally Albright. She's positive, romantic, and a little naïve. These names are blatantly obvious, and they give you a quick snapshot of each character's personality.

Comedic characters need appropriate names too. Guybrush Threepwood, SpongeBob Squarepants, and Larry Laffer aren't heroic-sounding names, but they are totally appropriate for the humorous games they are in. The only rule of thumb is that when you look at an image of the character, the name fits what you see.

---

[13] Did you know that Luke Skywalker's original name was Luke Starkiller? This name change provides a great lesson: never give your character a name that gives away the ending of your story!

That's all I have to say about naming characters. And now for something completely different:

A Few Pointers on Writing for Kids of All Ages

Here's some advice when writing games for kids: just because you are writing game stories for kids doesn't mean the story has to be simplistic. The most common mistake kid-game writers make is trying to make the story too simple. I have often heard developers protest over using complex ideas and themes because "it's for kids!" But think about children's literature. Children's classics like *Where the Wild Things Are, Heidi,* and *The Chronicles of Narnia* are full of complex themes, interactions, and emotions. If it's good enough for kids' books, it should be good enough for kids' games. Coming of age doesn't only mean that the main character can carry a sword!

Another great thing about kids' games (heck, this applies to all games) is that you can teach your players things without their even knowing it. I'm not talking about "edutainment," but the type of entertainment you used to find in movies and comic books. As a kid, I remember a *Batman* comic book in which I learned about famous comedians of the 1920s, the opera *Pagliacci,* African masks, and how paraffin wax discolors with age. That's some pretty impressive knowledge to gain from a "kiddie story." Don't be afraid to educate as well as entertain. Who knows, your players may learn something while they are having fun . . . and you may learn something as you are writing your story.

Writing for Licenses

A **licensed game** is one you create based on a pre-existing intellectual property (or *IP*), such as a character or world first seen in a movie, comic book, real life, television, or even another video game.[14] *Star Wars, Batman, Harry Potter,* and *SpongeBob Squarepants* are all licensed characters and worlds, known as **properties**. The property is licensed by a publisher or developer, which means that a fee is paid to use the property for a game (or several games). The group or individual who owns the original property is called the **licensor.** Licensors include groups such as Lucasfilm, DC Comics, J.K. Rowling, or Nickelodeon (to use the preceding examples). However, just because the **licensee** has paid to make a game using the character, that doesn't mean he can make any game he wants. A licensee must work with the licensor to adhere to the brand. For example, a licensor may not want a character to kill enemies. Therefore, the developer has

---

[14] There are also plenty of IPs that exist in the public domain: *Cinderella, The Wizard of Oz, Dracula, The Three Musketeers, The Bible, Dante's Inferno,* to name a few. Remember to base your own work on the original material and not on someone else's interpretation.

to design the game around these "brand limitations." Some properties are pretty lenient about what developers can do with them, whereas others are very strictly moderated.

Don't be dismayed about having to stay within the confines of a license. With a good licensing partner, you can design a game that allows room for creativity. For example, my team was working on a licensed game that had seen more than ten games previously based on it. Not looking forward to making just "another installment" of the property, we discussed making the new game a genre that wasn't just a standard platformer. After we made our pitch, the licensor confessed being tired of creating the same style of game over and over, but had never considered taking the gameplay in another direction. The licensor gave us a lot more freedom than we had previously thought we would have and, in the end, we produced a solid game. Just because you are working on a licensed game, don't assume that you are locked in to the "same old, same old." It never hurts to ask.

Here are a few tips I've picked up from working on licensed games:

- Find out about the license inside and out. Read, watch, and play everything you can on it. Go deep whenever possible. If you go in directions that aren't obvious or use characters that are more obscure, the fans of the brand will appreciate it. Every licensed game should be a celebration of the license and a big "thank you" to the fans.

- Uncover the "big issues" early. Talk to your licensor and find out what the big "no no" issues are. Doing this will save you a lot of headaches and prevent you from making resources that will have to be changed later in production. For example, one game used hamburgers as a power-up. When the character ate them, he became invulnerable. However, even though it was never mentioned in any of the license's episodes, one of the main characters (one that was a playable character in our game) was a vegetarian. We had to change the power-up because the show's creators didn't like that we had their character eating meat.

- Remember that licensors can have final approval and be very tricky to work with. On one project, the licensor would repeatedly reject the project because a rock was the wrong color blue.[15] But unfortunately, there's often not much you can do about this behavior. If it's not important, follow their request and move on.

- Get as much material as possible from the licensor. Television shows have "bibles"—detailed documents that outline the show characters and worlds. Established comic books have years of back issues that make great reference material. If your license is still in production (for example, if you are making a game for a movie with a simultaneous release), get hold of scripts, animatics, storyboards, and production photos as soon as possible.

---

[15] Seriously, this happened. It happened so much on one project my teammates started calling this kind of request "blue rocking." The term has stuck in my personal vocabulary.

- If you are working on a game based on a movie or TV show, try to go to the set (if applicable) and take your own reference pictures. Try to get anything you might need to help you replicate the world of the license as closely as possible.

- Respect the license, but find ways to make it your own. A two-hour movie may not have enough material to allow you to create an eight- to ten-hour game. Work with the licensor to expand the fiction to help you "fill in the gaps." Don't be afraid to bring your own interests to the party; those interests may fit in better to the brand's license than you may think.

There is much more I could tell you about writing stories, but I won't. This description should get you started with *your* stories. Next, let's get back on track and talk about the foundations of gameplay: what I call the Three Cs!

Level 3's Universal Truths and Clever Ideas

- Some games need a story. Some games don't. All games need gameplay.
- A story always has a beginning, a middle, and an end.
- Never mistake story for gameplay.
- Almost ANYTHING can be made into gameplay.
- Create a world that players will want to play in, and they will come back to play.
- Make death matter.
- Players care about NPCs when those characters contribute something to the gameplay.
- Keep names short and descriptive.
- Don't underestimate kids: they're smarter than you think.
- Stay true to a license, but don't be afraid to "make it your own."

Level 4

You Can Design a Game, but Can You Do the Paperwork?

A JAPANESE GAME director once visited the studio where I worked to impart his wisdom to our team about his philosophy of game design, which mainly had to do with how much money his latest game had made. As he was leaving, he asked our team a cryptic question: "I believe making games is like fishing," he said. "When I return, you will tell me why this is so." If he had been wearing a cape, I'm sure he would have swooshed it mysteriously as he left.

I spent a lot of time thinking about just exactly how making games was like fishing. In the end, I decided that making games is **nothing** like fishing. Fishing is quiet and slow and involves waiting for something to happen that may never happen.[1] I also decided that this game director was full of crap. So I developed my own analogy.

Making games is like making chili (bear with me—it'll make sense soon). Like making chili, making games means you first need a recipe, and that recipe is the game's design. Having the right recipe is important. You are not making soup or stew. You want to make sure your documentation covers not only what is in your game, but how it can be made—just like a recipe. Be sure to follow the recipe, but be mindful that it will have to change, especially if something doesn't go right. And, just as when you're making chili, you must remember that

---

[1] You may be able to tell from this statement that I do not enjoy fishing.

you can season to taste. Some parts of the game will be "meatier" than others, so you will need to adjust your game to make those parts more pronounced.

The next step is to assemble the ingredients. Just as a chili needs ingredients, a game's design needs gameplay elements. The developers are the chefs. They make sure everything is prepared and cooking like it should. You need the right tools—code that runs the game and scripting tools to create the gameplay—just like you need spoons and pots and pans and a stove to make your chili. However, you might not have exactly what you need at hand. Sometimes you might have the team and resources you want, and sometimes you have to improvise with what is available. That's OK; I hear cowboys made some pretty good chili using nothing more than a campfire and a tin can. Prepare and add the ingredients in the right order. Simmer the beans and the vegetables first. Brown the meat **before** you add it to the pot. (I learned that one the hard way.)

In chili, everything is brought to a boil and then left to simmer. The **game's production** reminds me of boiling—a burst of energy and effort to get everything in and running. However, if you leave the pot boiling too hot for too long, you can ruin the chili, burn the pot, and catch the stove (and the chefs) on fire. Games and studios have been destroyed by too much **crunch time**, so be responsible. **Game polishing** and **bug squashing** remind me of chili simmering. Chili isn't ready the moment you finish assembling it. You need to take the time to make it just right, to fine-tune the seasonings and let the ingredients meld to create a richer taste. Games, just like chili, need time to be iterated on, improved, and seasoned. **Bugs,** code, art, and design problems with the game need to be found and fixed. That takes time. Allow for that time, just like you need to allow for cooking time with chili. Sometimes it's good to let the team play with a part of the game to find out what works and what doesn't. I find that chili always tastes better the day after you have made it.

You may need to add something to your chili at the last minute to make it work. Unless you've royally screwed it up, chili can usually be salvaged. However, I don't recommend making games this way. It can lead to stomach upset. Chili can also deceive. It may look horrible but still taste delicious. Some games may not be perfect, or even pretty, but if they have good gameplay, they can still entertain. Good games and good chili satisfy the soul as well as the stomach. (Or the head, if you think with your stomach.)

You see? Making games is **exactly** like making chili. Take that, Japanese game director![2]

Achievement Unlocked
20 G - Exactly Like Making Chili

---

[2] I don't blame him for his bad analogy. They might not have very good chili in Japan.

So you've learned how to make chili, but what about making games? To make a game, you need to create a **game design document,** or **GDD** for short. A game design document defines everything in your game. Sound like a tall order? It is! But don't be scared, there are actually four documents that will guide you through preproduction as you build towards making your GDD:

1. The one-sheet

2. The ten-pager

3. The beat chart

4. The game design document

While each of these documents has a specific use during the preproduction/production, the first three each build upon the content from the previous document and eventually end up composing the content found in the GDD.

Check out Bonus Levels 1, 2, and 3 for templates of these documents.   **NOTE**

The length of your GDD is going to be dictated by the complexity of your game. A GDD for a mobile game might only need a 30 page document. A console game might require a document over 300 pages. Game designers have struggled with just how long a game design document should be. There is a movement within the game development community to keep the game design document as short as possible, for a variety of reasons. In the end, I believe a GDD should be just long enough to accurately describe what is going on in the game. However, don't let that intimidate you. The other documents—the one-sheet, the ten-pager, and the beat chart—are all steps to help you reach your goal of a completed GDD.

Speaking of the basics, you should make sure your document is readable. I'm not just talking about using proper grammar or using correct spelling and punctuation—all of which are very important in making your documents look professional. I'm referring to using the right body font. **Font** refers to a particular style of typeface. Fonts can be used to convey feeling when you only have words to play with, and I explain how to do that later in this chapter. What I'm referring to is the main body of text of your document—much like the words in a book. You should avoid fancy fonts; otherwise, your readers won't be able read your document. Keep things simple and legible.[3]

---

[3] I suggest a simple font like Arial, Calibri, Helvetica, or Times New Roman.

Speaking of fonts, I recommend never using more than two font styles in one document unless you absolutely have to. You can use a fancy (but legible) font for the title page and things like headings, but try to keep your font size around 22 points or larger. For the body text of your document, keep your font size around 12 points. Anything smaller can be hard for some people to read. If you are creating a PowerPoint presentation for your game, I suggest using body text no smaller than 24 points.

By the way, there is no official format for any of these game design documents. What I'm showing you here is just one way to present the information. For example, video game consultant Mark Cerny presents his GDD material in a single page per topic, bullet point format. He claims this simple presentation is easier for his teammates to read and digest. Use what works best for you. Just remember, the goal of great game design documentation is **communication**—communication to the player, to your team members, and to your publishing partners. The clearer the communication, the easier it is going to be to get your coworkers excited about your ideas. Got it? Good. Let's start writing!

Writing the GDD, Step 1: The One-Sheet

The one-sheet is a simple overview of your game. A variety of people will read it, including your teammates and publisher, so you need to keep it interesting, informative, and most importantly, short. It should be no longer than . . . you guessed it . . . a single page. You will find two examples of one-sheets in Bonus Level 1. You can create them anyway you'd like, just as long as you include the following information:

- Game title
- Intended game systems
- Target age of players
- Intended Entertainment Software Rating Board (ESRB) rating
- A summary of the game's story, focusing on gameplay
- Distinct modes of gameplay
- Unique selling points
- Competitive products

Most of these terms are self-explanatory, but the following sections describe a few you may not know.

ESRB Ratings

The ESRB is a self-regulatory organization that enforces a rating system as well as advertising and online privacy principles for software in the United States and Canada.[4] The ESRB's creation is similar to the comic book industry's Comics Code Authority, which was created to enforce content and morality guidelines in conjunction with concerned parent groups. However, the ESRB's rating system more closely resembles that of the MPAA's movie rating system (G, PG, PG-13, R, X). Games are reviewed and assigned a letter rating according to content.

Currently, the ESRB can assign six ratings:

- **eC (Early Childhood)**—Contains no material parents would find inappropriate.

- **E (Everyone)** —May contain fantasy, cartoon or mild violence, and infrequent use of mild language.

- **E10 (Everyone 10+)**—May contain more fantasy, cartoon or mild violence, and mild language and suggestive themes.

- **T (Teen)** —May contain violence, suggestive themes, crude humor, minimal blood, and infrequent use of strong language.

- **M (Mature 17+)**—May contain intense violence, blood and gore, sexual content, and strong language.

- **AO (Adults Only 18+)**—Not suitable for people under 18; may contain prolonged scenes of intense violence, graphic sexual content, and nudity.

Although the ESRB's guidelines are effective in informing parents what titles are appropriate for their children, stigma is attached to some of the ratings within the development community and fanbase.

Many gamers consider eC to be for "baby games" because this rating most frequently appears on edutainment and licensed titles for young audiences. At the other end of the scale, no brick-and-mortar retailer in America will carry a game with the AO rating. It's the industry's equivalent of an X rating in film. Therefore, most publishers and developers won't even consider making games for this rating and will take great pains to prevent their titles from having this rating.[5]

---

[4] The ESRB is the American rating system. There are several other international systems including the Pan-European Games Information (PEGI), the UK's British Board of Film Classification (BBFC), and Germany's Unterhaltungssoftware Selbstkontrolle (USK). Their age and content restrictions vary by country.

[5] This situation happened on *The Punisher* (THQ, 2005), where players could curb-stomp and feed criminals into a woodchipper during interrogations. The scenes were so graphic that the developer changed the camera angles and displayed the action in black-and-white to bring the AO rating down to an M.

An advantage to publishing iOS and Android games is that developers don't need to submit their games to the ESRB to sell them. However, Apple, Google, and Microsoft have best practices and guidelines on certain content such as pornography, so you can forget about selling your X-rated platformer on the iPhone.

Unique Selling Points

Unique selling points (or **USPs**) are the "bullet points" found on the back of the box. As a rule of thumb, you should have around five USPs. (A number I developed when I realized I could really fit only five bullet points on the back of a game box.) Remember that "amazing graphics" and "awesome story" or "sequel to the award-winning game" don't count. All games should have or be these things (though only if your game actually is a sequel in the case of the last one). Besides, gamers can spot that marketing lingo a mile away. USPs should be the unique features that make your game stand out from the crowd. Here are some examples. Let the spin begin!

- "Multiple gameplay modes, including the mind-blistering 256-player death match!"

- "Over 1,000 tunes from the universe's greatest bands!"

- "Explore gaming's biggest open-world, where players can go anywhere!"

- "Mow through your enemies using the blastinator, the skull-defiler, and the awesome fire-ant extinguisher!"

- "Experience better-than-reality physics and eyeball-numbing special effects with the new Realitech engine!"

As you can see, USPs should get readers excited about the features of a game without going into lengthy detail about them. Exposing more of that detail is what the ten-pager is all about.

Competitive Products

Competitive products (or **"comps"**) are games that are similar to your game design idea that have already been released. Listing comps in your one-sheet helps your readers understand what your game is going to be about. However, make sure that when you choose your comps, you pick games that (a) people are very familiar with or (b) are successful. Publishers and marketers are very aware of how well or poorly a game sold. If you choose a comp of a game that did badly, a potential publisher may get scared off. Like I say, "Always pick a winning horse."

Writing the GDD, Step 2: The Ten-Pager

Now that you have completed your game outline, it is time to expand that information and flesh out the details.

The **ten-pager** is a "broad stroke" design document that lays out the spine of your game. The intent is for readers to quickly understand the basics of the final product without going into excruciating detail. Keeping your ten-pager interesting may be the most important part of your document. Remember, the people who are going to finance your game are going to read this document. Be sure to provide plenty of visuals but keep them relevant. Don't go overboard with fancy fonts and ornate layouts. Readability is the key. Creating your ten-pager in PowerPoint or a similar program will assist you with formatting, and will enable you can present it electronically during a pitch meeting or print it out as a "leave behind" handout.

No matter which document you are creating, the goal is to make it interesting enough so your readers want to continue reading it. As you write your ten-pager, ask yourself, "Who is my audience?" There is a big difference between a ten-pager that is being circulated around your team versus one that will be presented to a marketing department. Here are some examples of how you should skew the information in your ten-pager for each audience type:

Production Team	Marketing/Executives
Provide clear diagrams of gameplay.	Show exciting conceptual images.
Use short, punchy sentences.	Organize text in bullet-point form.
Use specific terminology to get your intention across clearly.	Use vivid, descriptive examples.
Compare gameplay to appropriate games, even vintage titles.	Use successful, modern games as comparative titles.

Although the preceding examples show two different audiences for a ten-pager, that doesn't mean you have to write two different documents. Just remember that both audiences will be reading it.[6]

---

[6] Then again, sometimes you might want to make a version that caters to one audience over another . . . it never hurts to be prepared.

Keep in mind that the ten pages of a ten-pager are more what you might call "guidelines" than actual rules. Feel free to go over or under[7] the ten-page count as long as you succinctly communicate the basics of your game design. By the way, you will find an example of a ten-pager in Bonus Level 2.

The Rule of Threes

Before you start writing, here is a **very important rule of thumb** that I use when creating a ten-pager:

THREE IS A MAGIC NUMBER

History has observed that all good things come in threes. Don't believe me? Observe:

- The Hindu Trimurti
- The *Back to the Future* trilogy
- *The Three Musketeers*
- *Three's Company*
- Arthur C. Clarke's three laws
- *The Three Stooges*
- "Third time's a charm"

This rule will come up again later in this book, but for now, my point is that people like things in threes, especially when you are providing examples.[8] The logic behind the **rule of threes** is this:

- The first example gives readers an idea of what you are talking about but can still mislead them.
- The second example gives readers something to compare or contrast the first example with.
- The third example can complement or contrast the other two, keeping your examples from feeling binary or contrived.
- Anything past three just gets too long and boring: never be too long or boring.

---

[7] Preferably under.

[8] Unlike the above. Sheesh.

Now that you know the rule of threes, use this power for good! When you are listing your examples in your ten-pager, group them in threes. History will thank you.

Ready for the details? Onward to . . .

The Ten-Pager Outline

As you read through this part, you might want to check out the example ten-pager in Bonus Level 2.

Page 1: Title Page

Your title page should include the following items:

- Game title

- Intended game systems

- Target age of players

- Intended ESRB rating

- Projected ship date

Game logos—When you are creating the game title for your ten-pager, I suggest creating a placeholder logo. Choosing the proper font for your title allows you to convey the genre of your game quickly without the need for pictures. See if you can guess the game genres suggested by the following fonts:

Page 2: Game Outline

Your game outline page should include two elements:

- **Game story summary**—Using your one-sheet's story outline as a starting point, flesh out your game's story. Keep in mind that your story outline still shouldn't be more than a few paragraphs long, but that limitation shouldn't stop you from telling the beginning, middle, and end. Your readers will want to know whether your hero ever rescues the princess! (He does.)

- **Game flow**—Briefly describe the flow of the game's action in the context of the locations the players will find themselves in. For example: "*Tomb Raider* (2013) is a third-person action-adventure that finds young archeologist Lara Croft searching for the lost city of Yamatai, an island off the coast of Japan. The island is rumored to be the home of the Sun Queen, a mythical ruler who possessed magical powers to control the weather." This brief game flow outline tells players who they are playing (Lara Croft), the camera angle (third person), and the genre of gameplay (action-adventure); plus, it paints a picture of game locations (Yamatai and the coast of Japan) and the players' goals (solve the mystery of the Sun Queen).

Go ahead and list the environments that the players will find themselves in. Make sure you point out any special gameplay that may occur in these locations.

Here are some other questions that should be answered by the game flow:

- What are the challenges players encounter and the methods by which they can overcome them?

- How does the progression/reward system work? How do players grow as the challenges increase?

- How does the gameplay tie into the story? Do players encounter puzzles that grant access to new areas when solved? Do players have to fight bosses that bar their progression?

- What is the victory condition for players? Save the universe? Kill all the enemies? Collect 100 stars? All of the above?

If your game doesn't feature a character, concentrate on the environments that the levels of play represent. For example, while the puzzle game *Peggle* has no main character, each level represents the challenges of a "Peggle Master" who lives in a particular location.

If you are working on a sports game, are there any special events like bowl games or stadiums that players will compete in? If you are making a driving game, concentrate on tracks or races. The key is always to take readers through the gameplay experience while creating vivid images of the game's locales and activities.

Page 3: Character

Up to this point in your ten-pager, you have gone into some detail about the character the player is controlling (or the vehicle they are driving) in regards to the story. On page 3, you want to highlight a few specifics about your character. Age, sex, and other dossier-style background material can go here . . . as long as you feel this information does your character justice. Don't bother listing your character's blood type if this detail doesn't add anything to your game. But if it does, mention it.

Concept art is a must when dealing with characters. What does your character look like?

What is the character's backstory? How did she end up in this predicament? What is her personality type? How does she respond to the challenges in the game? For example, when I worked on *God of War*, we were constantly referring to Kratos as "brutal," and everything he did in the game, from killing enemies to opening treasure chests, had to reflect that personality.

How does all this information about the character relate back to gameplay? Does the character have any signature moves, abilities, weapons, or attacks? For example, Mario has his jump-and-stomp attack, whereas Simon Belmont from *Castlevania* has his whip. What other gameplay does the character do? Driving, flying, or swimming? Make sure you allude to every major style of play in your game.

Show a basic map of the character controls. Find an image of the controller (you can easily find such images online) that will be used to play your game, whether it's a mouse and a keyboard or a Wii Remote, and show where the controls are going to go. For example, here is a control map for a PS3 action game:

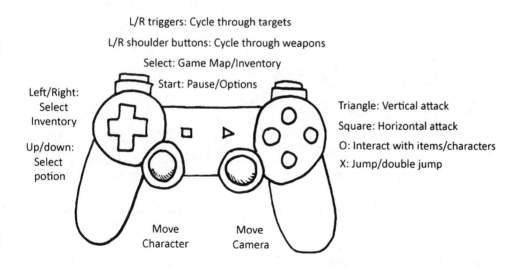

Page 4: Gameplay

Remember that big list of game genres from Level 1? On page 4, you apply those game genres to your game. Start with the gameplay and detail how the sequence of play is presented. Are there multiple story chapters? Or is your game divided into levels or rounds? Does it have any cool scenarios such as driving while shooting or running away from a giant boulder? Call attention to them. Include your big set pieces because they will get your readers interested in your game. Use your USPs from your concept overview here. Don't forget to outline any minigames, and include a short description and illustration. Diagrams are a great way to illustrate otherwise hard-to-imagine gameplay concepts. If your game utilizes touch or motion controls, use descriptive words like "move," "tap," "swipe," or "pinch" to give readers a good idea of how they will be playing the game.

After you write about your gameplay, go into detail about any platform-specific features. What game features capitalize on the platform's hardware? Does your game utilize a memory card or a hard drive, or is it downloadable? Does it use a camera or a motion controller? Is your multiplayer mode played split screen? Cover these details because they will be important for readers to understand what technology requirements will be needed to produce your game.

Page 5: Game World

On page 5, present some images and descriptions of the game world. List all the environments mentioned in the story. Provide short descriptions that outline what the players will find there. How do these locations tie into your story? What mood is being invoked in each world? What music will be used? How are all the locations connected within the game world as well as for the players? Include a simple map or flowchart diagram to show how players would navigate the world.

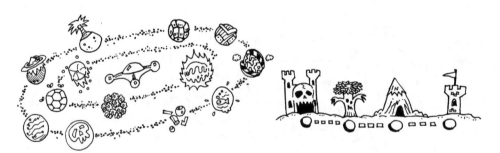

It doesn't matter if your map is a path or a galaxy, as long as it shows the player where to go.

Page 6: Game Experience

The fancy German word **"gestalt"** translates as "the whole" of something. "Gestalt" is often used by stuffy film and art critics to describe the overall feeling of a work of art or the ambiance of a restaurant. But don't let the term's fancy-pantsy-ness fool you; the concept of gestalt is fantastically useful when applied to video games. To make a game feel like a complete experience, on page 6 you need to account for the feel of the starting screens, your cinematics, your music, your sound design, the camera . . . in other words, the whole, or the gestalt of your game.

So now that you know what "gestalt" means, what is the overall gestalt of your game? Humorous? Horrific? Thrilling? Hardcore? Foreboding? Sexy? How is this feeling going to be presented to the players from the beginning of your product? Look to DVD movie menus and packaging (especially deluxe editions) as inspiration because they usually do a great job of capturing the feel of the movie with just a little music, some fonts, and a few visuals.

Does your gameplay use any unique interfaces? These can be modes that enhance existing gameplay like "detective vision" in *Batman: Arkham Origins*, for example.

Here are a few other important questions about the game's experience you should answer for those reading your ten-pager:

- What do players first see when they start the game?

- What emotions/moods are meant to be invoked by your game?

- How are music and sound used to convey your game's feel?

- How do players navigate the shell of the game? Include a simple flowchart diagram showing how players would navigate this interface. (You'd be surprised how many games have lousy interfaces because the team never thought about this issue!)

Does your game have any minigames? Make sure you provide a brief description explaining how to play them. Does your game have an additional play mode such as driving, flying, or swimming? Describe that mode. Does your game have a variant play style like *Plant vs. Zombie*'s bowling minigame? Describe it. Does your game have unique gameplay such as the "strike force mission" gameplay in *Call of Duty: Black Ops II*? Describe it. Describe it. Describe it. If your game has *anything* that will get readers excited about your gameplay, make sure to describe it.

How about movies or cutscenes? Do you have them in your game? How will they be used to tell your story? How will they be presented to players? Describe the method by which they will be created including (but not limited to) CG, in-game animation, and puppet show.[9] Describe when players will be seeing these—during the game, at the headers and footers of levels, and so on. Make sure to mention any attract mode movies too.

Page 7: Gameplay Mechanics

Terminology time! Learn these two valuable terms to sound like a real game designer!

First, mechanics and hazards—what's the difference?

---

[9] Don't fear; I cover all these terms later in the book.

A **mechanic** is an item or element that players interact with to create or aid with gameplay. Here are a few examples of mechanics to get you started: moving platforms, opening doors, rope swings, slippery ice.

A **hazard** is a mechanic that can harm or kill players but doesn't possess intelligence. Here are a few examples of hazards: electrified platforms, spike pits, swinging guillotine blades, jets of flame.

On page 7, describe a few of the mechanics and hazards in your game (you don't need all of them; I find that three are sufficient at this stage of your outline). What kinds of unique mechanics are in the game? How do they relate to the players' actions? How will they be used in the environment?

A **power-up** is an item that players collect to help them with gameplay. Examples include ammo, extra lives, and invulnerability. Although not all games use power-ups, you can still find them in many different genres of games from platformers to racing games. Provide some examples of your power-ups and describe what they do.

Collectibles are items that are collected (well, duh) by the player that don't have an immediate impact on gameplay. They can be coins, puzzle pieces, or trophy items. What do players collect? What is the benefit of collecting them? Can they be used to buy items, access new abilities, unlock material later in the game? Will they earn players trophies or achievements?

If your game has an **economy system**, briefly touch on that as well. Describe how players will be able to collect money and buy things in the game. Briefly describe the shopping environment (is it via a store or a peddler, and so on?).

Page 8: Enemies
If a hazard uses **artificial intelligence** (or **AI**), it qualifies as an **enemy character**. Be sure to include this info on page 8. What enemies do we find in the game world? What makes them unique? How do players overcome them?

Boss characters are larger, more fearsome enemies usually found at the ends of levels or chapters. Bosses are different because many of them have unique personalities. They are the villains of the story. Who are these boss characters? What environments do they appear in? How does the player defeat them? What does the player earn for defeating them? Your readers will want to know! Boss characters are fun and make for great visuals in your document. Show 'em off!

Page 9: Multiplayer and Bonus Materials

On page 9, you should mention any bonus materials, unlockables, and achievements that will encourage players to replay the game. Provide examples of this content. What is the players' incentive to play your game again? How will achievements be awarded? Will it use an in-game system, or will it be supported by an external system like Xbox Live or Game Center?

Does your game offer multiplayer capability? For how many players? Will the multiplayer capability offer gameplay that the standard game doesn't support? How many maps will it support? Can players create and share their own content?

Page 10: Monetization

Monetization has become increasingly important to game developers and publishers. Many mobile game publishers and developers utilize a "free-to-play" system where the players can freely download the core game but have the option to pay to extend their play experience. Other games charge a nominal fee but allow players to buy extra content to improve their experience or ensure victory.

What are players buying for their money? Time? Power? Customization? For example, *Kingdom Rush Frontiers* players can buy power-ups to give their character more health, upgradable hero characters, and the ability to freeze and explode enemies. *Dr. Jolt* lets players buy batteries that extend gameplay time. *Plants vs. Zombies 2* players can purchase new plant types and gameplay bonuses to improve scores. *Team Fortress 2* players can buy new weapons, gear, and amusing hats. *LittleBigPlanet*'s customers can buy costumes to turn their Sackboy avatar into characters as diverse as The Muppet's Kermit the Frog, Metal Gear Solid's Solid Snake, Marvel Comics' Spider-Man, or 2000 AD's Judge Dredd. Some developers use downloadable content (DLC) as an opportunity to expand the core mechanics to their game. *LittleBigPlanet* added an entire fluid dynamics mechanic to the game with its *Pirates of the Caribbean*-themed DLC.

On page 10, make sure to describe how your game will use monetization. These kinds of games utilize an in-game store where players can pay to download virtual content. How does the in-game store link into the game experience? What can players buy, and how can they buy it? Because games do not allow players to directly pay cash, they have to buy a proxy currency to pay for this content. What is it, and how does it tie into the game? *Jet Pack Joyride* allows players to buy coins to pay for additional content, whereas *Card Hunter*'s currency is pizza slices. In an attempt to sweeten the deal, publishers have been offering bundles and "season passes" that bundle together DLC that is not immediately available upon the game's release. Other kinds of season passes provide an opportunity to buy episodes or content as a bundle at a reduced price. Make sure you mention these monetization methods because they will impact your game's content creation time and your game's release plan.

Monetization doesn't stop with virtual goods. *Skylanders'* and *Disney Infinity*'s publishers sell physical toys and "power discs" that add characters, environments, and gameplay mechanics when used with an electronic interface. If these physical goods are important to your game, make sure you describe how they work!

If you want to see an example of what a ten-pager looks like in action, just jump over to Bonus Level 2 at the back of the book. Don't worry; I'll wait for you.

Welcome back! You also need to be specific when thinking about how the gameplay will unfold to the players over the course of the game. How this happens is called **progression.**

Writing the GDD, Step 3: Gameplay Progression

Introducing gameplay to players can be a tricky thing. Here are several suggestions on how you can start your game:

- Players start from ground zero (or level 1) with no skills, gear, or abilities.

- Players have several skills that are presented to them at the beginning of the game but have to be unlocked over time. The gating mechanism can be experience, money, or some other factor.

- Players have several skills but have no knowledge of how to use them . . . yet.[10]

- Players have significant power that they can use immediately . . . only to lose it after a boss fight or initial confrontation.

---

[10] The character with amnesia is one of the oldest cliches in video games. Unless you have an exceptionally clever way to use this story point, I highly recommend not using it. Nothing makes gamers' eyes roll faster. Except for maybe the character realizing that "it was all a dream."

■ Players have significant power that they can use immediately . . . only to have to "start back at zero" as the game story is structured as a flashback.

No matter which method you choose, make sure it is fair and satisfying to the players. Players are willing to put up with some shenanigans at the beginning of a game (for example, the "start back at zero"), but they like it best when they feel as though they are advancing quickly and earn lots of new things such as weapons, gear, and abilities.

Just as you need to know how your game begins, you also need to know how it ends. This is why the beat chart is extremely helpful.

Writing the GDD, Step 4: The Beat Chart

The **beat chart** is a handy-dandy tool that not only can help you develop the content of your GDD but also provides a "map" of the structure of your game; this is extremely important when examining the gameplay progression. Every beat chart requires the following elements:

■ Level/environment name

■ File name (level/environment designation)

■ Time of day (in context of the game)

■ Story elements for level

■ Progression: gameplay focus of the level

■ Estimated play time of level

■ Color scheme of level/environment

■ Enemies/bosses introduced and used

■ Mechanics introduced and used

■ Hazards introduced and used

■ Power-ups found in level/environment

■ New abilities, weapons, or gear introduced/unlocked

■ Treasure amount and type the players can find

■ Bonus material found in level/environment

■ Music track(s) to be used in this level/environment

Here is an example of a beat chart for a couple of levels from *Maximo: Ghosts to Glory*.

Level: World 1-1 Name: Grave Danger (Boneyard)	Level: World 1-2 Name: Dead Heat (Boneyard)
TOD: Night	**TOD:** Night
Story: Maximo enters the graveyard, fighting his way through undead creatures that bar his way.	**Story:** Achille's drill has cracked open the earth, causing lava pits to open up throughout the graveyard.
Progression: Player taught basic movement, combat and defensive moves. Player learns how to collect and map abilities.	**Progression:** Player masters hazardous jumps and more intense combat.
Est. play time: 15 min	**Est. play time:** 15 min
Color map: Green (trees), brown (trees/rock), purples (tombstones)	**Color map:** Red (lava), brown (trees/rock), purples (tombstones)
Enemies: Skeleton (basic), sword skeleton (red), skeleton (axe), ghost, zombie (basic), wooden coffin, chest mimic	**Enemies:** Skeleton (basic), skeleton (axe), sword skeleton (red), sword skeleton (blue), skeleton (guardian), zombie (basic), raven, ghost
Mechanics: Holy ground, breakable tombstone, breakable torch, breakable crypt lid, breakable rocks, Achille key statue, key lock, opening gate (door), opening gate (cave), prize wheel, treasure chest, locked chest, hidden chest, end plinth	**Mechanics:** Holy ground, breakable tombstone, breakable torch, breakable crypt lid, key statue, key lock, opening gate (door), enemy coffin, floating platform, prize wheel, treasure chest, locked chest, hidden chest, end plinth
Hazards: Unholy ground, Achille statue, fall-away ground, skull tower, breakaway bridge, deep water, lava pit	**Hazards:** Unholy ground, swinging gate, skull tower, flame jet, lava pit
Power-ups: Koin, koin bag, diamond, death koin, spirit, life up, flametongue, shield recharge, sword recharge, half health, full health, iron key, gold key, armor up	**Power-ups:** Koin, koin bag, diamond, death koin, spirit, life up, flametongue, shield recharge, sword recharge, half health, full health, gold key, armor up
Abilities: Second strike, mighty blow, magic bolt, doomstrike, foot cheese	**Abilities:** Second strike, mighty blow, magic bolt, doomstrike, throw shield
Economy: 200 koins, 2 death koins	**Economy:** 200 koins, 1 death koin
Bonus materials: N/A	**Bonus materials:** N/A
Music track: Graveyard 1	**Music track:** Graveyard 2

When you compare two or more columns of a beat chart, certain patterns start to emerge regarding the introduction of new enemies, mechanics, items, and abilities. You can then identify deficiencies in the design and start to move elements around. Filling in holes here, shifting bloated areas there.

Here are a few things to look out for:

- Beware of "clumping"—too many new enemies or mechanics being introduced at once. Spread these out over the course of the game. Remember, the first level of the game always has several elements, so technically it doesn't count.

- Also beware of "samey-ness"—too many identical combinations of enemies and mechanics. You want to mix things up to keep interaction fresh.

- Alternate your time of day and color schemes. If you have too many of the same lighting or color schemes in a row, things are going to feel and look repetitive. It's easier for players to notice change and feel progression in the world if things are colored differently.

- Alternate your music tracks. Players will get bored listening to the same music over and over again.

- Watch out for problems in game economy. Make sure players have enough money to buy items to use in the world. Also, make sure players don't have so much money that it becomes worthless or buy so much stuff that game becomes too easy.

- Introduce mechanics and enemies in conjunction with the items and abilities required to defeat them.

- Determine when players will have "everything" in the game—all weapons, all skills, all vehicles, all armor upgrades. Make sure players have time to play with them. I try to make sure players have everything by three-fourths of the way through the game so the last quarter lets players use all their cool stuff.

- Introduce elements in a reasonable way. As a rule of thumb, I try to introduce two or three new mechanics, enemies, and rewards per level.

- Look out for too much story. How long are players going without playing? A game is a game because you play it. Otherwise, it's a movie.

Writing the GDD, Step 5: The Game Design Document (and the Awful Truth about Writing It)

Now that you have some meat on your game design's bones, it's time to flesh it out with a GDD. A GDD outlines everything that will be in the game. It defines the entire scope of the game. Programmers read the GDD to define a TDD—the **Technical Design Document**—that is used to build the game. If the GDD doesn't detail a feature from the start, the team might not be able to add it to the game later without a lot of pain. Needless to say, it's a very important document that the entire team will refer to during the production of your game.

Some people confuse a **game bible** with a GDD. Don't make this mistake. "Show bible" is a term taken from television production. A game bible, like a show bible, emphasizes the rules of the world and the backgrounds and relationships of the characters. This is an important document to create, especially if information about your world and characters is going to be shared with other individuals (like those working on marketing materials such as websites, comic book adaptations, and merchandising), but remember that the game bible has nothing to do with gameplay. That's what the GDD is for.

The horrible irony is, even though writing a GDD takes lots of time and effort, no one on your team wants to read it. Why? Because most GDDs are very long and intimidating documents filled with information ranging from the useful to the arcane. When I was writing GDDs, I found that everyone was interested in them, but no one wanted to take the time to read them. So, if no one wants to read my design, why am I spending all my time writing it?

Well, eventually, YOU will need to read your own GDD. Creating documentation will help you as much as your teammates. If you keep the game "in your head," I guarantee there is going to be a moment when you have too much to keep track of and you will get overwhelmed or, even worse, you will forget about your great idea like the gun that shoots fire ants.

Unlike scripts for movies, a GDD has no "official" or mandatory form. Each game designer usually finds what works best for him. For example, because I like to draw, I illustrated my design documents. I found that my teammates understood concepts quickly when I drew pictures for them. The image on the next page shows a single page from my GDD:

MAXIMO III: Merged Grim Form

Maximo 3 starts with Maximo and his band in **bad shape**. In their quest for Sophia, the heroes have encountered the **Cult of Chut**; death-worshipers who find "a man who walks with Death" an affront to their beliefs. As a result, **Baron has been killed, Tinker maimed** (she now sports Zin parts) and **Maximo and Grim have been merged** into one, thanks to a **curse**. Maximo and Tinker have been hunting down cultist sects when they arrive in Mashhad, seeking revenge and a cure to Maximo's condition.

Maximo is covered in **tattoos,** which are actually the external manifestation of the **cultist's curse** that has trapped Grim within him. With the press of a button, Maximo transforms into Grim, allowing him several **abilities.**

As a result of the curse on Maximo, turning into Grim **drains Maximo's health.** Stay as Grim for too long and Maximo will **lose a life.** Only by collecting the souls of the evil cultists can Maximo sustain himself in Grim form.

As a phantom, Grim can **slide up walls, flow like a shadow along walls** give an little extra distance to a **jump and glide down** from long drops.

At some point in the game, Maximo will use Grim's form as a disguise to **infiltrate** the cult's tower during the **Chut Holy Day.** Gameplay will have the player **switching** between the two forms.

While in Grim form, the player cannot talk to innocents (they are too scared). However, Grim's attack will free **innocents of the cult's influence.** Turning them from enemies to normal **innocents** that Maximo must rescue from other enemies.

In addition, the player can perform several attacks with his scythe. Grim attacks **do not always kill,** rather they are used to "**prep**" an enemy for Maximo's attacks; such as **breaking a** cultist's protection spell or "**mortalizing**" **ghostly foes.**

Grim "prep's" enemies

The **High Priest's plot** is to lure Maximo to their temple and transfer Grim into their own vessel: **Sophia.**

Remember, this is the way *I* created my GDD because I found it easy (and fun!) to create, and this document effectively communicated my ideas to the other team members. Not all designers will want to work this way, and finding your own way is always best. As a starting point, there is a GDD outline in Bonus Level 3.

However, it doesn't matter how you communicate your ideas, just as long as you are clear. There are plenty of techniques that you can use to get this information across:

- **Storyboards**—Just like movies, gameplay can be storyboarded. It doesn't matter whether you can draw detailed images or stick figures; there is truth to the old saying "a picture is worth a thousand words." If you are having trouble coming up with ideas, you can use published movie storyboards, comic books, or even the gameplay diagrams in this book for inspiration.

- **Diagrams**—If you are worried about your art skills (you shouldn't be; even a stick figure conveys information), you can always diagram your gameplay examples. Use consistent shapes and colors to represent elements of your game. Make sure you include a legend so readers know what your icons and shapes mean.

- **Animatics**—Using your storyboards or diagrams as a starting point, you (or an artist friend) can animate them with programs like PowerPoint or Flash. Although this approach takes more time, seeing your gameplay examples in motion leaves very little room for misinterpretation.

- **The beat chart**—A beat chart is a document that covers the entire span of the game. The advantage is that it allows readers to grok[11] a lot of information on one page, and to compare and contrast the flow of information within the game. Hold on to your horses, cowboy; I talk more about beat charts in a moment.

- **The team wiki**—Rather than killing trees, why not publish your GDD electronically on a wiki or in a Google doc? It's a great way for your team members to be kept up to date on the latest and greatest game material, especially because they can contribute to its creation. But be careful; as preproduction moves into production, the design team can very easily neglect a wiki so that it becomes out of date.

A GDD is first and foremost about gameplay—how the character interacts with the world rather than relates to it. It's a subtle difference, but an important one nonetheless. I find bibles important, especially when communicating your game's universe to other interested parties, but it really should be done *after* you have started to flesh out your GDD.

---

[11] "Grok" means "to understand completely" and is a slang term created by sci-fi writer Robert Heinlein. Now do you grok?

While writing the game design document, always keep this **very important thing** in mind:

EVERYTHING IS LIQUID

This means that game designs are living things. Game designs change: they flow, they mutate, they evolve. If you don't let your game idea simmer (like chili!), you may not think of a great idea, or you may miss an opportunity to create some truly great gameplay. Eventually, many of the things you write in your document will become obsolete. At a certain point, writing things down becomes counterproductive, and it all becomes about finishing the game. But you need a starting point, and a GDD gives you that launching pad from which to soar.

Just as you did with your ten-pager, you need to know who your audience is for your GDD. This is a bit easier because your primary audience includes four types of people: the producer, the designer, the artist, and the programmer. Knowing how these different disciplines think and work and prioritize information is very important to getting your point across. Remember this **very important thing:**

THE MOST IMPORTANT PART OF A GAME DESIGNER'S JOB IS COMMUNICATION

Take the time to talk to your teammates to find out what they are most interested in about the design. If you have to adjust some information in your GDD's format, then do so. In the long run, your teammates will appreciate your effort.

Speaking of communication, remember that words are very powerful. Make sure you provide very specific examples and terms for the elements in your game design document, especially when referring to characters and game mechanics. If an accurate term doesn't exist, go ahead and make one up!

For example, when I was working on *Maximo vs. Army of Zin*, I first referred to the game's enemies, the Zin, as robots. I quickly learned that everyone on my team had a different mental image of what a robot was, ranging from C-3PO to the Iron Giant. I realized that my team would be on the wrong page unless I provided a clearer description for them. The image I had in my head of the Zin was of a metal skeleton made out of riveted brass with turning gears for guts. I started using the term "clockwork undead" to describe the Zin. I found that when I focused my language to something very specific, my teammates were able to better visualize the image I had in my head.

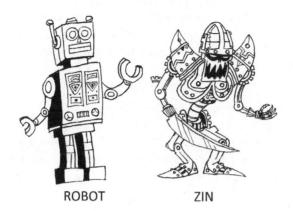

ROBOT   ZIN

There is some debate as to which is better: a shorter, "bite-size" play experience or a longer, more involved one. To be honest, I think the choice totally depends on your game genre, but now that mobile games have exploded onto the market, players are getting used to shorter gameplay experiences (averaging around 15 minutes a session). Even longer games like RPGs and action-adventure games are carving up their game experiences into encapsulated sessions. Whichever way you go, what matters the most is that you give your players their money's worth.

I usually advise teams making a big action game to aim for a minimum of eight to ten hours of gameplay. I advise teams making smaller mobile games to aim for no more than two to five minutes per level. This doesn't include replay time or time spent watching cutscenes or reading dialogue. Remember, it never hurts to have more content. However, if you have to cut out a level, remember that you still need to integrate that content (mechanic, item, enemy, etc.) someplace else. If it's just hanging out at the start of the next level for no apparent reason other than it was needed, the player will be left with a feeling that the game is shoddy. You will learn about some tricks to help determine playing time and avoid cutting features in Level 9.

Writing the GDD, Step 6: Above All, Don't Be a Jerk

Creating all these design documents is important, but your designs mean nothing if you aren't a responsible game designer. Some of the following advice may seem like common sense, but I've also learned that common sense isn't always that common:

- **A good idea can come from anywhere.** I have seen many teams suffer from what I call the **"not invented here syndrome,"** a belief that any idea from someone who isn't on the design team isn't valid. Pardon my French, but only a colossally arrogant idiot would believe that. Good designers always have their ears to the ground for great suggestions from others. Always share your ideas and designs with others. They may disagree with you, but you don't always have to take their advice either.

- **Make a decision and stick with it.** Although game designs are always changing, the worst thing you can do is keep redoing and redoing work. It's no crime to be a perfectionist, but many design issues can be thought out and designed on paper first before a single pixel is rendered or a line of code typed. I have seen many projects drain away time, resources, and team morale when design leads are unable to commit to a direction.

- **Update often.** Send out e-mails, make comments on documents, use a version control system and in-document comments or text highlighting to make sure your colleagues are kept up to date when changes occur.

- **Talk to your teammates.** I'm a big believer in "face time"—getting up out of your chair and going to talk to a teammate in person. Some ideas are just better communicated in person. Plus, you never know what great idea might arise during the course of a conversation.

- **Tackle the tough ones first.** Talk to your art and programming leads ahead of time about how they work and what issues in your design they think are going to be trouble spots. Don't leave these difficult design issues until the last minute. Sort them out first. If they don't work out, you will still have time to make course corrections with your design.

- **Trust your instincts . . .** There are moments when you are going to have an idea for something in your game that no one else is going to believe will work. Sometimes you just have to dig in and fight for it. Don't be afraid to fight for a good idea. You may be right in the end.

- **. . . Or don't.** First make sure your idea is a good one and worth fighting for. Shop it around to other team mates. Get opinions. Try someone else's idea for a change. Better to let Darwinism weed out the bad ideas. You don't want to end up fighting for a bad idea. It's a waste of time and energy and makes you look foolish. Don't make everything a drama. That will just turn off your teammates, and you'll get branded as a prima donna.

- **Respect the abilities of your peers and be mindful of their limitations.** Certain team members are better at certain things. Work with your producer to find out who would be the best person for the job. The last thing you want is a teammate working on an aspect of your design that he doesn't have the talent for or an interest in. Conversely, talk to your teammates about what they'd like to work on. Everything else being equal, you will always get better results if your teammates are into what they are working on.

- **Save often and always.** Accidents happen, vacations are taken, babies are born during the course of production. Any of these things can cause designers to not be around at a critical moment in production. Make sure your designs are accessible to all the pertinent team members, especially your producer. Use version control programs such as Git, Perforce, Alien Brain, Google Documents, WorkSpace, Dropbox, or Subversion to store documents on a drive that is backed up regularly. Don't keep the contents of the game in your head. Write those things down. Make sure you have some system of filing so you can find your work too!

- **Stay organized.** When creating files and documents, use naming conventions that humans can understand. For example, if you have a forest level, make sure the word "forest" or at least the letter "f" is part of the name. Add the YEAR-MONTH-DAY to the end of your documents, especially when multiple documents exist. It's easier to sort and find your documents using this numbering convention. Naming files by date is helpful, especially when your project spans longer than a single calendar year. Make sure you use consistent naming of everything in your game.

- **Be prepared.** Eventually, you will need ways for others to get around your game. Have your game include level skips; a flexible cheat camera so others can take screenshots of your gameplay; and cheat codes that enable invulnerability, grant power-ups and money, and so on. Talk to your publishing/marketing partners about their needs early in the development of your game. Sometimes they will want additional content such as extra levels, costumes, or bonus materials to market and sell the game. Be prepared to create this material; don't leave it until the last minute of production. Be aware that you may have to make a demo of your game. Think about what you would want to have in your game demo to show it off in its best possible light. Earmark potential content such as specific levels or experiences that may be used for a demo later down the line.

Arm yourself with this advice, and I guarantee you, your project will go a lot smoother in the long run.

Now that you have some good habits and documentation examples, you're ready to dig into one of the pillars of game design, something I call the Three Cs. Level 5 will get you started on the first C, Character.

Level 4's Universal Truths and Clever Ideas

- A game is like chili: it needs the right recipe, tools, ingredients, and time to come out right.
- A game design document should be just long enough to describe the action in a game.
- Know your intended ESRB target rating and design toward it.
- Work your way up from one-sheet to ten-pager to game design document.
- Use tools like beat charts to help find problems early in your game design.
- No one likes to read long design documents, so find the best way to communicate your design ideas to your team.
- Everything is liquid; your game design WILL change over the course of production.
- Give your players their money's worth.
- Be smart when naming and organizing documents and files.
- Save your documents and game content often and always.

Level 5
The Three Cs, Part 1: Character

ALTHOUGH MUCH OF your game design is always changing, you need to establish three fundamentals early in your preproduction. I call them the "**Three Cs**":

1. Character

2. Camera

3. Control

If you change any of the Three Cs during the course of your production, you risk massive problems with your gameplay, which may require extra reworking, and you risk endangering your game. Don't give me that look. I know this sounds dramatic, but so many game elements hinge on the Three Cs that changing one thing will have a ripple effect throughout your entire game. I have seen teams catastrophically screw up and cancel their games because of their failure to stick to the plans of their Three Cs. Although you learned about writing a character in Level 3, here I use the term in a different context. In this level I talk about the way the character is presented to the player and the activities the player does with that character. The **very important rule** about character design is

FORM FOLLOWS FUNCTION

Let this rule be your motto when designing anything. It will come into play more importantly later in the book, but it should be your guide, especially when designing your game character. You can find several great books on how to design a character visually,[1] so I don't go into great detail about this topic, but let me pass on some of the high-level things to keep in mind.

---

[1] Some of my personal favorites include *Disney Animation: The Illusion of Life* by Frank Thomas and Ollie Johnston (Abbeville Press, 1984), *The Art of Star Wars* (Episodes I–VI) series (Del Rey, 1976–2007), and Ben Caldwell's cartooning series *Fantasy! Cartooning* and *Action Cartooning* (Sterling Publishing, 2005).

Who Do You Want To Be Today?

As you are creating your character, you need to think about his or her personality. What are the three personality traits that you would use to describe your hero?

Mario—Courageous, bouncy, happy

Sonic—Fast, cool, edgy

Kratos—Brutal, vicious, selfish

Apply these traits to your character's physical appearance. Animators have known for decades that the shapes you use for your character's design will help communicate his or her personality. Circles are used to make a character feel friendly. Squares are often used for strong or dumb characters, depending on just how big the square is. Triangles are interesting. A downward-pointing triangle is often used to give a heroic character a powerful frame. However, if you use that same downward-pointing triangle for the character's head, he seems sinister. Try rotating, mixing, and matching shapes to create compelling characters.

Another old trick that all professional character designers and animators use is the **silhouette.** A strong, clear silhouette of a character is important for many reasons:

- Tells you the character's personality at a glance
- Helps distinguish one character from another
- Identifies "friendly" or "enemy" characters
- Helps the character stand out against background and world elements

For example, look at the silhouettes of the player characters of *Team Fortress 2.*

Due to their unique silhouettes, you can immediately distinguish one character from another. In the preceding image, the Heavy is clearly distinguished from the Pyro from the Spy. Body language also plays a huge part in creating unique personalities. Each character's silhouette not only gives you a snapshot of their personality, but also indicates differences between characters. This was no happy accident. It was an intentional decision by the game's designers. They knew that making their characters distinct and instantly recognizable was important to gameplay. This way the player would know which enemy was gunning for them—or more importantly, who is in their sights. Boom. Headshot.

If you're designing several characters that appear on-screen at once, as in multiplayer games, design them together. Use their silhouettes to make your characters "fit together" even when they are standing apart. This is an especially useful trick when creating "duo characters" like Jak and Daxter (tall and short) or SpongeBob Squarepants and Patrick Star (square and pointy) or Mario and Luigi (fat and thin).

Other ways to distinguish your characters from each other include using color and texture. Super heroes in early comic books usually wore bright patriotic colors like red and blue, whereas villains were dressed in darker, "opposite colors" like greens and purples. In the original *Star Wars,* the heroes (Luke, Leia, and Han) wore black and white baggy and flowing clothing. Although Darth Vader and the Stormtroopers also wore black and white, their costumes were hard edged and metallic.

Of course, what determines whether your character is good or bad, noble or evil, is personality.

Personality: Do We Really Need Another Kratos?

I have found that there are three types of video game characters. The first two are humorous and heroic. And of course you can have a heroic, humorous character. Or a humorous, heroic character. Is there a difference? Either way, here are a couple of tips on creating these types of characters:

Humorous character:

- **Says funny things**—Writing funny dialogue is hard. If you can't write something funny, hire a professional writer.

- **Does funny things**—Do me a favor and try not to resort to farting or burping. Not only is it puerile, which makes you look as though you couldn't think of anything funny to write, but all that gas flying around impacts your ESRB rating.

- **Looks funny or cute**—Funny characters and cute characters share many traits, including expressive eyes, oversized hands and feet (whether due to anatomy or costuming), and stubby or very lean bodies. Expressive body language used for physical comedy is a must, too. These cute and humorous characters are often known as **mascot characters** because (a) they resemble the mascots used by sports teams, entertainment corporations, and small business owners; and (b) they often end up being the mascot of the hardware system.

- **Funny doesn't always mean jokes**—Remember the *Batman* TV program from the 1960s? Batman was a funny character, not because actor Adam West was goofy, but because he played the character deadly serious—as if wearing a bat costume and driving around in a bat-shaped car and pulling bat-shark repellent out of his belt were the most normal thing in the world. It was the contrast of this absurdity that made the show so funny.

Heroic character:

- **Does heroic things**—The hero saves the princess, the world, the day. Whatever your hero does, make sure it matters. But you can also make sure your character is good without becoming sappy.

- **Is always good at something**—Lara Croft is good at finding treasure. Sonic is good at running. Simon Belmont is an expert with a whip. Make sure your hero has a specialty, whether it's a weapon or a skill.

- **Can come in all forms**—Look at Abe from the Oddworld series, Kirby, Kratos. No matter how creepy, strange, or brutal these characters look, they still manage to look brave, heroic, and even friendly compared to the other inhabitants of their world.

■ **However . . . no one is perfect**—A good hero is relatable, and that means he has problems just like us. Phobias, unrealized ambitions, relationship issues: they all make the character more real. But it's one thing for a character to have these problems, and it's another thing to make it part of your gameplay. Indiana Jones is afraid of snakes. What happens when he comes across a chamber full of them? It can't just be business as usual. The hero of *Trauma Center: Under the Knife* (Altus, 2005) lacks self-confidence in his own abilities, which adds to the drama of the story. In the MMO *Champions Online* (Atari, 2009), players may choose disadvantages, such as a vulnerability to fire or cold attacks. I guarantee that these disadvantages will end up inspiring some memorable moments in your game.

Go back to your three character traits. Let them guide your character's creation and everything he does in the game. How does he walk? Fight? Open a door? Celebrate? What does he do when he's bored and waiting for you to continue playing?

One other kind of character is prevalent in video games nowadays: the hardcore tough guy— think Kratos from *God of War*.[2] Remember, video games are all about wish fulfillment. And like you, I wish I were Kratos or Lara Croft. But since I am not a tough guy in real life (Lord knows I've tried), my only recourse is to live out my dream life in a video game.

Anyway, like a humorous or heroic character, a tough guy has to be carefully created; otherwise, you just end up with a lame character.

Tough guy character:

■ **Does hardcore things**—No matter whether it is killing enemies or opening doors. Does it with style.

■ **Isn't a nice person**—Sure, just about everyone in video games kills and steals, but a tough guy seems to enjoy this behavior a little bit more. He goes out of his way to add insult to injury and then revel in the results.

■ **Says cool things but (almost) never shouts**—Because this character is so tough, he never needs to shout. Just be careful: a stoic character can be easily mistaken for one without a personality.

■ **Looks like a bad guy**—Black clothing, leather, chains, spikes, skulls, a deadly arsenal of weapons, a wild haircut, scars—all the things that make a villain look like a villain are true for a tough guy. The only difference is the tough guy looks like a villain but acts (mostly) like a hero.

---

[2] The hardcore tough guy is known in more scholarly circles as the "anti-hero."

The general public often gives video games a bad rap for teaching kids bad behavior. True, there are some game characters that I don't think are great role models. Unfortunately, beating the audience over the head with morality is generally considered bad form. If you have an issue with this, don't fret: there are subtle (read: sneaky) ways you can steer your character toward being good. Good doesn't always have to equal dumb, sappy, or annoying.

If you are like me and prefer your good guys to be good, here is a trick I pulled in *Maximo vs. Army of Zin* to sneak a little morality into the game. In the original game, the main character Maximo was just in the adventure for himself. He wanted to rescue the princess, defeat the bad guy, and collect as much treasure as possible. But to me, he didn't really come off as a heroic character. So in the sequel, I wanted him to act like a hero and do good things, but I couldn't force the player to do good things they didn't want to and I didn't want to be too preachy.

Instead, my team created victims that the players encountered being menaced by the Zin enemies throughout the levels. It was up to the players to rescue the victims or not (sometimes they had to go out of their way to do so). There was no penalty for not saving them, but if the players did save them, they would give Maximo a reward: a few coins here, an armor power-up there. When play testing the game, players immediately started to become concerned about these villager characters and would feel bad if they didn't rescue them in time. While progression was still the players' primary objective, they would make sure to try to save the villagers. After the session, they would mention that they liked being a "hero"—exactly the feeling I wanted them to experience.

Of course, the other side of the coin is presenting players with bad deeds to avoid. In *inFAMOUS* (SCE, 2009), the character doesn't have to be bad, but if he chooses to do bad things (such as steal from non-player characters or kill civilians) and becomes "evil," the locals start to shout abuse and throw bricks!

Let's Get Personal

Remember when you learned about naming characters back in Level 3? First of all, make sure your characters' appearance matches their name. Which of the following characters do you think looks like a "Dirk Steele"?

I learned an important lesson about naming characters while playing the classic computer game *X-Com: UFO Defense*. In the game, you command an international military team that battles an invading alien threat. The team members you recruit are given rather non-descript names. Then I learned that you could rename them. All of a sudden, my team of previously generic soldiers suddenly gained personalities. And something funny happened . . . I started to care about them. Whereas I previously didn't care whether they died or lived, I now wanted to give them good weapons, heal

Dirk Steele   Dirk Steele

them, and make sure they returned safely from each mission. What this taught me was the power of **customization.**

Now keep in mind, not all games *need* customizable characters. If your game features a story-based character or a licensed character, like Nathan Drake or Batman or Kratos, there is no need to let the player rename the character. After all, the player is playing the game to play *that* specific character. However, if your game doesn't feature a licensed character, why not let the players name the character themselves? Heck, even though Link is one of the most loved characters in gamedom, the designers of every *Legend of Zelda* game allow you to rename him. Just remember that if the character's name is mentioned in voice-over or in a cutscene, a changed name might feel jarring. Zelda gets away with this because all of the dialogue uses text. Regardless, anything you can do to let the players customize their character furthers their feeling of ownership.

Many games are now offering players greater and deeper customization tools to allow them to make just about any character they want. *DC Heroes Online, Saints Row 3,* and *Skyrim* all offer incredibly deep character customization tools to build very detailed heroes; you can spend hours before you even start "playing" the game. *Grand Theft Auto: San Andreas* (Rockstar Games, 2004) allowed players to customize their character's physique. If your character ate nothing but fast food, eventually he would get fat.

Spore's (EA, 2008) creature creator goes even further: players have used it to build a staggeringly creative array of fantastical creatures from gorgeously detailed dragons to living game controllers! No matter what you build in the editor, the anatomy and physical traits of your character affect the way your creature moves and acts within the game. You don't even need talent to create your hero in the *Drawn to Life* series (THQ, 2007), which allows you to draw your character from scratch even if you can draw only a stick figure.

The level of player customization will only increase as time goes on. *Graffiti Kingdom's* (Taito, 2004) deep customizing tools allow you to insert your own sounds and choose your character's animations. *LittleBigPlanet 2* (SCEE, 2011) even lets you "customize" your character's emotional state! Did you grab the prize bubble before your friend? Make your Sackboy smile. If your friend got it first, you can make him frown . . . or scowl and "reward" your friend with a slap to the head!

Customization doesn't begin and end with the player character: it extends to choosing costumes, picking weapons, or decorating the character's home base. As I always say, "Every player likes to play house."

Give the players options for personalization. Allow the players to customize any of the following:

- **Name**—Not just of character, but of weapons, vehicles
- **Appearance**—Hair/skin/eye color, ethnicity, height, weight
- **Clothing, armor and gear**—Style, color, texture
- **Vehicles**—Paint job, weapon and tech load outs, decals, hubcaps, even the thing that hangs from the rearview mirror
- **Home base**—Furnishing, lighting, decorations
- **Weapons**—Appearance, decoration, ammo loads, special effects

Traditional role-playing game characters are often "blank slates" defined more by their role (Fighter, Magic User, Thief, Soldier, Medic, and so on) and gear than their appearance or personality. But that doesn't mean these characters can't have character: you just have to surface it through the play styles. For example, at first glance the wizard character in *Card Hunter* (Blue Manchu, 2013) may only seem to be a template for staffs, robes, and arcane items. The character has no predetermined personality. His name, visual, and gear are all editable, meaning you could change core aspects about him at any time. You could even change his character to female. However, it is the depth of gear selections that helps craft the wizard's character. Because the different spells possess different attributes—for example, lightning attacks can be used to hit specific targets at a distance versus fire attacks that work at close range to damage both friends and foes—a play style emerges that starts to create a character. I found my lightning-throwing wizard became more cautious and more of a team player, whereas my fire-casting wizard was reckless and burned anyone who got in his way. You can see this happening frequently in MMORPGs like *World of Warcraft* and FPSs like *Team Fortress 2* where the play styles of characters and the weapons they use inform the characters' personality regardless of who is playing the part.

Speaking of weapons and equipment, you may choose to give your character a signature weapon and gear/appearance. In this case, they shouldn't be customizable. These weapons are part of the character's identity. Most licensed characters use signature weapons and gear to keep them unique. Can you imagine a Ghostbuster without his proton pack? Dante without his trench coat? Cloud Strife without his humongous sword?

Think about how the players are going to be using these items for gameplay. Make the items appropriate to the action. Although I advocate form following function, sometimes these items can help inspire the design to determine the players' actions.

Sometimes the most important item in a character's design isn't even one that character can use. Because most video game characters are viewed from behind, it's important to have something that creates the feeling of movement. For example, many characters have an object swinging from their back. With Lara Croft, it was her ponytail. With Batman, it was his cape. While these objects added movement and personality, they required both unique and sometimes complex code to create. Talk to your art and programming leads to make sure these visual markers are feasible.

While video game character design allows for a wide variety of stylization, the goal of many video game art directors is to create realistic characters. But be aware of the phenomenon called the **"uncanny valley,"** in which a character doesn't look quite right to the viewers. It can be distracting for the players, especially during cutscenes, if this occurs. Here are a few tips to remember when creating realistic-looking characters:

- **Facial proportions**—Realistic human characters look odd if given features used to enhance personality traits. Watch out for features such as large eyes, exaggerated chins, and wide mouths that can make characters look inhuman.

- **Movement**—The more realistic the model, the worse animation tends to look precisely because of the uncanny valley. Be careful of stiff-limbed movement in the arms and shoulders. Hands can be particularly troublesome because most game art can't support jointed fingers and treats the hands as simple objects, which end up looking like hams. A human is a very flexible being, so make sure your character moves realistically. Put the effort into rigging your character's skeleton to be so.

- **Humanity**—If a character looks extremely human (especially a non-human character, like an alien or robot), people will expect it to do human things and have a human personality. However, you can give humanity to non-human characters. Claptrap from *Borderlands* is a great example of playing against this expectation.

Now, for the other side of the coin, here are some tips to remember when creating stylized characters:

- **Facial proportions**—Enlarge facial features such as eyes, chins, and mouths to convey greater expression and range of emotion. You find this all the time in Japanese games and anime.

- **Movement**—If you don't have the time and money to spend on motion capturing, you might be better off using stylized character animations. The more stylized your characters, the more exaggerated the movements can be. Watch and learn from old Tex Avery cartoons (for example) to see just how far you can go with exaggerated character movement.

- **Humanity**—The great thing about stylized characters is that they don't have to be human. Humanized animals have a long-standing place in video games ever since Donkey Kong captured Pauline. Anthropomorphic characters like Ratchet (and Clank), Sly Cooper, and Aero the Acrobat can provide just as much emotion and player investment as human ones can.

Realistic or stylized? It's a choice that comes down to what is best for your game. For example, the *Team Fortress 2* team started building their game with realistically designed characters and then did a 180 with character designs inspired by artists J. C. Leyendecker, Dean Cornwell, and Norman Rockwell by way of Pixar. It was a great choice—one that changed the tone of the entire franchise for the better.

Using All the Parts

As you are designing your characters, try using them to communicate information to the players. Think about it: players spend the majority of their time looking at the characters. What better way to display their in-game status? Personally, I like this method because I find it extremely clear as to what the players' status is at all times. All aspects of the players can be treated visually. Here are some other ways to communicate information through visuals and animation:

- **Movement**
    - Give subtle clues, like a character's head turning to look at interesting and interactive items in the world.
    - Make characters automatically reach out for pickups or door handles.
    - Make your characters respond positively to favorite things, negatively to perilous things. Maybe go as far as to refuse to go into sure-death situations.
    - Characters' health can be reflected by their movement. In the *Resident Evil* series, wounded characters limp and move at a reduced speed.

- **Appearance**

  - Make characters' health be reflected by their appearance. Many games have the characters' physical appearance become more battered and bruised the more damage they take. In *Batman: Arkham City,* the more often the player "dies," the more tattered Batman's costume becomes. Taking a cue from the *Ghosts N' Goblins* series, we had Maximo lose armor and clothes the closer he reached zero health.

  - Make status part of the character design. Isaac, the main character in the *Dead Space* series, wears a space suit with a glowing spine that doubles as a health meter, as well as readouts that show oxygen and weapon status.

  - Use visual effects to represent state. Have wounded characters bleed out, leak oil, or shoot out sparks.

- **Inventory**

  - Players' gear can be part of the character, rather than hidden within an inventory screen. When designing *Maximo: Ghosts to Glory,* we had inventory items like keys appear on the main character's belt. This allowed players to always know what they had without having to check their inventory system.

  - Any major ability upgrade should have a model and/or animation component to it. Evolving characters keep thing interesting for the players, who are looking at the same characters for the entire game. Even better, take a page from *World of Warcraft* and allow players to dress up and customize their characters whenever they gain new gear and abilities.

- **Weapons**

  - Rather than just adding a +3 upgrade to a weapon, give it a physical manifestation of that new power. Have it glow or spit flame; add runes, sights, nozzles, or other "bits" to reflect the weapon's new capabilities. The *Borderland* games do a good job of representing every upgrade with a new part.

  - If you don't want to change the weapon's appearance, consider changing the animation of the player character. A more powerful gun requires a different shooting stance than a lighter one.

In short: keep it clear, expressive, and visual, and you can't go wrong.

Games Without Characters

Not every game has a main character. Who is the main character of *Bejeweled*? Or the *Grand Turismo* series? Or *Sid Meir's Civilization V*? The answer, of course, is YOU! However, because the game designers haven't met you (and probably never will), they sadly can't design their games around you. Therefore, they need a proxy, a character to stand in for the player. There are a few ways to do this:

- **Guide character**—This character is the emcee, host, or "front man" of the game. He often interacts with the player to provide story, help, and challenges but doesn't necessarily have to be the player's friend or guru.

- **The story is the guide**—Many puzzle games have a loose (or precise) story framing to tie all the levels and experience together. *Angry Birds Star Wars II* is based on the *Star Wars Prequel Trilogy*, whereas *Where's My Water 2* uses an original storyline to connect the puzzle levels together.

- **The world is the character**—Some games, particularly social and construction management games, don't have characters in them. So, instead, the world becomes the character. It has a personality all its own that keeps players engaged. The players want to see "what happens" to the world and how it is changed by their play decisions.

Regardless of what genre your game is, remember that players love stories, and a little story can go a long way.

We Are Not Alone

In early video games, players were a single hero battling against computer enemies or a human opponent. Games like *Double Dragon* and *Teenage Mutant Ninja Turtles* allowed a friend to help out, as long as you didn't mind that person bumping into you as you played. While cooperative gameplay with multiple players has advanced greatly in the MMO and FPS space, console games have pushed the envelope in the other direction—the **second character.** When creating gameplay with a second character, you have to decide whether the character is **playable** or a **companion.**

OY!
Howcum he always gets
the sexy companion
and I always get
the talking squirrel?

A second playable character (or SPC) lets the player swap or "zap" between controlling multiple characters. When control is relinquished on one character, the second becomes controlled by artificial intelligence. This concept originates from *Ultima III: Exodus* (Origin Systems, 1983) in which players can "control" each of the party members to battle enemies during the combat sequence. The idea quickly spread across the Pacific to American action and sports games like *The Goonies* (Datasoft, 1985) and over the Atlantic to the UK with *Head over Heels* (Ocean, 1987) and *Speedball* (Bitmap Brothers, 1988). However, control would revert back to a single character for navigation purposes during the rise of consoles like the Famicom (aka the Nintendo Entertainment System), partially due to hardware limitations.

In *Mario & Luigi: Superstar Saga* (Nintendo, 2003), players can control either Mario or Luigi for the duration of the game—although there isn't too much difference between them. However, the characters in the Lego games like *Lego Batman2* (WBI, 2012) have unique abilities used to solve puzzles. Keep the "player zapping"[3] to a single button press to allow players to quickly jump to the other character. If players can swap with more than one SPC, determine the method by which the players will be able to make the choice quickly:

- The player chooses the SPC positioned closest to the player character.

- The player cycles through a preset list of characters.

- A "compass-style" selection window allows the player to select directly rather than in a cyclic order.

- A predetermined location in the level automatically switches characters.

The difference between an SPC and a companion character is that a companion is controlled by the game's AI. In some cases, a companion is the second player character, as in the *Lego Star Wars* games or *Army of Two*.

Originally, AI-controlled characters were a bit of a pain—standing right where you wanted to be and being pretty useless in a fight. But thankfully games have evolved. Companions can be useful in combat (*Resident Evil 2, F.E.A.R. 2*), provide navigational support and advice (*The Legend of Zelda: The Wind Waker, Darksiders*), aid players in puzzle solving (*GoldenEye, Mark of Kri*), or even heal or help the players when they are in physical danger (*Ghostbusters, Gears of War 2*). These characters don't even have to be human, like the canine Shadow in *Dead to Rights 2* (Namco, 2005), the dog in the *Fable* series (Lionhead Studios, 2008), Dogmeat in *Fallout 3* (Bethesda, 2008), or the inanimate weighted companion cube in *Portal* (Valve, 2007).

---

[3] "Player zapping" was the charming term used for SPC switching in *Resident Evil 0* (Capcom, 2002).

An interesting phenomenon related to AI characters is the "dadification" of games, particularly in action and adventure games. In these games, the main character is a father figure (or an actual father) who feels protective toward a child or female AI character. By playing on traditional gender and paternal roles, designers are able to create a "short-hand" relationship that players quickly understand and (hopefully) will adopt during play. A *Walking Dead Season One* player might feel protective of Clementine and will often (if not always) skew their choices in favor of protecting her. The companion character can be passive and somewhat helpless, but it helps if he or she offers something to the relationship in return.

Although companion characters are helpful in gameplay, be aware that creating companion characters is often a significant dedication to game assets because they require complex AI and animations as robust as the main character's. However, the more varied and intelligent these characters are, the more real they will become. And the more real the companions are, the more the players are going to care about them.

When creating these companions, remember that **opposites attract.** Give character abilities, strengths, and limitations that complement and contrast each other. A perfect example can be found in *Resident Evil 2* with Claire Redfield and Sherry Birkin. The two characters couldn't be more different: Claire is a capable fighter, and Sherry is a scared and defenseless little girl. Claire wields two guns to take out zombies, whereas Sherry can crawl into hiding places and access areas to find puzzle pieces and items. Each character couldn't survive without the other, and that's the feeling you have to convey with a companion.

A game's puzzles and progression can be designed around how to utilize the companion to help both characters progress. *Ico* and *Army of Two*'s heroes **need** their companions' help to complete the game. Because players are going to be spending the entire game with the companion character, you want to create a relationship early in the game so you don't have to do much AI programming to sell the companion's personalities later. Victor "Sully" Sullivan in *Uncharted: Drake's Fortune* and Captain Price in *Call of Duty: Modern Warfare* are two strong examples of companions with well-written personalities and motivations.

When More Is More

Sometimes two characters aren't enough. *Mortal Kombat: Armageddon* (Midway, 2006) has 63 unique playable characters! Games with large casts can be found in many game genres: fighting, car combat, RPG, RTS, FPS, and survival horror games.

Start your character creation process by creating a stereotype: the old "fighter, magic-user, thief, cleric" class/profession model, for example. Wait a second, what about creating unique, compelling characters? Yeah, yeah, that stuff's all great, but sometimes players will need to judge a book by its cover. At the beginning of many games, players don't have the luxury of a storyline; they're just going to pick a character that looks the coolest or that they identify with the most.

But that doesn't mean your characters have to be stereotypes, particularly in the way they play. Your characters should have something significantly different to offer to gameplay. It helps to build an abilities matrix to compare and contrast your characters so none of them have the same abilities. The characters in *Team Fortress 2* live in one of three classes: offensive, defensive, and support. They have three categories that impact gameplay: health, speed, and attack. Let's see how they stack up:

Offensive Class	Defensive Class	Support Class
Soldier	**DemoMan**	**Medic**
High health	Medium health	Medium health
Mid to strong attack	Slow to mid speed	Medium speed
Medium speed	Strong attack	Medium attack

continued

continued

Offensive Class	Defensive Class	Support Class
Heavy	**Pyro**	**Sniper**
High health	Medium health	Weak health
Slow speed	Medium speed	Medium speed
Strong attack	Strong short-range/weak long-range attack	Medium attack (headshot does instant kill)
Scout	**Engineer**	**Spy**
Weak health	Weak health	Weak health
Very fast speed	Medium speed	Fast speed
Weak to mid attack	Medium attack (gun turret can be improved from weak to very strong attack)	Weak attack (backstab does instant kill)

As you can see, the characters in *TF2* are very finely balanced. No two characters share the same attribute specs, and weaknesses are counterbalanced with strengths. Where the heavy is slow, he has the strongest attack. Where the scout has a weak attack, he is very fast. Even the most statistically average character in the game, the medic, can heal and grant temporary invulnerability to the other players—an ability that is totally unique to this character. This balancing act is like a game of Rock, Paper, Scissors, where each character has a weakness and a strength.

To design a Rock, Paper, Scissors (or RPS) system you need clarity. An RPS system gives the player three choices to choose from. Those choices need to be simple and clear for the player to understand so they can make the right choice. For example, in a fighting game, there are three types of moves: an attack, a throw, and a reversal. Attacking beats throwing, throwing beats blocking or reversing, and blocking and reversing beat attacking. Making sure the player understands what choices are available and what the possible results of that choice will make for a good RPS system.[4]

These characters also support different types of gameplay: the sniper, heavy, and engineer all work best when they root themselves in place. Notice how one of these types occurs in each class? Your characters will become more balanced the more classifications there are to gauge them against, such as

- Movement speed

- Movement type

---

[4] For more on Rock Paper Scissor systems read www.sirlinx.net/articles/rock-paper-scissors-in-strategy-games.html.

- Attack speed and rate

- Attack strength

- Attack range and duration

- Armor strength

- Health

- Encumbrance

- Advantages (such as health or puzzle solving)

Be careful to make sure these values and traits are easily editable; if you need to make a global change in your game, you don't want to spend all your time tweaking values.

Who Are the People in Your Neighborhood?

The general. The con-artist. The innkeeper. The service robot.

Non-player characters (or NPCs, as the kids call them) come from all walks of life: kings that assign quests and award trophies for completing them, blacksmiths that craft new weapons and armor. You know what the great thing is about them? YOU (as the player) are the center of their universe! They solely exist to help (or hinder) you! How's that for stroking your ego? That's why, in some way, every NPC needs to provide the answer to this question:

WHAT DOES THE PLAYER NEED TO SUCCEED?

What **does** the player need to succeed? Good question. I'm glad you asked. Every NPC needs a role. A job. A reason for living. All NPCs should provide one or more of the following:

- Objectives for the player

- Access to new locations where objectives await (anything from keys to maps to pointing in the right direction)

- Methods for the players to travel to said locations

- Rewards for completing objectives (can be economic or pride rewards)

- Tools to defeat enemies

- Gear to protect players from said enemies

- Answers to puzzles and problems

- Backstory about the world and its characters—just don't be too long winded

- Players' instruction on gameplay (although you should never tell the players something they already know)

- Compliments to your hero on his heroic awesomeness (or to suitably quake in fear if your hero is evil)

- Humor

While your NPCs are waiting to provide help to players, give them something to do. NPCs are the "extras" in the video game universe, and just like extras, they need to be given "business." In movie-making lingo, business is what extras do in the background of a scene to make it look as if life is going on regardless of what the actors are doing: eating, talking, chopping wood, washing the floors. Simple animations are a good start. Complex activities are even better. In some games, NPCs perform different activities depending on the time of day.[5] Just don't make players have to chase the NPCs around to talk to them.

---

[5] In life simulators like *Harvest Moon* and *Animal Crossing*, NPCs will go to bed if it's late enough. That means that many players will not be able to interact with some characters because they're sleeping. Make sure you take this into account, because you don't want to waste production time creating assets that the players will never see!

When putting NPCs into your game worlds and levels, be sure to place them within eyesight of where players are traveling. Make them easy to find. Place them on the game's mini-map if you have one. Don't make players have to hunt them down. Unless your story calls for it, don't put them in strange locations either: an innkeeper should be found in the inn, the police captain in the police station, and so on. Let players know they can interact with them. Don't be afraid to make it obvious. If necessary, put a large arrow over their heads.

Have your NPCs be physically distinct in dress and body language. A soldier is going to look and act very differently than a gang member. Use as many visual cues as possible to help players remember which character has what information or which guy is gonna sell them that phase plasma pistol for a good price.

If having lots of unique NPCs in your game isn't possible due to budget or time, you can still distinguish them with different "voices." This can be done through text as well as voice acting. The lead designer of *BioShock* told a story of how players had trouble distinguishing the NPCs from one another until they were written with strong international accents. Not all NPCs tend bar, dispensing advice in outrageous accents.

Replacing a gameplay mechanic like a switch or crate with an NPC makes your game feel less contrived and predictable. How about making your NPC the interface for the save system? That way you can place it anywhere a person can stand. Just be aware that talking to an NPC will slow down the pace of your game because players will have to actually have a conversation to open a door rather than just turn a handle.

Interaction with an NPC can also initiate a puzzle, activate a mechanic, or start a countdown clock. Protecting an NPC on escort missions or in battle arenas is another common gameplay mechanic. Or if you don't want your NPCs to be so helpless, have them taunt and spur your player into action. In *Darksiders,* a counter pops up when the smith Ulthane challenges War to see who can kill the most enemies. This not only indicates the start of the contest, but also changes the players' mindset into one of competition.

Study other games and see what they do with their NPCs. Use any good ideas you find and create your own. Making your NPCs less predictable will keep the players on their toes and curious to see who they will meet around the next corner.

Finally, We Talk About Gameplay

Now that we've discussed what the character looks like, let's talk about what he does. All gameplay flows from the main character. You have to think about the character's relationship to the world. How tall is your character? How tall or short are all the other characters and enemies in relationship to the main character? How long is the character's reach? If your character is a quadruped or a vehicle, how long and wide is it? As you create your character, you determine these proportions. These proportions become the basis of the character's **metrics:** the cornerstone of your gameplay and design.

But before we dive into metrics, let's talk about fencing.

When you fence, you learn how far you travel when you step forward, how far your weapon goes when you extend your arm. As a fencer, you learn that those distances get greater as you lunge at an opponent. It's important to know these distances to help you gauge how far away you are from your opponent and how close you have to be to score a touch on her. As a fencer, you get accustomed to these distances and adjust your fencing style to compensate for them.

Video game players do the same thing. Metrics are especially important to players because they use them to gauge movement and jump distances "by eye," whether they know it or not. When playing, they get a feel for what is and isn't obtainable, and anything that changes that constant will throw off the players and feel wrong.

Determining metrics starts with the basic height of the character, the speed that character travels, and the height that the character can reach. I always use the hero character as a yard-stick for the rest of the world. For example, in *Maximo: Ghost to Glory*, our measurement was called "1 Maximo unit," which was obviously based on the height and width of the main character. All game distances, widths, and heights were expressed in this way.

Use metrics to determine the following:

- **Height**—The height of the player character
- **Width of passage**—Usually wider than the player character
- **Walking speed**—How far the character travels per second or unit of time
- **Running speed**—Same as walking speed, but faster

- **Jump distance**—The jump takes the player farther in one jump than he would travel while walking, but not while running. Usually based on the character's height and width. The shorter or wider the character, the smaller the jump distance.

- **Jump height**—Based on the character's height. A jump is half the character's height, and a double jump can be twice as tall as the character

- **Melee attack distance**—Usually not much farther than the length of the character's arm and weapon

- **Projectile distance**—Can be as short as the character's reach or width to as far as the character can see

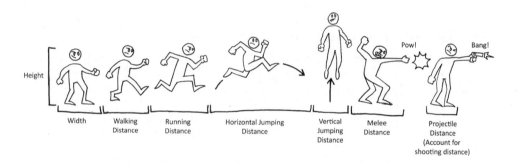

The cliff ledge shown in the following graphic is obviously completely unobtainable with a normal jump/double jump distance. Players will know that they won't ever be able to reach this height and will look for another way to get to their destination.

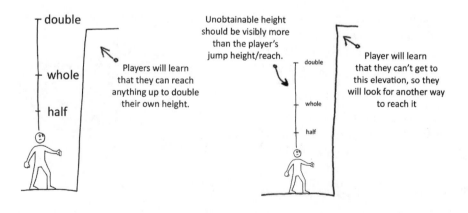

Metrics for Non-Characters

Although the majority of the preceding examples focused on metrics for human characters, you can still apply these principles to determine metrics for non-character games. These include puzzle games, driving games, flying games, and strategy games. However, non-character games draw attention to one thing in particular, and that's the feel or rhythm of the game. For example, Tetris players get used to the time required to rotate a piece into place and the time required for a piece to drop. Or Angry Birds players get used to the "feel" of how far they have to pull back the slingshot to launch a bird. If the metrics for either of these examples were changed mid-game or randomized, they would totally throw off players and mess up the play experience. Just as you do with metrics for game characters, you want to lock down your metrics early on so players get used to how the game feels.

Be Kind to Our Four-Legged Friends

Not every game features a bipedal character. The beauty of video games is that a player can be a dog, a spider, or a spider-dog . . . just about anything. But when you are creating non-bipedal characters, there are a few things to keep in mind:

- Quadrupeds need a wider turning radius. Build these wider-than-normal lengths and turning times into your metrics.

- Four legs generally mean these characters can move faster than bipedal ones. Take into account these characters' acceleration and deceleration.

- A longer character means more body mass to hang off an edge or fill up an environment. Adjust your characters to world metrics accordingly. Be doubly mindful of the Wile E. Coyote effect.

- Many quadruped characters are shorter than average human height. Make sure you account for this difference when having characters perform attacks or simple tasks such as opening doors or chests.

Let me reiterate: the key to avoiding problems with quadruped characters is to make sure your metrics are built around them.

Why Walk When You Can Run?

Let's talk about bipedal characters for a moment. Every character walks. But many gamers will complain if a character walks too slowly. Instead, try making the walk work for you. If you really want to mess with your players, here is something I have learned.

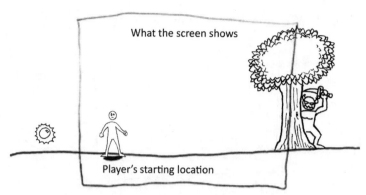

Use the screen to hide surprises and secrets.

Westerners are accustomed to reading things left to right. You can use this impulse to get players to go where you want them to go. In the preceding image, players will usually go toward the interesting object on-screen (in this case, the tree) rather than to the left where I have hidden a goodie.

Why have I done this hateful thing? Because making the character walk to the left makes people feel "ill at ease" and can be used to psychological effect. If you really want to mess with your players' heads, make them travel to the left for an entire level. Most of them won't be able to figure out what is "wrong" about the level, just that something is (quite literally) not right.

Although it's fun to mess with players' heads, there is something that many designers forget when designing their levels. If you are describing the action in your level walkthroughs and you find yourself telling your colleagues ". . .and then the character walks through here," this should set off very loud klaxons. Why? Because

WALKING IS NOT GAMEPLAY!

Don't fall into the trap of assuming your players will find gathering collectibles as interesting as you find placing them. While alternating the pace of your action is good, having your player travel for long stretches, no matter how much beautiful art she looks at, is just boring. Keep it interesting even if a player is just walking. Why have this:

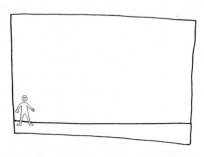

When you can have this?

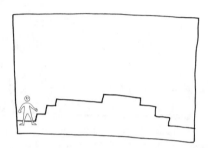

They both do the same thing: get the character from point A to point B. However, the second path is more interesting because it allows the character to use a variety of moves to traverse the terrain rather than just walking.

I often ask the developers I work with, "Do you really need a walk?" Although it would seem unusual not to have a walk cycle for your characters, I have found that players will always choose a faster move over walking, be it jumping, rolling, or dashing. For example, when we were making *God of War,* Kratos could do a tumble/roll move. More often than not, the designers would roll their way around the levels even though doing so looked stupid. We used this move because it felt faster than walking.

What I'm ultimately getting at is that if you are going to have your character walk, make sure the pace is fast enough to be useful.

A walk is useful when navigating edges and ledges. I have found that most players will walk to an edge because they are afraid that they may fall off. There are other tools that you can use in conjunction with the edge—such as a teeter or hoist (more on those in a moment)—but the walk is what the players will use most because it makes them feel safe and in control. There is a trade-off to the teeter. Players can't attack during a teeter state (at least, I've never played a game that has allowed me to), and a teeter reduces the player's movement to zero, which is useful when keeping the player from falling to his death, but not so useful for getting away from that fast-approaching enemy! So maybe having that walk cycle isn't such a bad thing after all.

If your character is a vehicle (as in a driving, flying, or rail shooter) or rides in a vehicle, remember that driving (or flying or jet-skiing or whatever) should always move faster than the character's standard walk. Remember to account for the vehicle's weight, too. If you don't have the vehicle's weight built in to your basic movement and metrics, the vehicle will feel "floaty" and not realistic. When dealing with larger-than-normal characters such as cars, hovertanks, and motorbikes, you will be dealing with even more extreme weight differences that can affect the feel of your vehicle.

Weight, in general, makes a character, be it a car or a person, feel as if it is connected to the world. But with weight comes sliding and skidding. You need to compensate for these characteristics in the player's metrics. In some games, particularly platformers, the skid is part of the player's movement. In *LittleBigPlanet*, players can very easily skid off a platform or ledge if they don't land in the right place.

I'm torn about the usefulness of the skid. I find it to be very frustrating, but without it, the character movement feels stiff and artificial. Ultimately, you need to choose what is best for your own game.[6]

Whether your game character is a person or a vehicle, you should ask yourself, "What is the speed of my gameplay? Fast or slow?"

If your game is fast, the majority of your gameplay should be fast. This includes

- Running
- Jumping
- Flying
- Driving
- Shooting

- Bouncing
- Fighting
- Spinning
- Falling

Slow-moving moves include

- Walking
- Ducking
- Crouching
- Sneaking

- Swimming
- Hiding
- Hoisting
- Climbing

I find it best to alternate between fast experiences and slow ones to keep the game's pacing interesting.

When thinking about running, ask what is it being used for. I prefer gameplay in which the run speed is drastically different than the walk. The *Resident Evil* series uses the run not only as a way to move fast but as a way for the character to push through and escape from slow-moving zombies.

---

[6] Which seems to be a running theme in this chapter, doesn't it?

The **dash** is the run's cousin. A dash is usually a faster run that expires after a time limit. It is often used to get through timing puzzles such as closing doorways and fire jets, or as a combat move either to escape an enemy's attack or drive home an extra-powerful blow. To prevent your players from exploiting a dash, give them a cooldown: a short period of time (usually a few seconds) before they can use the dash move again.

Let's slow down and talk about "slow walking," aka **stealth.**

I admit I have mixed feelings about characters moving stealthily in games. As a general rule, I don't like characters to move slowly, unless the entire game (or a whole experience, like a level) is based on stealth gameplay. Whenever I play games with stealth mixed in (not dedicated), I always end up running around blasting away at the enemies because I get tired with moving so slowly when I could be moving quickly instead. Because this isn't the intention of the game, I usually lose a lot of lives playing like this.[7] But I know my frustration comes from the character moving so slowly.

When you make your characters move stealthily, make a significant difference in speed. It's the same principle as walking versus running. A **creep** is useful if the character is ducking or is behind cover, is getting into position to snipe, or in humorous situations such as when the character is trying not to wake a sleeping dragon. The creep move should be a mode that players can activate at any time, but a creep works best when it is given some context.

But creeping aside, I think that the instinct to make stealth gameplay automatically equal a slow-moving character is incorrect. Have you ever seen SWAT team members or ninjas move around? They don't really creep as much as move in short bursts. Stealth comes into play when they have to wait or hide as something happens or some clueless guard with a very slittable neck passes by. This is where the tension that defines good stealth gameplay comes from. The gameplay of waiting.

---

[7] When you are designing a stealth game, make sure your character looks, or at least acts, stealthy. I once played a really well-made game that featured a burly barbarian hero as the main character. I fully anticipated the game to be a brawler because the hero was armed with several huge weapons that allowed me to cut up the enemies into messy chunks. However, as I played the game, I continually found myself dying in battle after battle. I got so frustrated with the game that I stopped playing it even though I really wanted to like it. I mentioned my regret to a coworker and he said, "You aren't playing the game correctly." Before I could make him take back such a dire insult, he said "It's not an action game; it's a stealth game." Armed with that information, I replayed the game stealthily and eventually finished it—which I may have never otherwise done due to the mixed signals the game gave the player.

The Art of Doing Nothing

Even slower than stealth gameplay is no gameplay. However, just because a character is standing still doesn't mean he has to do nothing. An **idle** is an animation that plays while a character isn't moving, triggered after a few seconds of the player being idle. Did you see that? How the word describing the player's in-action is also the name of the move? Pretty clever, those early video game designers.

The first idle that made an impression on me was in *Sonic the Hedgehog*. When the player stopped running, Sonic would look out at the player with an annoyed look on his face and tap his foot impatiently. That guy wanted to run! Pretty soon humorous idles were a staple of platform games through the 1990s. But they aren't just for laughs. An idle can convey personality and even a little narrative to the player. At the very least, it provides some movement on the screen even when nothing else is going on. Keep in mind, other than adding character or humor, idles (usually) have no gameplay benefit whatsoever. Some cover shooters like the *Halo* series give the players back health during the idle, but that is meant to be an advantage to keeping in cover. If you add a benefit during an idle, you might end up encouraging the player to do nothing, when you really want them to play the game.

Remember, when creating idles, you don't want to create long and involved animations, because players can press a button at any time and interrupt the idle. In fact, any idle that creates a poor transition into players' moves will cause a problem, no matter what the length. Keep them short and snappy. Don't have any ideas for idles? Here are a few to start with:

- Twirl, reload, or "shoulder" weapon
- Stretch and jog in place
- Glance around or be startled at an imagined noise
- Shiver with cold or wipe sweat from the character's brow
- Knock dirt from the soles of the character's shoes
- Adjust armor or pack
- Crack neck or pop knuckles
- Play air guitar or do a little dance
- Check a map or guide or talk on a cell phone
- Whistle and rock on heels as if waiting
- Eat or drink something
- Scratch self in embarrassing location
- Check watch
- Yawn or fall asleep

Might as Well Jump

Of all the basic moves in video gaming, the **jump** is the most mysterious, the most majestic, and the most misunderstood.

To fully understand the jump, take a look at one with the help of my patented "slo-mo" graphic:

1. The player is at rest: this is when the player is walking, running, and so on.

2. The player presses the action button. The jump has to happen immediately because so many jumps are the player's response to danger. In some cases, the jump may need a brief animation to sell the anticipation of the leap, but this animation should be kept as short as possible.

3. Make sure the jump rises to the maximum height quickly.

    A. If the player is given the opportunity to do a double jump, allow him to do so before reaching the apex (top height) of the jump. Any time after the apex feels weird.

4. Falling is like jumping in reverse. Don't make the fall last too long, or it will feel "floaty," which is a negative sensation to the player and screws with the player's sense of metrics—unless the player has some sort of power-up or ability that allows him to glide or float down to safety.

5. The landing can take a little longer than the jump, but it needs to "stick" to make it feel good and solid. I am not a fan of jumps that end in skids or slides because it is easy for a player to make a jump and still slide off the edge of a platform. This is one instance in which I have found that "game physics" works better than "real-world physics."

Let's take a second to talk about physics. Should you model your game physics on the real world or use "game" physics? Or should you abandon the laws of physics entirely? Good questions! And you better know the answer!

Since Sir Isaac Newton did all the hard work back in 1687, one would assume this would be easy, right? Real-world physics are based on the laws of physics we live with every day. But a certain fidelity to real life is necessary to sell real-world physics, and trying to create something that precisely emulates real-world physics usually ends up inferior to something tweaked. For example, gravity in games is not 9.8 m/s^2 no matter what the real world says. In fact, some games even use different gravitational constants on different objects!

This is where game physics come into play. Programmers can "tweak" the real-world values to fit the gameplay needs. Running speeds, jumping heights and distances, and collision bounciness always feel better when adjusted. Most people in the real world can't jump higher than their own waist, but the average platform game character can easily double his own height in a single bound.

What if your game takes place in outerspace? Or occurs on a planet with low or high gravity? Or you can make exceptionally powerful jumps like *Jumping Flash* or *Doodle Jump*? You need to work all this out ahead of time to make sure your metrics match your physics. Tackle this task early and don't change it, or you will cause huge problems.

Okay, let's jump back to jumping. Because platform games were the most popular game genre in the 16-bit days, you can understand how the art of jumping has been taken to its furthest limits—more than any other player character movement. By my count, there are five major ways to jump:

- **Single jump**—The player jumps once—either vertically or horizontally.

- **Double jump**—The player makes a second vertical or horizontal jump that starts while the character is still in mid-air after the initial jump.

- **Triple jump**—The player makes a third jump that can be done after the second jump, usually requiring something for the player to bounce off and most often horizontal.

- **Contextual jump**—This "automatic" jump happens when the player approaches a pre-tagged area such as a ledge.

- **Wall jump**—This special case jump is performed after the player jumps "into" or toward a wall. If the player presses a button while colliding with the wall, she will jump off the wall in the opposite direction. The player can gain altitude by chaining wall jumps, which allows her to "climb walls" by wall jumping between two opposite-facing surfaces. A wall jump can be treated as either a "natural move" that the player has from the beginning of the game (like in *Super Meat Boy*), or it can derive from an earned skill or equipment (as in *Ratchet and Clank*).

Even as the character hurtles through the air, there are design decisions to be made. Some games treat jumping realistically and don't allow the player to change the character's trajectory after jumping, whereas others allow the player to course correct the character. Other games will allow the character to jump higher and further depending on the amount of time the button is pressed.

After years of making "hoppy-skippy" games (as I call them), I have discovered some curious things about jumping. Players usually do not jump from the edge of a ledge, but from a little way back. Edges make players nervous. They leap from an area I call the **"jump zone,"** which can be up to half a jump's distance to the edge of the platform.

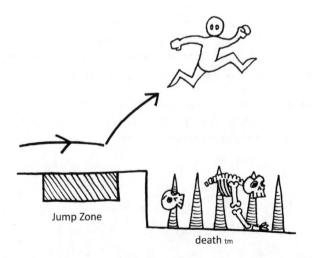

Jump Zone

death tm

The target the player is trying to hit is a safe spot about half a jump's length away from the edge of the opposite ledge. However, landing right on the edge makes a player nervous! This means that when you create your jump, make sure to add one more jump length to your distances to make the player feel confident and secure when landing.

For smaller and floating platforms, the target should be the dead center of the platform. Make sure there is enough space to land. There's not a lot of room on most floating/single platforms, which is why I don't recommend having a post-landing slide animation to your jump.

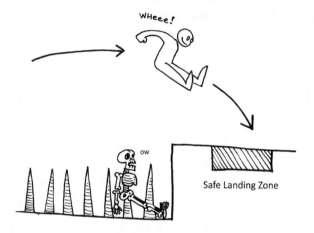

When a player gets nervous, she tends to jump again. If the target is too small, she will usually jump herself to her death. Save the really small platforms for expert jumping puzzles. (Usually found late in the game.)

Hoists and Teeters

Hoists and **teeters** are two very useful tools for players to help them get around and avoid dying. A hoist allows players to reach a height slightly higher than their jump allows. The teeter acts as a warning to players that they are too close to an edge and may fall.

Not all games have or need hoists and teeters. However, if you are going to use these moves, make sure you account for them when creating your player metrics. A hoist generally adds up to a full body length of the character to his jump height.

When a player is in a hoist position but hasn't moved back up onto the ledge or dropped down to the ground below, this position is called a **hang.** Some games will bypass this state entirely by having a player automatically hoist himself back up, whereas other games use the hang for gameplay, allowing the player to hang from objects and surfaces while waiting for timing puzzles and other hazards to pass on by.

I have found hoists, hangs, and teeters really good opportunities to add character to your players. For example, you can have characters react humorously to the fact that they are hanging for their life or about to fall off a cliff! Remember, these animations need to cycle because the players may leave their characters literally in a cliff-hanger!

You will have to be careful of what I call the "Wile E. Coyote effect." Remember in those old Chuck Jones[8] cartoons where Wile E. Coyote chases the Road Runner off a cliff? And then he stands on thin air for a beat before he plummets down into a little poof of dust at the bottom of a canyon?

---

[8] Charles "Chuck" Jones (1912–2002), director and animator of some of the best cartoons in existence, including *What's Opera, Doc?*, *Duck Amuck*, and *How the Grinch Stole Christmas*. He created the characters of Road Runner and Wile E. Coyote, among others. Do yourself a favor and watch all of these.

What Goes Up Must Fall Down

Speaking of **falling**, let's talk about it. Using the power of the slo-mo graphic, let's examine a typical fall off a cliff:

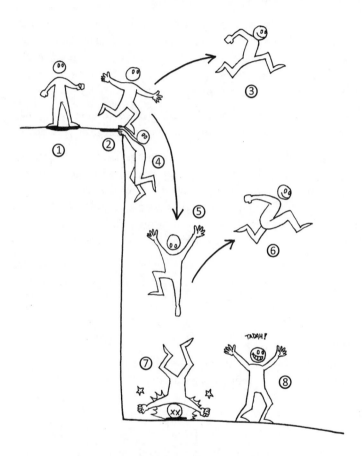

1. The player will usually approach an edge with caution. If he plans on jumping, he will usually do it from the jump zone.

2. Does the character teeter? This acts as a warning to the player, but it can also disrupt the player's control.

3. Give the player a chance to jump out of a teeter so he can get to where he wants to go. If the result of missing a jump is death, let him see the bottom/death zone as he makes the jump. Blind leaps of faith make players very nervous.

4. Does the character have a hoist? If so, the player can use the hoist to abort a jump or as a "last-ditch effort" save option to keep from falling to his death. Because some games use distance to ground as a variable to determine whether the player will take damage upon falling from a great height, a hoist can make the difference between a safe drop and death.

5. When the player is falling, does he have control over the fall? Many games allow for course correction, and some allow for flat-out in-air maneuvering. Make sure the animation of the character falling communicates whether or not the player has control. An out-of-control fall may have the character flailing about or screaming in terror, whereas an in-control fall may reuse the same animation as at the end of a jump.

6. Can the player "air jump" out of a fall? How will this ability be communicated to the player? Make sure there are plenty of gameplay situations that capitalize on this move.

7. What happens to the character when he hits the ground? Does he land on his feet like a cat and take no damage? Does he land hard on the ground and have a longer recovery animation, which would make him vulnerable to approaching enemies? Does he bounce off the ground like a rag doll and die? Make sure the player knows early on in the game whether or not there is any penalty for hitting the ground. And be consistent with this rule. Nothing messes with the player more than inconsistent results.

8. Whether or not your player takes damage from hitting the ground, let him recover quickly so he can get back in control of his character and get moving again. Nothing is worse than waiting for a "get up" animation to finish playing.

Me and My Shadow

As you are building your character in the game, it is important not to forget the player's **shadow.** Having a shadow provides several benefits to the player:

- A shadow acts as a reference point in 3-D space for the player—particularly important when gauging jumps.

- A shadow grounds the player in the world; it adds to the illusion that the character has weight and mass.

- A shadow helps players with edge detection. If their shadow doesn't "lie" on ground, they will get one more hint that it's not meant for them to stand on.

- A shadow conveys lighting and mood. In some survival horror games, the shadow can be a disquieting distraction to the players, literally making them "jump at their own shadow."

- A shadow can be used for gameplay: The Xenomorph in *Alien: Isolation* (Sega, 2014) uses shadow detection as part of the enemy's AI. This can be especially important in stealth or survival horror games.

- If you don't have a shadow, you don't have a soul! (At least according to Egyptian mythology!)

There are many ways to technologically represent a shadow in video games. It can be a complex shape that matches the silhouette and motions of the player character, it can be a rough form that follows the player, or it can be a simple black shadowy spot (or **drop shadow**) on the ground.

While a drop shadow looks less realistic, it is very effective as a device to let players know precisely where they are in the level, particularly while making jumps, where the players can use the drop shadow to determine where they are going to land. However, some gameplay mechanics, like small or moving platforms, can make using the drop shadow as a guide tricky—just one more instance where visual realism can be at odds with gameplay.

No matter what your character's shadow looks like, you should still include it, preferably during the early stage of your production. A few things to keep in mind about shadows:

- Watch out for your character's shadow being in two places at once. While this phenomenon does happen in real life, it will look as if it is a bug in a game.

- Watch out for your shadow "casting" itself through surfaces, especially onto platforms that are above other geometry.

- Shadows react in different ways under different lights and on different surface textures. Although you don't have to adhere to reality, it may seem weird to a player if a shadow shows up underwater.

The Water's Fine . . . or Is It?

While we're speaking of water, be aware that designing gameplay around swimming can be a difficult task. In the earlier days of game design, video games avoided water traversal altogether, resulting in a long tradition of "water = death" in video games. If you choose to go that route, keep your messaging consistent; otherwise, the players will get confused. Don't expect players to be able to differentiate between water that is safe and water that is deadly. My rule of thumb is that water within a single environment should be one or the other. There is no deep end to the pool. It's either all shallow/safe or deep/deadly. If you must have transitional water, give your players adequate cues and warnings of the danger of swimming too far. One game I worked on had a shark fin appear and swim near players when they strayed out too far. If they ignored the warning and kept going, they got chomped on by a great white!

However, water gameplay can be quite interesting because it lends itself to exploration and exotic environments. But you must always consider several gameplay rules when considering swimming:

- How do players enter/exit water? Always make sure water entrances and exits are clearly marked for players. These markings can take the form of clearly marked ledges, sloping ramp geometry, or those little pool ladders—just as long as players can tell "this is where I get out."

- Can characters swim under water or just on the surface? Sometimes the ability to dive isn't given to a character until later in the game. Sometimes not at all.

- If characters can swim underwater, can they stay underwater for an extended period of time? Is there some sort of a timer that gauges air supply or pressure that prevents characters from staying underwater for extended periods of time?

- Does air matter? Can characters die due to lack of air? Do they need to collect power-ups or have some other method to sustain their air supply?

- Can characters attack underwater? Do they carry their weapon and swim at the same time? A typical swim stroke may look strange or cause sorting issues if a player is carrying a weapon at the same time.

- How do characters react when they reach the bottom? Can they glide along the bottom? Or do they bob back up toward the surface?

- Can characters do any actions underwater that they can do on land? Can they pull switches or operate those submarine hatches you always seem to find in underwater levels?

- Do characters travel at a consistent speed or can they "swim faster"?

- Changing directions or elevation underwater can cause problems for the camera as it attempts to match the characters' orientation. Quick underwater moves can cause a camera to struggle to keep up with a character and flip around.

Before we flip the page to the next of the Three Cs—the camera—let's look at:

Level 5's Universal Truths and Clever Ideas

- Form follows function: your characters' actions and personality should determine their appearance.

- Give your characters distinct shapes, silhouettes, colors, and textures.

- Name your hero appropriately.

- Customization will increase player attachment.

- Use the player character to reflect in-game status.

- Companions and SPCs require a fair amount of work to get right. Make them complement the player character.

- Balance multiple player characters to maximize effectiveness.

- Give your NPCs gameplay functions.

- Use the player character to determine game metrics.

- Walking is NOT gameplay.

Level 6
The Three Cs, Part 2: Camera

DO YOU HEAR that crashing sound? That is the sound of a video game controller being thrown through a 50" 1080p HDTV plasma panel with a 600Hz subfield drive. And why was this fine piece of technology utterly pulverized? Because your game has a really bad camera.

Did you know that over 1 billion TVs are destroyed a year because of really bad game cameras?[1] Nothing will cause players to stop playing your game faster than a poor camera. This is why it is so important to get it right.

---

[1] This is a completely made-up statistic.

Get It Right: Camera Views

Choosing the right camera for your game not only is very important for determining how to program the camera, but also impacts how you design your game, map your controls, and create your artwork. It's pretty common for a game to have more than one style of camera, but you should stick with one "main" camera style for the majority of your gameplay and use other camera views only for specific gameplay situations.

A **static camera** does not change position, focal distance, or field of view and stays fixed onto a single screen, location, and image. The earliest video games used static cameras because (a) the scrolling camera hadn't been invented yet (duh!) and (b) it was easier for players to track all the elements if they were kept to one screen. Early video gamers just weren't that sophisticated. But it didn't take long for them to adapt and evolve . . .

Even though the static camera's roots are old school, this view is still very popular in many current games like *Candy Crush Saga, Crabitron* and *Plants Vs. Zombies 2*. A clever use of the static camera is to set the mood as found in early survival horror titles like *Alone in the Dark* and *Resident Evil*. These developers not only used the static camera shot to represent a single room, but also used it to set up the camera for maximum effectiveness. It maximizes the game's artwork by requiring only art that would be seen only "from certain angles." An item in a game world that is viewed from only one angle doesn't need a backside, which saves on production and object rendering time.

Another advantage is that you can easily use it to set up story-related events in your game world because you don't run the risk of players looking the other way when it happens. However, you have to be careful with static screens because they aren't very dynamic. Make sure to compensate for this problem with lots of animation and effects to keep your screen lively.

If you aren't satisfied with a camera that stays put, you can always ask your programmer nicely to make it into a **scrolling camera** instead.

Pretend you are looking down at a desktop. Or use this picture if you are bad at pretending. On this hypothetical desktop, you can interact with all the elements on the desk, but hey— you just can't find your pen. In the picture, what you can see is represented by the gray box. By moving or "**scrolling**" the camera (in this case your eyes) to another part of the desk— voilà!—you find your missing pen beside a book. Amazing!

A scrollable camera offers all the advantages of static camera but with the added advantages of (a) movement, which keeps players engaged in the act of moving the camera, and (b) your ability to hide stuff off-screen or reveal it in a big dramatic way. This is why you will find it being used in many old-school adventure games like *Day of the Tentacle* or the *Monkey Island* series. If you use a scrollable camera with a God-mode or isometric view (which I talk about later), you can simulate a table top to simulate miniature games. This is why a scrollable camera is used in RTS and dungeon crawl games like *Dawn of War* and *Diablo III*. Make sure your controls for moving your camera are simple and relative to your players' controllers. You don't need anything fancy to move a camera around.

Work with your programmer to **tune the hydraulics** of your camera—the speed at which the camera accelerates/decelerates. The wrong speed can cause the camera to drift past the character or abruptly stop short, which can be very frustrating as the player goes through a process of overshooting back and forth, a condition that eventually leads to insanity and/or a destroyed monitor. Conversely, don't make your camera scroll too slowly. This can be particularly catastrophic in a game in which your little army's platoons are in danger of being wiped out by enemy tanks and your scrolling camera is too slow to get to them in time. Oh, the humanity!

Why not let the players decide what speed they want the screen to scroll? It's an uncommon option in RTS and strategy games, but it could work for any genre of game with a scrolling camera. I suggest making this option a sliding scale with several speeds to choose from. Just "fast" and "slow" won't cut it.

In the beginning, there was the static screen. The static screen was fine for *Invaders from Space* and the *Kongs of Donkey*. And then game players cried out for more. So in 1982, the great Irem descended from the heavens in *Moon Patrol's* purple moon buggy and introduced **parallax scrolling** to the video games world.

As a parallax scrolling camera moves, the world moves with it. This camera view revolutionized video games, allowing game developers to create longer and deeper game worlds in which to play. There are two different ways you can treat parallax scrolling. First is plain ol' scrolling. The camera is controlled by a player's movement: the player essentially stays in the center of the screen as the world moves past him just like in those old-fashioned western films. Giddyup!

When using this type of scrolling, be careful to play out how your game level loads because your players may be able to "outrun the load." Always play your game level backward to make sure that your players can't break your game.

Another type of scrolling is the **forced scroll.** Players are forced to "keep up" with a scrolling camera, which is why it was first used on driving and flying games like *Moon Patrol* or *Scramble*. It can be used with 2-D, 2-D parallax and 3-D scrolling games. It became popular with first person shooters like *Operation Wolf* and third person rail shooters like *Panzer Dragoon* and was later used for "chase" sequences like those found in *Crash Bandicoot*. More often than not, if a player fails to keep up with the camera, something horrible (such as death) happens

to him. This makes a forced scroll camera great for gameplay where you really want to put pressure on players, but keep in mind that you don't want to use it consistently in a game—that is, unless your whole game is based on this idea.

Scrolling games dominated home video games throughout the 1990s (really—I was there). There were tons of them! When you have a bunch of people making a genre of game over and over again, innovation eventually sneaks in. And it happened. Twice, in fact.

The first was **Mode 7,** named after the seventh (out of eight) background layer on the Super Nintendo entertainment system.[2] The hardware would convert 2-D art into a 3-D plane which, when scrolled, created the illusion of a background infinitely moving toward or away from the horizon. Add a forward-facing or rear-facing sprite, and you would create the illusion of a car or character traveling toward or away from the screen. Excellent examples of Mode 7

can be seen in *Mario Kart*, *F-Zero*, and *Super Star Wars*. However, designing a level for Mode 7 gameplay can be tricky because your level has no true back wall, only a horizon the players can never reach. While technology has advanced to allow programmers to easily create 3-D worlds without any special graphic mode, the term still remains in use by some (albeit ancient) game developers.

---

[2] The scrolling ground plane actually existed before the SNES's Mode 7. Racing games like *Night Racer* (Micronetics, 1977) and *Pole Position* (Namco, 1982) were some of the first games to feature a scrolling ground plane that gave the illusion of 3-D space.

In addition to scrolling the camera, programmers found inspiration from the **multiplane camera** used in traditional animation. This camera gives the illusion of depth by zooming the camera toward and away from the screen. By having a camera that tracked in and out of the **Z-axis,** developers were able to create level designs with parallel paths. Games like Disney's *Hercules Action Game* (Virgin Interactive, 1997) used the multiplane camera to create **bidimensional** gameplay, the forerunner to what is known as **two and a half D.** A side effect of the zooming effect in bidimensional games was severe pixilation that occurred when the camera zoomed in on a nonscaling sprite. You can still find this effect being intentionally imitated in "retro"-style games.

First Person Camera

As gameplay moved into the Z-axis, game creators explored more cinematic camera views. Although a few games in the 1970s featured a **first person camera**, it wasn't until *Wolfenstein 3D* (Apogee Software, 1992) and its successor, *Doom* (id Software, 1993), that the camera view became popularized. The camera is used in a variety of game genres, from racing to platform; it became most associated with the **first person shooter**.

Despite the popularity of the first person camera, it's hard to discern whether it is really the best camera for gameplay. Here's a quick comparison of the pros and cons of the first person camera:

Advantages	Disadvantages
Aiming weapons is easier.	Gauging jump and movement distance is hard.
Players view their characters as "self," allowing for greater immersion in game world.	Players can't see their characters and can lose emotional connection.
Creating atmospheric situations (like horror) is easier.	Players do not always look where the designer wants them to look.
Players get a close look at weapons, world objects, and puzzle items.	Game objects (like pickups) have to be exaggerated in scale to compensate for distance.

As you can see, the arguments for and against the first person camera are pretty darn even. But regardless, you can pull off some pretty fun visual effects when using a first person camera:

- **Blood splatter**—Many current FPSs use a blood splatter effect on the screen to show that a player has taken damage. You can also have the screen start to "grow dark" or dim to represent the player dying. Some games use this effect heavily and some games do it light, but I feel it's pretty unfair to punish a dying player with the additional disadvantage of not being able to see the gameplay (or where the damage is coming from!). My advice is to use this effect sparingly.

- **Raindrops/mist/lens flare**—This effect obscures the camera lens with weather effects. Raindrops on the windshield of a car in driving games can increase the feeling of speed. Lens flares in the eyes of a player can increase the realism of a sunset. Mist obscuring the details of a silent and lonely town can make things a little more creepy.

- **"Predator vision"**—Based on the thermal camera effect seen in the movie *Predator*, you can simulate these effects in a first person view to make players actually feel as if they are using high-tech or alien gear, such as night-vision goggles. Just make sure the effect actually gives players a gameplay advantage in addition to looking cool.

- **Blurry/drunken cam**—First person view gives the designer a chance to put a player in the character's shoes. As long as the altered state doesn't interfere too much with the player's control of the game for too long, there's no problem with giving the player a good whack in the head now and then—or at least an awful simulated hangover.

Those effects sound pretty fun, right? Remember, many of these effects can be used with a third person camera too, but using them with the first person camera really makes you feel as though you are "in the action." But wait, before you pass judgment, let's "toss" one more "chunk" of information into the "pot."

DIMS stands for **Doom-induced motion sickness,** and it is a very real thing. It's what happens when your eyes register movement and your inner ear (responsible for balance) doesn't. Motion sickness is heavily influenced by the field of view of the game's camera. So, the larger the field of view, the more people will feel motion sick.[3] Victims of this form of motion sickness can suffer from clammy skin, sweating, dizziness, headache, and nausea.

To avoid having your players vomit all over your game, try the following remedies:

- Get the game's frame rate as close to 60 frames per second as possible. Avoid bobbing foreground elements, like your player's weapon.

- Keep your floor as level as possible.[4]

- Add large stationary objects to your environments to give the players something to focus on.

- Don't whip the camera around too much.

- Try not to have your players change their elevation view (looking up and down) too quickly or often.

- And although I am not a doctor and don't even play one on television, I recommend getting some fresh air, drinking a glass of water, and taking nondrowsy motion sickness medicine if you end up experiencing any of these symptoms.

Third Person Camera

Another good way to avoid turning your game into a puke-a-rama is to pull the view back into the **third person view.** Now remember, this isn't a solve-all solution, but I have found that when players have something to focus on, the effects of DIMS seems to decrease. A third person camera also lets players get a better view of the world, the action, and what's coming up behind them. Watch out, Lara! That mercenary has a machete!

---

[3] This is the reason why I never sit closer than the seventh row from the front when I go to the movies.
[4] This is what killed me when I played *Goldeneye* on the N64. Don't get me wrong; this is a brilliant game, but there was one level with an undulating floor that, after I played it for a half hour, made me wanna throw up and I had to stop playing. I haven't finished it since.

Pulling the camera back behind the player offers many advantages over the first person view. First off, the player can get a clear view of his character . . . 's butt.[5] Well, you can fix that by allowing the character to turn around and run toward the camera. But then you have to make sure the camera can track backward with the player. Does that mean the controls become camera relative or player relative? And how does the player restore the camera back to its original position? Hmmm. This may be more complicated than I first thought.

Getting a third person camera to work correctly may be the biggest challenge a team has to face. Although many things can go wrong with your camera, let's see what you need to be concerned with to get them right:

- **Camera movement**—When I was in high school, I had an after-school job videotaping sporting events. As I concentrated on filming the game, I lost track of everything else that was going on around me. As a result, I tended to back into the coaches and trip over the gear lying on the sidelines, which (a) didn't result in great footage and (b) generally annoyed the coaching staff. To solve this problem, I recruited a friend to act as a spotter as I filmed to make sure the collisions were kept to a minimum.

---

[5] The story goes that Toby Gard, one of the designers of *Tomb Raider* (Eidos Interactive, 1996), made his lead character a woman because he didn't want to spend the entire game's production staring at a guy's rear-end.

Having that experience made me realize that every camera needs a spotter—even ones that live within video games, which is why I say "treat the camera like it's a person." As you program your camera and build your world, give the camera room to maneuver and the player a way to manipulate it. This style of camera is commonly called a **follow cam** because it follows after the player. After my years of working on 3-D follow cams, here's what I've learned to watch out for:

- **Sorting**—Sorting is what happens when a camera moves through a character or geometry with collision. Nothing breaks the illusion of a real world faster than this. It makes the world feel unsubstantial. What's worse, in many cases, the sorting camera will expose the background layer of the world, which in most cases is a sky or flat color layer. It looks bad and you should take great pains to make sure this doesn't happen in your game.

You can avoid sorting by paying attention to the camera and its relationship to the geometry. One way is to give your camera a detection radius so that it can avoid passing through world objects by moving over, under, or around objects. If you don't want your game to process that much collision detection (which causes the game to slow down), have world objects turn translucent. This approach works pretty well with objects within the confines of the walls but shouldn't be used for perimeter walls because they can ruin the entire illusion of your level. Players get disoriented when elements in the level flicker in and out of existence! (And it looks bad.)

- **Controls**—Think about how your camera is going to operate in regards to controls. Many games won't work properly if the player is pointing the camera straight up or straight down. Personally, I dislike "airplane controls." Unless I'm flying an airplane, don't make me push up on the analog stick to make my character go down. To me, it makes no sense to give a FPS character airplane controls. However, if you must have this camera-relative control option, at least give the player the option of changing it. Even better, make the character-relative controls the default and make the airplane controls the option.

- **Camera flipping**—Also called "ping-ponging" or "bouncing," this problem occurs when the camera tries to find a good place to come to rest but ends up bouncing between two or more objects. It's due to a lack of mathematical sophistication, but you'll have to bring that up with your programmer.

The number one cause of camera flipping is **corners.** Instead of trying to come up with an overly complicated camera system to combat flipping (and believe me, it usually ends up being overly complicated), just keep players out of corners in the first place. But rather than creating invisible geometry (oh, how I hate invisible geometry; more ranting on this later), build blocking geometry such as small retaining walls, shrubberies, boulders, or fencing, which tell the players to "stay out!" of corners. Don't invite trouble: keep your collectibles out of corners. Keep your enemy's AI path/detection zones out of corners. Move your gameplay elements to the middle of the room. Stay out of corners! I mean it!

OK, so you didn't listen to me. You HAVE to have that one power-up nestled in the corner of that room. Then, as your character walks into the corner, make sure your camera goes up the wall. Imagine that the Amazing Spider-Man is your camera man. What does Spidey do when he reaches a wall? He climbs up. Have the camera scoot up along the surface of the wall to look at the player from a bird's-eye view (or would that be spider's-eye view?). But avoid having the camera show the player from a direct top-down view. Not only does the view look bad, but it just invites flipping when the camera tries to decide where to look at the player.

- **Obstruction**—This problem occurs when something in the world gets in between the camera and the player, blocking the player's view. If something gets in the way, I suggest treating like a person . . . in this case that person is Spider-Man! Make that camera climb up walls, leap over items, or swing up into the air. Anything to quickly get the camera into a location to provide a clear view of the action.

- **Position**—A topic of disagreement among the world's greatest designers is whether the camera should strictly follow the player as if it were attached to a stick that is stuck to the character OR whether the camera should be more laid back and follow the character around freely. Don't stress it, dude; the camera will catch up with the player when it feels like it. (Or when the player chooses to reset it.)

Maybe it's because I grew up in Southern California, but I am definitely in favor of the second method for the following reasons: there are fewer chances for obstruction, you see the character's face from time to time, you can set up gameplay where players have to deal with enemies that sneak up behind them, and it's easier to orchestrate "chase"-style gameplay. Why this is such a contentious topic is not because the world's greatest designers are against such concepts but because they would have to give up control of the camera.

Giving Up Control

Bad things happen when players are given control of the game camera. They start sticking it in places they shouldn't be sticking it. They find ways to get the camera stuck into geometry. They generally screw things up. And I can tell you that nothing pisses off a game designer more than watching some idiot screw around with the camera. So you, the game designer, have three choices to solve this issue. Loosen up your sphincter and let the players take control of the camera, or channel the dictator within you and make that camera all yours! *Or* you could decide when they need control and when they don't. You are the designer; you call the shots!

Make your choice, adventurer!

READ THE NEXT SECTION to let players have control of the game camera.

SKIP THE NEXT SECTION AND MOVE AHEAD ONE to take away control of the game camera.

SKIP THE NEXT TWO SECTIONS AND MOVE AHEAD TWO to let players sometimes have control and sometimes not.

So You've Decided to Let the Player Control the Camera

In the past I've used three methods to give players control over the game camera.

The first method is to **allow players complete control over the follow cam.** By using the analog stick (or a mouse for PC games), players can move the game camera to look around 360 degrees at any time—while running, standing still, waging combat, whatever. The disadvantage of this is that players can get quickly disoriented, miss interesting and important level events and clues, or suffer DIMS.

The second method is a **free-look camera.** This camera allows players to stop and look around the world (effectively a first person view). The free-look camera is usually initiated by a button press, which activates a mode in which players can use the analog stick (the one that is usually used to move players) to rotate the camera around 360 degrees. I have seen versions of this camera in which the free-look cam is restricted to a little less than 180 degrees in an attempt to mimic the natural rotation of the

human neck. When players press the button to return back to the third person view, they are usually reoriented in the direction that the free-look cam was facing.

Speaking of reorientation, players usually appreciate your giving them the option to reorient the camera to its default position (behind a character in the case of a third person camera). This approach comes in particularly useful during combat and platform jumping scenarios. Players usually achieve reorientation with a quick, single button press.

Be mindful of the speed of your third person camera as players rotate it around. A good camera feels as if it has hydraulics; it never stops dead, but rather slows down slightly as it decelerates. This will keep players from suffering from DIMS. Because a player character is usually in motion, another trick I learned is to have the camera slightly overshoot its target when players stop and creep back to center on the players if they stay still long enough. Just remember, you NEVER want players to get out of the camera's view.

The third method is to **give players selective control over the camera.** Like with the first person free-look cam, this mode is activated by a button press, which brings the camera in for a closer look at an object's detail or into a special mode like a sniper's scope. The difference between selective control and a free-look camera is context.

With the free-look camera, you are simulating the turning of the character's head. With selective control, you are simulating a piece of equipment, such as binoculars or a telescope. Any limitations this camera may have should mirror the limitations of the object the character is using. This realism sells this view, so let reality be your guide.

Some game designers find the transition from third person to first person to be jarring and feel it risks taking players out of the carefully constructed atmosphere they've created. *Resident Evil 4* created a unique solution for its shooting gameplay. As a player aims his firearm, the camera viewpoint shifts down to hover behind the character's shoulder.

Another infrequently used alternative is to use **second person view,** where the camera mode is given to an entirely different character. In the *Mark of Kri* (SCEA, 2002), players "see" through the eyes of Kuzo, a bird that can be flown on spy missions. In *The Darkness* (2K Games, 2007), players can control a "tentacle cam" to see around corners and further than the players' POV. When players see what they want, a button press returns the view back to the third player view.

So You've Decided Not to Let the Player Have Control over the Camera

Good call. The last thing you need is someone screwing around with the camera making your game look bad. You will realize that there are many benefits to taking away the players' control over the camera:

- Removing camera control gives players one less thing to worry about. If they aren't wrestling with the camera, players are free to concentrate on what's important: playing your game.

- You get more visual bang for your buck. A camera where YOU determine what it's looking at means that game art can be built to maximize polygon and texturing limitations. In *God of War*, the environments were built like theater sets, not in full 3-D. Why build the back of a building if you are never going to see it?

- You can treat your game like a dark ride. Disneyland's *Haunted Mansion* is the perfect real-world example of a designer-controlled camera, as its omni-mover carts[6] always have the guests looking at the most interesting scenes in the ride. You commonly find this kind of **rail camera** in first person shooters like *Time Crisis* (Namco, 1995) and *House of the Dead* (Sega, 1996).

- Your game world simply looks better. Taking away camera control means you can set up shots. Want a worm's-eye view to make the boss look more menacing? No problem. Want to skew the camera to make the world look demented or creepy? Go right ahead. No one is going to be able to screw it up.

- What did I miss? Have an important clue or event happening in your game world? Want the players to be able to see the Tower of Doom looming in the background or that giant spider that is creeping up on them? No problem. Without camera control, you don't risk players missing anything important in your game.

---

[6] Which they call "doom buggies." Heh.

- Want to have the camera do a barrel roll? Zip in and out between columns? Move around pillars or over or under objects? Match players' movement as they crawl under obstacles and through narrow passages? Go right ahead and go nuts with those complex camera moves. Using a rail camera, you can set up elaborate and cinematic camera angles. You don't have to worry about players wrestling to regain control of the camera. Just make sure your gameplay controls remain consistent during any of these fancy camera moves.

- If you decide to obstruct or let characters get out of the players' view, make sure that your character-relative controls let the players guide the characters back into view. For example, if a player moves her character behind a fence, she should be able to keep pushing the control stick in the same direction with the assumption that the character will eventually emerge on the other side. Don't place hazards behind the obstruction or widen the path in these areas, which would allow for movement in the Z-axis: the players could get unjustly hurt or lost when not in view. These situations, however, are great places to hide goodies.

But the most important point to remember when removing the players' control of the camera is to make it clear they don't have control over it. Once they realize this, they can focus on the gameplay and not worry about the camera.

Two-dimensional versus three-dimensional? In the end, all that matters is that you use the camera that is best for your gameplay.

So You've Decided to Let Players Sometimes Have Control over the Camera

You are a fair and balanced individual who knows the meaning of moderation. Now go back and read about the other two options so you can actually learn something, you know-it-all.

Two and a Half D

Crash Bandicoot (SCEA, 1996) was one of the first games to take two-dimensional platform gameplay and move it into the third dimension. Unlike bidimensional gameplay, which uses sprites for the game world and characters, two and a half D uses three-dimensional character and world models but limits the camera movement in the same manner as a bi-dimensional game: up, down, and in/out on the Z-axis.

When making your two and a half D games, just follow the same rules as with a parallax scrolling camera, with the guidelines of taking control away from the players as listed previously.

Isometric Camera

Introduced with *Zaxxon* (Sega, 1982), the isometric camera gave players a new way to look at the playing field. Not quite side view and not quite top down, the end result creates a rather toy-like view of the world. This and the smooth scrolling 3-D world on a 2-D display contribute to why the isometric view is popular with building and simulation games.

There are some advantages to an isometric (or iso) camera. Players get a quick snapshot of an environment's layout and the relationship of items within it, which makes it good for environmental puzzle solving. Hordes of enemies seem more impressive when seen from this camera view, as exhibited in games like *Diablo* and *Starcraft*. That said, elevation can cause some problems in iso view. Determining whether something is higher up and closer than something farther away and lower can be difficult, as they both appear to be in the same spot on-screen. Regardless of how small their subjects look compared to their first and third person cousins, iso games can still be quite detailed and beautiful. However, if your gameplay is less concerned about getting a detailed look at the inhabitants of your world, go ahead and step into the sandals of the divine with **God view**.

Because details aren't as important in God view, you will find it in games that are concerned with controlling cities or dominating land masses like *Spore* or *Supreme Commander*. God view is essentially an isometric camera, but the player is given a wider field of vision over the world, sometimes as high as low orbit.

Here's a pro tip for your artist teammates about creating art for isometric levels: They can draw the game characters from a side view and they'll still work—as long as your game's art style isn't too realistic. Don't believe me? Take a look at games like *Kingdom Rush: Frontiers* (Ironhide, 2013) and *Plants vs. Zombies 2* (Popcap, 2013).

Top-Down Camera

Although it is considered to be an "old-fashioned" camera view, you can still occasionally find action arcade games presented in a **top-down view.** Classic games like *Smash TV* and *Gauntlet* are examples that used this camera view. It has some disadvantages, such as not being able to get a good look at the game character or the game world, and concepts like depth should be avoided from this perspective.

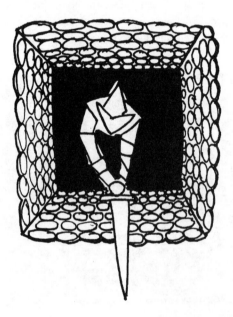

An interesting variation on the top-down camera view is the **top-down/side view** camera, also known as "forced-perspective" view. Although some elements in the game level are presented from a top-down view (usually world elements and power-ups), other elements (like characters) are presented from a side view. This view has a certain charm to it, similar to how characters in Egyptian tomb art are always shown from the side view. *Snake* and *Tower Defense* are some of the more recent types of games that use this quirky camera view.

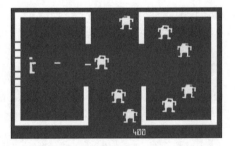

AR Cameras

In augmented reality (or AR for short) games, virtual characters "appear" in the real world when the player points the camera in the right direction. Since the introduction of cameras in mobile devices and camera-based controllers like the EyeToy and Kinect, AR games such as *Wonderbook: Book of Spells (Sony, 2012)*, *Star Wars Falcon Arcade Gunner* (THQ, 2010), *AR GAMES* (Nintendo, 2011), and *AR Defender 2* (BulkyPix, 2012) have become increasingly popular—promising to blur the line between the game and reality.

There are two styles of AR games. The first requires a printed card—much like a QR code— for the camera to look at. As long as the player keeps the camera trained on or near the patterned image, the game's elements can be displayed. If the player moves the camera, the characters will disappear and gameplay will suspend.

The other style of AR games displays virtual characters, vehicles, and effects "on top of" the camera's image. For example, *AR Invaders (Soulbit7, 2012)* displays spaceships and a HUD over the background of whatever you are looking at—be it a city skyline or inside your kitchen.

When designing AR games, try not to clutter up the screen with HUD elements or large virtual objects because the main appeal is seeing the virtual characters in the real world. Also make sure your game elements are scalable because players can change their distance from the printed card as easily as taking a few steps backward.

Special Case Cameras

Okay, so you've decided what camera to use for your game. You're ready to go, right? Wrong! What about the camera for special instances? Designing a camera to work underwater or while flying adds another layer of complexity.

Here are a few red flags to be aware of and tricks to keep in mind when adding these extra layers to your own game:

- Make sure your camera is always moving along with the player while flying or swimming. Don't let the player rise or fall off-screen.

- If your player flies or swims straight up or down, make sure your camera doesn't sort through floor geometry.

- While a player is swimming, keep your camera underwater with the player. Don't have it pop out of the water unless the player is swimming on the surface. Try to keep a clear distinction between "in water" and "on land."

- Try to resist the urge to have your camera realistically bob while underwater. Effects like these make players suffer from DIMS.

Tunnel Vision

Another camera problem can occur when the player is moving through tight environments like caves, sewers, or dungeons. Low ceilings, narrow passageways, and doorways can cause all sorts of trouble to the camera.

I find that if you restrict the movement using a rail camera in these troublesome locations, you not only alleviate any camera problems but also help maintain the feeling of claustrophobia. Avoid low angles; instead, keep the camera at the character's shoulder height or slightly above the player—but watch out for low-hanging stalactites that will cause camera sorting issues.

Camera Shot Guide

Now that you've seen all the ways a camera can present the game, it's time to see all the ways the camera can present the story as well. Let's go to the 5-second film school and find out how to set up your camera to get the best shot—just like those Hollywood professionals!

- **Extreme wide shot (EWS)**—This shot shows a character or location from a very far distance. It is perfect for showing castles looming in the distance or a planet-killing space station in orbit.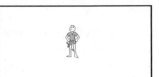

- **Very wide shot (VWS)**—This shot is closer than an extreme wide shot so that you can make out some details. It is usually used for establishing shots of buildings or other large things like space ships or to set the tone that the player is stranded out at sea or in a desert.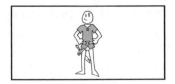

- **Wide shot (WS)**—The entire subject (be it a car or person) can be seen in frame on a wide shot. It is usually used when first establishing a main character or vehicle so the player can get a good look at it in its entirety.

- **Medium shot (MS)**—About half of the figure or the subject can be seen in frame—usually your character from the waist up. This means your character doesn't need to wear pants that day.

- **Medium close-up (MCU)**—Also called a "head and shoulders shot," this view is most commonly used when a character is talking. Make sure to animate hands to keep the character on the screen lively.

- **Close-up (CU)**—This is also called a "head shot": the camera is tight into a character's face to show expression. When you get this close to a CG character model, you start to see flaws (such as in the interiors of mouths or close views on textures). I recommend using this shot sparingly.

- **Extreme close-up (ECU)**—Wham! Right up the nose with this one. This shot is great for focusing on the expression in eyes like in spaghetti westerns and old horror movies. Or you can use it to show details on objects such as puzzle clues or even the puzzles themselves.

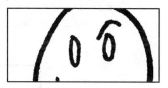

- **Cutaway**—You know when the hero says "I need to get that magic sword" and the next shot is a magic sword? That's a cutaway. A cutaway can be used for a character reaction shot too.

- **Cut in**—Here, our hero says "I need to examine this clue," and then the camera shows a close-up detail of the clue. That's a cut in.

■ **Two shot**—This is called a two shot because it features two elements (usually talking characters) shown on-screen at the same time.

■ **Over-the-shoulder shot (OSS)**—This shot is taken from over the shoulder of a character. It's a good opportunity to show hidden things too, such as characters revealing that they have a gun strapped to their back or are crossing their fingers as they promise not to kill the bad guy.

- **Noddy**—In this shot, a character is reacting to what someone else is saying ("nodding" in response to the speaker). You see this shot a lot with news interviews.

- **Point-of-view shot (POV)**—This shot is from the perspective of someone or something. It is usually shown from the eyes of the player but can be from the point of view of a watching enemy, a floating power-up, whatever you want!

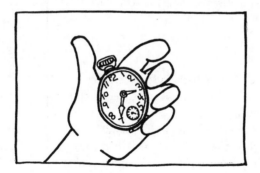

Camera Angle Guide

Now that you know what kind of camera you are using and what your shot is going to look like, let's place the camera to make things look as cool as possible:

- **Eye level**—The camera is aiming level at the eyes of your subject.

- **High angle**—The camera is above the subject, looking down on it. This angle can make things look less impressive. A good shot for showing elements in relationship to each other.

- **Low angle**—The camera is below the subject, looking up at it. This makes things look more menacing or impressive. Great for boss fights.

- **Worm's-eye view**—The camera is literally on the floor looking up, as if a worm were watching the action.

- **Bird's-eye view**—This shot is taken from high up in the sky, as if a bird were watching the action.

- **Dutch tilt**—We did this trick in *Maximo: Ghosts to Glory*. We wanted our in-game camera to feel slightly creepy or wacky, like shots you see in a Sam Raimi horror movie or the 1960s *Batman* TV show. Tilt the camera so everything seems to be cockeyed. If you do a Dutch tilt subtly, it has a great effect on the player, who realizes something is wrong but isn't sure what. If you do it severely, it really makes things feel screwed up.

Camera Movement Guide

Moving the camera is an art all unto itself. Here are the most common ways to move a camera. See whether you can incorporate these moves into your game camera to make it feel more cinematic:

- **Arc**—The camera follows or dollies around a subject in an arc. A common technique is to have the camera arc around the player for 360 degrees if something amazing or wondrous is happening to the character (for example, he's just gained a new power).

- **Dolly zoom**—The camera adjusts the focal length but is moved forward or back to keep the subject the same size on camera. You see this shot a lot in Steven Spielberg movies where a character is amazed by something or comes to a realization that something bad is going to happen.

- **Follow**—The camera moves with the subject. Depending on the style of your cutscene, you can try to make your follow a little shaky as if it were taken by a handheld camera.

- **Pedestal**—The camera moves up to match the subject. Like a tracking shot, but vertical. Having the camera pedestal move past objects in the foreground helps add to the illusion of speed, especially if you are trying to show something rise up suddenly or powerfully.

- **Pan**—The camera moves to the left or the right. Play around with your pans: move them around and past objects. Place items in the foreground to make more interesting shots.

- **Tilt**—The camera's focus is moved up or down, but the camera's position stays the same. Effects like lens flare can make a tilt more interesting.

- **Dolly**—The camera is moved smoothly toward or away from the subject. This is also called a tracking or crab shot. Speed can really make a dolly more interesting—a slow crawl if something is mysterious or suspenseful, or really rocket forward if something is dangerous or dramatic. Play around with starting and ending your tracking before your subject starts moving to make things feel more dynamic.

■ **Zoom**—The focal length of the lens changes, giving the illusion of the camera moving. Be careful not to zoom in through items (sorting) or zoom too close to characters or world objects that aren't very detailed. Seeing textures go from fine to pixilated breaks reality for the viewer.

Other Camera Notes

Now that you are an expert cinematographer, you can work on your directing skills.

Nothing kills a good shot faster than having unappealing composition. The most basic guideline for composition is called **the rule of thirds.**

In this image, see how the screen has three imaginary lines running through it? The rule is that you want to put the item of focus either a third of the way up or a third of the way to one side or another. Of course, after you have mastered the rule of thirds, you will want to break it. That's OK too. After all, you are an ar-teest.

Another tried-and-true rule is called **crossing the line.** Just like in the rule of thirds, an imaginary line cuts through the middle of your scene or environment. Let's say you have your hero running away from a deadly trap.

The hero has just crossed the line, which makes it look as though he is running first to the right and then to the left, which just looks weird and doesn't convey that the hero is running in the same direction. Instead, add a shot of the hero from the front to show that this is the same guy in the same place.

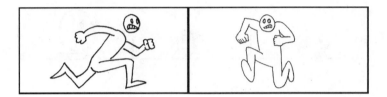

You also want to apply crossing the line when you have two characters talking to each other; otherwise, they'll look as though they are talking to someone else off-screen.

Always Point the Camera to the Objective

An excellent rule of directing your shot, whether it is in-game or in a cutscene, is that the camera should tell the players what they should be looking at. For example, you enter a mysterious, underground chamber. Players can be told any number of things by the camera's movement: where puzzle elements can be found, the appearance or location of enemies, a dramatic reveal of a beautiful piece of architecture, or where the exit is. Or even better, all of the above. Playwright Anton Chekhov said, "If in the first act you have hung a pistol on the wall, then in the following one it should be fired. Otherwise don't put it there."[7] In other words, show everything that the players need for the entire room or scene. You can spool clues out to them, but don't make them blindly guess.

---

[7] *Anton Chekhov: A Life*, Donald Rayfield (Henry Holt and Company, 1997).

Even if players can't see the objective, give them tools to find another way to see it. *Batman: Arkham Origins* uses a "detective mode" (literally a pair of X-ray specs) that allows Batman (the player) to see hostiles as well as to point the way to secret paths. *Heavenly Sword* (SCEE, 2007) displays a picture-in-picture view to show puzzle clues and "beauty shots" of the enemies during boss fights.

Never Let the Character Get out of the Camera's Sight

Oy. I can hear all the kvetching now. "How can I keep my camera on the character ALL the time? But what if my character goes behind a wall or hides behind a very dense shrub?" Feh. Not a problem. There are several tricks you can do to help players keep track of where they are in the game. Observe:

- Show an arrow, name tag, or "ghost image" outline of a player through geometry.

- Have the screen react as if it were an X-ray or thermal imaging device and show the player's skeleton or heat signature while he is behind the object.

- Make the wall or object turn transparent to show the character behind it.

- If your character gets off-screen (this can happen in multiplayer mode[8]), have an arrow or icon point to where he is.

- Zoom into first person mode to show the character's POV.

- Build your geometry to make sure you can always see a little bit of the character. Tinted windows, arrow slits, and grating with gaps all go a long way to show the movement of the player behind it.

While players are in this obscured view, the camera should NOT act any differently: the last thing players need is to have to wrestle with the camera when they can't see their character.

Multiple-Player Cameras

Keeping a camera on a player is tricky enough but what if you have more than one player? I have seen many a game designer go mad trying to determine a workable camera scheme for multiple players. Fortunately, I have done all the hard work for you and will save you a trip to a padded cell.

- **Split screen**—*GoldenEye 007* (Nintendo, 1997) had a great four-player split screen mode that worked pretty well as long as you didn't expect to make out any detail on the screen. *War of the Monsters* (SCEA, 2003) used a split screen that engaged only

---

[8] But it won't because you aren't going to let your main character get out of the camera's sight, right?

when the two combatants were far enough away from each other to trigger it. Now, in the age of giant plasma screens, split screen works better because each player can actually see what is going on.

■ **Zooming screen**—*LittleBigPlanet* zooms out whenever there is more than one character on-screen. If any of the characters get off-screen, they use an arrow to keep track of the player's location. If they stay off-screen for too long, the player is "killed" until the next checkpoint is reached. *Power Stone* does something similar, but dynamically scales in and out because there can be up to four players on-screen at once. The characters get pretty tiny at times, but coupled with an indicator arrow system, you can keep track of your character pretty well.

- **Camera in picture**—You can also go with the camera-in-picture route. A main character is represented on the "big screen" with additional characters shown on smaller insert camera views. It's not the best solution for some types of multiplayer games like FPSs, but it works pretty well for sports titles.

Whew. I think we've exhausted the topic of cameras. Time to move on to the last of the Three Cs: Controls.

Level 6's Universal Truths and Clever Ideas

- Choose the right camera for your game.
- Prevent DIMS by minding frame rate, speed of camera movement, and level topography.
- First person camera allows for greater player immersion.
- Third person camera allows players to get a good view of their character and the world.
- Treat the camera like it is the player's "spotter."
- Remove camera control whenever it becomes a problem.
- When removing camera control, make sure players know it.
- Use Hollywood-style camera angles and shots to heighten game visuals and drama.
- Never let the character out of the camera's sight.
- Accommodate multiple players using the game camera.

Level 7
The Three Cs, Part 3: Controls

WELCOME TO THE last of the "Three Cs"—**controls.** It's worth mentioning that out of all Three Cs, only controls are universally applicable to every style of game. The first C, character, applies only when you have a character. Abstract puzzle games, vehicle simulators, and many sports games don't have a distinct or playable character. The second C, camera, only applies to games that use a game camera: old school, fixed screen cameras don't use any of the fancy camera moves we covered. This makes this third C the most important one of all. Which is why it pains me so much to recount this true story . . .

Once upon a time, I joined the team of a console game that had been in production for three years. I was asked to take a look at the current state of the game and report back any issues I had. Overall, the game was really good, but there was one thing that bothered me. One of the enemies could be defeated only with a quick-time event (see Level 8 for more details on these events), and even though I'm awesome at playing action games, I just couldn't seem to press the button fast enough to win the contest and kill the monster.

I went to the creative director and told him that I thought the controls for the minigame were too hard. He asked me, "How did you hold the controller?" This is what I showed him:

He said, "Oh, no wonder. You are holding the controller wrong." Whaaa? As far as I knew, there was only one way to hold the controller. Keeping things respectful, I asked: how did *he* recommend I hold it? This is what he showed me:

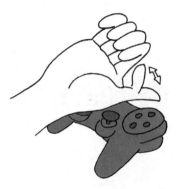

I wasn't sure whether he was joking. "I don't believe that players would change their hand positions midway through the game. It just doesn't seem very natural." He became insulted and proceeded to tell me that not only was this the proper way to hold the controller, but that *everyone else* on the team held it that way as well. "Hmm. Did you *tell them* how to hold it that way?" I asked. "Yes," he replied. I gave his way a try but still didn't win the fight. If anything, the new hand position made things worse. I returned to his office and told him, "Sorry, but I think players are going to have difficulty playing this." Pointing his finger at me, he said "You are 100% WRONG!" and stormed off.

Three months later, after testing revealed that the quick-time event (QTE) was too hard to play, the controls were adjusted. What **very important thing** did I take away from this experience?

ALWAYS REMEMBER THAT HUMANS ARE PLAYING THESE GAMES

Not six-fingered mutants or multi-tentacled squid men from Praxis Prime. It's *Homo sapiens* who play video games, most of them possessing short if not stubby fingers and mediocre motor skills coordination, which is why it is important to consider ergonomics when you are creating your control schemes.

Control Is in Your Hand

Ergonomics is the study of fitting equipment to the worker. Hardware developers take great pains to see how players hold and use the controller. This is the reason it never made any sense to me that a developer would create a control scheme that forced players to twist up their hands like pretzels. To help with this problem, I created this rule of thumb (BAA DUM! TISH![1]) that I call the **"Gamers' Guide to Flex-O-Fingering."**

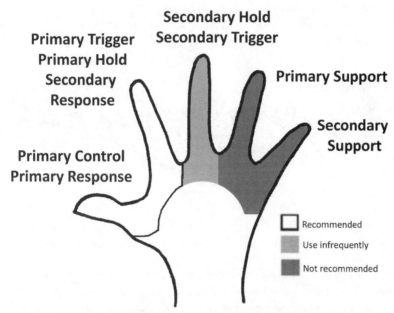

Thumb: flexible with reach. Good for steering and fast response.
Index: strong and fast. Used for response or hold moves.
Middle: weaker but usable for hold moves. Decent reach.
Ring: weak with poor reach. Better for stabilization
Pinkie: poor strength. Reach requires hand support.

When you are designing controls, try establishing design rules for your control schemes based on hand placement (for example, in FPS games, it's common to use the keyboard for character movement and the mouse for aiming and shooting). Not only is this approach helpful when determining what controls go where on the controller, but players will begin to associate muscle movement with a certain action even if they don't realize they are doing it.

Speaking of keyboards, just because you have a whole keyboard available for use doesn't mean you have to use every single key. Keeping your keyboard controls localized around commonly used key groupings like QWERTY or ASWD makes it easier for players to adapt to.

---

[1] Thank you, thank you. I'll be here all week, folks. Try the veal.

Another way to assign controls is thematically. In *Tak and the Guardians of Gross* (THQ, 2008), the motion-controlled Wii Remote was used for all of the player's magic powers while the analog stick/nunchuck controlled all of Tak's real-world capabilities such as interacting with objects and fighting. If players had any question on how to perform a move, they would usually try the thematically related controller first. Just make sure that you don't cross signals and start intermingling your themes. That just leads to confusion and sadness.

The preceding tricks are really no big secret; it boils down to this: you just need to understand the control needs of your audience. Here are a few more tips (exclusive to buyers of this book![2]):

- If you are designing for really young (8 and younger) players, keep the button presses simple. Don't create complex combinations because these younger fingers just can't make them. Or if you are designing a kid's game using the keyboard, try not to spread out your key commands too far because most kids tend to "hunt and peck" the keys—which isn't good if you want them to make quick actions.

- MMO and FPS players often create hotkeys and macros to chain attacks or spell effects. Give them the option to customize their controls. You never know when you'll need to cast "Combustion," "Icy Veins," and "Fireball" to boost your dps. In addition, customizable controls have the benefit of being disabled gamer friendly.

- Fighting gamers, like fans of Capcom's *Street Fighter* series, pride themselves on mastering ultracomplex control schemes, but remember, not everyone can pull off the dragon punch move in *Street Fighter II*. If you want to keep your game accessible to other types of players, don't go nuts with the ubercomplex controls.

- *Track and Field* (Konami, 1983) was a very popular game that required manic button pressing to make the little athlete character run. However, it was impossible to accurately do this move without the aid of a pencil (see image), resulting in what we kids called the **"pencil trick."** However, the pencil trick destroyed game controllers. While I'm sure that controller manufacturers loved the pencil trick—because of all the replacement arcade

---

machines they sold—it's unfair to make your players have to resort to a stop-gap measure just so they can succeed at your game.

"the pencil trick"

- Although experimenting with unconventional control schemes is fine, make sure players have the option to revert back to a more traditional one.

- On that note, offer players several control options. Or, even better, let the players map their own controls in the options screen.

- For Zeus's sake, don't reverse your flight controls! Pulling back on the stick should make the plane go up, and pushing forward should make the plane go down. Nobody likes those reversed controls, and anyone who tells you otherwise should be forced to play the super-awful *Superman 64* and fly through rings for a week straight.

You've Got the Touch

While joysticks are great, we humans come with our own controllers—ten of them in fact! Fingers are great stand-ins for anything a game designer can imagine . . . a sword, a slingshot, a gun sight, a laser pointer, a joystick, or even a finger! Since the explosion of touchscreen gaming on mobile devices, understanding how to create simple and responsive controls is more important than ever before. But before you start designing your touchscreen game, you really should learn what a finger can do!

- A **tap** is a quick press used to make a selection or make a character perform an action, shoot a weapon, or quickly place an item.

- A **double tap** can be used to verify a selection, open and close selection windows, or indicate a direction for a character to move.

- A **timed tap** requires the player to tap in time with the gameplay—like you would find in a rhythm game.

- More complex or random sequences require **staccato pokes.** You can also use them for moments of intense action such as a finishing move.

- Because true two-hand typing isn't possible on the tiny screens of mobile devices, the player will have to **peck** instead. Unlike timed tapping, pecking usually has no time constraint assigned to it. Players are able to type with one finger (and correct those stoopid autocorrect mistakes) at their leisure.

- **Touch and hold** works well when you need to hold a moving object in place.

- **Hold and drag** is the best move to use when you need to move around inventory items, dressing characters in their finest armor and gear or tossing stuff into the trash or the *Little Inferno* oven.

- A **flick** mimics the action of a character tossing something like a hockey puck, a wadded-up paper ball, or an advancing zombie in a specific direction.

- **Page Up or Down** is a flick that works in multiple directions. It's best used to scroll through pages of text or menu options.

- The **pull and release** move is most famously known for launching birds toward pigs, but it can be used for any action that mimics "rubber banding" or springs, such as pinball plungers.

- **Scrubbing** is used to erase or cover something on-screen with a rapid back-and-forth motion.

- A **swipe** is used for indicating directional lines. I find swiping feels better if players associate the motion with using a real-world function such as swinging a sword or drawing a line.

- **Shape drawing** enables players to use a finger as a pen/pencil/crayon. Make sure the players can change the size of their brush. Giving them a little color selection doesn't hurt either.

- **Shape tracing** is often found in games in which spells are cast. Players trace or draw a shape such as a circle, square, triangle, or zig-zag on-screen to get the desired effect. Be wary, however, that your game code doesn't mistake similar shapes with each other.

- If you want to size something up or down, use a **pinch.** Since most touchscreens support several fingers, you can do fun things like use four fingers at once, as with the pinchy claws of the space crab *Crabitron.*

- A **swirl** is used to draw circles. Remember that your character or object will spin slower or faster depending on how tight the curl is.

Even you have plenty of touch control schemes to choose from, the secret is to use as few as possible to minimize confusion. *Canabalt, Jetpack Joyride,* and *Fruit Ninja* all utilize "one-touch" control schemes and still have deep and engaging gameplay.

Another common touchscreen scheme is the **virtual controller.** A virtual controller is exactly that—a digital representation of the game's controller and buttons. Virtual controllers are primarily used when adapting games from other systems (like arcades, for example) to mobile devices. Unfortunately, many virtual controllers have been poorly executed in the past, causing many members of the game development community to view them as an undesirable option. If you must use a virtual controller for your game, I suggest using the following techniques to minimize suckage:

- Clearly delineate the directions players can move their stick. Stick to the eight directions of the compass wherever possible.

- Have your joystick "snap back" to the center of the controller to prevent drifting. Make the center a "dead zone" so nothing happens until the stick is pushed in a direction.

- Make the visual of your joystick as big as possible without obscuring gameplay. But don't make it so big that it actually takes time to move it to the extremes.

- Keep your joystick and buttons away from the edges of the screen so players don't miss by sliding off the device! Even better, mark off "zones" on the screen dedicated to a single action like moving left or right, jumping up, or crouching down.

No matter which control scheme you use for your touchscreen game . . . or any type of game for that matter, it helps to first consider *how* your game is going to be played.

Dance, Monkey, Dance

A good designer will think about how the game is played in the real world as well as in the game world. Think about how players are going to move those fingers over the controller. Avoid repetition and strive for an uncomplicated control scheme. If you get it right, you create what I call the "dance of the buttons" for players. If your controls get too complex or repetitive, you end up with your players resorting to **button mashing.**

Button mashing is a derogatory term used to describe when players aren't sure how to control the game, resulting in wildly and/or rapidly hitting the buttons randomly to get any sort of positive result. This situation usually happens in action and fighting games when either the control scheme is too complex or the players aren't getting satisfactory feedback.

Button mashing contributes to player fatigue and "gamers' thumb" (otherwise known as "occupational overuse syndrome"), characterized by stiffness, burning or cold sensations, numbness, or weakness. The American Physical Therapy Association[3] recommends the following exercises and advice:

- Keep your wrists straight (don't let them droop) as you hold the controller.

- Sit comfortably in a chair with good back support.

- Stretch every 20 minutes to give your head, neck, and shoulder muscles a break.

---

[3] Exercises courtesy of the APTA website (`www.apta.org`).

■ Tap each finger with the thumb of the same hand. Repeat five times.

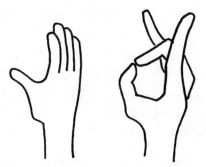

■ Alternate tapping your palm and the back of your hand against your thigh as quickly as you can. Repeat 20 times.

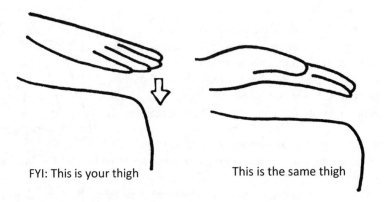

FYI: This is your thigh   This is the same thigh

■ Open your hands and spread fingers as far apart as possible. Hold for 10 seconds. Repeat eight times.

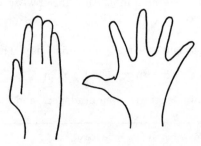

- Clasp your hands together, turn your hands away from your body, and extend your arms forward. Hold for 10 seconds and repeat eight times.

- Fold your hands together, turn your palms away from your body, and extend your arms overhead. You should feel the stretch in your upper torso and from your shoulders to your hands. Hold for 10 seconds. Repeat eight times.

However, not all button mashing is bad; you may be able to use it to your advantage. I have observed that the first thing players do when they start a game is to press all the buttons on the controller. This is because (a) players want to see what happens, and (b) no one ever reads the game manual. So how do you get players to learn if their first instinct is to just mash buttons?

Simple. Have the character do something cool whenever players press a button, even if they don't understand how they're doing it. *God of War* does this fantastically well: Kratos pulls off some awesome attack moves even when you just mash buttons—and it's completely intentional. When the players see these moves happen a few times, they will slow down to try to dissect how they pulled them off.

Never have a button do nothing when pressed. Here are some ways to deal with this:

- Play a "negative response" sound effect or animation to make it clear to players that this control isn't available. I always liked that the character in *Dark Castle* shrugged his shoulders if he was out of ammo or missing a key.

- Make it clear during your training mode that a button is inactive. Then make a big deal when it is unlocked. *Brütal Legend* stops the game dead and shows a full-screen graphic whenever the main character gets a new move. Just remember: (a) don't teach more than one new move at a time, and (b) don't jam new moves down the players' throats too quickly. Players tune out if they get overloaded with information.

- Assign a redundant but related function. If the triangle button is slated for a projectile attack that players don't have yet, assign the melee attack to the button until they find that kill-o-zap blaster. The players will mentally equate the triangle button with combat until the "true" move is unlocked.

- Go the *Batman: Arkham* series route and don't have the button do anything until it's needed. The triangle button doesn't do anything unless Batman can perform a silent takedown or needs to counter an attack during combat. Then the triangle icon appears, reminding players what button to press. Not only does this technique save players the hassle of memorizing a bat-load of controls, but it also creates a mini-QTE, adding some delicious tension to the gameplay.

With the advent of motion controls like the Wii Remote, PlayStation Move, and Xbox 360's Kinect, designers now have an opportunity to re-create real-world controls for moves. But before we get into that, let's talk about how to get the most reality out of traditional controllers.

One of the best examples of re-creating real-world moves using an analog stick can be found in *Pitfall: The Lost Expedition*. (Activision, 2004). In the game, water is health and the character carries a canteen to hold water. Whenever the character comes across a cistern, the player pushes the stick forward to fill the canteen. When he pulls back on the stick, the hero Harry takes a drink from the canteen to replenish his health. The clever combination of intention and animation makes this feel very satisfying. Mapping the moves to logical control locations helps immerse the player into the game world. In *Maximo: Ghosts to Glory*, the goal was to create an "out-of-game" correlation between Maximo's moves and the real-world PlayStation 2 controller.

Maximo's overhead swing is performed by pressing the triangle, the button at the "top" of the controller—echoing the swing from high to low, while the horizontal swing is mapped to the square button on the horizontal plane of the buttons. The jump, which starts on the ground, is mapped to the X button, the lowest button on the pad, while the shield throw is mapped to the circle button—the shape of the button icon matching that of the shield.

Some genres of games like FPS, RTS, and platformers have widely accepted control schemes. For example, the spacebar, X, or A button usually makes the character jump in a platformer. The more your control scheme resembles that of other successful games in the same genre, the more easily new players will be able to quickly master it.

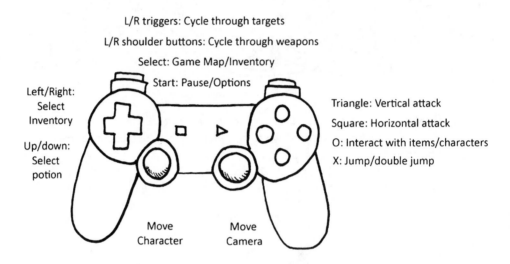

L/R triggers: Cycle through targets
L/R shoulder buttons: Cycle through weapons
Select: Game Map/Inventory
Start: Pause/Options
Left/Right: Select Inventory
Up/down: Select potion
Triangle: Vertical attack
Square: Horizontal attack
O: Interact with items/characters
X: Jump/double jump
Move Character
Move Camera

Shoulder buttons can be found on most modern console controllers, but you should consider the actual button size when mapping controls. For example, on an Xbox 360 controller, the left and right shoulder buttons are physically smaller than the left and right shoulder triggers. You should assign "quick move" functions to the shoulder triggers, such as shooting, braking, and acceleration or melee attacks. Why? In the heat of combat or as a character skids around a corner, the player will want to quickly respond to the situation. With the smaller shoulder button, there is a risk of the player's finger slipping off. Use these smaller buttons for "slow move" functions, such as precision aiming, looking at a map screen, or swapping inventory.

Speaking of "quick moves," I can't believe I've gone this far into the chapter without mentioning this **very important thing** about controls:

AS THE BUTTON IS PRESSED, THE ACTION SHOULD HAPPEN

Don't get me wrong, I love beautiful character animation as much as the next guy, but nothing pisses off a player faster than pressing a button and then having to wait for the gorgeous animation to finish playing. The only thing that happens quickly in these situations is the character dying due to misjudged timing or stray enemy attacks. Save the nice animation for the finish of the move. Or in other words, when the player presses jump, the game should ask "how high?"

Long animation and controls do have their place, as long as there is a balance between the risk and reward. Make sure the control represents this, too. Your game can consider a tap to be one action and hold to be something else. For example, in a hockey game, the power of the shot is proportional to the time the button was held before releasing it. A tap will make a quick shot while a hold will shoot a more powerful shot. Have the animation reflect the action. Many action and fighting games use long wind-up animations for the most powerful attacks in the game. When you hit an enemy with one of those suckers, he isn't getting back up again. The risk is the wind-up; the reward is the high damage, powerful shot or the instant kill.

Character or Camera Relative?

A common snare that game designers can get into is creating controls that alternate between being **character relative** and **camera relative.** Because of the frustration it can cause to players, the designer needs to pick one control scheme or the other for the duration of the game and STICK WITH IT.

With a camera-relative control scheme, the controls change depending on which way the character is facing the camera. Say you are playing the survival horror game *Terror Zombie Death Mansion 3,* and your stalwart hero stands in a hallway.

When you press left on the analog stick, the character walks to the left. The room he enters has the camera pointing at the hero—in the opposite direction from the shot in the hallway.[4]

---

[4] Tsk, tsk! Someone has "crossed the line" with the camera. Didn't you read Level 6?

Now when you press the stick to the left, the character walks to the right—because the controls have been mapped to how the game camera sees the character, rather than from the character's orientation. Unfortunately, thanks to the backward controls, the hero has walked right into the arms of a zombie, who proceeds to chew out his brains.

This is why I'm not such a big fan of the camera-relative control scheme. I much prefer a character-relative control scheme. In a character-relative control scheme, the game controls are always relative to the player character. If the control stick is moved to the left, the character will always move to the left no matter where the camera is facing. The game compensates for the player's movement even if the camera turns 180 degrees around.

You don't need to get fancy with the controls . . . unless you are designing for one of those newfangled motion controllers.

Shake, Rattle, and Roll

Most modern game controllers are outfitted with **actuators** and **gyroscopes.** They are the devices that make most motion controllers like the ones found on the Wii or the PS3 possible.

An actuator gives feedback to players in the form of vibrations. As with control schemes, make sure the language of your actuator usage is consistent. Rather than blasting the thing off all the time, limit it to when players take damage or when they earn a reward. You can have a lot of fun with actuators—if you take the time to play with them.

My favorite use of an actuator was in *Silent Hill* (Konami, 1999). The developer figured out how to vibrate the two actuators at different frequencies to simulate a heartbeat. Whenever the character was scared or hurt, the controller's "heart" would vibrate, telling players that they were in trouble. This result was really creepy and effective.

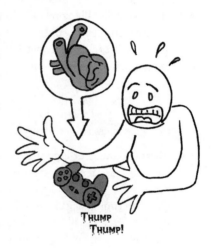

THUMP
THUMP!

A gyroscope allows players to rotate the controller as another way to manipulate an on-screen element. The control applications for gyroscopes can be quite robust. I have played games that allow players to nudge arrows while in flight (*Heavenly Sword*), maneuver falling characters (*Ratchet and Clank: Tools of Destruction*), or even flip over an entire level (*Super Mario Galaxy*).

Gyroscopic controls—also called **tilt controls**—have especially taken hold in mobile games. Some titles like the *Rolando* series, *Doodle Jump,* and *Tilt to Live* use tilt controls exclusively to control gameplay. Because a mobile device fits in one hand, it is easier for players to quickly tilt and shift direction. Tilt controls don't have to be used exclusively to move a player character around. Why not make the player shake the controller or device to roll dice, reload a gun, toss bad guys around, or even jump?

The most important point to remember about having players use gyroscopes is to clearly communicate the direction they have to turn the controller. As the gyroscope is "hidden" within the mechanism of the controller, players can easily forget that this is a control option; make sure to remind players that this function is available.

Whatever the action, I find that players respond best when the moves match a real-world action. If you tell players to swing the controller like a sword (or a tennis racket or a bowling ball or a conductor's baton . . .), they get it. The trick is to design and tune your in-game sword to *feel* like a sword through animation and physics. Game animations with the right timing, speed, and feel of friction in the world will make them feel less "floaty" and "gamey"— a feeling that is always less desirable to players.

Camera-based motion controllers such as the Microsoft Kinect and the Sony EyeToy use a combination of infrared sensors and computer vision to track players' movements to control gameplay. These controllers allow for a more natural way of interacting with video games. The strength of these motion controls is how they correlate to actual activities. You want your character to punch? Just punch. You need to avoid a swinging hazard? Just duck. You no longer have to mentally convert a button, stick, or even finger move into its real-world analogy. As a result, these controllers have transformed the home console space into a more active place—with the players getting up and moving to take part in the action. With that change come a few considerations:

- Many players don't play video games to exercise. Unless the goal of your game is for players to lose weight, don't forget to build in breaks and changes in control motions to keep players from wearing out or suffering repetitive stress injuries.

- Always account for **lag**—the time it takes between performing an action and when it happens on-screen. Lag occurs because it takes time for the console or computer to process the video and figure out what the players are doing. Because most games are based on timing, lag can be extremely frustrating for the player. This is especially true for rhythm games like *Rock Band* and fighting games like *Street Fighter*, where lag issues can screw up the player's timing and the game becomes too frustrating to play. *Guitar Hero* even allows the player to adjust the lag to match the player's skill level.

- An issue with online games is **latency**—a communication delay in the time it takes for game data to be received and decoded. Latency can cause control lock-up, sound distortion or game freeze. Even if care is taken to transmit only the minimal amount of data, it takes time for that data to go cross country. At 60 Hz, it's pretty common to have delays as much as six frames between when data is sent and received. Sadly, latency is an inescapable fact of life for Internet multiplayer games.

- Keep your players' movements broad. Precise and subtle motions tend not to register on the game cameras.

- Ensure your gestures make sense and match their real-world counterparts. Point to aim, grab to collect, wave to engage, grip to move, type to write.

- Players tend to stick to a single input style or movement unless they have a reason to change. If the input isn't reliable or consistent, players will look for alternative methods of control. If you are going to switch an input style or move, make sure it happens intuitively or at a natural transition point.

- Help guide the players' motions by using on-screen graphics. For example, *Fruit Ninja* for the Xbox 360 uses the player silhouettes to help guide where their hands (and their ninja swords) are in relationship to their fruit targets.

- Keep verifying the players' successes. Sometimes motion control players aren't sure whether their moves are being registered. Constant feedback will help reduce their confusion.

- When drawing shapes or glyphs, keep the shapes simple, like circles, triangles, and lines. Even seemingly uncomplicated shapes like figure eights and squares can get misinterpreted by motion-detecting controllers and cameras.

- Don't overdo it. Already many motion-controlled games are getting dinged for being **"waggle-fests,"** where the designers make every game action use the motion control just for the sake of it. Make your game controls a mix of traditional analog stick, button press, and controller motions.

Congratulations! You've mastered the Three Cs! But how are you going to communicate these newly minted design ideas to the player? Come with me to the remarkable Level 8 . . .

Level 7's Universal Truths and Clever Ideas

- Let ergonomics play a role in designing control schemes.
- Consider assigning control functions thematically.
- Consider emulating control schemes of other games in the same genre. Familiarity relieves confusion.
- As the button is pressed, the action should happen.
- Use negative responses as well as positive ones.
- Give your players a break to avoid "gamer's thumb" and other health problems (take a break yourself while you are at it).
- Camera-relative controls or character-relative controls? Pick one and stick with it.
- Avoid creating controls that are contrary to the game's visuals.
- Use the game controller's special features to make your controls more intuitive to the players.
- Be aware of the special needs of touch and motion controls and design to their strengths.
- Players' movement with motion controllers should be broad and mimic reality.

Level 8
Sign Language: HUD and Icon Design

PICTURE, IF YOU will, another dimension balanced between game and the real—a dimension of sight and sound, a realm of things and ideas. No, it isn't the *Twilight Zone,* but the zone known as the **HUD.**

Heads Up!

Named after the **heads-up display** found in modern aircraft, the HUD is the most effective way of communicating with players. The HUD refers to a visual screen overlay that communicates information to the player. The mini-screens and icons found in a HUD are some of the best tools in a video game designer's bag of tricks. They can communicate information, emotion, even tell players where to go and what to do. Let's look at some of the HUD elements found on an average game screen:

1. Health bar/lives

2. Targeting reticule

3. Ammunition gauge

4. Inventory

5. Score/experience

6. Radar/map

7. Context-sensitive prompt

Health Bar

A staple of action, adventure, platform, and shooter games, the **health bar** represents how close players are to death, or at least how close they are to restarting the game or a level. Health bars are the most flexible of the HUD elements and come in a variety of forms and imagery depending on the game:

- Many health bars are bars "filled" with color (often red) or icons. As players take damage, they lose a percentage of the bar, or the color empties from the icon. You can even make the color change—from green when healthy to red when damaged. When the bar is gone, that player dies.

- Or vice versa; you can have a **damage bar.** When this bar is full, the player dies.

- The health bar may represent the status of some sort of on-board defense system, as seen in the *Metroid* games.

- Both shields and health can be expressed as a numeric percentage (as seen in *Doom*). Health can be represented as shields. When all the shields are gone, the last hit destroys the player, as seen in *Star Wars: X-Wing* (LucasArts, 1993).

- Health can be represented as a story device. In the *Assassin's Creed* series, the health bar represents the game's narrative. Stray too far from the "correct story," and the narrator says, "That's not the way it happened." Then the character is "reset" back to the proper point in the story.

- Just because players lose health, that doesn't mean they can't get it back. If *Halo* players find cover and wait, their health bar eventually recharges back to full. This "wait for health" technique is becoming increasingly popular in action games, and I think it's a pretty good compromise in lieu of a game over/death screen, which pulls players out of the game. On the downside, the pace of the game really slows down as the player waits around to heal.

- Recently, health bars have been replaced by first-person-style effects that are also used in third-person view. In *Uncharted 3: Drake's Deception* (SCEA, 2012), damage is indicated by blood smears or a red blur effect that "points" in the direction of the source of damage. Just don't obscure the players' view so much that they can't see the action.

- In *Metroid Prime* and *Batman: Arkham Origins*, if players are hit by an electrical attack, the screen "fritzes" for a brief moment.

- As players take damage in the *Call of Duty* titles as well as *Uncharted 3*, the screen darkens, accompanied by heavy breathing and a heartbeat sound effect. In *Silent Hill,* the controller's actuator simulates a heartbeat as the player is dying.

Targeting Reticule

A **targeting reticule** helps players locate and/or lock onto ranged targets. Types of reticules can vary from a simple "dot" of a laser sight to a complex lock-on system that also provides target information such as health and range.

sights can be simple or complex

- A reticule shouldn't dominate the screen, but you should not make it so small that it's hard to see.

- Although I have seen reticules rendered in white, this can make them hard to see on some surfaces and backgrounds.

- Reticules are commonly activated in a zoomed-in mode, such as a sniper's scope. Some reticules change size to allow for more precise targeting when zoomed in, as seen in *Red Faction: Armageddon* (THQ, 2011).

- Have the reticule change color or "sharpen focus" when over a target. This gives players a clue when to fire.

- Give your reticule some "stickiness," also known as "aim assist." When it is aimed at a target, make the reticule gravitate toward it, allowing for faster targeting. This works great for vehicular weapon targeting.

- Build gameplay into your reticule. *Team Fortress 2*'s zoomed-in sniper's reticule also projects a laser pointer spot. If enemy players see this spot on walls, they can make an effort to avoid being shot.

Ammo Gauge

Whether your **ammunition gauge** displays bullets or a simple number, it will be one of the most watched gauges on-screen. Because some games sparsely distribute ammo (*Resident Evil 2*, I'm looking at you!), placing this gauge in an easy-to-see location is particularly important.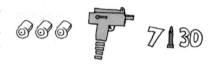

- If you have the screen space, display both clips and individual bullets, like in *Operation Wolf* (Taito, 1987).

- If the player has to track multiple types of ammo, such as grenades or rockets, make sure that they can be brought up with a button press (as they are in *Ratchet & Clank: Tools of Destruction*).

- I know this one seems like a no-brainer, but always display the ammo gauge of the weapon currently armed by the player.

- Even if your player's weapon holds an infinite number of shots, still display it to let the player know what weapon is armed. (The *Metal Slug* games do this.) Replace the number with an infinity symbol.

Inventory

A staple in adventure games and RPGs, **inventory** allows players to track and manipulate objects collected during the game. Keys, potions, puzzle items, and weapons are common inventory items.

- Players need quick access to items such as potions and spell components. Hotkey or drag-and-drop systems will help players grab items quickly.

- Allow players a location to see their inventory items in all their glory. *Tomb Raider* (Eidos, 1995) shows the items in Lara's backpack on a larger scale for easier inspection.

- *Diablo* has a limited inventory in which each item has a specific size. Inventory becomes a bit of a puzzle if the player has to fit as many items as possible into a limited space.

- If you have lots of inventory items, let players sort them by type, name, rarity, and so on.

- Inventory items can be represented either realistically or as icons. Whichever graphic style you choose, make sure that the items have clear silhouettes and use simple color schemes.

- If you are going to create a restricted inventory system, allow players to expand it later in the game. For example, start with a pouch, expand to a backpack, and eventually expand it to a magic bag of infinite holding.

- Make sure players have another permanent location in the game (such as their home base) where they can store their items. Players don't like losing their stuff, especially stuff they've bought.

- Why not use a "magic box" for storage, as in *Resident Evil 2*? Whatever items are stored in the box appear in boxes found further in the game. That way, players never have to run back and forth through the game world.

Score/Experience

In the beginning, there was **scoring.**

Achievement Unlocked
10G - You have reached Chapter 8

Can you believe the earliest video games had only single-digit scores (*Pong* and *Computer Space*)? I guess no one expected games to last that long! Scoring quickly jumped to four digits (*Space Invaders*), then six (*Galaxian*), and by the time the arcade boom started in the early 1980s, the high score was king. Entering your initials into a game's high score table was the sign of true mastery—provided the arcade owner didn't reset the machine and wipe it out!

As the home market grew, high score became less important in games (perhaps without networking, there was no one to brag to!) and stat tracking replaced high-scores. Percentages of the game completed became more important than scores. Text-based **combo meters** replaced score bars in games like *Devil May Cry* (Capcom, 2001). Players would be congratulated (or judged) on their performance. It's one thing to earn a low score, but another when the game criticizes your performance! And whoever thought up *Resident Evil*'s rating system must have been traumatized by grade school. There's nothing more insulting than surviving the zombie apocalypse only to be told you are graded a "C." Sheesh. However, with the increased popularity of online gaming **leaderboards,** scoring has returned to live harmoniously alongside combo meters, stats, and achievements.

Scoring indicators can take a variety of forms. They are still most commonly found in arcade-style games and Japanese RPGs like the *Final Fantasy* series, but scoring is starting to creep into Western-developed RPGs like *Borderlands* (2K Games, 2009).[1]

Positive Messaging

A high score provides validation to the player, but there are other ways to do that as well. *Mortal Kombat's* "Finish Him!" and "Fatality!" text and voice prompts are just as rewarding as seeing high score points flash across the screen. Other games will display "Good job!" and "Awesome!" messages to keep the player excited about their performance. Author Jane McGonigal postulates in her book *Reality is Broken*[2] that one of the reasons why video games are so popular is that players are getting the positive re-enforcement for their actions in games that they don't receive for their actions in their everyday lives. I think she makes a valid point. (Good job, Jane!)

Whatever form these positive messages take, make sure that when it happens, it's big and flashy. Video game developers are great at making players feel unskilled and stupid, but bad at making them feel good. There's no such thing as overdoing it when congratulating players. *Zack & Wiki: Quest for Barbaros' Treasure* (Capcom, 2007) does a great job of making even the worst player feel like the smartest, most skilled player in the world. Every little successful action results in a shower of fireworks, congratulatory text, and happy pirate rabbits flipping through the air! And let me tell you, nothing stokes your ego more than back-flipping bunnies!

---

[1] *Borderlands*' developers call it an RPS—a role-playing shooter—but would that qualify as picking nits?

[2] *Reality Is Broken: Why Games Make Us Better and How They Can Change the World*, by Jane McGonigal, Penguin Books, 2011.

Here are a few pointers to make your rewarding feel more rewarding:

- Use voice and sound effects to call attention any time a player gets a reward.

- Match your voice-over talent and music to the tone of your game. *Candy Crush Saga* (King.com Ltd., 2012) has the strangest mix of cheery candyland graphics and depressing funeral parlor music topped off with a dour sounding narrator. It's distracting and downright bizarre.

- Freeze gameplay to allow players to savor the moment of reward or have the hero celebrate along with players with victory animations, sounds, and effects.

- You can never have too many particles, especially when celebrating an achievement or awarding a high score.

- Players need to see a clear "cause and effect" for scoring so that they understand how they achieved their score. For example, as a player collects a gold coin in the world, the coin "travels" up to a tally. Don't forget the cool "Las Vegas-style" sound effects. Cha-ching!

- Choose an easy-to-read font. Ornate fonts (like medieval script) with heavy stylization or even serifs can be hard to read. Watch text length because you may run out of screen space!

- Fill up as much of the screen as possible with your celebratory effects, but don't interrupt or cover up gameplay.

Radar/Map

The first game **radar/map** was found in *Rally-X* (Namco, 1980), which allowed players to see the location of power-ups without seeing the game map or enemy cars. Since then, map screens have provided much more detail to players, from outlining the playfield to revealing secret clues.

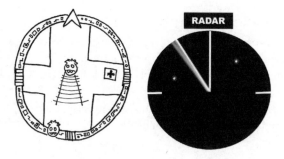

- Make your map large enough to be legible, but not so big that it fills up the whole screen. If you must have the map fill up the whole screen, do your players a favor and pause the gameplay.

- Make it easy for players to move/travel and look at the map at the same time. It's too much of a chore to open a map, memorize the locations, and then close the map to return to the game. Modern sandbox game designers let the players add markers onto the map, which lead players right to the objective!

- Create a legend for your map's icons so players can easily identify and find checkpoints, doorways, quest items, traversal goals, or story points. Also include pop-ups or some other text to remind players what these icons represent.

- Be sure to indicate changes in elevation on your map if you have them in your game world. Players can easily get confused when dealing with levels with multiple elevations. Use a color code or an "onion-skin" effect to show what layer players are currently on.

- Show the players' current direction by using an arrow or some other icon. Alternatively, rotate the map to face the direction the players are facing. This way, players won't have to reorient themselves in relationship to their goals.

- The **fog of war** occurs when a map is obscured until players actually "clear the fog" from the area by moving through it. You can always give your players ways to expose the whole map. Refogging areas is common in RTS games and is part of the strategy, but I have to admit, I'm not a fan of this mechanic. I find players can get lost when areas are refogged. If you need to have it in your game, fine. But don't come crying to me when your players complain.

- Add other information to your map to aid players. *Batman: Arkham Origins* provides a distance-to-goal counter, and the *Metal Gear* series shows the "detection cone" of enemy guards. *Harry Potter and the Order of the Phoenix* (EA, 2007) displays the names of NPCs on the "Marauder's Map."

- Incorporate visual themes into your mini-map. Fantasy maps look good on parchment, a sci-fi game might use a high-tech holographic display, and so on. Even the map can add to the game's **gestalt.**[3]

Context-Sensitive Prompts

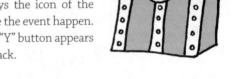

A **context-sensitive prompt** is an icon or text that appears when players are next to an object or character with which it interacts. The most common context-sensitive prompt displays the icon of the button or control that players have to use to make the event happen. For example, in *Grand Theft Auto 3*, an icon of the "Y" button appears whenever players stand next to a car they can hijack.

---

[3] *Die Gestalt* is German for "whole." In the context of games, it applies to the overall feel of an experience.

Using context-sensitive prompts is a great way to teach players what to do without having them resort to button mashing, memorizing control schemes, or even reading a manual. An added benefit is that using these prompts makes players feel more in character. Because the context-sensitive prompts in the *Batman: Arkham* series let you know when you can carry out an awesome move like a silent takedown or interrogation move, you end up feeling more like Batman.

In *Maximo: Ghosts to Glory*, we created a variation of context-sensitive prompts called **plings**—emoticons that told players when they couldn't do an action as well as when they could. Need ideas to know when to use these guys? Here's a short list of suggested uses for context-sensitive prompts:

- Use prompts to indicate whether doors, gates, and/or hatches can be opened or are locked.

- Use prompts to indicate what controls are required to operate mechanics such as cranks, levers, and pushable objects.

- Use them as NPCs. Because they are not only for talking anymore, you can use plings and emoticons to show their emotional state. Catch them in a good mood, and you'll get a better response/reward than if they're angry, scared, or sad.

- Use context-sensitive text to see what items and weapons players can collect. Take a page out of the *Uncharted* series to show players where compatible ammo can be collected or from the *Borderland* series to see if an item drop is better than the one you are currently have equipped.

- Use context-sensitive prompts to indicate use of a vehicle or minigame. Numerous games allow players to man a machine gun turret during the middle of regular gameplay.

- It seems a bit strange, but you can use context-sensitive buttons to indicate where players can jump, as in *The Legend of Zelda: The Wind Waker*. Because Link cannot jump on his own, the prompts teach players where they can interact with the world and where they can't.

- Use them as quick-time event prompts, as seen in the *God of War* series: a preset sequence of events that progress if you press the right button (see the quick-time event section later in this chapter).

- Use them as combat notification—icons that show when an enemy is vulnerable to a certain type of attack or even warn when an attack is about to happen so players can perform a blocking or counter move.

- Use them as secret treasure items. Have your icon appear when players are close to a hidden item.

In addition, some HUD elements are self-explanatory, such as fuel gauges, speedometers, and countdown timers. As with the others mentioned previously, keeping it clear, clean, and simple is the winning formula for making a successful HUD system.

The Clean Screen

Ah, reality. It's a double-edged sword. You want your game to look like a . . . dare I say . . . *cinematic* experience . . . but you still need to communicate gameplay and controls to your players. What to do, what to do?

Well, the first step in keeping your screen clear is to make your HUD elements move or fade off-screen while they are inactive. Of course, they need to reappear whenever they are valid (such as when players are taking damage or collecting treasure), and you should always make sure that players have a quick and easy way to bring them back up if they need to know the information. A simple shoulder button press usually does the trick.

Some games strive to remove HUD elements altogether. Peter Jackson's *King Kong: The Official Game of the Movie* (Ubisoft, 2005) utilized a few prompts at the beginning of the game but mostly conveyed game information through sound, animation, and visual effects. The result made for a very cinematic and immersive experience. If you want to go this route, here are some suggestions:

- Have characters react to things in the world to indicate function or interaction. Have them look at collectable items, reach for places they can get to, comment on things in the world that they are supposed to interact with, and so on.

- Opt for full-screen-sized effects over smaller or subtle ones. It never hurts to overemphasize. Use whatever you can to get your point across—sound, voice, visual effects, color, and lighting.

- Use glows or other attention-drawing effects on items to make them stand out. Or use what I call the "Scooby Doo effect."[4]

---

[4] The "Scooby Doo effect" is named after a by-product seen in Hanna-Barbera cartoons of the late 1960s and 1970s. While the background image of the cartoon is beautifully painted, the animated elements (such as a character or prop) are more flatly colored (usually lacking shading), making them unintentionally stand out against the more detailed background.

- Use cinematic characters to lead your players through the world. If you can't afford that much work or it doesn't fit your story or gameplay needs, at least illuminate the path using color or lighting effects. You could even give a subtle clue such as having leaves blow in the direction players need to travel. Something is better than nothing at all.

If you don't completely want to eschew (bless you!) the HUDs, you can at least keep them out of the way. Using a **temporary HUD** is a good way of keeping things clear. I remember *Crash Bandicoot* having one of the first HUDs that "got out of the way" when it wasn't being used. If players collected a mango or an extra life or they took a hit, the HUD would pop onto the screen. If it went a minute or more without any of these events happening, the HUD would slide back off-screen, keeping the screen clear so players could enjoy the pretty game art. The *Infinity Blade* series displays a directional arrow only as players perform a move. This arrow acts more like a guide than a true control path, but it helps eliminate any confusion as to where players need to swipe.

If video game interfaces were a galaxy of planets and on one side of the galaxy was the planet "No Interface," then all the way on the other side of the galaxy would be the planet "Gobs of Interface." I might add that both of these are very dumb names for planets; I mean, what do the inhabitants of these planets call themselves? "No Interfacians" or "Goblings"? But I digress. This is where the RPGs, RTSs, simulations, adventure games, and some slumming shooters all live. Hello there, friendly life forms of planet Gobs of Interface; let's examine your interesting markings and plumage.

Icon Has Cheezburger?[5]

The first thing you'll notice on many RTS and adventure games is that there are lots of **icons** on-screen. Icons for tracking stats, icons for weapons, icons for magic spells, icons for the contents of bags of holding and whatnot. I believe part of the allure of these icon-heavy games is that players make lots of choices and have lots of things to build and collect. That's OK; not every game needs to be like one made by Oscar-winner Peter Jackson.[6]

---

[5] Yeah, I know; that's a really, really bad pun. Sorry.

[6] 2004 for *The Lord of the Rings: Return of the King*. He did that HUD-less King Kong game too. Weren't you paying attention?

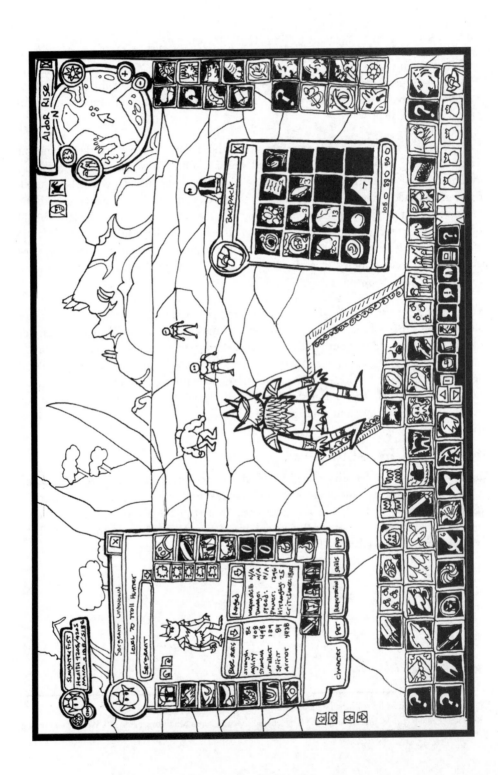

So, because you are making icons for your game, here are 157[7] things to think about:

- Pick the right image for your icon. If pressing your icon builds tanks, then guess what picture should be on the icon?[8]

- Make sure the image that you use is current and accurate. I was working with a team who had an icon for a stamp function (like an ink stamp) that looked like a postage stamp. Many of the younger testers didn't even know what a postage stamp was! Kids these days!

- Color-code your icons. Fiery punch? Make it red! (Or at least orange.) Chilling hand of frost? I'll give you one guess (blue). You can take color coding one step further and make the image or background of the icon a representative color. For example, all the icons that advance players to the next screen could be green, and your sword combat icons could all have a red background or feature that colors in the artwork (make sure it's a different shade of red than the one you are using for fire attacks!). The goal is for players to understand similarities between icons and be able to choose the correct one at a glance.

- If color isn't enough, use shapes as a differentiator—circles for ammo, squares for health pickups, and so on.

- Try to avoid text in your icons. Not only will you have to change them for localization, but they may be too small to read.

- If you are going to use text (like a word) as an icon, make sure it is legible and looks more like a button than straight text.

- Never, ever combine several visual elements (such as text and a character and a logo) on one icon. Keep them separate graphic files for easier editing, especially when localizing for different languages.

- Surround your icon with a strong black or white outline to make it "pop" off the background or give it a soft surrounding glow or a drop shadow.

- Look at all your icons together to make sure you aren't creating any similar-looking ones. Try to make each one of them as individual as possible.

- A good trick is to have text of an item's name ("spell" or whatever) appear if players move their cursor over the icon. Any reminder for the players never hurts!

- Ensure artists create the icons. Don't leave it up to other team members.

---

[7] Give or take 141 or so.

[8] I can't believe you are actually looking down here for an answer!

■ Learn from the experts. Apple, Adobe, and Microsoft have dedicated icon artists who create clear and clever icons for their software and operating systems. Go online and see what icons others have used for their websites. Games that use lots of icons like RTSs and sims are great sources of inspiration. When we were making Maximo's ability icons, we were inspired by the designs on Boy Scout merit badges. You can find icons everywhere. Don't feel you have to reinvent the wheel.

■ When players select the icon, make it do SOMETHING. Change color, make a clicky sound effect—anything to register user interaction. I recommend that you avoid using a voice effect, though, because players don't want to hear "Good choice, commander!" every time they press a button. If you need voice, repeat it only once every three or so clicks. And make sure to record a few extra voice cues to avoid repetition. So, to make this point clearer,[9] think of it this way: click no. 1, "Yes, sir!"; click no. 2, "Right away!"; click no. 3, "I'm on it!"; click no. 4, "Yes sir!"; click no. 5, "Right away!" . . . you get the idea.

■ The most important button on the interface should be the biggest.

■ Make the most-used buttons easy to reach from the middle of the screen or wherever the players' cursor will spend the most time.

■ Make your icons a little "sticky" so the cursor will easily gravitate toward them.

Creating Icons for Mobile Games

In mobile gaming, an icon is used to represent your game in the marketplace. It might just be the most important piece of art you will create for your game. It's like a movie poster or a book cover. Some customers might buy your game just because the icon looks cool, or conversely, choose to skip it because your icon looks lame. When designing your game's icon, strive to give your icon the following traits:

■ **Clarity**—Make the images in your icon easy to see. Use silhouettes to create simple, easy-to-understand images. The stronger the silhouette is, the easier it will be to "read."

■ **Iconic design**—I often compare a game's icon to the logo on a superhero's chest. It should represent the character in a single image. Make it memorable, cool, or funny—whatever you think will best sum up your game. Because your icon will become your game's identity, make sure it looks great. Try not to use multiple images in one icon. Stick with one image that sums up your game—whether it is your main character, a puzzle piece, or an image that captures the game's tone.

---

[9] Or possibly to make this understandable at all.

- **Color**—Use color to your advantage. There are lots of books on color theory that can help guide you. For example, primary colors like red and yellow always grab the eye more than dark blues, purples, and blacks. Plus, they're easier to see on small screens. Contrasting colors (like blue and orange or black and white) make images pop. Pick a simple color scheme that will visually represent your game.

- **No text or numbers**—If you use raster artwork, text runs the risk of aliasing or blending together to become unreadable, especially when scaled down. Consider skipping text altogether if you want your game to be sold to an international audience.

Ultimately, the rule of thumb when creating icons is

KYSS = KEEP YOUR SYMBOLS SIMPLE

Today's audiences are familiar with icons, from comics and cartoons[10] to the desktop of their computer, so take advantage of this familiarity. Over the years, video games have developed their own vocabulary of icons. Here are a few classic examples:

- **Red cross**—Designates healing items.[11]

- **1 Up**—Is universal video game-ese for an extra life. Also, the head or little "doll" version of the character works well for this.

- **Heart**—Can be used as a replacement for a red cross or 1 up.

- **Food/soda can/pills**—Means energy or healing, as in "Elf needs food badly."

- **Exclamation point**—Shows surprise when put above enemies' heads. Put one above your hero's head to show he can interact with something.

---

[10] Icons in comics and cartoons? Sure! From stars and tweeting birds over Daffy Duck's head to "Pow!" bursts when Batman throws a punch to scratchy marks over Charlie Brown's head to show that he's mad to those swirly circular "rootbeer-ootles" coming out of Opus, the penguin, to show that he's tanked on A&W, you can find icons all over comics and cartoons.

[11] The Canadian Red Cross has contacted game developers about using the red-colored cross image in "violent video games." The organization interprets the use of the image as a misuse of their trademark. The video game industry as a whole has not officially addressed this complaint.

- **"No" symbol**—Means that players cannot use or do not need this item. Also used for busting ghosts.

- **Skull**—Means poison, death, or danger. And sometimes pirates.

- **Coin**—Represents money, gelt, dough-re-mi. How about a nice big sack o' cash lusted after by bank robbers?

- **Controller icons**—Used as a shorthand to prompt players to press a specific control for a specific action. You find these a lot in quick-time events, which I describe next. And here we are!

Don't Get QTE

Quick, press the button!

Now press it again. Too late! You died. Congratulations. You have just lost the first book-based **quick-time event.** Fortunately for you, you have an extra life.

Originally called a "quick-timer event," a quick-time event (or **QTE**) is a prompt that forces players to make a split-second action or suffer usually painful or fatal consequences. Other times it is used to make cutscenes more interactive.

Dragon's Lair (Cinematronics, 1983) first featured QTE gameplay—heck, the entire game is a quick-time event—but after a brief spurt of similar arcade games (*Cliffhanger, Space Ace, Thayer's Quest*), QTEs almost went the way of the text adventure. *Shenmue* (Sega, 1999) brought them back and christened them QTEs at the same time. They've become a gameplay staple since *Resident Evil 4* and *God of War* popularized them. In motion-controlled games, you can use player motions to replace the button press of the QTE, but the effect is still the same: the player has to quickly react to an on-game action. QTEs are pretty flexible, which is why game designers like them.

Here are just a few things you can use QTEs for:

- Avoiding getting hit by a bolt out of the blue like a falling object, moving car, or soccer ball.

- Fighting off an attack from a biting dog, a hungry hydra, or a killer crocodile man.

- Finishing off a boss with a life-or-death shot or throwing a hail-mary knife at an escaping villain.

- Doing extra damage to an enemy during combat or countering, blocking, or disarming an enemy's attack. You can even throw a grenade back at an enemy!

- Responding to a moral choice such as choosing whom to save from a horde of zombies.

Players either love or hate QTEs, but they are here to stay. There's no need to hate them, though; they're just one more gameplay tool in a designer's toolkit. The trick is to use them responsibly:

- Never use a QTE for something players can do for themselves in the game. I prefer to use them as shortcuts to cinematic sequences. Save QTEs for big exciting moments and nigh-impossible actions.

- Timing is everything. Give players a "beat" to process the appearance of a QTE icon and another "beat" to press the appropriate button.

- Don't string them out for too long; most QTEs need to be repeated if the player fails the sequence, and there is nothing worse than having to repeat the QTE over and over and over again.

- Wait! There is something worse than repeating a QTE, and that's a QTE that doesn't play fair. While using random QTE icons sounds like a good way to introduce variety, this is the one time you want predictability in your game. Once players memorize the pattern, they can concentrate on watching the cool actions. Now, I know what you're saying. "Wait a second! There are video games with random QTEs in them." And I'd respond, "You are correct." However, I just don't like them. They make players feel as if they won because they were lucky, not by their own skill.

- Keep your QTE controls to a single set of controls. Most games use the buttons or sometimes a stick. Try not to use the harder-to-reach shoulder buttons.

- Make sure the QTE icons are big and easy to see. Keep their placement consistent; don't move them around.

- Try not making the QTE mandatory. Both *Uncharted 2* and *Batman: Arkham Asylum* offer QTEs as options for dispatching enemies; however, if players miss that opportunity, they still have plenty of other ways to take out the bad guys.

- A "button mashing" QTE, in which players repeatedly press the button, can heighten an emotional situation or simulate physical effort.

- You can use QTEs for purely emotional effect such as in *Heavy Rain*'s infamous "Press X to Jason"—in which the player must press the X button to call out for his lost son.

- When using motion-controlled QTEs, keep the waggling short. And if you are going to make players waggle the controller, don't do it too many times in a row. Gamers want to play your game, not get wrist injuries.

HUDs and Where to Stick 'Em

Now that you have created a whole mess of beautiful icons, what are you going to do with 'em? Why, slap 'em up onto the screen, of course! But before you start displaying them willy-nilly, let's see where they can go. Our zombie friend is going to help us out with this one.

Because the middle of the screen is where the action is, please refrain from putting your HUD there. (Unless it's for targeting, or identifying game objects.) If you have to bring up a full-screen display, consider making it translucent like the holographic screen in *Dead Space* (EA, 2008). This way, players don't get disjointed from their environment and "lose their place" in the game world.

The upper left side of the screen is traditionally used for the most important information: health, score, and so on. As the (Westerner's[12]) eye travels from left to right when reading information, putting icons to the left so the eye can travel back "into" the game on the right usually feels comfortable to the player.

Displaying icons along the bottom of the screen works well too, as long as you watch out for **clipping** that can occur if a player is using a monitor or TV screen that isn't calibrated for your game. Assume at least 50% of your audience have a crappy television set; heck, even gamers with excellent HD LCD rear-projection sets still can get clipped images on the sides of their screen. Get that information as close to the safe frame as possible (and always offer screen calibration options).

---

[12] Although many Asian and Middle Eastern languages read right to left, I can't think of a single video game that displays information on the screen in this way.

If you are going to use the right, left, and bottom of the screen, be careful of the "bracketing effect" that happens; this will make your game screen seem smaller and claustrophobic. I've seen some RTS screens so filled with HUD elements that it felt as though I was looking out of a mail slot!

If you are going to have lots of icons on-screen, why not consider letting players choose which ones they want and prioritize where they should go. This way, the players can choose what they feel are the most important icons for them. Just make sure you don't give them the option to obstruct the main gameplay field.

Some icons open up other screens, like inventory lists. Make sure players have a quick way to get back to the game. You may want to consider allowing players to pause the game so they don't get bushwhacked by an enemy while they are trying to find their +6 rod of killing. Of course, you could be like the designers of *Dead Space* and intentionally allow enemies to attack while your character is rooting around in his holographic space backpack for another air canister. According to interviews with the team members, this was an intentional choice: they wanted players not to be able to rely on the "gamey" mechanic of the world freezing (as happens in, say, *Resident Evil*) while looking for inventory items. This type of gameplay really conveys the sense of dread as necromorphs are bearing down on you when you realize that you just don't have time for a break.

There Are Other Screens Than the HUD

Oh, video game screens. There are so many of you. Where to start? At the start, of course!

The first thing your players see (other than the box cover[13]) is the title/start screen, so it's important to set the right mood. The problem is, there are so many styles to choose from! Let's see:

- The **movie poster** title screen that mirrors the cover of the box.

---

[13] Okay, technically, players also see a warning screen, a publisher logo, a developer logo, and the logos of the companies of any technologies leased by the development team, but starting with those wouldn't make for a very exciting list, would it? Stop making me get ahead of myself!

- The **heroic pose** title screen where the hero is standing on some high bluff, long hair blowing in the breeze, giant sword and/or gun at the ready.

- The **enigmatic** image that brings up all sorts of questions: Why am I in a jungle? What is that monkey statue doing there? Is it a relic I will be raiding? The image is something important to the game, but players have no idea because they haven't played the game yet. When they finally learn the significance, their minds will be blown!

- The **logo** screen, where a large image of the game's logo is displayed. Not very exciting but effective. Make it more exciting with strobing colors, rotating effects, bouncing text, anything to get some motion in there.

Title screens often feature menus that offer selections such as save/load, number of players, options, bonus features, and difficulty. How much you include depends on how many button presses you want the players to make before they get into the meat of the game. I find that players just want to get to the good stuff, so you should keep the button pressing to a minimum. Remember, this **very important rule** I never, ever try to break:

YOU SHOULD NEVER HAVE TO PRESS A BUTTON MORE THAN THREE TIMES TO REACH ANY GAME SCREEN

Why? Because players don't want to spend the entire game pressing buttons to reach interface and inventory screens! They want to play the game! Let them play the game! Why aren't you letting them play the game? Think of the children! Oh, the humanity!

Sorry. Lost it there for a moment.

Seriously, don't make the players dig to find the options and get to the gameplay. Make everything in the game reachable within a button press or two. Consolidate screens if you have to, but keep track of how many button presses it takes to get to that information. I once managed to reduce the "start to play" from 16 button presses to 4 button presses. Not too shabby if I do say so myself.

- **Pause**—The well-designed pause screen can do more than give players a break. It can be used to save a game; access the options screen, game map, or inventory screen; or even just exist to be enjoyed, as with *Banjo-Kazooie*'s (Nintendo, 1998) lovely acoustic version of the theme. Whatever you do, just make sure players don't feel that they are missing any of the game by pausing. Remember, most people use pause screens to take bathroom breaks. Of course, you can always remove the option of a pause screen altogether, like in *Dead Space*, but that could be taxing on their bladders.

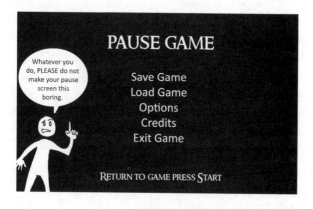

When designers create pause screens, they have this bad habit of making the first choice "resume" and the next one down something like "options." Usually, the map and save game options appear a few more choices down in the list. This placement makes no sense to me. Let's say you use the start button to bring up the pause screen. Think of all the times you are going to have to press the start button, then D-pad down the list to the "save game" selection, save the game, and then return back up to the resume button? Why not use the start button to close it again? Why do you even *need* the resume option? If the save button is the most common selection the players will be making, make it the first thing they can select. If it isn't, make it the map or the inventory. Plan out your pause screen as carefully as you do your level! Your players will thank you for it.

Wow! Look at this next graphic. All these options can stem from a pause screen:

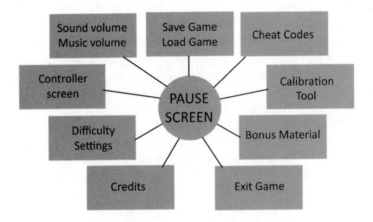

- **Options**—Like the ancient labyrinth, the option screen usually leads to more screens. But don't lose your players in a maze of choices. Think of the option screen as a hub, with the choices the spokes that radiate from it. Sound and music volume controls, controller settings, difficulty settings, and even bonus and cheat codes can be placed under the options heading.

- **Calibration tool**—If your game is particularly moody and dark in theme and visuals, I suggest having a screen calibration tool. A calibration tool allows players to adjust the screen's contrast on a dark-colored image or set of color bars. While it's fine for this tool to live in the options screen, I prefer to have players adjust it before starting the game, to see the game in the best light . . . er . . . darkness possible.

- **Save/load game**—This option is one of the most important aspects of your game, so keep it simple and automate the process whenever possible. Always start a new game with the option to create a new save file. Don't make players hunt around for this option, and make sure they quickly pick up on where it is—even in the tutorial if possible.

I highly recommend that you allow players to have several (at least three) save files. Players often restart new games after completion, want backup files in case they make catastrophic choices during gameplay, or even just want to let someone else play the game concurrently.

Customization goes a long way when creating a save file. Let the players name their own files. Store playtime, titles of game levels or chapters, and even inventory items like lives or gear to help the players remember their progress. Show icons or images to help jog the players' memory further. Everything helps.

Autosave is a useful function that acts as a backup if players are too engrossed in playing. Give players the option to load a game from a saved file or the autosave. Make sure you display an icon warning players that the game is autosaving so they don't shut off the system and lose their file.

When designing the save system, be careful that it doesn't become a "reset system." In many games, it is easier and faster for players to reload the game than to die and start again. Don't let players use the save system as a gameplay mechanic because it breaks the immersion of the play experience.

- **Loading screen**—Many players consider loading screens as a necessary annoyance, but that's just because developers fail to treat these screens as part of the game. Eliminating loading screens can be difficult to implement technically. It may even be impossible to do, given the technical limitations of the game. As a designer, you need to know the limitations of your game code up front.

More recent games strive for a "seamless" loading-screen-free experience by disguising the loading screen with slowly opening doors, long elevator rides, or dissipating fog. Just don't make what happens on the loading screen too complex—loading screens need to be loaded too!

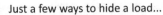

Just a few ways to hide a load...

abnormally long corridors   very slowly unlocking doors   microwaving popcorn

If you must have loading screens, here are some ways to spruce them up:

- Show concept art.

- Ask trivia questions.

- Have a playable minigame.[14]

- Display the game map.

- Display a character bio.

- Provide tips on gameplay or control (but be careful not to repeat them; even the most useful tip becomes annoying after several viewings, so don't display control tips that players have already seen).

- Fill in gaps in the game story or provide a recap of players' progress and remind them of their goals.

- Play a short video briefing players on the upcoming mission or location.

- Have players fight endless waves of enemies or destroy a large object.

- Provide "beauty shots" of your character or items in the game.

- Have players manipulate an interactive object such as the game's logo or a significant story item.

Hardware manufacturers require that there be some moving image on a loading screen so players know that the game hasn't crashed. No matter what your loading screen displays, you should provide a progress bar or percentage loaded indicator so players know how long they have to wait.

- **Controls**—When showing the control screen, first and foremost, you need to display an image of the game controller, as shown in the following image:

---

[14] Unless you work for Namco, you may want to avoid this one because it owns the U.S. patent (#5,718,632).

L Bumper: Block
L Trigger: Activate Force Shield

R Bumper: Crouch/Cover
R Trigger: Shoot/Melee/Throw Grenade

Back: Map   Start: Pause

Y: Vent Cooling
X: Special
    Talk

L Analog Stick:
Move Character
Press to Run

B: Grab Object/Enemy
A: Jump/Vault

Inventory
Up: Health
Down:
Left: Cycle through weapons
Right: Cycle through weapons

R Analog Stick: Move Camera
Press to Zoom

Some games show the character that performs an action when you press the appropriate button. At the very least, display text explaining the control.

Make sure the controls screen is easily accessible from the game for quick player reference. Also, consider allowing players to customize the controls or at least give them several options to remap controls schemes.

- **Scoring/stats**—Otherwise known as a "tally screen," the scoring/stats screen appears at the end of a level. It displays the players' progress and performance in the game. You can tally just about anything on a tally screen. Here are just a few ideas:

TALLY SCREEN

Whatever you do, PLEASE do not make your tally screen this boring.

GOLD COLLECTED   1138 GP
TREASURE CHESTS FOUND   18/20
...CHES/MONKEYS DEFILED   5/5
PIRATES SLAUGHTERED   182/200
SHOOTING ACCURACY   72 PERCENT
SECRETS DISCOVERED   13/20

OVERALL GRADE   C+

RETURN TO GAME PRESS START

- Score

- Time of completion

- Accuracy of shooting

- Enemies slain

- Money remaining/collected/spent

- Number of lives

- Rating (can be an A–B–C grade or a "word" rating, like "Awesome dude" or "Master of the Universe")

- Objectives reached/completed

- Secrets found (usually expressed as an X/Y value)

- Gallons of blood spilled/distance traveled/chests smashed . . . you get the idea

- **Legal/copyright**—These screens are required by publishers and hardware manufacturers. Make sure that they are legible and, more importantly, accurate. Just remember that console manufacturers require that they cannot be skipped.

- **Credits**—Allow me to pull out my soapbox for a moment. People work very hard on games. Too many people in the video game industry get screwed out of the credit they deserve due to egos, politics, and old-fashioned neglect. I am a firm believer that if you work on a game, you should get a credit. That credit should reflect the title on the person's business card. Sadly, it doesn't always happen that way: it's something in the gaming industry that needs to change. I like to follow this simple but **very important thing:**

GIVE CREDIT WHERE CREDIT IS DUE

Credit screens are an important part of the game. They are a celebration of the people who made and contributed to the final game. They deserve to be seen, but these screens should be as entertaining as possible. Some games get it: *LittleBigPlanet,* for example, has an amazingly entertaining credit sequence. *Typing of the Dead* (Sega, 2000) has a playable minigame where the player can type the credits!

If you need more inspiration for great-looking screens or credit sequences, take a look at most movie DVDs. DVD designers do a great job at creating a gestalt built around the film. This level of attention to detail takes a lot of time and effort on behalf of the art director and designers, but it's always worthwhile.[15]

There are other screens to consider as well, such as the **game over, bonus materials,** and **store** screens. Don't worry; I cover these screens in greater depth later in the book.

---

[15] Some excellent examples of gestalt in games include *Twisted Metal Black* (SCEA, 2001), *Brütal Legend* (EA, 2009), and *House of the Dead: Overkill* (Sega, 2009).

A Final Word on Fonts

As you make your HUD and display screens, you need to think about fonts. I find that fonts follow many of the same rules as icons when it comes to legibility and clarity. However, they do present some of their own issues:

- Theme your font to your game, but don't use overly ornate fonts that are hard to read.

- In many cases, fonts require a license to use. I know of a game that had to be re-worked at the eleventh hour because the developer didn't have the rights to use the font. Fonts are like any other piece of artwork. It's only fair to pay the artist for his work.

- Be mindful of the color of your font and your background. For example, never place red text over a black background, because it usually blurs on many TVs, particularly older ones or ones where the console is hooked up on composite cables.

- Now that HDTVs are the industry standard, developers should use higher resolution fonts. I have found that any font size under 18 points is very hard to read on a standard definition television. Remember that not every player has a state-of-the-art screen![16]

Remember, the goal of all these screens is to communicate clearly and efficiently to the players. Now let's move on to the good stuff: the game itself! But first, the obligatory Universal Truths and Clever ideas section . . .

Level 8's Universal Truths and Clever Ideas

- The HUD communicates game concepts to players.
- Players should be able to access the HUD information quickly.
- Keep HUD elements away from the sides of the screen and closer to the safe frame.
- Design easy-to-see and -read icons.
- Make QTEs fair and easy to perform.
- Players should never have to press a button more than three times to reach anything in the game.
- Don't make players dig through screens for important information.
- Fonts should be easy to read. Don't make them too small or too fancy.
- Even the most "boring" screens can be exciting and interesting.
- Give credit where credit is due.

---

[16] The text displayed in *Dead Rising* (Capcom, 2006) was so small that players couldn't read mission objectives—rendering the game unplayable to those with standard definition sets.

Level 9

Everything I Learned About Level Design, I Learned from Level 9

YOU CAN'T EXPECT a book called *Level Up!* not to have a chapter on level design. But what do I mean by **level**? Much like the word **score,**[1] its definition changes when used in different contexts. Observe:

Level: An environment or location where game play occurs. "If you are on the Death Star level, you are near the end of the game."

and

Level: A term favored by developers that describes how to break up physical space based on a specific gameplay experience. "I must have died a dozen times on the mine cart level."

and

Level: A unit of counting a player's progression, especially when repetitive gameplay is involved. "I'm up to level 20 on *Tetris*."

and

Level: The rank of a player based on earned score, experience, or skills. A term for marking character progression and improvement, as in "I finally leveled up my third *WoW* character to 70." The most common use of "level" in this context can be found in RPGs.

---

[1] Score: (1) To gain something (as in "I scored a battle axe off that weapon drop"), (2) to calculate a total (as when a high score is tallied), (3) to cut without cutting all the way through (like scoring metal with a light saber).

A possible explanation for "level" having four definitions in the video game industry is that video game developers have extremely limited vocabularies.

Another reason for the multiple definitions is that developers have used the term "level" in different contexts for so long that it's too late to get everyone to agree to call it something else like a **floobit** or a **placenheimer.** So level it is. But why level? Most ancient game designers believe that the term came from *Dungeons and Dragons*, when players would travel down many dungeon levels (like floors of a building) to reach the dragon. (Hence, the title of the game.) Why no one thought to call it "floors" is beyond me.

In fact, to complicate things further, often a level isn't even called a level. I've played games with rounds, waves, stages, acts, chapters, maps, and worlds, but even these have their specific definitions. Let's review:

- **Rounds** can be found in games where you play the same action, if not similar gameplay, over and over again. This term can be used for sports games as in a round of golf or boxing where the activity is the same, or there can be variation in the gameplay like rounds of *Peggle* or *Diner Dash*.

- **Waves** usually refers to combat, as in "wave after wave of enemies assaulted the stalwart heroes!" Pretty exciting stuff, but you are still doing the same thing—beating up bad guys.[2] Whole games can be made of waves of enemies as in *Plants vs. Zombies* and *Defend My Castle*, or waves can be a sequence of play like those found in *Gears of War 2* or *Uncharted 2*.[3]

- **Stage** is usually interchangeable with the term "wave," but it's often used when describing an experience that has clear separations that relate to the activity—much like the separate stages of a rocket.[4] "Stage" is often used when referring to the actions of a boss enemy.

- **Acts** and **chapters** are often used when the developer wants players to concentrate on the story of the game. These titles make a game feel classier. They're not fooling anyone; they're really just game levels.

- Levels are often referred to as **maps** or by the location of the environment (like "Power Plant" or "Insane Asylum"). This is most common in FPSs, where players associate the location with a style or method of gameplay.

The term **world** is often confused with level, but I blame this on its origin. "World" was first used in *Super Mario Bros.* with the famous "World 1-1." The game was extremely successful, and the term was immediately embraced by developers. However, by my own definition, World 1-1 should actually be called Level 1-1. A world is a video game location that is distinguished primarily by its visual or genre theme and may be composed of multiple locations that share this theme.

world 1-1

---

[2] And by beating, I mean punching, stabbing, shooting, karate-chopping, decapitating, rocketing, and exploding.

[3] You can find waves in any action game, not just ones with "2" at the end of their names.

[4] Remember, these terms were first created and used by early game creators: the same guys who were in your high school rocket club. Sorry, cool kids; the nerds have taken over the world.

In early video games, players would refer to the levels as "worlds," as in "Fire World," "Ice World," and so on. However, as the home market demanded longer play experiences and developers wisely learned to create multiple levels using the same texture sets and/or mechanics, worlds gained additional sequences—most famously seen in *Super Mario Bros.*'s World 1-1. However, World 1-1 is just the first of four levels of the first world.[5] We needed a term to define these separate sections of play, hence the term "level."

The Top 10 Cliché Video Game Themes

Because so many game worlds have been introduced over the years, some of them have become hoary clichés. Most developers run screaming from these, but they still have their uses. I therefore present them to you:

1. **Outer space**—You can easily see how a black television screen may have served as inspiration to early game developers as the perfect stand-in for outer space. Brightly displayed vector-drawn stars looked great on those early CRT screens. Player-controlled spaceships meant no animations. Spaceships could be rendered in simple geometric shapes. Gameplay could be based primarily on physics: an important advantage to those early programmers during the days prior to game designers and artists. As the earliest game genre—the shooter—evolved, outer space continued to be a popular locale for video game battles to be waged. Outer space also allows for all the tropes of sci-fi: aliens, spaceships, computers, and futuristic weapons. All things beloved by the geeky game developer community.

---

[5] World 1-1 is grassland, 1-2 is an underground cavern, 1-3 are is made up of mountain-like platforms, and 1-4 is the interior of a castle. These levels are all part of a world known as the Mushroom Kingdom. And now you know.

2. **Fire/ice**—These levels swiftly became popular for three reasons: first, fire and ice levels created hazards that were easy to program—flames and low-friction surfaces. These hazardous terrains created perfect timing puzzles that caused the players to "break their rhythm," making the level more challenging. Second, fire and ice environments lent themselves to a wide array of deadly inhabitants, from lava men and flame-breathing dragons to snowmen both of the abominable and frosty varieties. And third, fire and ice levels added color (red and blue) to the palette of gameplay worlds, especially important to distinguish screenshots on the back of home console boxes in those early 8-bit days. Today, fire and ice levels are camouflaged as snow-bound train wrecks and lava-filled temples, but as long as the color, feel, and mechanics are represented, they'll always be fire and ice levels to me.

3. **Dungeon/cavern/tomb**—The connections between *Dungeons and Dragons* and Tolkien's *Middle Earth* run strong and deep in the DNA of video game developers. Dungeons are laden with traps to avoid, puzzles to solve, and mechanics to circumvent. Dungeons offer up waves of enemies (without a whiff of explanation as to why they live there), and of course, there was always lots of collectable treasure to be gleaned. Even when the game world isn't themed to medieval fantasy, players still thrill in raiding uncharted dusty tombs. Technically, dungeon locations offer game artists many advantages: great opportunities for dramatic lighting and intricate carvings and statues. Even in the early days of gaming, cave wall textures were made from easily repeatable (or "tiled") art.

4. **Factory**—Factory levels became a staple of platform games, especially as the platform game genre exploded on home gaming systems. The dynamic mechanics offer game developers easily created, combined, and repurposed hazards that can be tuned to a wide variety of difficulty levels. These adaptable factory mechanics quickly spread to other locations too: moving platforms, conveyer belts, and turning gears were present in the tombs, circuses, and space stations of just about every action and platform game.[6]

---

[6] I consider it a triumph of the video game industry that *Star Wars* creator George Lucas, at the last minute, added a factory level to his 2002 movie *Attack of the Clones*. The movie's heroes ride conveyer belts and make timed jumps through smashing presses worthy of a sequence right out of a Nintendo platformer.

5. **Jungle**—The jungle theme allows video game designers the flexibility of the dungeon but without the dull colors and right angles. With its exotic traps (like quicksand and pongee-covered knife-lined pits) and exotic creatures (such as crocodiles, snakes, and scorpions) set in a colorful outdoor environment, jungle levels quickly became a prevalent video game level theme as game art became a focus. Jungle levels lend themselves to robust mechanics—swinging vines, tree branch platforms from which to leap, and rivers with moving logs à la *Frogger*—that keep a player's heart beating like a jungle drum.

6. **Spooky/haunted house/graveyard**—Spooky environments are great when your game requires mood and story. Players slowly explore creepy environments, punctuated by unsuspected "scares" in the form of play mechanics or enemies that seemingly spring out of nowhere. But scaring people is an art; you must build pacing into your levels. Allow moments of quiet, followed by moments of distraction, before you scare your players. Music and sound design is critical to the spooky theme; it goes hand-in-hand with encounter and puzzle design. But be careful you don't tip your hand too much. You can easily give away your scares if you don't choreograph things correctly. After years of making haunted houses in my garage, I find the best scare is one players expect but don't know where it's coming from.

The spooky theme is also the most adaptable theme of the video game tropes. There have been spooky adventures, platformers, RPGs, FPSs, and even puzzle games. Everything's more fun when it's scary!

7. **Pirate (ship/town/island)**—The spiritual brother to the spooky level is the pirate level.[7] The pirate theme is perfect for high action gameplay, melee combat, and of course, lots and lots of treasure. Many pirate levels capitalize on the pirate's natural form of transportation: the pirate ship. And then there are the pirate skeletons. Who doesn't love these guys? Like the spooky theme, the pirate theme is treated as a "catch-all" that can be applied to almost any genre of game to increase its sales.

---

[7] The only reason I can fathom why pirate and spooky levels are often found in the same game is the designer's love for Disneyland. "Pirates of the Caribbean" and "Haunted Mansion" attractions are found in the park's "world" of New Orleans Square. I know that's the reason I put them together in *Pac-Man World*.

8. **Gritty urban**—No matter whether it's populated by criminals, punks, mutants, or supervillains, the gritty urban theme allows for fantastic action in a realistic and relatable setting. That relatability is part of the genre's appeal. Artistically, it's easier for artists to create the world outside their window. Densely detailed environments just keep looking better and better as system processors and game polygon counts rise. Although it's ironic that players would want to play in a world that mirrors the one right outside, they get a choice that most people never do: to improve it or destroy it.

9. **Space station**—The space station has become the stand-in for the dungeon in sci-fi games (especially in the FPS and survival horror genres), all strongly influenced by the 1986 film *Aliens*. In video games, most space station halls are infested with horrible aliens and malfunctioning robots. The space station theme lends itself to a variety of tech-based mechanics including laser-based force fields and factory-style moving platforms. Space stations allow the art team to show off when creating spectacular visual effects, whether it is holographic computer displays or stunning starscapes.

10. **Sewer**—While you could eat off the floor of *Mario Bros.*'s sewer, video game sewers got more disgusting as game graphics improved. This modern analog for the fantasy dungeon[8] grew more complex and deadly with hazards ranging from giant rats and albino alligators to fetid water that caused instant death upon immersion. You can also find the harmonious addition of factory-level mechanics in sewers, such as whirling ventilation fans and sinking platforms to challenge players. Just be glad that smell-o-vision never caught on.[9]

Just because the preceding themes are considered clichés doesn't mean that they are unusable. To give them a twist, just apply the **Mexican pizza** technique.

Back in the 1990s, Taco Bell introduced the "Mexican pizza": a pizza-shaped snack made with Mexican food fixings. To me, it sounded vaguely disgusting. However, curiosity got the better of me and I tried it. It wasn't bad. But what I learned was that you can combine two things you wouldn't think go together to get something surprisingly good and, more importantly, completely original.

While designing *Maximo: Ghosts to Glory*, we applied the Mexican pizza technique. Instead of just a regular graveyard, our graveyard was cracked apart by volcanic eruptions that blasted out flashes of fire. A fire graveyard, if you will. We also made a pirate level that was enshrouded in ice—you get the idea. We took hoary level themes and breathed new life into them simply by combining them with each other.

The Name Game

Now that you have your level's theme, give it a name. However, keep in mind that a level always has two names: one for the development team and one for the players. The level name

---

[8] Didja know that early D&D players would play live-action sessions in sewer and drainage systems? The forerunner to today's live-action role playing (or LARPing).

[9] There have been several attempts to bring smell hardware into gaming. The most recent device, ScentScape, blasted player's noses with the smells of a pine forest, a briny ocean, and shotgun fire.

is a file name, created to be referenced with the game's code. Here are a few things to remember when creating file names:

- Keep the name to eight characters max because (a) a short file name is easy for team members to remember and (b) it takes up less space in the code. Traditionally this was necessary because of technical limitations in DOS filenames. That restriction is no longer relevant. Note also that short file names are not always easier to remember as names might need to be truncated in weird ways; for example, frstclea.lvl might be the Forest Clearing level or something having to do with cleaning the Frost world.

- Players don't see the file names, so you don't have to be witty. For example, "Castle01" succinctly lets your team members know the most important info: location and order.

- For more complex titles, use abbreviated text: for example, "fac01s01" might stand for "factory 1, section 01."

- Make sure your naming conventions don't overlap. If "sec" stands for "section" in one area, don't use it for "secret" in another.

- Organize your levels. Keep files in folders where it is easy for other team members to find them. Use file-sharing software to make sure changes aren't made without the other team members knowing about them.

In the context of the game, the level's name is a different matter. Just as with naming characters, you need to give your level the right name—one that fits its feel. There are a few schools of thought to naming levels:

- **Functional**—A straight-up number system is a hallmark of retro gaming. It cuts to the chase and gives players an idea of progress. However, because most players aren't exposed to the highest number in advance, they have no way to accurately track overall progress. Another disadvantage to functional naming is that it lacks personality.

- **Location**—Police station. Sewer. Science lab. What's good about using the location names is that you immediately get an idea of what players will be seeing and/or encountering. However, these expectations are based on the players' knowledge—something that may not match what you are going for. Using the right words is important when naming a location.

- **Descriptive**—"A nasty surprise." "On the road again." "Death from above." Descriptive level names read more like chapters of a book. This type of naming is great for providing foreshadowing or tone. Be careful not to tip your hand too much and ruin any surprises your plot or level may hold. Or you can be tricky like the *Dead Space* designers and have the first word in every level spell out a secret message!

- **Punny**—If you are feeling particularly creative, try writing a punny title for your game level. Punny titles were all the rage in the late 1990s, starting with *Crash Bandicoot*. Usually, you want to reserve this type of naming for games with a sense of humor.

Remember, level names provide your level's first impression, so put your best foot forward!

Everything I Learned About Level Design, I Learned from Disneyland

The world is the best narrator.
    —Ken Levine[10]

I believe that it is within a game's level where the story should actually be told. Using space to tell a story isn't a new concept; this approach has been used in architectural design for centuries. When I first started designing game levels, I found that theme parks held the answers to many of my questions on how to tell a story as well as inform players. I pored over theme park maps[11] and studied how they were laid out. I found that theme parks are designed to move guests from one adventure to the next in the most effective way possible, much like a well-designed game level.

Disneyland, in particular, proved to be a source of great inspiration. I read about Walt Disney's imagineers and how they went about designing their own world. Walt Disney had a deep love of miniature railroads, and Disneyland was structured around a train track. The imagineers needed something to fill in the middle of the track, so five "lands" were created, each inspired by Disney's passions: history, progress, nature, his animated movies, and nostalgia for his childhood hometown. These became Frontierland, Tomorrowland, Adventureland, Fantasyland, and Main Street.

The imagineers filled these lands with attractions, themed adventures that allowed guests to "ride the Disney movies." These attractions were built as storytelling experiences within a physical space, and detailed attention was given to each scene as guests passed through it.

I noticed that the creation and structure of Disneyland bore a strong resemblance to creating and structuring a video game world. The basic progression of creation is this:

- **Disneyland:** *World* to *land* to *attraction* to *scene*.
- **Video game:** *World* to *level* to *experience* to *moment-to-moment gameplay*.

---

[10] Ken Levine is the creative director of *BioShock* series, a highly rated FPS whose fully realized worlds have become the gold standard for level design.

[11] I used to love to collect theme park brochures during family road trips to other, more educational destinations—souvenirs of places I never actually visited. Who knew they'd come in so useful in the future!

The world of Disneyland contains many lands. Within each themed land are attractions, each with its own story. The "story" of the attraction is composed of scenes.

The world of the video game contains many levels, each with its own part of the story. Within each themed level are encounters, challenges, and story points that move players through the level. Connecting these experiences is the moment-to-moment gameplay that keeps players engaged.

Mapping the World

This notion of working from the "top down" helped me approach a game world and determine what the confines are and what lives within it; to determine that, you need to make a **game world map.**

Some designers really got into creating their world map and loved to share it with players. Common pack-ins with early computer games were lovingly rendered maps printed on parchment, cloth, and even faux leather. But you don't need to create anything so fancy. Your world map can be something as simple as a flow chart created in Visio. It only needs to chart out where the players are going and what they'll find there. A map can also define the spatial relationships of locations in the world: this can help the designer determine how players are going to get around and in what order.

The game world map is important not only to help your team understand the connection of all the levels to one another but also to offer players several advantages.

One of the earliest arcade games to expose players to a map of sorts was *Donkey Kong*. It was a simple graphic of several Donkey Kongs stacked on top of one another with the challenge "how high can you get?" There was room for four Donkey Kongs on the screen. With each progressive level, the game added a Donkey Kong. The player could figure out by the space on the screen how many Donkey Kongs could fit on the stack and therefore realize there were four distinct environments in the game.

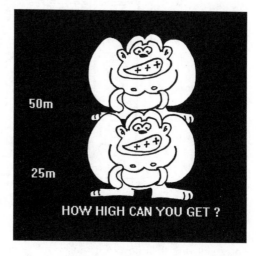

The next great advance in mapping came with the arcade game *Ghosts 'n' Goblins*. Before gameplay started, a map was displayed with a little icon of the player at his current location: "You are here." The camera then panned over the entire world, teasing the player with everything that was to come. I remember seeing this and thinking, "I wonder what's in that ice level at the far end of the map?"

Even if your characters don't physically travel anywhere in your game, you can still use a map to show progression. The fighting game *Mortal Kombat* displays a screen full of characters' headshots, with most of them "locked up" at the beginning of the game. But by showing all the locked windows, the game's map of opponents provides foreshadowing that players will eventually fight many characters. As more opponents are unlocked, players are then compelled to "collect them all."

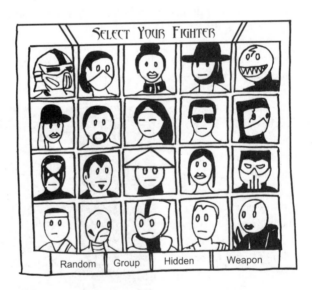

Foreshadowing

Foreshadowing is a powerful tool to get players excited about the activities and dangers found in a level. Building anticipation is just as important as delivering on it. In all my years of making haunted houses, I've found that a scare is bigger and better if the victims know it's coming. It's waiting for the scare to happen that drives them nuts.

You can use lighting, sound effects, and geometry to make a level look foreboding. And remember, nothing says "beware" like a pile of skulls.

Another lesson I learned from Disneyland is to provide foreshadowing with **posters.** Guests pass by posters advertising attractions as they enter the park. While the guests don't understand the significance of the images they're seeing, the posters provide foreshadowing to future adventures. In games, one of the best uses of posters is in *BioShock* when the player, first entering Rapture, sees posters advertising the superpower-giving plasmids. Only when the player learns about plasmids and what they can do is their significance understood.

Goal Setting

Much like a game map, the level itself should help transport players through the level from story point to story point. The always eloquent imagineers of Disneyland describe it this way:

> When we began designing Disneyland, we looked at it just as we do a motion picture. We had to tell a story, or in this case, a series of stories. In filmmaking, we develop a logical flow of events or scenes that will take our audience from point to point through a story. If I were to 'leapfrog' from Scene One to Scene Three, leaving out Scene Two, it would be like sending the entire audience out to the lobby for popcorn in the middle of the film.[12]

Disneyland's attractions tell four different stories to their guests. I have found these stories have parallels with the players' goals within a video game level:

- Escape/survive
- Explore
- Educate
- Provide a moral

With the **escape/survive** goal, players have to survive being in a place they have no business being in—whether it's a ghost-infested manor or a crazy factory where one misstep means being ground up into cat food. Storytelling is shown through **action** and **location,** which move the player along quickly, using gameplay centered on movement and combat.

---

[12] *Disneyland The First Quarter Century*, Walt Disney Productions, 1979.

The **explore** goal allows players to discover the story at their own pace. The village of Skyloft in *The Legend of Zelda: The Skyward Sword* and city of Los Santos in *Grand Theft Auto 5* let players explore the environment and create the story in their own order. **Freedom of mobility** and **conversation** are important storytelling tools when exploring is the players' goal.

Although there are many educational games, the **educate** goal has yet to make the full transition into entertainment games. Educational games carry a stigma that they are only for younger or "non-gamer" audiences. There are exceptions. The *Assassin's Creed* series exposes players to historical characters and events. *Rock Band* focuses on teaching players the same skills needed to actually play music (at least in the case of vocals and drums). Emphasize **observation** and **imitation** when determining the players' goals and gameplay.

Examples of the goal of learning a **moral** can be found in many of Disneyland's attractions. Mr. Toad's Wild Ride's moral message is: "Drive recklessly and you'll crash and burn." Quite a statement for the happiest place on Earth! But we're talking about video games. Morals and consequences have been in games since the early adventure games. Adventure games like *Star Wars: The Knights of the Old Republic* and the *Mass Effect* series allow players to experience "good" or "bad" endings based on choices made during the game. But recently, players are being morally tested beyond "good and evil" with themes such as morality during wartime (*Spec Ops: The Line*), loyalty to individuals versus groups (*The Walking Dead: Season One*), and even whether or not to perform torture (*Call of Duty: Black Ops*). These games use choice and consequence to deliver the level's moral goal and then make those choices impact gameplay.

In addition to these goals, you need to ask, "What is the players' objective in this level?" Some levels exist to teach a specific gameplay move such as jumping, engaging in combat, driving, or simply how to play the game. Answering this question will guide and focus how you design the players' moment-to-moment gameplay within the level and even how you construct and pace the level. Make sure players stay focused on the specific level-oriented goal because it's easy to get distracted, especially when you have lots of choices. Use NPCs, story, quest goals, and even powers and gear to guide the players toward the goal you want them to reach.

Now that we've got our world figured out, the game's theme selected, and goals for the player planned out, we have one more important choice to make.

Following Procedure

The most common way to build a level during production is by using a **scripting tool** or **scripting editor**. A scripting tool is the program you use to create and place scripts. A script tells the game engine what to do and when to do it. Scripts control mechanics, enemies, cameras, and other in-level elements. Scripting is done by the designer during the game's production—so why are we talking about it here? Because there are two ways to build a game level, and the method the dev team uses will impact how you design your game during pre-production.

An alternative method is to create your levels *procedurally*. A **procedural game** has levels that are generated using an algorithm rather than using levels that are created in an editor. The advantage of procedural games is that they create unique environments so that every game level is different.

Procedurally generated content can vary depending on the game. *Candy Crush Saga* (King, 2012) and *Dungeon Raid* (Alex Kuptsov, 2011) procedurally generate how gems populate the game board. *Scribblenauts Unmasked* (5th Cell, 2013) procedurally generates puzzles with each new game. *Cargo Commander* (Serious Brew, 2012), *Spelunky* (Derek Yu and Andy Hull, 2009), and *Borderlands 2* (Gearbox, 2012) have procedurally generated levels and encounters. You can even procedurally generate entire worlds as seen in *Slaves to Armok: Gold of Blood Chapter II: Dwarf Fortress* (Tarn Adams, 2006), *Minecraft* (Mojang, 2009), and *No Man's Sky* (Hello Games). Using procedurally generated content is a powerful tool for both the development team and the player, but it's not without its problems. Here are a few tricks to help you make the most out of your procedural levels:

- **Know your metrics.** Even though procedural content is generated randomly, it still needs to follow the rules of your game. Knowing the distances your player can move and act will determine the parameters of your design. That way, the game isn't generating an invalid situation—one where the player can never hope to win.

- **Provide structure.** Even though the appeal of procedural levels for designers is randomness, players still need something to latch on to. Procedural levels have a tendency feel too random, too empty, or too unstructured. Create a standard for your level and use it as a top-down approach to how a level should be generated. As you generate new levels, pay attention to which elements repeat and how often, and adjust your values to provide maximum content without making the level too difficult.

- **Symmetry helps.** Symmetry helps players navigate the game as they look for patterns in the environment, the mechanics, and encounters. Build in instances of symmetry to act as guides for your player and too keep environments from getting too disorientating.

- **Use just a little randomness.** Just because your game uses procedural design doesn't mean everything in the game has to be generated procedurally. *Left 4 Dead* (Turtle Rock, 2008) uses an artificial intelligence called "The Director" to create procedural encounters and music cues as the players fight their way through pre-designed levels.

- **Mix in predesigned elements.** Just because a game is procedural doesn't mean the entire game has to be. Mix in some pre-designed gameplay to offset the randomness. The challenge is to make procedural gameplay feel designed and designed gameplay feel procedural. Why not have the best of both worlds?

The irony about procedurally generated gameplay is that when it's good, players won't notice it. You'll have to weigh the benefits and costs to your development team to see if procedural design is worth using.

You've Got the Beat

Now look at all the useful tools you have to help you: character, character actions, story, level themes, a world map. These tools are all you need to build an entire universe! To help organize my thoughts, I like to create a **beat chart** (remember these from Level 4?). A beat chart is a tool Hollywood writers and directors often use to help them organize and plan their movie's production. Creating a beat chart helps the designer determine gaps and clumping in your game. You can reorganize the game elements to spread things out and make the game feel more organic. Pretend you are making a game called *Relic Raider*. Your hero, Jake Hunter, travels the globe looking for lost treasure. You've developed the story and have brainstormed the gameplay and the game's environments and enemies.

Take a look at this sample beat chart and see if you spot any problems:

Relic Raider beat chart

Game Element	Level Name/File Name				
	Shanghai/ Roof01	Jungle 01/ Jung01	Jungle 02/ Jung02	Temple of the Hidden Skulls/ Jung03	Mountain Escape!/ Road01
Location	Shanghai rooftops	Jungle	Jungle	Ancient temple (int)	Mountain pass
Gameplay	Stealth, shooting, jumping	Shooting	Fighting	Platform, jumping	Driving
Objective	Find crime boss Wu-Fan	Jungle part 1	Jungle part 2	Reach chamber of skulls	Car chase
Story beat	Jake steals medallion, is caught by Wu-Fan	Jake explores jungle	Jake finds temple of skulls	Jake places medallion in statue; Nazi general Hauser shows up	Jake steals truck, flees Nazis
New weapon	.45, machine gun	Machete	No	No	No
Enemies	Tong thug, axe man, machine gunner	Jaguar, native (spear)	Jaguar	Jaguar, Nazi soldier	Nazi truck, Jeep w/ machine gun

continued

continued

| Game Element | Level Name/File Name | | | | |
	Shanghai/ Roof01	Jungle 01/ Jung01	Jungle 02/ Jung02	Temple of the Hidden Skulls/ Jung03	Mountain Escape!/ Road01
Mechanics	Swinging rope, zip line	Swinging rope, zip line	Zip line	Spiked pits, blow darts, crushing walls, fall-away floor	Falling rocks
NPC	Wu-Fan	Guide	None	Hauser	None
Bonus materials	Art gallery 1	Art gallery 2	Art gallery 3	Alt. costume	Art gallery 4
Time of day	Night	Night	Night	Day	Day
Color mapping	Blue/red	Green/brown	Green/brown	Green/gray	Tan/sky blue

Did you spot all the issues the beat chart exposed?

- Level naming is inconsistent. Rather than have generic titles like "jungle 01," find a way to give them more descriptive names like "temple of the hidden skulls."

- Roof01 and Road01 could be mistaken for each other. Name the Shanghai level "Shang01"; the more distinctive, the better.

- Since "Jung03" doesn't seem to share too many assets, I recommend calling it "temp01" to show that it's a different place than the other jungle levels.

- Do you need two jungle levels back to back? Perhaps the activities in "Jung01" and "Jung02" would be better combined to make one improved jungle level?

- The driving seems to be introduced a little late in the game. There seems to be four "on-foot" levels before that point. Find a way to bring the driving in sooner or lose a walking level.

- Although the other levels are very specific, the jungle objectives seem unfocused. Give the players more of a purpose.

- Introduction of weapons seems to ramp up quickly and peter out fast. That's a warning sign that you need more interesting things for players to do and toys for the players to use.

- The enemies are clumped up at the beginning of the game. Enemy AI could be repurposed for more effective use. Jungle 02, while listed as a fighting level, doesn't seem to have any enemies that would work well with fighting.

- Those jungle levels are re-using enemies too much. How about adding another enemy like a deadly python, some piranhas, or a pack of vicious apes?

- Repurpose mechanics like you would enemies. The temple has a lot of unique mechanics that will take time and effort to create. Can any of them be re-used in other ways?

- Art galleries are a pretty basic reward. What other bonuses can you give players rather than just the same thing over and over again?

- There are three night levels in a row. Break up some of this with morning, evening, atmospheric effects like rain or snow, and so on. And because the interior of a temple is going to be dark, it doesn't make a difference whether it's day.

- That color map has a lot of green. Make sure that the visuals offer a more diverse palette; otherwise, all the levels are going to feel the same.

Just by spending a few hours creating and observing the patterns created by a beat chart, you are able to make significant improvements to production, gameplay, and art before you build a single asset!

Re-using Re-use

While looking at the preceding beat chart, I noticed several different gameplay systems: platforming, shooting, driving, and stealth. These different systems add diversity to a game, but when it comes to creating them, they have nothing to do with each other. One of the most important design decisions you can make is how and when to re-use gameplay systems over the course of the game.

If you use a game system fewer than three times over the course of a game, it's not worth having. This doesn't mean that you need to have the same gameplay section over and over again. Instead, you can be smart with your art assets and repurpose them.

For example, a vehicle system can support a jeep, a hatchback, and a sedan. Creating the vehicle system costs more time and money than building the three different cars does. But remember, you can stretch your recycling only so far: the same system you use for your cars can't support a hovercraft or motorcycle. Although they are both ground vehicles, they behave quite differently.

There is always a trade-off between design and programming. Learn the limitations of the game system and craft your game accordingly. Create a small number of gameplay systems that you can re-use over and over again throughout your game. This way, you maximize your game as well as your schedule and budget. Use the limitations to your advantage. If you need examples, take a look at any game created by Japanese developer Treasure Co. Ltd. (*Gunstar Heroes*, *Dynamite Heady*, *Ikaruga*), which really knows how to milk a small palette of mechanics. When you are creating your beat chart, make sure you don't use the same gameplay systems back to back. Unless your game is specifically a driving game, don't follow a driving level with more driving.

> **TIP** You also can work with your artists on how to best re-use art assets. Simply recoloring and retexturing game items will make them look different from level to level.

The Gary Gygax[13] Memorial Mapping Section

There are many ways to start building level maps. The designers of the original *Metal Gear* built their levels out of LEGO blocks. Many developers do rapid-level prototyping in 3-D tools like Maya or 3D Studio Max. One designer I know liked to model his levels in clay. Myself, I like a ream of blank paper, a very sharp #2 pencil, and an eraser. I like making maps on paper because it reminds me of the good old days of creating *Dungeons and Dragon* levels.

I have found that there are two types of three-dimensional video game level design: **alleys** and **islands.**

Alleys create a directed gameplay experience: players have a goal to reach, and the level is built to help them reach it. Your alley can be narrow to create a sense of claustrophobia and tension, or it can be wider to give the feeling of sprawl and space.

---

[13] Ernest Gary Gygax (1938–2008) was the co-creator of the first role-playing fantasy game, *Dungeons and Dragons*. Creating dungeons and adventures for D&D served as the springboard for many a young game designer's career, myself included.

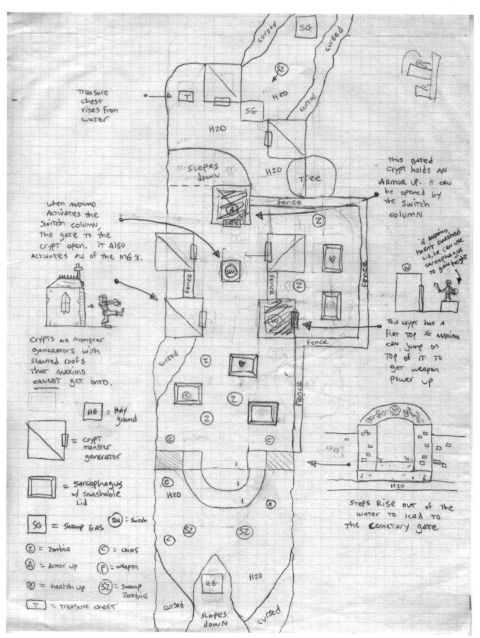

An example of "alley" level design

Alleys offer the following advantages to designers:

- Placing camera trigger zones is easier when you know where and how players will be entering and moving through the level.

- You can get dramatic with your camera movements to inform players or enhance the action and drama.

- You can remove the camera controls from the game, allowing players to concentrate on gameplay.

- You can create scripted, triggered gameplay events because you know where players are looking.

- It is easier to choreograph combat and traps since there is only one way for the player to go.

- Bottlenecks can be used to prevent backtracking.

- You can use illusional narrative (more on this in a moment) to tell the level's story.

The island level, in my opinion, is a bit more challenging to design and build. The game camera has to be flexible enough to accommodate a wide variety of widths and elevations. Scripted events are tough to execute because there's no guarantee that players will be looking in the right direction. Players can completely circumnavigate combat encounters. Even stagecraft-style tricks like façades are useless because players can view and interact with level geometry from all directions.

Despite these limitations, island level design offers expansive space that allows players the freedom to choose the order in which they want to experience the gameplay. *Mario 64* is one of the earliest examples of island level design in which players could choose to climb mountains, explore hills, or swim into underwater grottos in any order they liked. Islands allow players unparalleled freedom. In fact, an entire genre—the **sandbox**—has emerged as island level designs have grown bigger and bigger. *Just Cause 2*, *LEGO Batman 2*, and *LA Noire* are just huge island playgrounds.

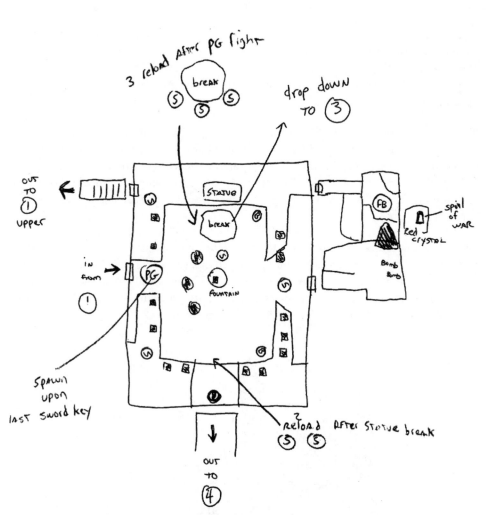

An example of "Island" level design

Sandbox Play

When creating these sandbox worlds, you should divide them up into distinct areas to aid the players' navigation and orientation, much like the "lands" of Disneyland. Disneyland goes through great pains to make each land visually distinct. Take Frontierland: it has everything you would expect in the Old West—watering troughs, wooden cigar-store Indians, wagons, cactus, and even those old video game standbys, crates and barrels. (Frontierland's main thoroughfare was originally dirt road until guests complained about dusty pants and shoes.) Disneyland even themes the trash cans! For example, Frontierland's trash cans are painted to look like wood, while Tomorrowland's are futuristic silver. You always know where you are even when throwing out the trash.

The game *Crackdown* uses this technique throughout its sandbox world of Pacific City. Not only is each zone themed to aid navigation, but the themes match the criminal gang that players have to overthrow. The Shai-Gen Corporation runs Chinatown while the tech-using Volk inhabit gleaming skyscrapers. To draw your viewers' attention, you should use as many cues as possible, such as color, sound, lighting, even weather, but first and foremost, I like to use weenies.

Disneyland's imagineers pioneered the use of architectural landmarks like Sleeping Beauty's castle, the Matterhorn, and Space Mountain, which they call **weenies.**[14] Weenies are used to get the interest of guests and draw them in their direction. Weenies don't have to be giant castles or mountains. They can be interesting architectural elements like statues, bridges, and buildings, or even natural elements like a distinct tree or rock.

---

[14] Walt Disney himself coined the term after the frankfurter that off-screen animal trainers would wave at their dog actors to get them to walk past the camera to where they wanted them to go.

Theoretically, you want to string your weenies along your path to keep players moving from one to the next. When creating 3-D maps, make sure the path is clearly marked with weenies. I once created a map that looked like this:

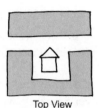

Top View

When I play tested this part of the level, players would travel down the road, see the path leading behind the house, and walk around the back of the house looking for treasure. When they emerged onto the road, they turned around and walked back down the way they came!

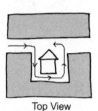

Top View

I realized that the area needed a landmark (marked on the map) so that when players came out, they were able to re-orient themselves.

This brings up an important truth about designing games: players will ALWAYS find a way to break your game, whether or not they are doing it intentionally. Tackle this issue head-on by making players play the game the way YOU want it to be played, but provide plenty of help to show them the way.

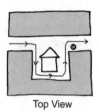

Top View

Islands work particularly well for multiplayer games because you can accommodate many different styles of playing. Do you like to sneak around the back of the map? Islands provide a back to sneak around. You can still charge up the front if you want, or you can camp over on that hill and snipe to your heart's content.[15]

That doesn't mean alleys and islands can't live together in perfect harmony. Islands can still have alley-like sections. *Red Faction Guerrilla* and *Team Fortress 2* use interior spaces that feel like alley level designs, but their freedom of approach and wide perimeter edges mark them as islands. The *Uncharted* series alternates between using alleys and islands frequently. *Darksiders* and the *Maximo* games use alleys for their dungeon levels and islands for their hubs and battle arenas. Whether to use island or alley all depends on the gameplay.

Islands have the following advantages:

- They give an extraordinary feeling of space and scale. It's quite an experience the first time you realize a level goes on and on.

- Islands promote exploration and encourage designers to fill in "in-between spaces" with secrets, additional missions, and objectives.

---

[15] Not that anyone reading this book would stoop so low as to be a camper. And remember, there is a special place in hell for spawn campers.

- Gameplay options are laid out in front of players like a smorgasbord.
- Vehicle gameplay (like racing and car combat) feels better in wide-open spaces than in tight alleys.

Sandboxes are tricky things because I have found that no matter what players tell you, a world where players can choose to do anything at any time can be intimidating and confusing. Despite the freedom that the sandbox world promises players, they should still get some prompting on what to do next even if they don't want to do it. There's a reason your annoying cousin is always calling to tell you your next mission in *Grand Theft Auto 4*.

Illusional Narrative

Another challenge for designers that a sandbox (or even a plain old level) provides is how to use the world to tell a story. **Illusional narrative** is a storytelling trick I first observed when riding the Peter Pan's Flight attraction at Disneyland. Having flown over London and to Never-Land, we have reached the part where Peter Pan and Captain Hook are engaged in a pitched sword duel on the deck of the pirate ship. The Darling children have been captured by the pirate crew and watch the battle.

The guest's ship flies around a corner (cleverly disguised as the sail of the pirate ship). Now Peter Pan is victorious, the Darlings are freed, and Captain Hook is keeping himself from being eaten by the crocodile.

Illusional narrative is the video game equivalent of what happens in the gutter of comic book panels or between edits in a movie: players fill in story when given two or more images or environments. With the proper transition and presentation, you could convince players that a train has crashed, a world has become overrun by aliens, or a character has crossed a room without animating a single element. The savings to production is significant. Real-time animations take time to produce and have to be ripped up and redone if the designer decides to change something in the level.

Here's a good example. In *Medal of Honor Allied Assault* (EA, 2002), your commanding officer meets you at the outskirts of a village with orders to attack a Nazi command post. He says that he'll meet you at the far end of the village. Now, the game could have had you follow the commander all the way through the command post, fighting side by side—the series had done this before—but instead, after you cut your way through the base, you reach the exit of the compound to find your commander, who congratulates you for a good job. If you viewed the level map from above, you'd see two commander models, and the illusion would be broken. But because you never see the two versions of the character together, in your (the player's) mind, it's the same character just at a different time.

Make sure that you use gating mechanisms in your level design such as bottlenecks, camera views, checkpoints, elements that turn on and off, or even plain ol' doors to keep players from breaking the illusion.

The Dave Arneson[16] Memorial Mapping Section

It's time to get cracking and get your game design down on paper with a map.

When creating a map, you first must determine a scale. When drawing a **top-down view map** on graph paper, the size of the player usually equals one square. All other elements, such as treasure, mechanics, enemies, or objects, are drawn in relation to the size of the player—much like how you determine player metrics. Represent these elements as icons on your map. Create a legend for the icons on your map so readers can determine what they are looking at. You should include

- Player's starting point

- Enemy starting locations

- Doors, teleporters, gates

- Puzzle mechanics (like levers and switches)

- Treasure chests and power-ups

- Traps and their areas of effect

- Significant landmarks (like statues, pools, pits, and so on)

I start my level map creation process by roughing out the major locations where I want big events to happen: a treasure chamber, a battle arena, a puzzle room, a mechanic that I want the player to learn, a spectacular view, and so on. Then I start to think about what I can use to connect those rooms together: hallways, mazes, chasms, or passages. Then I usually move on to graph paper, which helps me communicate the scale of the level to the level artist. Often I draw in elements such as the tombstones, crypts, mechanics, and enemies.

---

[16] David "Dave" Arneson (1947–2009) was the co-creator of *Dungeons and Dragons*. Arneson's pre-D&D campaign *Blackmoor* introduced the concept of hit points, armor class and the term "dungeon crawl" to gaming. We owe him much.

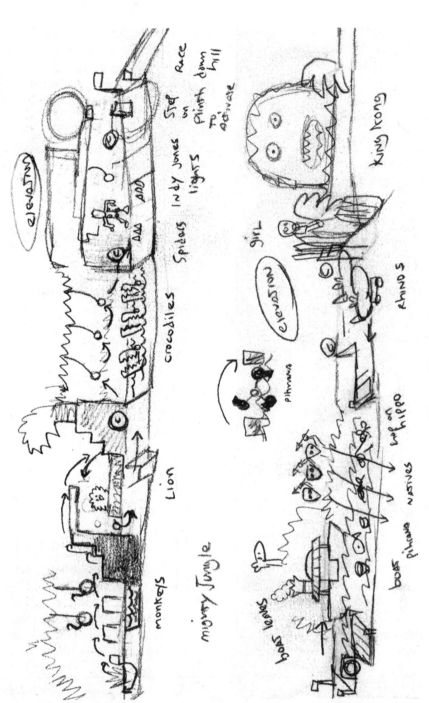

a (very rough) level outline

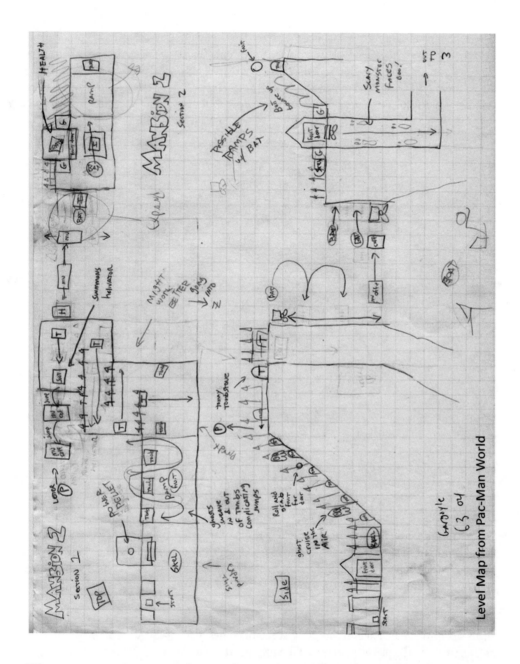

Level Map from Pac-Man World

When you are creating passages for a top-down view map for a 3-D level, I recommend making it five squares wide: that's the width of the player plus two more widths on either side. It provides enough room for the player to navigate, for combat to occur, and the camera to have some room to maneuver. However, I can guarantee that your first few efforts at level design will usually end up too small and too cramped, so don't be afraid to be generous with your proportions.

Use geometry and lighting to help move the player down the path. Players are drawn toward light, but they tend to avoid or overlook dark places. You can use shapes like diagonal lines to draw the player's eye in a specific direction. I learned my favorite trick from the designers at Naughty Dog, the creators of the *Crash Bandicoot* and *Uncharted* games. They use a trick they call the **squint test.** Take a look at the following image and squint your eyes until they are almost closed:

What's the brightest thing on the screen? The main path. You can do the same thing in your game using color and lighting. Even if players don't consciously notice this, they will still be able to see which way to go. If players have someplace to go, don't waste their time with needless wandering. Never intentionally try to get players lost. Instead, find ways for them to get quickly to the main objective. A good trick is to talk your way through a level design. For example, "The player is Astronaut Baker, who is finishing up testing the ODIN weapon platform. He and astronaut Mosely spacewalk back to the station, as a shuttle docks. As the astronauts enter, the new arrivals start killing the station's crew, forcing Baker and Mosely to flee. Baker is ambushed by an enemy and takes his gun in the fight. Baker and Mosley continue to battle their way through the station as they receive messages that ODIN is locking onto targets all around the U.S. The astronauts watch helplessly as ODIN fires on Los Angeles, San Diego, Phoenix, Houston, Miami. . . . Mission control detonates the station, and the two astronauts are sucked into space. Dodging debris, the two fight their way to ODIN. Opening ODIN's control panel, Baker blasts away at the fuel lines, making the weapon platform alter its trajectory. As the player's faceplate fills with fire, the last view is of ODIN burning up as it re-enters the Earth's atmosphere." Whew. That's the way to do a level!

This example not only tells an exciting story but also gives the audience an idea of the actions the players will be performing (spacewalking, fighting, opening the control panel, and shooting fuel lines) as well as how they will receive information (watching ODIN fire, hearing mission control give instructions, listening to astronaut Mosley). Just like the beat chart, this exercise will help you find lulls in the level design. If you ever find yourself saying, "Then the player walks over to here," cut that section out of your game. Because a **very important thing** is

WALKING IS NEVER, EVER GAMEPLAY!

Only **lazy designers** consider walking to be gameplay. You're not a lazy designer, are you? Of course, you aren't. You are an **active designer.** An active designer who creates active things for your active character to do. Actively. This is why you should think about your game in terms of what I call the **primary action.** The best game concepts can be described with *one action verb* (although sometimes it takes more). You remember what a verb is, right? It's a word that shows action or a state of being. All levels should support the primary action. *Pixel Junk Shooter* is all about shooting. *Katamari Damacy* is all about rolling. *Sneak Beat Bandit* is about sneaking. *Flight Control Rocket* is about directing rockets. *Muscle March* is about shape matching. Some games use more than one. The *Grand Theft Auto* games focus on shooting and driving. The *Batman Arkham* series splits the players' focus between sneaking and fighting.

Here are just a few more primary actions you can have your players perform:

- Jumping
- Collecting
- Climbing
- Swinging
- Breaking
- Adding
- Creating
- Flinging
- Drawing
- Exploring

Speaking of exploring, let's talk about multiple paths. Which one to take? The one that leads to the harem of 1,000 delights or the one that leads to the lava pits of Overfiend? Decisions, decisions.

I equate creating multiple paths in a level to a good action scene in a movie: you don't always see (or do) everything the first time around. The fact is, players want **variety.** It's what keeps most players playing games. They want to find out what's around the next corner, who the next enemy is, what the next power-up or weapon will be. The minute a game gets predictable, players get bored. Keep in mind, this is a different type of predictability than I mentioned earlier. I guess a better word would be "sameness." If things start to feel the same level after level, encounter after encounter, the player is going to get bored.

They also want **surprise,** but surprise is just variety that players don't expect. Of course, you can have both good and bad surprises, but if you don't play fair with your players, they will get frustrated and stop playing.

Getting back to giving players variety, you will need multiple paths, multiple things to interact with, multiple enemies, randomized AI behavior, randomized treasure drops, multiple storylines and endings. No matter which multiple choice you provide, creating this alternative content can be a tricky thing to deal with—especially with level design. Creating multiple paths raises multiple questions that need to be addressed: Which path will players choose? What can you do to entice players to go down one path over another? What can the designer do to promote players to use that alternative path? Hidden power-ups or cash prizes? Provide an achievement for all secrets discovered? Will the game change depending on which path you choose? You can design an entire game around the concept of choice—*the Stanley Parable* (Davey Wreden, 2013) did.

I've worked with producers who have balked at the idea of designing and building a level that players may never see. They feel the effort from the team doesn't justify the experience the players have. In some cases, those producers were right. In others, that variety has made a level design shine. Levels with multiple paths work better in some genres than others. For example, the wide-open worlds found in FPSs, RPGs, and driving games require multiple paths just to prevent regular traversal from getting boring and to create the feeling of a real world.

Whatever answer you decide on, make sure that your effort provides something significant to your level.

Some designers don't like **backtracking**, that is, when players have to go back to a part of the level they've already been to. I don't mind it. I think it's a good way to get the most out of a level. I like to use backtracking for puzzles. I always say "show players the door first and then let them find the key." Just don't make players go back and forth too many times. If you need to make players go to a location more than twice, do something to make that experience different: add gameplay like (new) combat or collectibles, change the topography by having an earthquake change a flat spot into jumpable hills. A nice natural (or unnatural) disaster can work wonders.

Another lesson I've learned from Disneyland is that there are three ways for players to get around a world. The first is the main path—using weenies and the tricks described earlier in this chapter—that helps guide players around the level. The second is to use secret paths and shortcuts; these are sneaky and tricky ways players learn as they explore and get more familiar with the level. Using these shortcuts makes players feel smarter. They can also be used for gameplay, such as time trials where getting from point A to point B as quickly as possible is the goal. The third way is to use circuit transportation. Like the train that circles Disneyland, players need a fast way to get around the level but one that provides a handful of stops. It has to be faster than traveling by foot. It doesn't have to be a train. It can be a car or a horse, or a mythical mount like a griffin or dragon. Let them catch a lift in a zeppelin or on a spaceship, or, if your fiction supports it, there's always the ever-popular teleporter.

Just be aware that traveling in vehicles can really chew up the real estate. You'll need to build that space into your levels. But it's a double-edged sword. Don't make the experience last too long, especially if it's something you will be doing often. Just remember this **very important thing** when it comes to traveling through levels:

IF IT EVER FEELS TOO LONG OR TOO BORING, THEN IT IS

Avoid boring levels! But how? Variety is one way. **Fingers** are another way of making a world feel deeper and fuller without having to build lots of complex geometry and multiple paths that players may never take. Picture a linear path:

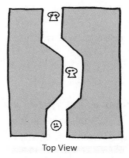

Top View

Not too exciting, huh? You can place all type of hazards and enemies along the way to make things challenging for players, but it's just going to feel like a straight path even if you crinkle it up and bend it around.

However, if you start to add fingers off your path, little dead ends for players to explore and go down, it makes the players feel as if they are exploring the level and not just promenading down it. These fingers expand the life of your level and you can promote the players exploring them. Take a look at the level now that a few fingers have been added off the main path:

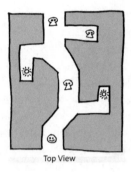

Top View

Now you have interesting places for players to explore as they work their way through a level. Although I wouldn't suggest putting something that is important to the critical path down a finger, you can place whatever you want along a finger: combat, treasure, bonus materials, or just something visual or fun. Remember this simple yet **very important thing:**

EVERY FINGER SHOULD HAVE A REWARD AT THE END, EVEN IF IT'S JUST A TRASH CAN[17]

The point of this? Variety. Avoiding boredom. Boredom in a game is worse than death. I can't count the number of times I've been bored with a video game. Video games should never be boring. They should be awesome! But coming up with ways to keep players entertained can be hard. Fortunately, I have done the hard work for you. Here are just a few ways to prevent players from getting bored:

- **Change modes.** Spice things up with a shooting level, a puzzle, a minigame.

- **Add beauty shots.** These moments of wonder help tell the story and make for a cool screenshot.

- **Make the familiar unfamiliar.** As in the *Poseidon Adventure*, turn the commonplace on its head to get double-duty from something you've already created. Turn the location of a boss fight into an arena battle against an army of foes.

- **Change the direction that players move.** Left to right, straight or spiral, take them up or drop them down. Changing elevation can work wonders.

- **Use texturing and color.** Change the time of day, the weather, anything to make your level feel different.

---

[17] Whether that trash can has trash or treasure in it is up to you.

Time of day and weather can be used to emphasize events and elements in your level. How would players traverse the level if it were covered in snow or took place during a blizzard? How would a fairy village look differently if it were set at night? Make sure that any weather effects extend to the player character, the mechanics, the enemies, and other elements in the level. If one element isn't affected by the weather, it will ruin the entire effect. Give your game levels a variety of atmospheric effects and times of day to keep things interesting.

Variety should be applied to the level geometry as well as to gameplay. Alternating interior and exterior spaces keeps your level from feeling like too much of the same physical space. You don't have to alternate the spaces in between every room, but break it up according to what feels natural. Players usually feel safer in large spaces. Tighter spaces feel more mysterious and dangerous. Be mindful of your camera placement throughout your level design. Allow enough room in tight spaces for the players and camera to move around, or just resort to a fixed or rail camera. When you are staging combat, larger spaces allow you to throw in bigger and larger groups of bad guys, whereas narrower spaces work better for one-on-one battles.

Verticality is very important when designing levels. Alternating elevation makes an environment feel natural, provides much-needed variety, and allows designers to set up "Kodak moments" of any impressive visuals like statues, vistas, and horizons. As players walk or climb up, they feel as though they are making progress and heading toward a goal.

However, as players travel downwards, they may try to skip elevations by jumping downward. If players can be killed by very long drops, make sure that they have a way to look down to gauge the metrics of the drop. There's nothing more annoying than falling to your death if it looks as though you can safely make the drop. If you don't want players to drop down, corral them in the direction you want them to travel with switchbacks, ladders, or other climbable surfaces.

My golden rule of level design is this **very important thing:**

IF IT LOOKS AS IF PLAYERS CAN GO THERE, THEY SHOULD BE ABLE TO

Establish a visual language within your level to clarify where players can and cannot go. Use low walls, shrubbery, or rock walls to indicate impassable areas in the level to players. They will learn that these visual cues mean "you can't go there." Whatever you do, please don't be a lazy designer and use **invisible walls.**

Nothing breaks immersion faster and makes a level feel less like a real place than smacking headlong into a big fat wall of nothing.

Want to screw with your players' heads? Have your character travel from right to left, particularly if you are making a 2-D game. Western audiences are used to reading and viewing information in a left-to-right orientation. Making a character walk from right to left can make players feel uneasy, even if they can't articulate why. I find this works best when the character is entering the boss lair at the end of the game.

I don't know, it just feels wrong...

Another fun way to torture your players using level geometry is to force them to walk across very thin platforms over great heights, boiling lava, or swirling whirlpools. Increase the danger by using a bird's-eye view camera to view the action. I call these perilous situations **sphincter twitchers** and use them in all my level designs. Even if players are never in danger of dying, they sure will feel as if they are!

When working with your artist, unless the surface is specifically designed like a ramp, stairs, or natural incline, make sure any geometry that players can stand on (like platforms) is relatively flat. Most characters are not programmed to adjust their body to uneven surfaces and, even if they are, they can "stutter" or misstep as they are playing their walking animations. Try to have smooth transitions between even small elevations to avoid this problem.

While making a level feel like a real place helps the designer create the level, remember that you shouldn't be bound by realism: this is a game after all, and you are limited only by how real you want to make it.

However, here is a cautionary tale about realism. A friend of mine was a designer on the team of an action shooter. The levels had already been created by the artists, who were extremely proud that they had created architecturally accurate buildings. These buildings had realistic nooks, stairwells, in-scale hallways, and even bathrooms on each level. The buildings were almost completely unusable in the game because the spaces didn't allow for gameplay or work well with the game camera. Think of it this way: in the movie *Star Wars*, we never saw the toilets on the Death Star. I'm sure they were there just off-camera, but because we didn't need to see them, we didn't have to see them. Omit any parts of your building, temple, city, and so on that don't help support telling the story that you want to tell.

Wrapping Up Mapping

Now that we've covered these topics, how do you communicate them to your team members? For example, designing elevations for a top-down view map can be a bit tricky, but here are a few tricks that might help:

- You can draw levels in different colors, but I find that approach gets visually crowded.

- Use tracing paper or paper and a light board to layer the elevations of your level, and break them up by the height of the players.

- Be sure to clearly mark which elevations are what so viewers can read them in the correct order.

- While you are at it, number the consecutive map pages or tape them together into one big map so they are easier to read.

- Just because a sheet of paper is square doesn't mean you have to design to a square shape. Cut, fold, extend—do whatever you have to do to make your map accurately represent your design.

- If you are drawing your map from the side view, determine the height of your character first and then draw the map to scale.

- It's a lot easier to show vertical gameplay from a side view. Sometimes you are going to need a combination of side and top view maps.

You don't need to be working on a game with an isometric camera to use an isometric map. This type of map is a little trickier to draw, and it requires some artistic skill to create, but it works great for showing things like elevation.

Side view level design

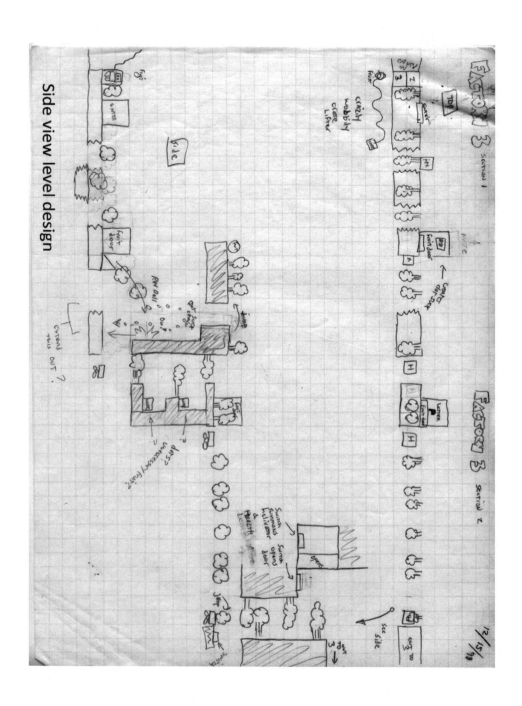

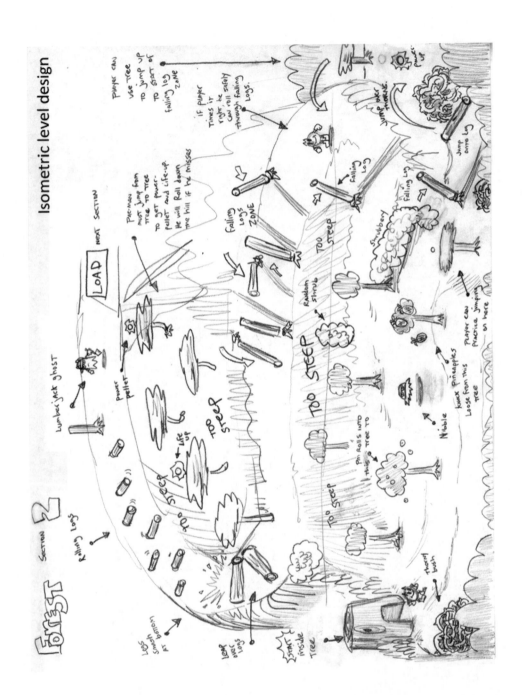

Isometric maps work best when representing games using a two and a half D camera. If you need to show depth or a part of the level that is obscured by geometry on your map, you can show the missing information using a cutaway or X-ray view. Or you can create a flap that the viewer can lift to see what lies underneath. Make as many layers as you need to convey your idea for your level. Some of my levels have had so many panels that they started to look like an advent calendar!

Here's some other information to include on your level design maps:

- Enemy spawn locations and detection/aggro radius
- "Bread crumb" collectibles (like coins or *Pac-Man* dots) that lead players through the level
- Secret entrances/breakable walls or other concealed locations
- Obstacles and barriers like walls, trees, tombstones, and so on
- Clearly marked terrain like cursed earth, swampy water, slippery ice, and hot lava

Gray Matters

Armed with your level maps, you are now ready to start building (or have an artist start building) your game levels. But hold on there, tiger! Before you even start thinking about enemies, mechanics, or even detailed geometry, you will have to flesh out your level in **gray box** form.

A **gray box level** is created within an art tool (Maya and 3D Studio Max are the two most common industry art tools, although others exist, like the open-source tool Blender). The gray box level shows the scale, size, and relationship of basic elements pertaining to camera and character metrics. It is pivotal in determining scale, camera, and pacing. Spend time running your game character around the gray box level. Have others play the level to find confusing areas and trouble spots. Iterate on your level while it's still easy to make big sweeping changes. You may find that a level works better if you rip out an entire section and stitch the remaining pieces together. A straight hallway may be more thrilling with plenty of twists and turns to transform "boring old" enemies, mechanics, and treasure into unexpected surprises.

As you are building your level, you might be wondering how long a level should be. Early in the production process, you should **pace out** a level to determine its overall length. Start your character at the beginning of your gray box level, and then start walking. Don't worry about hazards or combat or collecting every musical note in the level. Just walk from the start to the finish. Whatever time it took for you to get from point A to point B is roughly half the time it will take you in the final game. So if you need your levels to average a half-hour each, it should take 15 minutes to pace out the level. While it seems weird to do this, remember that many publishers and reviewers are concerned with the overall length of a game. I tell developers that a single-player action game should last at least eight to ten hours. Going longer than that is great; just make sure your production schedule and team plan for it.

Another pacing technique is to change the player's emotion every 15 to 20 minutes. Sadly, the gamut of emotions experienced in most video games is pretty limited,[18] but you can make a player go from mystery to wonder to fear to panic using geometry alone.

Divide your gameplay between "big moments" and "small moments." Don't stack too many big moments next to each other; you'll wear out your players. Conversely, small moments of calm and quiet will only feel boring if there are too many of them in a row. *Shadow of the Colossus* successfully balances the big moments of battling giant monsters and quiet moments of traveling through the expansive game world.

---

[18] I think it's fair to say that most video games let players experience only eight emotions: anger, panic, dread, surprise, wonder, satisfaction, joy, and disappointment. And some games only disappoint.

Stop! Wait! You haven't built your gray box levels yet, have you?

Good, because you will want to create a **playground** first. A playground is a gray box level not intended to be used in the game. It is a separate testing ground for game mechanics and hazards. All mechanics and hazards should be tested and tweaked in the playground until they feel right; then you can use them in your levels. Here are a few things to test in your own playground:

- Create ground angles to test basic walking, running, inverse kinematics (IK), and other technology to make sure the player looks good while moving even when not on level ground.

- Build several simple boxes at a variety of elevations to test the player's metrics with jumping, hoisting, teeter, and so on. You should create any specific length and height geometry to test double and wall jumps.

- Test mechanics and hazards to determine distance, timing, and lethality.

The sister to the playground is the **combat arena.** This is just like a playground but used by the dev team to test combat systems, cover systems, and enemies. Have a way to quickly spawn and test combinations of enemies to create the best combat experiences. I'd rather hold off on talking about this topic because—SPOILER ALERT—the next two chapters are all about combat and enemies!

Leave the Training Level for Last

The **training level** is the place where players learn all the basics of gameplay. It teaches players the game's basics. It provides players with their first impression of gameplay. It stokes their enthusiasm[19] for the rest of the game. You'd think that this is the most important level of the game.

You'd think!

Unfortunately, the training level is often left until the end of the game's production. Now, I know why this is done. Developers will argue that you won't know the most important lessons of the gameplay until everything is in the game. They will insist that because gameplay elements are often added during development, they should build the training level last after all the elements are set.

---

[19] Hey, I think I found a ninth emotion!

They state that by the end of the game's production, the art team is capable of creating the best-looking art and effects for the training level in order to give the first level of the game the biggest bang for the buck. Sometimes they claim the players will learn the basics over the course of the game. The reality is, production schedules get tight and priorities shift, resulting in the training level usually not getting the love and attention it deserves.

You may want to consider creating the training level first. Sure, it may not look as pretty, but your team can always go back and polish up the art. The advantage is that you, along with players, will be learning the basics and can accurately determine what the players should learn before the designer blinders kick in. A training level always benefits from a pair of fresh eyes.

Even better, don't have a training level at all. I have found that in the best games, players are always learning new moves, gaining new gear, experiencing new gameplay, and constantly learning. Why not make your **entire game** the training level?

Levels without Characters

Now that I've spent an entire chapter explaining how to make levels for primarily character-based games, what do you do if your level has no character? What if it's a puzzle game or a driving game or a flying game? Well, much of the advice from this chapter still applies, but here are a few more tips for these types of games:

- Make levels dependent on new mechanics. If players can now purchase nitro for their car, make sure there is a ramp that requires a nitro-powered jump to cross or a close race that can be won with the judicious application of a nitro-boost.

- Just because it's not an environment doesn't mean it can't have a theme. Many people don't realize even an abstract game like *Tetris* had a theme: each board was based on a cultural or architectural achievement of Soviet-era Russia.

- Even if you are designing a purely abstract game like *Super Hexagon, Hundreds,* or *Impossible Road,* changing the color of your level every so often helps indicates progress.

- If your game utilizes an "empty" environment like an open sky or outer space, changing objectives can still make the players' experience feel different. Think about how an escort mission would feel different than an all-out assault.

Now that you've started to create your levels, what are you going to fill them with? I have a sneaking suspicion you'll find out in the next chapter.

Level 9's Universal Truths and Clever Ideas

- Even a cliché can be made compelling.
- Use the "Mexican pizza" technique to make level themes unique.
- Level names can help convey mood and info to your players.
- Design from the top down: world, level, experience, to moment-to-moment gameplay.
- Use level maps and posters to give information and build anticipation.
- Determine the theme of your levels: escape/survive, explore, educate, or learn a moral.
- Decide early whether to use scripted or procedural gameplay.
- Use the beat chart to point out weaknesses in your game's overall design.
- Design your games using a tight set of gameplay systems and mechanics: maximize play through re-use.
- Players will always find a way to break your game.
- Is your level an alley or island? Design to each style's strength.
- Map and gray box your levels to plan camera placement and prevent architectural issues and gameplay problems.
- Walking is never, ever gameplay.
- Every finger should have a reward at the end, even if it's just a trash can.
- Players need variety, and surprise is just variety that players don't expect.
- If it looks like players can go there, they should be able to go there.
- Use playgrounds and combat arenas to test metrics and systems.
- The entire game should train players.
- Even games without a story can have a theme.

Level 10
The Elements of Combat

Every action is seen to fall into one of three main categories, guarding, hitting, or moving. Here, then, are the elements of combat, whether in war or pugilism.

B.H. Liddell Hart

BRITISH MILITARY THEORIST Sir Basil Liddell Hart may have died before video games became popular, but his quote neatly covers the basics of video game combat. Combat is a popular and major component of a video game player's moves and activities. A good combat system requires much thought and work from the development team to get it right. But before diving into combat, we need to open and look into the messy can of **violence.**

The simple truth is this: many video games are violent.

Let me amend that.

Video games are about **action.** Some of those actions, like hitting, shooting, stabbing, and killing, are violent.

However, anyone who assumes that all video games are violent obviously knows nothing about video games. A large number of video games don't rely on violence—from the first video game, *Tennis for Two,* all the way to the latest iPhone puzzle game. I could fill this entire book with a catalog of non-violent games. But somehow, it's always the *Dooms, Mortal Kombats,* and *Grand Theft Autos* that get all the attention. Why? Because:

1. Violence in video games is graphic, dramatic, and visceral.

2. As a result of the above, it offers a player the quickest positive response feedback loop.

The player does an action (hitting, shooting) and sees the immediate result (enemy is killed by attack), which grants a reward (experience, money, power-up). This elegant feedback loop allows for quick and frequent player-to-world interaction. It's Freud's pleasure principle in practice.[1] Ring the bell, a reward is gained. Why stop ringing the bell?

Another reason violence is common in video games is that other human interactions such as conversation, romance, humor, and manipulation are often hard to re-create in games! The results are (a) development teams do not explore alternate methods of gameplay as often as they do violent ones. (b) Because game players tend to buy the same types of games over and over, (c) publishers find that newer styles of play are harder to sell.[2] (d) Parents and other social groups who mean well don't always find out all the facts before leaping to the assumption that all video games are violent.

Let's avoid all this stress by doing our part as responsible members of society and keep mature games out of the hands of younger gamers. Plenty of alternative games are available out there. You wouldn't take little kids to an R-rated movie, so why would you let them play an M-rated video game?

As mentioned back in Level 4, the ESRB reviews and provides ratings for game content. At its website,[3] you can find the board's descriptors of violence found in games:

- **Comic mischief**—Depictions or dialogue involving slapstick or suggestive humor.

- **Cartoon violence**—Violent actions involving cartoon-like situations and characters. May include violence where a character is unharmed after the action has been inflicted.

- **Fantasy violence**—Violent actions of a fantasy nature, involving human or non-human characters in situations easily distinguishable from real life.

---

[1] The fact that a developer called "id" created the FPS, a genre that directly adheres to Freud's pleasure principle, is almost too delicious to ignore.

[2] EA's marketing team tried to cancel the company's bestselling game, *The Sims*, during its entire development; they thought no one would buy it!

[3] www.esrb.org/ratings/ratings_guide.jsp

- **Violence**—Scenes involving aggressive conflict. May contain bloodless dismemberment.

- **Intense violence**—Graphic and realistic-looking depictions of physical conflict. May involve extreme and/or realistic blood, gore, weapons, and depictions of human injury and death.

When designing violence in games, you should realize that it's all about context. The more violent activities the player does himself, the higher the rating. Ask yourself the following questions to help determine the proper rating for your game:

- Does the player do the violence himself? Does he use realistic weapons?

- How frequently does the player perform the violent act?

- Does the game reward the player for performing violent acts? Does the game show in any way that violence is "not appropriate?"

- How graphic is the violence? Is there dismemberment? Do the game visuals linger on the violence?

- Is there leftover residue like bloodstains or gibs? Better graphics equal more realistic graphics equal more realistic violence.

- Is the violence against "bad guys"?

- Do the enemies suffer as they are being killed or defeated?

Now that you know how violent your gameplay will be, you can start to design how it is going to happen.

400 Quatloos on the Newcomer!

When designing combat moves for your character, first consider your character's personality. Is your character acrobatic like Edward Kenway? Is your character jumpy like Rayman? Stealthy like Garrett? Brutal like Grayson Hunt? Each of these characters has a unique combat style because each has a unique personality.

So... you guys wanna fight?

* smoking kills

What genre is your game? What kinds of gameplay experiences do you want the players to have? These questions will help determine what weapons your character will use. Or maybe you just want to have your hero carry a laser scimitar *and* a phase-plasma pistol for no other reason than it looks awesome. You'll still want to consider the ramifications of his carrying both because it impacts your games and everything the player does in it.

In combat, the attack used totally depends on the player's distance from the target. Check out the four ranges of combat: close range, medium range, long range, and area effect.

- **Close-range combat** consists of grapples, punches, strikes, sweeps, tickle fights, and quick burst moves like head butts and upper cuts.

- **Medium-range combat** consists of weapon swings, flying kicks, and dash attacks.

- **Long-range combat** consists of shooting or throwing projectiles or spells at enemies.

- **Area effects,** like **smart bombs** and "super" attacks, will affect enemies at long range or on the entire screen.

Knowing what your character's combat range (or ranges) is going to be makes a huge difference in how the player approaches combat during gameplay. A *Mario* game is almost exclusively close/medium-range combat, whereas *Contra* is a long-range combat game. As a result, Mario must come into close contact with enemies to be able to defeat them, whereas in *Contra*, the player's goal is to keep away from enemies and keep them from ever getting close by shooting them at a distance.

In addition, attacks can be delivered from four different elevations to give combat variety: standing, low, high, and aerial. Although you don't have to use all four of these elevations in your game, you will have to make each of these elevations have its own set of attacks because they make the player deal with combat in very different ways:

- **Standing position** is the basic shoulder height of the player. Man-sized and larger opponents can be struck at this elevation.

- **Low position** strikes are at the waist height (or lower) of the enemy and delivered from a crouched or kneeling position.

- **High position** attacks are delivered over the head of an average height enemy. They can be done only by jumping and then attacking. High attacks are used against flying or large enemies like bosses.

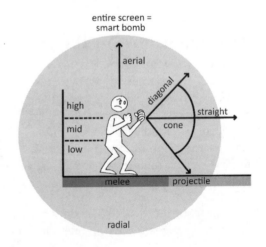

- **Aerial position** is achieved when a player jumps or flies into the air to attack. Aerial attacks can be extended jumps like those found in *Devil May Cry* and *Dante's Inferno*, or they can be true flying like in *Marvel Ultimate Alliance* or *Dark Void*.

Attacks from any elevation and range can be delivered both **vertically** and **horizontally.** In *Maximo: Ghosts to Glory*, we designed enemies that could be defeated by only one of the two attacks.

A skeleton guard wore an armored helmet that deflected Maximo's overhead vertical attack. Another skeleton warrior used a shield that blocked Maximo's horizontal attacks. The solution was to use the opposite direction attacks to smash the skeletons.

An **attack matrix** is useful to track important information about combat moves. An attack matrix should include the following data:

- Attack name

- Control scheme

- Range of attack

- Speed of attack

- Direction of attack

- Damage—in terms of strength as well numeric damage (usually expressed as a value or percentage)

- Special—anything that distinguishes the attack from other attack moves

Here's a nice example of an attack matrix:

Attack	Control	Range	Speed	Direction	Damage	Special
Slash	Square	Close	Med	Horizontal	Medium (10 hps)	Can be blocked by shield
Overhead strike	Triangle	Close	Med	Vertical	Medium (10 hps)	Can be thwarted by helmet
Thrust	Forward on stick, Triangle	Close	Fast	Forward	Strong (25 hps)	Knockback to target
Jump strike	X, down on stick, Triangle	Close/ medium	Slow	Downward	Strong (25 hps)	Stun to any target in two-unit radius

Feel free to add as many columns as you need to your attack matrix to accommodate degrees of severity, defensive items/moves, and so on.

You can use an attack matrix to track combat moves and compare and contrast values for maximum variety. Each attack should be distinct and usable in a specific combat situation.

Before you start whacking away with swords and blasting everything in sight with your guns, look first at the most dangerous weapon . . . the hand.

Put 'Em Up!

Hand-to-hand combat has been a staple of video games ever since early brawlers and fighters. How your character fights depends on who your character is. You won't find a better case study than the *Street Fighter* characters. Each one is a personification of a different martial arts style. Even if your character lives in a crazy fantasy world, you should study real-world fighting styles to make your character's attacks feel more realistic and distinct. Let's look at some different hand-to-hand fighting moves:

- **Strong and weak attacks**—Attacks in action and fighting games are often broken up into two categories: strong and weak (also called **heavy** and **light attacks**). Both types of attacks can be composed of punches or kicks or other moves, but what matters is the damage they do and the opponent's reaction to the attack when struck. Strong attacks do more damage than weak attacks. Strong attacks often have a longer animation. The time it takes for the attack to connect is the risk the player takes for the reward of the higher damage. Weak attacks are quick but do very little damage. However, weak attacks often act as the opening move for a chain of attacks leading up to a super-move. Weak attacks are often blockable, whereas strong attacks may not be. Strong attacks might act as shield breakers or cause stun or knockback to the enemy as an added benefit.

- **Punch**—A punch should happen quickly. When the player taps the button (or screen), the character should immediately throw a punch. The animation of the punch shouldn't have too long of a wind-up, unless it is for some spectacular finishing super-move. When animating a punch attack, be mindful of the distance between the character and where the punch lands. The distance can't be so short that the player doesn't see it happening thanks to poor camera placement or an enemy getting in the way. By throwing a fast punch, the player can **chain** punches—throw several punches within a short period of time. But speed isn't the only thing important to a punch. A punch feels powerful when the enemy reacts to it. Stronger punches, such as an **upper cut,** should really rock the enemy's world. A good reaction animation, sound effect, and special effect really help sell a punch. I talk more about how to do this correctly later.

- **Kick**—While you have to be flexible to do a kick, kicks are more flexible than punches. They can be a quick snap kick at an enemy's torso, a **sweep** at the legs to cause the enemy to lose balance and fall, or a **flying kick** attack—a dramatic mid-air cartwheel attack or a flurry of kicks like Chun-Li's famous *Hyakuretsu Kyaku* attack. Kicks provide a little more distance between the player and the enemy than a punch and often cause knockback. Because kicking offers so many variations in fighting games, entire games like *DiveKick* (One True Game studios, 2013) have been built around it.

- **Knock-up** and **juggling**—An especially powerful attack, known as a **launcher,** can hit an enemy so hard he goes flying up into the air. Depending on the time it takes the enemy to come back down, the player can jump into the air, intercepting him, and repeatedly attack to keep the enemy suspended in air, helpless to defend himself. The *Devil May Cry* series allows player character Dante to use his pistols and swords in several combinations to perform a spectacular array of juggling moves.

- **Stealth kill**—This quick attack is used to kill or disable an enemy in one move without alerting other enemies nearby. These moves are usually performed from a crouch or cover position or by positioning the player behind her target. They often use quick timer event-style prompts to activate and reward players with dramatic enemy kills. Make sure that stealth kills can be done only under certain conditions (in the right position, while under cover, while in shadow); otherwise, players will constantly use them over regular attacks as an exploit. Don't let a cool move become stale to the players.

- **Grapple**—This move is similar to a stealth kill in that a player can activate it under specific circumstances. A grapple is achieved when the character grabs another character to detain him and execute an additional attack. Grappling used to be rare early on in games because it was hard to program the collision needed to make a grapple look convincing. However, many wrestling games have perfected the grapple, and the move has found its way into more fighting and action games. Just as with grabbing items, you

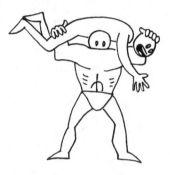

should make it easy for players to grab and release their opponents. Many games make this a context-sensitive move, as in Batman's interrogation move, which grabs an enemy and transitions into cutscenes of Batman demanding information from the enemy. The grapple is also the basis for a **piledriver attack,** in which the enemy is grabbed upside-down and driven head-first into the ground. Ow! That's gotta hurt!

- **Throw**—Throws are used to toss an enemy away from the player. The player grabs the enemy and then tosses him away in a desired direction. A throw can be used defensively, giving the player a little more time to prepare for the next attack, to clear some space when surrounded by foes, or as a way to set up another attack while the enemy is stunned on the ground. Throws can be used to toss enemies off ledges or platforms, often

to their death, and some games like *MadWorld* (Platnium Games, 2009) use throws to toss enemies into traps, doing the dirty work for the player.

- **Slap**—A slap is used to stun rather than to do damage. Slap fights aren't very common in gaming, but *Rose & Camellia* (Nigoro, 2007) features Victorian-era ladies slapping the heck out of each other. As in *Rose & Camellia*, an especially good slap reaction should really extend the enemy's neck and head to make the player really feel the sting. If your slap stuns an enemy, don't forget the stunned woozy stance, dancing stars, or tweeting birds flitting around the enemy's head. Slapping  the ground is known as a **ground pound.** In this move, the player smashes his fists into the ground Hulk-style, causing all standing enemies to lose their balance and fall to the ground. Ground pounds have big wind-ups and dramatic reactions, sending people, vehicles, and even stationary objects flying.

- **Block** and **Cancel**—Are you just going to take all those punches, kicks, and slaps? Of course not! Blocks and cancels allow the player (or the enemy) to keep from taking damage. Whereas a block stops an enemy's attack—sometimes at the risk of being thrown—a cancel (also known as an **interrupt**) actually interrupts the animation of an attack, allowing the opponent to make an attack of her own. Cancel systems are often used in conjunction with the blocking system, allowing the player to cancel out his own block move to perform a quick attack or one that takes advantage of an opening in the enemy's attack animation.

- **Parry** and **Counter**—While blocks prevent damage, parries allow the player to stop the attack, often stunning, disabling, or even disarming the enemy. Counters allow the player to not only stop the attack, but also strike back with an attack of her own! Action games like the *Batman: Arkham* series and *Uncharted* series warn the player of an incoming attack so the player can perform a counter move.

- **Focus attack**—Introduced in *Street Fighter IV*, focus moves allow the player to "charge up" an attack, which does major damage to the enemy upon release. There are often multiple stages to a focus attack, each level doing progressively more damage and allowing the player to follow up the attack with more attacks. However, focus attacks aren't always invincible; they can be "broken" by special **armor break** moves.

- **Taunt**—When your opponent won't fight you like a man (using a strategy known as **"turtling"**), you have no choice but to taunt him. Most taunts just mock your opponent, trying to make him angry enough to attack. Sometimes taunts can increase the player's health, decrease an opponent's power meter, or even cause damage like Pyro's Hadouken taunt in *Team Fortress 2*.

And a One and a Two . . .

Timing is one of the major keys to great combat. When the player presses a button, the character should immediately perform the attack. If you want your combat animations to feel smooth, you

must strive to have your game run at 60 frames per second. While many games run satisfactorily at 30 fps, lagging and stuttering that can happen at these lower frame rates will really impact your player's combat experience. Don't waste time with long and elaborate wind-up animations. If you do this, it will throw off the player's timing and he may end up missing or striking when he doesn't want to. Quick moves can be rapidly done in succession, but they tend to lead to button mashing.

When designing combat for touchscreens or motion controls, keep the moves localized. Don't expect the player to stretch all the way across the screen or room. Give the player lots of opportunities to stretch and take a break.

Lunges are more fluid thrusts that return the character back to his original standing position. By combining quick strikes and lunges, you can create a **combat chain** that will keep the player's basic attack from feeling boring.

To create a combat chain, create three or more attack moves that will run one after another. If the player presses the attack move once, play the first animation. If the player presses the button again within a short (usually within a second) time period, the player character goes into a second attack move. Usually, this second attack move deals more damage, so there is an advantage for the player to "chain" these attacks together. A third attack will do even more damage, and so on.

first button press   second button press   third button press

If the player is allowed to land multiple hits in a row, make sure that your animation (or game code) also moves the player character forward; otherwise, when the enemy is knocked back, the player won't be able to land the next attack in the chain. The hero in the following image misses because he doesn't translate forward. His attack succeeds only when he shifts forward.

OK, remember a few paragraphs ago when I said that you shouldn't do elaborate wind-up animations? I meant it—but only then. Elaborate wind-ups are awesome because they lead to powerful attacks that can knock a player into the air or chop an enemy in two! These moves work great when the player is wielding an oversized or heavy weapon. Because of the long wind-up, the player is forced to risk the wait for the reward of landing a more powerful attack! Risk versus reward. Remember it. It's gonna be big.

Speaking of rewards, use particle and visual effects to make attacks feel more dynamic and rewarding—from "slice streaks" on sword attacks and speed lines for dash moves like those seen in the *Onimusha* games—or resort to those old standbys, the fire trails and blood splatters like in *MadWorld* (Platinum Games, 2009). If an attack is going hurt, you can make the character's hands or weapon burst into flame, arc with lightning, or shine with mystical rays of light. Be big, be dynamic, and be dramatic! Give big action moves like ground pounds and smashing uppercuts big screen effects that fill the screen with debris, dust, screen flashes, and other eye-catchers. The more spectacular, the better!

The Big Finish

The most spectacular move in video games is the **super move.** These spectacular show-stopping attacks are often performed at the end of a combo chain or are the super moves originally found in fighters and JPRGs. They have blasted into other genres, making the final move as awesome as possible. Here are a few things you need to perform a super move:

- Super moves almost always require a charge to activate. The player must work up to earning the right to execute a super move.

- Super moves require a specific chain of controls. The moves are so awesome that the player shouldn't be able to press one button to perform it. She's going to have to earn it by completing a series of moves leading up to the super move.

- When the player finally performs the super move, stop the action and focus the player's attention on what's going on: dim the screen, drop out the background, bring in other characters. Games like *Power Stone*, *Darkstalkers,* the *Marvel vs. Capcom* series, and the *Final Fantasy* series have particularly cool super moves that you can look to for inspiration.

- Super moves require super visual effects. The screen should light up when the player is executing a super move, so much so that even the receiver of the beatdown should be able to appreciate the spectacle.

- Super moves do lots of damage or finish off the opponent. They're not called **"finishing moves"** for nothing!

- Super moves should award extra points or a bonus or some sort on execution. They're a great way to award a player an achievement.

- Super moves (almost) never miss. In fighting games, the opposing player should have an opportunity to counter a super move. There's nothing more satisfying than turning the tables on someone who thinks he has you dead to rights.

- If you use a super move in a multiplayer game, make sure there is a pause afterwards so the other players aren't unfairly penalized by the delay.

So what happens when that super move or any attack actually connects? Well, as I mentioned earlier, a strike without a reaction animation from the enemy doesn't feel as though the player has hit anything. It's as if the attack is merely skipping off the surface of the enemy. If you can't afford to let the enemy have reaction animations (due to memory limitations, for example), at least have visual effects and sound effects that indicate a successful hit has landed. Powerful sound effects make attacks feel more rewarding. Vocal reactions such as a big "Oof!" from enemies are always satisfying!

Exaggerate the impact of a powerful hit to heighten the feeling of strength of the attack and increase drama. The enemy should react to wherever he's been hit. Got cracked in the coconut? The enemy's head (and some teeth) should fly. Kick out his leg and a bone should splinter, or the enemy should at least topple to the ground. This kind of animation is getting easier to do within the game code using rag doll physics systems like Havok and PhysX, but sometimes nothing beats good old-fashioned key frame animation.

If conflict is drama, then combat should be a freakin' opera complete with flying, spear-carrying valkyries and a glass-shattering fat lady! Hype up that drama! A particularly powerful strike should be accompanied with a camera shake, a rumble from the controller's actuator, or combat slowing down to show off the power of the hit. Many games, from *Call of Duty* to *Peggle*, use slow motion to indicate that the player has defeated the last of the enemies in a combat encounter.

Before I forget, here's a pearl of wisdom: close battles are more exciting. Don't get me wrong, kicking hordes of enemies' butts can be quite satisfying, but just make sure that your player is evenly matched to his skill level for the majority of the game.

You can really pull out all the stops if you use a **cinematic finishing move** such that the action slows or freezes and the camera pans around the action. These finishes are frequently seen in fighting games like the *Soul Calibur* and *Street Fighter* titles, but they've crept into other action games because they just look so darn cool! This happened because of this **very important thing:**

PEOPLE WANT TO PLAY GAMES THAT MAKE THEM LOOK COOL

And nothing makes a player look cooler than a combo chain and a finishing move. Just look at the Mighty Bedbug in action here. You have to admit that pressing button prompts to create a choreographed combat sequence makes the battle look spectacular.

Case in point: Batman's combat in *Batman: Arkham Asylum* relies on QTEs to choreograph combat moves rather than leaving the player to flounder around on his own. Why? Because Batman would never miss a punch. Why should the player? The result? When the player successfully does the correct combat sequence, the player feels like an expert of combat—just like Batman.

Live by the Sword . . .

There has been a long history of heroes with signature weapons: King Arthur wielded Excalibur, the Monkey King fought with Ruyi Jingu Bang, Thor clobbered trolls with Mjolnir, and Honjo Shigenaga defeated armies with the Honjo Masamune.

Video game characters are no different. These new heroes have their own signature weapons: Link wields the Master Sword, Kratos thrashes monsters with his double-chained blades, Master Chief brandishes his plasma sword against the Covenant, and Batman uses a variety of bat-shaped weapons to defend Gotham City.

No matter what the weapon—swords, axes, daggers, hammers, clubs, chain-blades, staffs, boomerang, nunchucks—you will want to give your own hero a signature weapon. The weapon and how he fights with it become an extension of the character's personality. Your character's weapon is going to dictate how he fights. Rygar's throwable shield creates a different combat experience than Big Daddy's melee drill. Even if your hero uses an unconventional weapon like a giant spatula or bubble wand, you should have a variety of attacks and moves that the player can perform with them. The more original and memorable, the better!

Often in games, the camera is further back so the player doesn't get a good look at his weapon. Give him an opportunity to see it up close. This can be done when the weapon is first awarded to the player or through an inventory screen where the player can rotate and examine the weapon.

When designing how a weapon is used, think about its speed, range, the damage it does, and what other effects it may have, such as fire or poison. If a weapon is upgradable, make sure the effects are seen on the weapon. Merely adding a +3 to the stats doesn't provide the player with the gameplay information and visual rewards that she deserves.

While the player is swinging a weapon around, be mindful of it penetrating through objects. That just looks bad. Instead, have weapons respond to the world, such as rebounding off stone or metal surfaces or blades sinking into wooden ones. Be aware of the flipside of this: that the player's weapon will rebound off any non-breakable item in the world. Carefully design your combat environments to use this to the player's advantage and disadvantage. For example, a hero would learn he couldn't swing his giant axe around in an arena filled with unbreakable stone pillars lest  he risk rebounding off them, which would give the skeletons a chance to attack.

Don't forget the player character can use impromptu weapons as well—props or objects such as lead pipes, chairs, or even cars! Make it easy for players to find and pick up these items; provide on-screen prompts if you have to.

What's another way to make the player look like an expert? Use a **lock-on system.** *Mark of Kri* (SCEA, 2002) had an innovative lock-on system that had players use the DuelShock controller's analog stick to do a "radar-style" sweep to target a sequence of enemies that the players could program. This technique was patented by the game's creators. The *Legend of Zelda* games have a particularly good lock-on system in which players can lock on to the enemy closest/in front of them with a button press and flick the analog stick to select the next one over to the right or left. The characters can still perform sidestep and backup while locked on. As long as the button remains pressed, the player is locked on to an enemy. As each enemy is dispatched, the targeting system latches on to the next available enemy. Lock-on systems require HUD visuals to help players track their targets. Here are some examples:

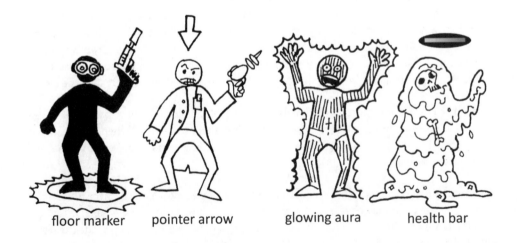

floor marker   pointer arrow   glowing aura   health bar

Now You Have to Kiss Me

Letting the player miss isn't such a bad thing. The player will be forced to become more skilled with his attacks, which will make him feel like more of a cool dude as he masters combat timing. Or if the player just doesn't get it, you can always increase an enemy's collision dynamically if the player misses or dies too many times in a row. Or you can offer to drop the game down to a lower difficulty setting. Do whatever you can to keep your players playing.

Let's Get Defensive

If you learn any martial art, you quickly are taught that defensive moves are just as important as attacking. The goal in a real-life fight[4] is to NOT get hit. Why should video games be any different? Allow your players moves that give them options for retreating or avoiding damage, and also ones that can be combined with combat moves for quicker or more powerful attacks.

Dodges and **rolls** allow players to get the heck out of dodge and quickly move out of the way of attacks. They should be quick and easy to perform too: a button press and single control stick move. Mind your metrics and keep an eye on your movement lengths, so the player doesn't roll off a platform or the edge of the world or fighting arena. A dodge move is done as a reflex to another danger. Don't turn a defensive maneuver into a disadvantage. Make sure your dodge lets the player get completely clear of wide-range attacks and longer-reaching weapons like halberds and huge swords, or radius-based attacks like explosions and magic spells; otherwise, you might be doing what, in *WOW*, they call "the graveyard hustle."

---

[4] Not that I'm advocating fighting in the real world: remember, the first rule of fight club is . . . oops, I've already said too much.

After the player does a dodge, there should be a beat to allow him to get back on his feet. Not only does this beat give the player a chance to reorient himself, but it keeps him from using the dodge as a movement exploit.

Allow players to use dodges and rolls to get past hazards. These movements add a nice moment of tension when the player character is dashing through a closing door or rolling under a swinging blade. But be careful. During a roll or dash, the camera has a tendency to collide with whatever the player is trying to avoid. I don't suggest having the camera pass through the hazard (that looks sloppy) or having the camera dip down with the player (because that gets disorienting). Consider the camera locking in place as the player dodges and then have it "catch up" with the player when he's cleared the obstacle.

Dashes are forward moves that can be used for defense or attack. Like dodges, dashes should be very quick to perform. Many action games like *Devil May Cry* (Capcom, 2001) and *Darksiders* (THQ, 2009) have dash moves that can be upgraded with more powerful sword or punch moves. Even your basic dash move should do something besides move the player. You want a dash to feel quick and powerful. And fast. And dare I say, dashing?

The player should be able to use the dash to ram into enemies or smash breakable objects. Even though a dash targets one enemy, you can have the player's momentum continue to have him hit several enemies at once or create a "sonic boom" to send bad guys flying! Whee!

While generally used for traversal, **jump** moves can be combat moves too. Where would Mario be without his famous **"butt bounce"** attack? The collision zone should be like a good pair of pants: there should be plenty of room in the butt. Don't make these pixel-perfect attacks. After the attack hits, apply **recoil bounce** to move the player a short distance away so the player doesn't land on or next to the enemy and take damage. If the enemy hasn't been killed by the butt bounce, minimize risk to the player by putting the enemy in a stunned state.

Many games allow the player to maneuver during this recoil bounce to let him chain bounce attacks off the heads of multiple enemies! Make sure you award an escalating bonus for each additional bad guy bounced. Make it a big moment for the player: he's just done something cool!

You don't have to be a short Italian plumber to do jump attacks. Weapon-wielding tough guys can do these moves too. Just make sure you follow these guidelines:

- Make sure the player's maximum jump is taller than the tallest enemy you can jump attack. Otherwise, you'll be colliding with the enemy's head or shoulders, which will look strange.

- When the player lands, apply the same rules as an attack impact: stop the action for a beat by freezing the enemy or world's action, generate explosive effects, rumble the controller—anything to make the attack feel more powerful.

- Even if the player misses, the strike could generate some radial effect—a stun or knockback for nearby enemies, for example.

- Allow the player a quick recovery; he'll want to get back into action immediately.

- Then again, you could give the player a delay as part of the risk/reward of performing the attack. For example, Mario firmly plants his butt into the ground after a butt bounce. If he misses an enemy, he's vulnerable for a beat to getting hurt by an enemy.

If jumping is a little too frivolous for your big bad space marine or soldier, you can have him **vault** over obstacles to add variety to battlefield movement. Vaulting works well with cover systems (see following sections) and ducking. *Gears of War 2* (Microsoft Games Studio, 2008) provides players with a prompt to notify them when they can vault over a low wall.

Dodging the Bullet

Combining a dodge with an attack, **bullet time** was first introduced in the 1999 movie *The Matrix*. Video game developers immediately fell in love with the visual of the player character leaping through the air, avoiding bad guys' bullets while blasting away with his own slow-motion projectiles. *Max Payne* (Remedy Entertainment, 2001) was the first game to use bullet time, and it's been a staple of 3-D person action games ever since. It doesn't matter if you call it Reaction Time (*Mirror's Edge*), Reflex (*FEAR*), DeadEye (*Red Dead Redemption*), or Tequila Time (*John Woo's Stranglehold*); here are a few tips when designing bullet time for your games:

- **Let the player know it's started.** Flash the screen with an effect, dial down the color saturation, play a distinctive "activation" sound effect— any clue to let the player know he's entered this hyper-reality state.

- **Outnumber the player.** Bullet time works best when the odds are against the player and all seems lost. Being able to take out individual foes amid the chaos of a large gun or fistfight makes the player feel unstoppable—at least until his meter runs out.

- **The player should still move faster than everyone else.** Let the player perform actions before any of the other characters can. You want the player to feel as if he's got the upper hand on the bad guys.

- **Give opportunities for precision shooting.** *Max Payne 3*'s bullet time increases Max's move set with each accurate shot the player makes. *Red Dead Revolver* lets the player shoot hats off heads and guns out of hands as well as precisely target lethal shots during DeadEye mode.

- **Make the soundtrack match the action.** Slow down the music or make the sound muffled as if it were running in slow motion.

- **You can never have too many effects.** Bullet casing, blooming muzzle flashes, exploding heads, or shattering glass, the star of bullet time is all the debris and flash that come with seeing the world in slow motion.

- **Make bullet time a "sometimes" mechanic or save it for special occasions.** If the player can use bullet time everywhere, she will abuse it. Limit its use by requiring the player to build up a charge or collect a power-up.

- **Save it for "super dramatic" moments.** The villain has a gun to the president's head and you have only seconds to make the shot. High noon has struck, and you're surrounded by banditos. You and your girlfriend have accidently stumbled onto a gangland crime scene. Is your superhero punching out the last baddie during a combat arena round? That's when you want to break out the bullet time.

On Guarding

WATCH OUT!

That's how fast you have to respond to an attack, so you'd better make sure your **block** is quick to pull off! Blocks can be either general or positional.

General blocks are found in action games—a single button press to cross weapons, cross arms, or lift a shield to block an incoming attack. These all-purpose blocks can be used for any situation or enemy. It doesn't matter whether your shield is a one-handed buckler or tall Roman Scuta; the function is still the same: the player blocks an attack with the press of a button, holding it aside during the rest of combat.

Don't underestimate the use of sound effects in conjunction with a block. A nice loud "CLANG!" lets the player know he's successfully executed a block. Sound cues provide important information to the player and help to differentiate between a miss and a block. Have the blocked hit create some sparks or some other effect (as long as it's not blood; you'll want to save that for when the character is hit) visually clue in the player. Some blocks displace the player back a little bit to make him have to move back in to hold his ground. Giving a successful block a disadvantage is a bit of a jerk move, but if you want to, then go ahead—it's your game.

Positional blocks correlate with a particular elevation and require a stick move and/or button press to block at the appropriate height, whether it's high or low. You find these blocks most often in fighting games. You'll have to decide whether or not a player can hold a block. Arm blocks are usually quick and drop down after a second or so. Other fighting and action games allow the player to hold the block indefinitely, or at least until an enemy performs an attack that breaks the player's block or knocks him off his feet. Shield blocks can last longer, allowing the player to "hide" behind the shield for an extended period of time. Some designers don't like letting the player camp a block, but that can be circumnavigated by using breakable shields, unblockable attacks or giving enemies knockback attacks. Oh, and don't let your shield sort through the ground when the player crouches to block low attacks.

As a designer, you need to decide whether or not your shield is breakable. This decision will make a big difference in how the player uses it. In the first *Maximo* game, we had a breakable shield. The player was able to upgrade it to a stronger shield through the course of the game. However, because it was still a limited resource, we found that players were reluctant to use it, preferring to jump and dodge out of the way of attacks instead. In the sequel, we wanted to promote shield usage, so we made shield unbreakable. Players were much happier to block because the worry of breakage was taken away. But shields aren't just for blocking anymore. You can use a shield to

- Clear obstacles when combined with a dash move

- Smash enemies at close range

- Throw as a short-range projectile

- Sled down steep inclines

- Protect from falling debris or lava when placed overhead

- Act as a crowbar to move large objects

- Protect from back-stabbing enemies when placed on the player's back

Heck, attach a shield to a chain like in *Rygar*, and it becomes a whole new weapon!

If a shield isn't enough protection, then **armor** will do the trick. There are several things to consider when giving the player armor. **Encumbrance** is one. The more armor the player wears, the slower (and noisier) he becomes. You usually find encumbrance in RPGs, not often in action games. It's fine if you are trying to be "realistic," but if your game's emphasis is on action and combat, not using it may be a better choice.

Perhaps your game makes a distinction between different parts of the body in combat? If so, you can use the "paper doll" approach to armor. The player has to armor his head, torso, arms, hands, legs, and feet. This feels more realistic and gives your player more items to buy and collect. However, it does require an interface—usually quite large, because it has to show the entire body. Make sure players can easily find, select, and change their armor. And discard or sell unwanted armor as well.

Your hero has finally defeated the first boss and won his prize: a new suit of armor. But don't cop out and just give the player a +2 chainmail shirt. Whenever the player earns an armor upgrade, make it look dramatically different. For example, full plate looks substantially different (and cooler) than a leather jerkin. When you visually improve the player's armor, the player can tell his "rank" at a glance.

Give it a unique name too, like the "Holy Armor of Protection" or "Dragon Scale Armor." This will make the player feel as if he's won something important and worth having.

But armor is not just for protection. Isaac's spacesuit in *Dead Space* has a health meter right down the spine. Players can check their status at a glance without the need for a HUD.

Ghosts 'N Goblins also shows health status . . . but in reverse: as the armor pops off, the player gets closer to death. This is a good trick for enemies too because it lets the player know how many hits are left to defeating a foe.

Armor upgrades are a great way to give a player a new ability. Can't move that heavy block? This hydraulically powered armor can help him move it. It doesn't even have to be a "suit of armor." Mario's Tanooki[5] suit not only added protection, but also let him fly, grow, and turn into an invincible statue.

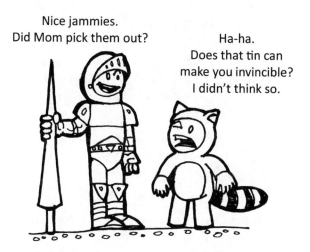

What's great about armor is that it's an easy way for players to customize their character without changing the base model—depending on the armor, of course. Chain mail wouldn't change the model, but plate mail armor or a full-head helmet would. The advantage to armor upgrades is that when another player sees your cool new helmet, she's gonna want one too. It's a great way to motivate players to spend more time seeking out cool loot in your game. It doesn't have to be armor; it can be hats, unique weapons, or mounts. The more unique gear you allow players to earn, find, and buy, the better.

State of the Art Bang Bang

Ooooh! Guns, guns, guns!
—Clarence Boddicker (RoboCop)

Shooting is simple. Aim the gun, pull the trigger. Right? But let's look at some of the most popular multiplayer shooters and see how wide they vary from each other:

- *Quake* has maps that promote linear action and predictable looping movement patterns. Weapon and armor pickups can change the dynamics of the action in a heartbeat.

---

[5] Tanuki are Japanese raccoon dogs. Mario wears Tanuki footie pajamas with raccoon ears. It's adorable. Really.

- *Halo* is played more like a sport, with game-like modes of play. The rhythm of the action is slower than many shooters, partially due to the player's regenerating health, and promotes "attack then retreat" strategies. Vehicles play a big part of the gameplay as well.

- The *Call of Duty* series has a multiplayer mode that concentrates on short-range combat with intense action. Players can concentrate on upgrading their weapons and characters like in an RPG.

- *Team Fortress 2* resembles an RPG, but the players assume widely varying skill-based roles. The game modes promote teamwork over single player actions. The turnover time from "play to death" is very quick compared to the preceding games because players can be killed with a single shot.

- The *Left4Dead* series is also all about teamwork; in fact, you can't win without it. While most multiplayer shooters match opponents one-to-one, *Left4Dead* pits a handful of players against an endless horde of zombies. Game modes resemble stories more than in other shooters.

Even in games where shooting isn't the main focus of play, **ranged combat** can immediately change the dynamic of the game. This is why I recommend that if a game isn't a shooter, guns should be saved until later in the game. Let players get used to their moves and attacks without a gun first. When you feel that they've learned all they can, go ahead and arm them.

Wait! I thought this was about ranged combat!?

Two feet is a range.

Creative Director Hardy LeBel, who has designed many successful shooters like *Halo: Combat Evolved* and *SOCOM 3*, says that ranged combat is about building a distinctive rhythm. Several factors influence that rhythm, such as targeting methods, reload times, weapon fire rate, weapon accuracy, rate of fire and lethality, the availability of ammunition, the availability of area-of-effect weapons like grenades, player health mechanics, and so on. Even level design, AI behavior, and mechanics contribute to that rhythm. Whew! That's a lot to digest at once, so let's start with the **three A's**: action, aiming, and ammo.

Action is the loading, firing, and unloading of a gun. Here are some questions you need to ask about a weapon's action:

- How quickly can the player reload his gun?

- Does the player need to reload with a button press, or does it occur automatically? You can create some great risk/reward gameplay around reloading a gun because the player is vulnerable during loading (such as in *Gears of War*, where a properly executed manual reload is faster, but a botched one is even slower and leaves the player defenseless for longer).

- Is there a limit to the ammo? Does the player even need to reload the gun at all?

- What is the gun's rate of fire? A faster firing gun is going to use ammo quicker than a single shot weapon. Can the weapon be fired one shot at a time or in bursts?

- Does the firing bloom obscure the player's view?

- Can a shot take out more than one target at a time?

Aiming is how the player sights a target. Aiming is a huge issue in games. It can make or break a shooter. Early shooters relied on the players' reflexes and skill in positioning the cursor over the target and pulling the trigger at the right time. Until *Halo: Combat Evolved* (Microsoft, 2001), most successful first person shooters were played on PCs—partially because of the ease of aiming with a mouse. To help players manage the tricky task of aiming with the Xbox's analog sticks, the game used aim assist such that the cursor became "sticky" when it was moved over a target. This made it easier for the players to lock on to a target. Since *Halo*, other aim assists have been developed, such as **reticule snapping,** in which the reticule immediately snaps to a target if it gets near, and **free-aiming,** in which players can shoot different parts of the target to gain different effects.

No matter what type of aiming method you use (aim assist, auto-aim, free aiming, and so on), you need to design and implement targeting mechanics for the tastes of your target audience:

- How does the player aim? Is there a scope? How much of the player's view does the scope obstruct?

- How does depth of field affect aiming? An effective visual trick is to have far-away objects that are blurry suddenly become clear when viewed through a long-range sight.

- Is aiming manual? Does the gun have drift? Can the player steady her shot? Some games allow the snipers to "hold their breath" to prevent drift. From how far away can a player make a shot?

- Is aiming automatic? Is there a quick-fire mode? Is there an auto-aiming/lock-on system?

- When you fire the gun, does it kick, throwing off the player's aim? Does it rise like a Thompson submachine gun?

- Are there systems to improve the player's aiming such as laser pointers, bullet time, or heat-seeking ammo?

- Can the player move while aiming? Are there limitations to where the player can aim, like diagonally or overhead?

- Does the scope detect other ways of seeing the target such as IR, motion detection, or heartbeat? Can the gun be modified in any way to become silenced or have additional add-on weapons like grenade launchers or bayonets?

- Can the player use shooting for puzzle solving or trick shooting? Shoot targets? Shoot locks off doors? Shoot the gun out of the hands of enemies? Ricochet a bullet into an enemy?

- Can the player disable the targeting mechanism or replace it with another style?

The targeting reticule and/or the iron sights on your weapons should be among the most sophisticated feedback mechanisms in your game. They will likely need to communicate aim, bullet spread, recoil, jamming, overheat, ammo, successful hits versus near misses, friend or foe, and the list goes on and on. And they will need to accomplish that while remaining useful and unobtrusive to the player.

Ammo is what the player shoots. Ammo raises its own questions:

- Where and how is ammo carried? Is there a limit to the amount of ammo carried by a player? Do you need the right ammo for the right gun?

- Does ammo have any special effects like incendiary, poisonous, heat-seeking, or armor-piercing properties?

- What happens when a shot misses a target? Does it impact against something in the environment? Does it affect that item? Break glass? Chip plaster? Ricochet off metal?

SPA-CHOW!

Put that thing away!
You're gonna get us killed!

Here are a few more tricks to make your gunplay more effective:

- Accentuate the excitement and danger of a gunfight with sound: weapon firing, bullet impacts, enemy gunfire, whizzing bullets, and so on.

- Play the SFX of the gunshot and bullet impact at full volume regardless of the target's distance to the player. This will let the player know whether he scored a successful shot. Don't forget to let the player hear his target reacting to being shot.

- Don't forget the weapon visual effects. Muzzle flash, spent shells kicking out, and smoke from the barrel all make the experience more realistic.

- In general, players like gunfights at shorter ranges because they are more exciting. Closer range not only makes it easier for players to aim, but allows them to see if they have successfully hit their target.

- Regardless of how graphic your weapon hits are, show some sort of impact effect when a bullet hits its target—from sparks to explosions to spraying gore.

■ Needless to say, level design IS game design when it comes to building the rhythm of ranged combat. If you design spaces that are long, open corridors and you have a high-lethality combat model, players will play cautiously. If you have lots of cover and break line of sight frequently PLUS use a regenerating health model, gunfights will feel like swirling dogfights as players engage and disengage to heal.

A great deal of time and writing could be dedicated to designing the targeting reticules for shooting, but suffice it to say this **very important thing** applies:

PLAY THE BEST SHOOTERS AND STUDY THEIR SOLUTIONS

Taking some time to deconstruct the mechanics and behaviors of the best-in-breed games will add immeasurably to your own gameplay.

Mr. LeBel leaves us with this important thought: "In general, players expect ranged combat to feel powerful and satisfying. It's an easy mistake to try and make ranged weapons weak to help offset the perception of too much power in the hands of the player; fight that impulse and try to remember to be 'generous' to the player[s], and they will thank you for it."

The Best Gun for You

When you're designing guns, even if you are creating made-up weapons, it's helpful to start with their real-life counterparts; after all, weapons are built for particular roles that can directly apply to their use in your game. But that will get you only halfway there. You should consider thinking about them in terms of effectiveness.

zap pistol = good

zap rifle = better

blazer cannon = best

kill-o-zap = freakin' awesome

But balancing weapons can be tricky, especially if you're basing them on real-world equivalents. There are gun-nut players who have their own opinions about which gun is better and how they should perform. You could go crazy trying to please everyone, so base your weapons on what fits the needs of your game first. Here are some guidelines to get you started:

- **Pistols** fire in a straight line (unless you are that guy from *Wanted*), which will dictate where you can shoot and whom you can shoot. A pistol shoots one enemy at a time unless your ammo pierces several enemies at once! That's going to keep the pace of shooting slow. Pistols usually require frequent reloading too, because their magazines carry from 6 to 15 rounds.

- **Rifles,** especially sniper rifles, mean the player has to aim and shoot. You usually can't fire from the hip with a rifle. That means the player is going to be vulnerable and usually looking down a scope, which means tunnel blindness. Sounds like a good opportunity for an enemy to sneak up. Many rifles carry large quantities of ammo: some have drum magazines that hold up to 100 rounds.

- **Shotguns** and **flamethrowers** fire in a cone, rather than a straight line. The cone is a shorter range than a pistol or rifle but can hit several targets at once. Both weapons do high damage to targets when hit at close range. Shotguns carry less ammo and have a slower rate of fire than guns or rifles, and flamethrowers go through propellant at a fast rate. A flamethrower's blast can be maintained for an extended time and does residual burning damage to an enemy.

- **Automatic weapons** allow you to fire quickly, but accuracy goes out the window. This high rate of fire also uses up ammo fast, regardless of larger magazine sizes. Designing your machine gun to have a little kick, drift, or spray will not only make it feel real, but push the player to master using the weapon accurately. Are your automatic weapons one handed or two? Can the player use two at the same time? This will determine what other actions the player can do while shooting.

- **Heavy weapons** pack a big punch, but usually take a while to warm up or cool down. The Heavy's **minigun** in *Team Fortress 2* takes a few beats to start spinning, but the player has a way to keep the gun spinning even when he isn't shooting with it. The disadvantage is that enemies hear you coming a mile away. **Grenade launchers** are also harder to aim but can do big damage to an enemy when they explode. They also let you shoot at enemies that might be hiding around a corner! There is an element of risk in using a grenade launcher as the projectile bounces around after shooting, which can make things dangerous for the player as well as his target. Magazine sizes vary from a dozen grenades to hundreds of rounds for fast-shooting miniguns. **Rocket launchers** (and their sci-fi cousin, the laser ray) allow the player to make a one-hit kill at the cost of a longer reload or recharge time. They often have limited ammo but work as effectively against armored vehicles as they do troops.

No matter what the weapon, think about its range, speed, and strength. You can use an attack matrix like the following one to track these values and compare and contrast your weapons for maximum variety.

Weapon	Range		
	Short	Medium	Long
Dual pistols	Strong	Weak	N/A
Assault rifle	Strong but slow	Very strong	Weak
Shotgun	Very strong	N/A	N/A
Sniper rifle	N/A	Medium	Very strong

Notice how there is very little overlap in weapon attributes, and any overlap that does exist has a disadvantage like shooting/reloading speed. Keeping the weapons distinct will help in making the game feel well rounded.

Ranged combat weapons aren't always guns. Fantasy games, for example, have a wide variety of projectiles, from arrows to magic missiles to cones of cold. Regardless of the genre, as long as you design your ranged combat with the guidelines set down for guns—range, damage, and the three A's—you should be fine.

One last question to ask in a multiplayer game is whether or not you should allow **friendly fire.** Your choice totally depends on the gameplay mode. Having friendly fire in a player versus player mode seems much more logical than in a cooperative mode. Whatever your choice, allow the player to turn it on or off.

Oh, no. You've just run out of bullets. Now what?

Players feel incredibly powerless when they're playing a shooter and have nothing to shoot with! So give your player a melee weapon that is always available. It can be a knife, fists, or even a pistol whip or clubbing attack with a rifle butt. Giving the player this option to bash the baddie allows things to feel fair and realistic. The *Gears of War* games don't mess around in this department: they have a chainsaw mounted onto their gun!

They say you can never have enough guns, but you don't want your player to be carrying around a golf bag full of firearms. Many games limit weapons to a main gun and a side arm. But if you do that, you'll need to be able to switch between them quickly, preferably with a single button press. *Call of Duty: Modern Warfare 2* allows you to draw your side arm faster than you can raise your rifle, which is helpful for those situations requiring a quick shot.

Since *Gears of War* came out, many action games have incorporated a **cover system.** This allows the player a way not only to take cover against a surface or barricade to avoid being shot, but also to fire "blindly" or in a limited manner at the enemy. The player is often penalized for avoiding risk by not being able to aim while under cover. Cover systems usually require the player to press a button or issue a command to move in and out of this mode. Be careful that your cover system doesn't become too "sticky" so that it takes time and effort for the player to disengage from cover; otherwise, the player may be going into cover when she doesn't want to.

"I was going to wait for him to empty it before I said anything."

Run and Gun

There are many, many ways to shoot at things in video games: from a plane, from a train, out of a box, at a fox—you name it! Take a look at this image of a shooting gallery gameplay and notice all the elements in it:

1. Turret showing weapon and player

2. Shootable object containing reward or power-up

3. Ground-based target

4. Visual element that indicates why the player can't shoot "past the screen"

5. Aerial target (note the clear indication to the player that the target has been hit)

6. Smaller aerial target (generally worth more points)

7. Smaller ground target (also worth more points)

One of the main styles of shooting gameplay is the **shooting gallery.** In some shooting gallery type games, the player is locked to a single screen and lots and lots of enemies and targets come in and out of the screen, as in *Duck Hunt* and *Start the Party*. **Mounted ranged combat** is this kind of shooting gallery-style gameplay, in which the players defend against waves of incoming enemies. Mounted ranged combat can take place in the middle of any-where; it offers a change in gameplay styles and lets players shoot up lots and lots of things. Players will tend to fire constantly if the weapon has unlimited ammo or in short bursts if it doesn't. You can also get the players to fire in bursts if the weapon needs a cool-down time. To help players aim, add tracer bullets. Not only do these bullets look cool, but they will help players get "leads" on fast-moving enemies or ones with erratic movement patterns. Let play-ers know the range of the weapon. If they can't reach a target, create a good visual justifica-tion as to why there are areas of the screen they can't hit.

Because both the target and the weapon move during **aerial combat** and **vehicular combat,** give the players opportunities to line up the target in their sights. If they have a chance to see the target coming, line up the target, and fire at it, they will feel in control. If too many tar-gets whip by the players without giving them a chance to react, they will resort to firing blindly, which will make the experience seem mindless and frustrating. Adjust the speed of the targets or the craft either naturally or artificially to give the players ample shooting opportunities.

Another type of shooting gallery game is the **rail shooter,** in which the player is locked into a scrolling environment where lots and lots of enemies and targets pop up for the player to shoot. Rail shooters take movement (other than aiming and shooting) and camera control out of the player's hands so he can just concentrate on the action—as if the player were mov-ing on a rail, hence the name. Clever, right? Games like *House of the Dead: Overkill* (Sega, 2009) and *The Shoot* (SCEA, 2010) are rail shooters.

A unique advantage of rail shooters is that the game developer has complete control over the game camera and the sequence of events. This allows the developer to create scripted action sequences and scares she knows the player will experience, without worrying about the player moving the camera and missing the cool event.

In fact, some rail shooters bear more resemblance to a theme park **dark ride** like Disneyland's *Haunted Mansion*[6] than a video game. Now, interactive dark rides have started to appear in theme parks around the world,[7] completing the circle of inspiration from dark ride to video game to dark ride.

Speaking of haunted places—mansions or otherwise—if you want to scare players during a rail shooter, or any other type of game for that matter, here are a few tricks you can use:

1. **Let players know they're going to be scared.** Nothing builds fear like anticipation. If they know the game is going to scare them, they will be much more susceptible to being scared.

2. **Don't be afraid to use "cheap scares."** These are things like a banging shutter, a blast of steam, or a jumping cat—a fast-moving distraction will make players jump.

3. **Don't rely solely on darkness.** Players can turn up the contrast. Or play the game in a lit room. There are too many ways players can make your game not-so-scary, so don't rely on just one trick to create mood.

---

[6] This reminds me of the time Disneyland's *Haunted Mansion* literally became a shooter. In the summer of 1974, a Disneyland guest wielding a .22 pistol took a shot at one of the duelist ghosts in the Ballroom scene. The bullet made a hole in the giant pane of glass used to create the scene's pepper ghost illusion. The management was frantic. Originally, a helicopter had been needed to install the giant sheet of glass, and they'd have to rip the ceiling off the ride to replace it. However, a clever imagineer took one look at the spider-web cracks in the glass and slapped a rubber spider over the bullet hole. Voilà, problem solved! The spider is there to this day.

[7] On your next vacation, why not travel the world playing interactive dark rides? *Buzz Lightyear's Space Ranger Spin* (Walt Disney World, Florida), *Men In Black: Alien Attack* (Universal Studios Florida), *Laser Raiders* (Legoland Windsor, UK), *Challenge of Tutankhamen* (Six Flags, Belgium), *Labyrinth of the Minotaur* (Terra Mitica Theme Park, Spain), and *Toy Story Midway Mania* (Disney's California Adventure)—all dark ride rail shooters.

4. **Sound is the scariest thing there is.** A player's mind is your most powerful weapon against him. Use sound to make players think there are things that aren't there, and soon enough they'll be jumping at any stray noise. It's even worse when they have to rely on sound to tell if something is coming, like the radio in *Silent Hill*.

5. **Don't stack scares.** If you constantly try to scare players, they aren't going to have time to relax. Only when they've relaxed between scares are they ready to be scared again. It's like a roller coaster: the lows are just as important as the highs.

6. **You can be gross, but don't be too gross.** Dead bodies and bloody or dirty environments in video games are missing two of the most important things that make them gross: touch and smell. If you rely too much on vile environments, players are going to get used to them. A small splash of blood in the middle of an otherwise clean room has far more impact than a room decorated with bodies that are strung up like Christmas ornaments.

7. **Boo!** (Did I scare you?) Nothing gets the blood going like something unexpectedly rushing in or leaping out at the players. If you really want to mess with the players' minds, let them hear a distinctive sound first before the scare happens. They'll get used to hearing that sound and start to panic when they hear it. Panicking almost certainly leads to player death.

Speaking of scares, when designing shooting gallery gameplay, you should give players time to recognize the threat, aim at the target, and shoot at it. Enemies and targets can appear at close range, which surprises players, or long range, which gives players a chance to anticipate and aim at a target. Alternating between these two distances will make a shooting gallery more robust.

Not Just Shooting

You don't really need a gun or melee weapon to defeat enemies. There are so many ways; one hardly knows what to choose! The more variety you introduce into your combat, the more fun the players will have.

When players are throwing **grenades,** allow them to predict the arc. *Gears of War* and the *Uncharted* series use "throw path" targeting aids to assist players. Don't neglect the effects when those suckers blow. When you blow up anything in a game, kick up dust and debris and blow props sky high to really sell the explosion.

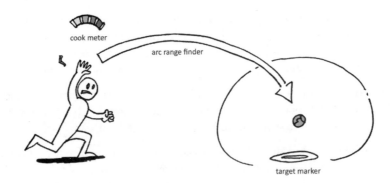

Throwing a grenade should always carry the risk or reward of having it accidently go off if held for too long or even bounce back at the player. Soldiers "cook" their grenades by holding on to them after pulling the pin to make sure they go off where they land. *Call of Duty: Modern Warfare* not only uses a HUD element to warn players of an incoming grenade, but allows players to pick it up and throw it back! Remember that grenades can also be shot from rifles and launchers for greater accuracy and range.

Because many players duck back under cover after throwing a grenade, make sure you provide enough sound, visual, and controller rumble cues to inform players when a grenade detonates, even if they aren't looking at the place where it landed. If players get too close to an exploding grenade, don't hesitate to blow them up as well.

Sometimes you just need to blow up everything. It doesn't matter whether you're calling it carpet bombing or a magical meteor storm; **smart bombs** are great one-shot solutions to keep the baddies off your back, if only for a few seconds. Show players the controls for a smart bomb so they don't confuse it with a regular attack. When activated, smart bombs should destroy everything on-screen save the player. If there are destructible items, they should blow up too.

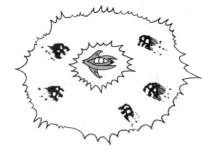

You have a few options for ways players can activate a smart bomb, depending on how much tension you want to create. In *Defender*, the smart bomb is immediate, whereas in *R-Type*, players have to charge up the smart bomb before firing it. Let players know what they are working toward so they can make an accurate decision as to when to use it. Be careful that you don't let the bomb charge up too fast or be used too frequently; otherwise, all the bad guys in your carefully designed combat encounters will be wiped out in the blink of an eye!

Wherever there are explosions, there is **fire.** Sometimes there's fire even without the explosions—things just need to be burned. Fire creates great-looking visuals and lingering damage to enemies and environments. But fire takes no sides: players should get hurt by fire if they stray into it. The fire should eventually burn out so that players don't paint themselves into a napalm-colored corner.

Fire also means flamethrowers. The closer players are to the enemy, the more damage a flamethrower should do. Flamethrowers are the weapon of choice for players who don't like to aim. Allow them to "fire and forget" or "hose down" enemies with flame. Burning damage allows players an opportunity to turn away from one threat and address another. That doesn't mean they can't be attacked by a flaming enemy, however.

Don't forget to use fire-based weapons as a gameplay mechanic too. Flaming swords and other weapons don't just do extra damage to ice-themed enemies; they can ignite braziers, detonate explosives, burn through rope, illuminate dark areas, or cauterize wounds. The gameplay possibilities are nearly endless.

Another lingering indirect attack is **poison.** Make sure you have an associated visual for poisoned items. A green gassy effect, a dripping blade, a hovering "death's head" effect—all are traditional video game indicators of poison. Players should be able to tell when they are wielding a poisoned item or have poisoned an enemy—make the visual unique and distinct. As a poisoned character loses health, make sure each increment that the poison takes has a clear sound effect and visual effect associated with it. You are creating a timer in which the players' focus will shift from regular gameplay to "find and administer the antidote." If the antidote is an inventory-based item, don't make it too hard for players to retrieve it. Even if poison is uncommon, make the antidote more common. There is no worse feeling in a video game than making players feel like death is inevitable. Always give them a fighting chance.

Another horrible feeling for players is to take away their control. While **stunning, knock-back, transformation, loss of balance,** and **sliding** are worthwhile tools to use in lieu of taking damage, the designer should use them judiciously.

- **Stun**—When hit by a stun, the player loses all control of the character for a short period of time, usually leaving the character in danger of being hit by an enemy attack or finishing move. Stuns are usually accompanied by visual (like cartoony stars or "tweeting birds") and sound effects.

- **Knockback**—The player is knocked back through the air a short distance and then falls to the ground. A knockback (or KB) can be lethal if a player is on a platform or next to a ledge. Be careful not to put the player into a situation in which he can be "double bolted"[8] by KBs.

- **Knockdown**—The player is knocked to the ground, which requires a second or two to get back up. While on the ground, the player is vulnerable to additional attacks. In some games, getting back up is automatic; in others it requires button mashing, stick waggling, or a QTE.

- **Latching on**—An enemy grabs or latches on to the player, pinning his arms and restricting his movement. Enemies can cause damage for every second they are latched on. Enemies can be shaken off by waggling the controls or performing jump or spin moves.

stunned   knockback   knockdown   grabbed   transformed   off-balance

---

[8] The term "double bolting" comes from the LEGO video games when a player is hit by an enemy and loses bolts, the game's unit of currency. The bolts disappear if not collected after a period of time. However, in some situations, the player is knocked by an enemy into another hazard or enemy, which causes more bolts to fly out of the player. The player is stunned by the attack and cannot regain control fast enough to collect any of the first bolts before they disappear, let alone the ones that were just knocked out of him. Thus, the player loses double the bolts from the initial attack.

- **Transformation**—The player has been hit by a magic spell that transforms the character into some other form. In *Ghosts 'N Goblins*, Arthur turned into a frog. In *Maximo: Ghosts to Glory*, the hero could be transformed into a hopping old man and a tottering baby. In all cases, the player's move set becomes limited; he cannot attack or jump and, in some cases, loses almost all control. During a transformation, game controls can be reversed to sow player confusion (for example, push controls left and the character moves right). While players might find this funny or surprising, I recommend ending the transformation quickly as the novelty wears off after the player loses control. Reserve transformations for special occasions because the players will tire of them if used too often.

- **Loss of balance**—This animation is used as a teeter move. The player briefly loses complete control as the character reacts to losing her balance. This works well as an indicator rather than a disabling move.

- **Sliding/skidding**—After a run, dash, or jump move, the character slides to regain her balance. While this animation adds quite a bit of personality to the character, it can be annoying, especially when it happens several times in a row as the player struggles to bring the character to a stop. Like a KB, a skid can slide a character right off the edge of a narrow platform.

Don't let enemies have all the fun! Design enemy-disabling attacks to give your players the advantage in combat. Use caution when creating attacks with these types of results, however. Consider what they add to the gameplay. Tell yourself this **very important thing:**

ALWAYS STRIVE TO ENABLE THE PLAYERS, EVEN WHEN YOU'RE DISABLING THEM

Remember, don't let enemies have all the fun! Design enemy-disabling attacks to give your players the advantage in combat. They'll thank you for it.

Dang it, Jones! Where *Doesn't* It Hurt?

For all this combat to mean anything, the player must have something to lose. That means **health** and **lives.**

To calculate the player's starting health, I suggest calculating in terms of the maximum damage the player can take. For example, at the beginning of the game, your hero can take 20 hits from enemies before losing a life and without replenishing health. Next, determine how much damage an average enemy's attack does. In this example, a normal hit will cause 10 **hit points** of damage. That means the player's starting health should be 10 × 20 hit points = 200 health.

There are many ways to represent losing that health to the player. **Numbers** are simple and transparent but boring. They stand out against cluttered HUDs, like those found in MMOs and RPGs. Just keep the font legible.

A **health bar** doesn't take much space running along the top or side of the screen. It can be framed with themed artwork to make it look more interesting and part of the HUD. However, telling when small amounts of damage have been taken can be difficult. A health bar can be segmented for readability.

If you're feeling artistic, **icons** can represent the player's health with simple visuals: human outlines that go from green to red (*WWE Smackdown*), crystal globes of blood (*Diablo*), or hearts (*Legend of Zelda*).

Some platform games use a **companion character** as the player's health meter. For example, *Crash Bandicoot* is followed by a tiki head that loses feathers with each hit the player takes. The problem with this system is that it cannot support a large amount of health.

Things are more direct with **character-based health** systems. *Ghosts 'N Goblins* represents health with armor that pops off the player. *Dead Space* and *Ghostbusters* have status meters as part of the character's armor or equipment. The characters of *Resident Evil* clutch their midsections and limp when they've taken damage. Many car combat and driving games show visible damage to the vehicle. You know your car is close to exploding in *Grand Theft Auto* when you are dragging a bumper and your engine is smoking! Whatever method you use, you need to have some sort of feedback: players can't always keep their eyes on the health bar, so these character-based feedback mechanisms make it possible for players to gauge how close to death or restart they are. They can then adjust their strategy (retreat, heal themselves, and so on) based on this knowledge. Just make sure these systems don't interfere with the character's movement or attacks.

(That Elf needs food badly!)

Many modern games have moved toward a **HUD-less health system.** As the player takes damage, the screen becomes splattered with blood, which gets thicker as more damage is taken. More dramatic effects, like turning the whole screen blood red, monochromatic, or blurry, can be used too. Sound and music can drop off and be replaced by heavy breathing and a heartbeat.

Other systems that defy classification have shown up over the years. In *Sonic the Hedgehog*, as long as the player held one collectable ring, he could not be killed. Or at the other end of the scale, *Bushido Blade 2* featured one-hit kill attacks, so the health bar was completely dropped.

Players can regain health with the aid of power-ups, increases in level or experience, and even time. *Halo: Combat Evolved* pioneered the concept of regenerating health in first-person shooters. As long as the player wasn't taking damage, the health meter would refill at a slow but steady rate. The *Ratchet and Clank* games ditched health altogether because the developer wanted the player to reach the end of the game, not constantly see a Game Over screen.

Whatever method of displaying health is used, players should clearly know when they are getting hurt and losing health. Don't skimp on the dramatic animations and particle effects. Both a **hit sound effect** and a **vocal reaction** ("ow!" "oomph!" and so on) should play. Health should deplete in a very obvious manner because with every hit players are closer to losing their lives.

Death: What Is It Good For?

Some game designers think that **lives** and the **Game Over screen** are outmoded concepts.

When video games first arrived, their goal was to suck quarters as fast as possible out of players' pockets. The best way to achieve that was to make players want to keep playing despite being killed as often as possible. Additional lives became a good short-term goal for players to keep in the game. When game characters became little people in lieu of blips and spaceships, the concept of dying came with them. (After all, a spaceship doesn't die, does it?) The emotional impact of the finality of dying (Unless . . . Quick! Get that next quarter into the slot!) was too good to pass up. When games moved to home systems, lives followed—but the players had paid for their game, and there were no more quarters to gain. So why kill players?

Another problem with killing off players often is that it discourages players from continuing the game fairly. If players are threatened with the loss of equipment, skills or money by dying, they will just revert back to an earlier save point. For example, players of *Doom* (id,1993) found that it was easier to restart the game from a saved file than it was from an in-game checkpoint. By using this exploit, players ceased to worry about death and never even saw the game over screen.

Many developers have caught on to this workaround and abandoned the concept of player lives. Instead of killing players and ending the game, players are reset to checkpoints within the level, where they can keep trying over and over until they succeed. In *Prince of Persia: The Sands of Time*, players can "rewind time" to a point where the character is safe. This type of mechanic has to be carefully implemented, though; it is possible for players to get into a situation in which they can't rewind far enough to avoid death and would die all over again. A narrator tells players "that's not how the story happened" before the character restarts from a checkpoint. In *Batman: Arkham Asylum*, players are given a chance to save the caped crusader from a fall to death by pressing a QTE button. If they are successful, Batman climbs back up to safety.

Lives and **Game Over screens** are necessary for many genres such as survival horror and first person shooters. If you *have* to kill your character, remember the following:

- Let players know that they have lives and that they will be lost. Players become protective of their character and will fear for their safety.

- Display lives clearly in the HUD. Make it clear when the character is losing a life.

- Allow players plenty of opportunities to regain lives. These opportunities can happen during level-ups or be power-ups or rewards for collecting objects.

- When killing a player character, do it quickly. Don't create a long, drawn-out death animation that players have to watch over and over again when things get hard in the game.

- The same goes for Game Over screens. Don't make players sit through long death sequence cutscenes. Make the path to restarting gameplay after death as quick as possible.

- When killing a character, make it as violent as your rating allows. Let players really feel some pain when it happens. Empathy toward the game character will motivate players towards self-preservation.

- If players earn something during one life, don't double punish them by taking it away from them when they lose that life.

- If killing the character during a boss round, don't make players have to play the whole sequence all over again. Why not let them continue on with the fight as if nothing ever happened, or only punish them with a little bit of boss health regained?

- That said, the threat of death is a great motivator for players to do better and learn that skill or control. Just use this power judiciously, okay? I trust you.

- If using alternative death systems, such as the player dying if his NPC partner dies, make it clear that (a) players need to protect the partner character with their lives, and (b) they will die if they don't.

Think very carefully about using lives in your game. If you don't think killing players will make the game experience better or more exciting, or you think it will actually be more frustrating, don't do it. Because this **very important thing** applies:

YOU WANT TO KEEP THEM PLAYING

Never give players a good reason to stop. Once you've lost them, you may never get them back. Instead of a Game Over screen, why not create a **"keep going" screen**? When a player dies or leaves the game, show a preview of the next level; the next story point; or the next treasure item, weapon, or power-up? Give players a sneak peek to get them so excited that they won't want to stop playing!

Conflict Without Combat

Although many critics of video games claim all games all super-violent, nothing could be further from the truth. For every *Splatterhouse*, there is a *Braid*. For every *Manhunt*, there is *The Act*. For every *Mortal Kombat*, there is a *Katamari Damancy*. In truth, the super-violent games are the exception, not the rule. And that's not counting the hundreds of thousands of puzzle games, music games, sports games, adventure games, farming games . . . to name just a few. However, these games do need conflict. Programmer John Rose states that the cornerstone of conflict is tension . . . and release.[9] Here are a few ways to interject some conflict into a game without a trigger being pulled or a punch being thrown:

- **Timer**—Whether you have to race against time to find a hidden object, assemble a puzzle, or drive a lap around a track, nothing gets the heart beating like a ticking clock. Make sure your clock allows players just enough time to get the task done. Don't force your players to be perfect to the second because, odds are, they won't be. I have quit playing many a game because of a timer that didn't give me a fair amount of time.

- **Speed**—If you want to make things tenser, just make the game go faster. *Tetris* is the king of racking up tension using speed. The further the player progresses, the faster the pieces drop. This was a common trick back in the days of arcade games when the code could make moves faster than the human player ever could. Go too fast, and it feels unfair to players.

- **Limited options**—Limit the number of moves players can make, or allow them to move their pieces only in a limited capacity—like in *Chess*. Limited options will force players to start thinking strategically because every move counts.

- **Limited space**—If players can move only within a limited area, they will have to be extra careful with their movements, making the tension rise. However, you must make sure there is a little room for mistakes, even if players don't realize it's there.

- **Precision**—Precision can create tension, and often players will mess up if they have to be too precise. Rhythm games often use precision as a way to make players sweat.

- **Moral dilemmas**—We talked about this issue in Level 9. Making players choose between right and wrong or even two different options when both paths are clear to the players will really drive up the tension. They spend the rest of the game wondering what would have happened if they had taken the "other path."

- **Cost**—When players have to start thinking about what things cost, they feel pressure to spend their money wisely. Make sure players have lots of choices and limited finances so the decision becomes even more excruciating. Of course, every choice should have its pros and cons.

Now that I've covered all types of fighting and conflict, it's time to look at who is causing all this trouble: enemies!

[9] John Rose, "Addressing Conflict: Tension and Release in Games," 2010, www.starming.com/index.php?action=plugin&v=wave&tpl=union&ac=viewgrouppost&gid=56&tid=8033

Level 10's Universal Truths and Clever Ideas

- Be mindful of ESRB guidelines when creating violent gameplay.
- Violence is all about context: a violent act is going to feel more violent if it is the player who does it.
- Give your character a signature attack or weapon.
- Create an attack matrix to track your combat moves and reactions.
- People want to play games that make them look cool.
- Use a lock-on system to enable players during combat.
- Close battles are more exciting.
- Use QTEs to heighten combat drama, but don't overdo them because they get old.
- Fighting enemies is supposed to be fun.
- Be aware of the three As when designing projectile combat.
- Use attacks to hamper and incapacitate players rather than kill.
- Make it clear to players that they have taken damage.
- Always strive to enable players even when disabling them.
- Keep the players playing.
- You can add conflict without having combat.

Level 11
They All Want You Dead

Video games are populated with a plethora of beings that want to kill you: aliens and androids, pirates and parasites, mercenaries and mushroom people. However, I realize not every video game features slobbering, sword-wielding enemies—often they use guns too!

Yes, yes. I realize that plenty of other video games use other forms of conflict, such as time, human competitors, or even the players' own skill, to challenge the players. But I'm not talking about those types of games.[1] As I flip back to Level 3, I am reminded of three types of conflict found in stories: **man versus nature** (like a hurricane or a giant white whale); **man versus self** (where the hero is struggling with an internal issue such as "where to go for lunch"[2]); and **man versus man**, or in the case of video games, man versus zombie or man versus ninja pirate or man versus hideous-alien-creature-made-from-the-skins-of-your-dead-crewmates.

Those are the types of enemies I talk about here. While zombies and ninja pirates and alien thingee enemies are great fun to design, you first need to follow this **very important** golden rule:

FORM FOLLOWS FUNCTION

Hey! I saw you trying to design that winged skeleton enemy without thinking about how he's going to attack.[3] Put down the pencil as I repeat myself because **THIS REALLY IS VERY IMPORTANT:**

FORM FOLLOWS FUNCTION!

You *need* to (not "would kinda like to") determine the function of your enemies first. So many things are resting on the decisions in your design: how the programmer will code it, how the animator will build the rigging model, how the artist will texture it. These important enemy attributes are

- Size
- Behavior
- Speed
- Movement
- Attacks

---

[1] Yet.

[2] I have seen large groups of full-grown people completely paralyzed by this internal conflict.

[3] He does look pretty awesome though.

- **Aggression**[4]
- **Health**

All these attributes, along with your level's theme, will allow you to determine who your enemies are, what they will end up looking like, and how well they will work together when they are placed in the game. Having to redo an enemy character again and again and again is a big morale killer for your team and a huge waste of time and money.[5]

Sizing Up the Enemy

Speaking of huge, enemies come in a wide range of **sizes:**

Short enemies are no taller than the player character's waist.

Average enemies are roughly the same height as the player character.

Large enemies are several heads taller than the player character.[6]

Huge enemies are at least twice the player character's own size.

Gigantic enemies are so large that they can be completely seen only from a distance.

short   average   large   huge

---

[4] I realize that aggression is considered part of behavior, but because designers often treat combat as its own system, it deserved its own heading.

[5] And irresponsible. Please do not be an irresponsible designer.

[6] Artists measure characters in terms of "heads"—literally the height of one average human head. For example, an average six-foot human is seven heads tall, whereas a heroic character is eight-and-a-half heads tall.

The size of the enemy will determine how the player will fight it. For example, a short enemy can be fought only by crouching or with a low attack like an upward sweep or radial spin attack. On the other end of the scale, a huge enemy with a vulnerable head can be reached only with a jump attack. Design your combat so the player character "fights his way up" the enemy: the player character should be able to hit an average enemy using a low or medium attack; the player character should be able to hit a huge enemy using a low, medium, or high attack; and so on.

Hey!
Quit it, you
big bully!

Size also influences health. Larger enemies traditionally have more health (are harder to kill) than smaller ones. This might account for why many bosses are so darn big. Size will also dictate the enemies' reaction to attacks. Hit a short enemy with a knockback attack, and he should go flying. Hit a large enemy with the same attack, and he may not even budge. You'd be lucky if a gigantic enemy even notices your attack, let alone reacts to it.

They say variety is the spice of life. I don't know about spice, but I do know it is variety that keeps a player from getting bored. Size can influence a player's emotions too. Defeating a huge enemy can make a player feel heroic, whereas defeating a short one can make him feel like a bully.

Bad Behavior

Now that you've determined size, ask yourself, what is the enemy's **behavior?**

- How does the enemy move?

- What does the enemy do when in combat?

- What does the enemy do when he is hurt?

Answer these questions, and you will have the foundation to build robust enemies. When you are designing enemy behavior, the goal is to not have different enemy characters repeat the same behaviors. Even better, design your enemies' behaviors to complement each other.

A **patroller** moves back and forth or up and down in a mechanical fashion. The path of movement can be more involved than this, but the movement is always predictable.

A **chaser** pursues a player if approached or some other condition is met. In many games, patrollers can turn into chasers when they see the player or the player attacks them.

A **shooter** is an enemy that fires a projectile. Shooting patrollers and chasers will fire at the player once they've been spotted. Due to the nature of the attack, this enemy will try to keep distance between himself and the player rather than engage him.

A **guard** is an enemy whose AI priority is to guard an item or location (like a doorway) rather than actively pursue the player. Guard behavior can be easily combined with chasing or shooting if the player manages to steal the item or get past the guard.

A **flyer** is an enemy that, well . . . flies. Flyers are aerial patrollers, but because the flying adds another dimension (literally) to the movement, these characters deserve their own classification. Flyers can swoop down to attack players, or they can fire projectiles from a safe distance. Flyers are more advanced enemies for the player to deal with because their movement and attack patterns can be difficult to predict. Players trying to attack flyers usually stop to target or make a jump attack.

A **bomber** is a flyer that attacks from above. Give the player warning that a bomber is above to drop down (or drop its payload) so it doesn't come as a nasty surprise. In a game that uses a third-person camera, bombers can be difficult for a player to see as they fly above the player to attack.

A **burrower** is an enemy with an invulnerable state that allows him to get into an advantageous position to attack the player. The player must wait for the enemy to emerge before he can attack.

A **teleporter** is an enemy that can change position around the playfield. The player must attack quickly lest the enemy teleport out of harm's way. The teleporter varies from the burrower in that the teleportation is instantaneous, giving the player no time to attack. Give your player a way to disrupt the enemy's teleportation, such as a stun or another disruptive attack.

A **blocker** is an enemy that defends himself against the player's attack with a shield or other defensive device. The shield can either be circumnavigated with an attack from another direction or elevation (such as from down low or from behind), or the player can disarm the enemy with a specific move or attack. Shields can make the enemy temporarily invulnerable, requiring the player to break the shield with a specific move or action, or wait around until the invulnerable state passes.

A **doppelganger** is an enemy that looks like the player; he moves, attacks, and uses AI that mimics the player's own. Doppelganger enemies force players to use moves or weapons in an unusual manner in order to defeat "themselves."

The goal of having all these different behavior types is to have enemies that complement each other. Enemies should "live harmoniously" with each other, creating interesting combat challenges for the players to solve.

Once you create enemy behaviors that work well together, it will create gameplay. In dealing with these enemy combinations, players will learn how to perform **threat analysis.** They'll find that sometimes it's easy to take out the weak enemies first and other times it will be better to tackle the deadlier foe and ignore the little guys. As a designer, you can force the player to make these kinds of interesting decisions during combat.

Here are a few interesting enemy combinations that I've found work well together:

- A blocker with a shooter positioned behind him. As the player tries to whittle down the blocker, the shooter is taking pot-shots at the player.

- A big chaser and a group of smaller flyers. While the player goes after the big guy, the little guys attack. However, if the player leaves the big guy alone and goes after the flyers, he's gonna get thumped.

- A teleporter and a chaser. As the player tries to catch the teleporter, he leaves himself open to the chaser's attacks.

- A guard and a bomber. While the player is tied up with the guard, the bomber attacks from above.

How Rapid is Rapid?

Depending on **speed** and **movement,** an enemy can be more dangerous, harder to target, and more frightening. Use the different speeds **stationary, slow, medium, fast,** and **quick** for your enemies.

The difference between a hazard and an enemy is mobility and AI, but every rule has its exceptions. Just because an enemy is **non-mobile** doesn't mean he can't move. Movement = character and life. A humongous Cthulhu-esque creature may be to too big to walk or fly around, but players would still consider him an enemy. Even an "inanimate object" like a turret can be smart enough to make life difficult for players. Design ways to keep players engaged as they attack non-mobile enemies, whether it's a timing puzzle that stands between the enemy and the players, or even a puzzle that's part of the enemy itself.

TK-421
Don't just stand
there,get him!

The speed, size, and strength[7] of an enemy are inversely proportional: small enemies are fast but not strong, big enemies are strong but are not fast. Medium-sized enemies can be either strong or fast, but if you give them both attributes, they end up feeling **"cheap"** because they've been given an advantage that the player cannot match. Whenever an enemy is extremely overpowered or too perfect at making attacks, it feels as though the player is fighting artificial intelligence rather than an actual living creature.

But I digress.

Slow enemies work best when there are lots of them. One zombie isn't very threatening, but a dozen of the slow-moving undead can make even the most stalwart hero a little nervous. Often, a slow enemy packs a big wallop: if players get hit, it's their own darn fault. Or you can give a slow-moving enemy a fast attack to keep players on their toes. Slow enemies often have built-in defenses, allowing them to brace themselves against a player's attack or casually

---

[7] Hey! It's the three Ss!

swat him aside. If you want your enemies to feel powerful, have them move slowly like the Tyrant, Nemesis, and Dr. Salvador from the *Resident Evil* series. The inevitability of the bad guy advancing on the hero can make the player panic and make fatal mistakes.

Medium speed is just what it sounds like: the speed of the enemy's movement and attacks will likely match the player's own speed. Medium speed may be a little predictable, but it's useful for most situations. I've found it's helpful to make medium-speed enemies run slightly slower than the player character, especially when chasing him. This allows the player to retreat at running speed if necessary without fear of getting cut down from behind. The player can then reorient himself and face the enemy in time to deliver an attack or effectively defend. It's OK to tweak speed values here and there to get the effect you want. There's no hard and fast rule when it comes to this; you've just got to do what feels right and fair.

Fast enemies either dart forward to quickly strike and back away, or they move quickly around and then jump in to do multiple attacks. Fast enemies work great in horror and action games. Players will have less time to react to an incoming enemy and may panic and make dumb mistakes—until they learn to keep their cool. However, don't make fast enemies constantly attack the players because they get frustrated by getting hit by something they can't hit back—unless this is the strategy you want. The smaller the enemies, the quicker they are. Give fast-moving enemies an erratic movement pattern to give your players a real challenge.

Quick enemies move in bursts. They can move blindingly fast—so fast that it may seem unfair to players, but you can balance that by limiting their attacks and moves. Help players see quick moves coming by playing a warning animation. This will allow players to dodge, block, or strike before an enemy completes its quick move.

Movement Style

What is your enemy's **movement style?** Does your enemy charge the player like an angry bull? Does he zigzag erratically to avoid taking fire? Does he make a beeline and then retreat? Does he jump from cover to cover? Does he crawl on the walls to ambush the player from above? Does he run away and never fight at all?[8] Knowing your enemy's movement styles will not only determine his attacks but also his personality.

Determine whether your enemy moves randomly or predictably. Avoid extremes and insert variety. Too random and the player might feel the enemy moves too arbitrarily. Too predictable and an enemy feels too "game-y."

The best solution doesn't include unpredictability. For *Crash Bandicoot 2,* Naughty Dog tried creating more behavioral AI with fewer simple patterns. Focus groups found them inferior. The players liked the challenge of figuring out the enemy's patterns. On the flipside, players like unpredictability in sports games. Predictable patterns become "holes" for players to exploit, which ruins the realism of the experience.

Coordinating several enemies' movements adds complexity. Consider how your enemies behave and group together during a fight. Some enemies can use flocking behavior to create realistic group movement.

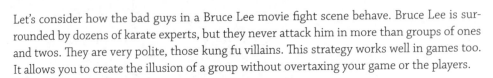

Look at the movement behaviors of different animals, birds, and insects for inspiration. Humans usually move in straight lines. Predatory mammals like wolves and tigers move in looping arcs as they circle their prey. Crabs move sideways rather than straight ahead. Birds fly in swooping patterns as they catch updrafts to aid their flight. Insects zigzag as they course-correct during flight. Giving your enemies different movement patterns will make them feel more realistic.

Let's consider how the bad guys in a Bruce Lee movie fight scene behave. Bruce Lee is surrounded by dozens of karate experts, but they never attack him in more than groups of ones and twos. They are very polite, those kung fu villains. This strategy works well in games too. It allows you to create the illusion of a group without overtaxing your game or the players.

---

[8] Personally, I think enemies are more fun when you can fight them.

This might go better
if we all went at once...

Work with your programmer to create **pathing AI.** Determine the needs of your enemies to figure out how they are going to move around. Here are some questions that you should address when creating pathing and behavior AI:

- **How mobile are your enemies?** Do they have more than one movement speed? Can they can break into a run or slide to a stop? Do they leap over obstacles or use doors?

- **How aggressive are your enemies?** Fast-moving frothing berserkers or slowly advancing stone-cold killers? Enemies can even be cautious or cowardly, afraid to get hurt or die. Giving enemies a sense of self-preservation makes them feel like real people.

- **How much like team players are your enemies?** Do your enemies raise the alarm and alert other enemies to assist them? Will they try to keep a player pinned down while another closes in for a melee attack or better shot? Will they try to flush a player into the open where another enemy will have the advantage? Will one grab and grapple the player while another attacks? Do they have a "partner," like a guard dog or attack drone?

- **How defensive are your enemies?** Do they crouch or duck behind objects? Do they use cover or hold the line? Do they act stealthily when they spot a player? Do they try to attack from behind and sneak up on a player? Do they have defensive items like shields or defense systems?

- **How versatile are your enemies?** Can they pick up and use dropped weapons or health? Do they drive vehicles or man weapon emplacements? Can they take over functions for other enemies if they are killed? Can they fly or use non-ground-based movement?

Most AI characters use a **waypoint navigation system** to move around. The designer lays out a grid or path that determines where the AI moves. As the AI moves, the programmer can determine what movement and animations are played to create specific AI behavior. Areas can be designated as "go" or "no-go" areas based on world geometry or to achieve a specific AI behavior.

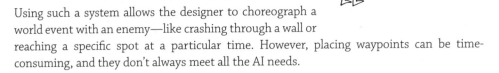

All this means is that your bad guys either travel along a preplanned network of paths or wander around within the confines of an invisible box (or sphere).

Using such a system allows the designer to choreograph a world event with an enemy—like crashing through a wall or reaching a specific spot at a particular time. However, placing waypoints can be time-consuming, and they don't always meet all the AI needs.

Because most waypoint-guided enemies are programmed to determine the shortest and quickest path to the player, be careful of enemies clipping corners and objects. You can fix this issue by tweaking your waypoint paths. Pull the waypoints in a bit at corners or near objects to compensate for this movement.

Bring on the Bad Guys

The player is walking through a graveyard winding his way through the tombstones when he sees a skeleton blocking his path, ready to fight.

Wait a second. Rewind. There's a much more dramatic way to introduce this bad guy into your world.

The player is walking through a graveyard, winding his way through the tombstones. One of them shakes as he passes by. Suddenly, the camera zooms in on the player's face as the screen shakes and the controller rumbles. The camera whip-pans around to a grave as a bony hand thrusts out of the ground! The tombstone shatters into a million shards as a skeleton warrior bursts from the grave, its eyes glowing evilly and bony fingers clenched, ready to fight!

Now that's exciting!

Enemy introductions are a really effective way to tell players that they've encountered something new, exciting, and dangerous:

- Freeze the camera or zoom in on the creature: let players get a good look at what's about to kick their butt!

- Display the name of the enemy on-screen. Players like to put a name to an enemy.

- Foreshadow what will happen. *Resident Evil 2* provides a great "what the heck was that?" moment when a licker enemy runs past a window right before the player encounters him. Foreshadowing builds up suspense for the moment when the licker actually appears to the player. Make it an event!

- Introduce your enemies in a very dramatic way. Have them smash through a window, kick down a door, blast into the world in an explosion of special effects—anything to let your bad guys make a good first impression!

Keep in mind, not all games warrant an enemy introduction. Players of a multiplayer games wouldn't want their own game play stopped while the introduction occurs. (Maybe they would if they could attack the player who is watching the introduction!)

Spawning enemies into the world is just as important as removing them. You want to make sure that players aren't able to slaughter the enemies before they get a chance to arrive on the scene. Some games make enemies invulnerable upon spawning or have them spawn from off-screen where players can't reach them. You may consider creating a hazard or mechanic that allows enemies to spawn on the playfield without getting killed.

In *Maximo: Ghosts to Glory,* we created coffins that burst through the ground to deliver enemies into the world. If the player collided with them, he would be knocked backwards. If he swung at them, he would shatter the coffin, but the enemy inside wouldn't be hurt and would start attacking. We wanted to make sure the enemy survived entering the world long enough to fight the player.

Why go through all this trouble? Because of this **very important thing:**

FIGHTING ENEMIES IS SUPPOSED TO BE FUN!

Before I forget, here's another **very important thing:**

ENEMIES SHOULD BE FOUGHT, NOT AVOIDED

I'm not talking about enemies that you have to dodge out before they hit you during a fight. No. I'm talking about the "this enemy is too hard, too cheap, too much of a hassle to fight so I don't want to fight him" type of enemy. And yet, I always see the following type of enemy in a game:

Some days you can't get rid of a bomb!

This enemy has a bomb or some other explosive device. The enemy runs toward the player. If the player doesn't get exploded, he will run away. Although this might sound exciting, in my experience this type of enemy always causes problems.

When the player runs, if the game is in third person, the camera tends to flip around to show the back of the player. In first person, the player can't even see the enemy following him. In either case, the player can't see the enemy at all. When the enemy explodes, it comes as a nasty surprise. Sure, you can give the player a warning with a HUD or in-game warning indicator, but in the end, you are going to design all kinds of stop-gap measures to help the player spot the enemy—but then that kind of defeats the purpose of the enemy, doesn't it? Ultimately, this kind of explodey enemy just isn't very good design.

In an action game, you are going to be fighting a lot of enemies, so do whatever you can to make the action **awesome**! Explosive effects, funny or dramatic hit reaction animations, cool and/or gory kills and, of course, lots of feedback and rewards.[9] Why fight enemies?

- **They have the loot.** Gold, items, bolts, experience points, health—it doesn't matter what it is as long as they have it and you want it.

---

[9] I talk about how to make the most of rewards in Level 13.

- **They block the path.** You can block the player artificially to force a fight, like a battle arena.

- **They have the key.** And you need that key to get through the gate that leads to the next room, section, or level. I've always wondered: why is it the last enemy you fight is always the one who is holding the key?

- **You need to take their power.** Tired of getting shot at? Defeat those enemies and take their bigger, better guns! Want to upgrade your +1 mace to a +2? You're going to have to fight that orc to get it!

- **They're making fun of you.** Taunts are a great way to motivate players into fighting. Having enemies taunt or challenge players if they're standing still for too long not only can force a player into attacking, but also is a great way to get some character into the enemies. Taunts work great in multiplayer fighting games like *Street Fighter* where the player takes a risk by taking a break from combat or defense to mock his opponent.

- **It's fun to fight.** Nothing will keep a player fighting more than having a solid combat system. To achieve that, see Level 10.

Don't forget to let enemies have a chance to be bad too! Give your enemies some sweet attacks like these:

- **Melee attacks**—Do they use hands/claws/tentacles/feet? Do they have raking attacks or punches? Do they know martial arts? Can they grab or ensnare? Can they perform throws? Can they "ground pound" or cause earthquake attacks?

- **Weapon combat**—Do they use weapons? One-handed or two-handed weapons? Are they barbaric or skilled fighters? Can they disarm or be disarmed by the players? Can their weapon be used by the players? Can the weapon extend, be thrown, or boomerang?

- **Projectile combat**—Do they use guns/magic spells/ranged weapons? How accurate are they with their attacks? Will they blindly fire or wait for the perfect shot? Do they track movement or lead when aiming? Do they need to reload? Is their projectile explosive? Can they be disarmed? Do they have a close-range melee attack if engaged or disarmed?

- **Persistent damage**—Does your enemies' attack have a side effect like acid/poison/fire? Does it do damage with the attack or as a lingering effect? Can it be healed by the players, or does it wear off over time? Can it be countered by player equipment/gear?

Telegraphing attacks is important for effective enemy combat. An enemy should have a "tell" animation that informs observant players that the enemy is about to go all stabby, shooty, or clawey. Tells include

- Cocking a fist back to punch

- Growling or yelling before swinging a weapon or charging

- Moving part of the anatomy (like a twitching tail or reptilian fins) before attacking

- The weapon's laser sight acquiring a target before firing

- A weapon or spell "charging up" before firing

Not every attack needs to do damage to the player. There are plenty of ways to give the player grief without doing permanent harm:

- **Block/parry**—The enemy can block or parry the player's attack, causing a stagger in the player's combat flow. This can break combat chains, reset combo meters, and cause the player's weapon to rebound or ricochet. Whatever the source of the block, be it a force field, an actual shield, or a defensive grab, don't ever make the player wonder why it happened.

- **Knock back**—Rather than taking damage, the player is knocked backward when hit. Putting distance between the enemy and player can upset any combat chain or disrupt any activity the player was engaged in, like spell casting or operating a mechanic. It is particularly effective when the player is hit while standing on a narrow platform, knocking him off or to his death.

- **Stun**—The player is stunned into a defenseless state. The player should lose momentary control—just as long as it doesn't last too long, which can be very frustrating for the player. Circling stars and tweeting birds effects are optional.

- **Freeze/paralyze/capture**—This type of attack acts like a stun, but the player can break out of it by button mashing or **furiously** waggling the control stick. Characters are often entombed with a freeze attack, snared by a spider's web, or caught in some sort of netting. The player may or may not take damage during this attack. Make sure you have a cool "victorious breaking free" animation and effect when the player finally regains control.

- **Repair/heal**—The enemy regains health. I suggest using this behavior infrequently because it can feel unfair to the player. It works best if the enemy has a healing animation as well as a health bar to show that he's **returned** to his fully (or partially) healed state. Consider allowing the player to attack the enemy to disrupt his heal.

■ **Buff**—This effect works like the heal, but the enemy gains power to charge an attack. Usually, this effect can be found when charging magical attacks. You also find it in shooters when the bad guy is charging up his weapon to unleash his wrath on the player. The enemy can be in either an invulnerable state while buffing up or the reverse, which would cause the enemy to lose the advantage he sought.

This is just getting unfair.

■ **Steal**—The enemy steals money or equipment from the player, causing the gameplay dynamic to shift from "fight the enemy" to "get that creep who just stole my chainmail!" Make sure the player has a fair opportunity to get back what's been stolen. Never steal anything the player has bought or won as part of progression; make it something that is (somewhat) easily replaceable.

■ **Leech**—The enemy drains the player's "charged up" resources. This can be super meter power, mana, shield power, or even fuel. Usually, the player doesn't have an opportunity to regain the resource from the enemy that attacked it. Once it's gone, it's **gone.** Players will soon pick up that leeching enemies should be dispatched as soon as possible.

■ **Perform unexpected behaviors**—If the player is expecting a movement pattern or attack, having another up his sleeve adds a nice bit of variety to the encounter. The variety adds to the illusion that the enemy is learning to react and defend against the player. The player will have to adjust his battle plan as he goes rather than falling into the same old routine.

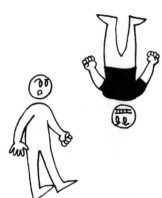

- **Show vulnerabilities** or **resistances**— Make sure they're clear to the player and follow logic. Of course, that murderous snow angel is going to be vulnerable to fire, just like **that** flaming pyre corpse is just going to laugh in your face when you wave that burning torch in front of him. Let the player make logical connections; don't ever let him wonder why something doesn't work. Enemy taunts are great for conveying that information. The more

smug or cutting the enemy's taunt, the better. Just don't overdo it; even the funniest or best-delivered line gets boring after the third time.

Even if an enemy has fierce attacks, nimble defenses, and cool behaviors, there still has to be a way to kill him. You determine an enemy's health the same way you would for player characters. Balance your enemy's health in relationship to the player's attack. Start with how many hits you want your enemy to take before he dies. Consider all the different attacks your hero has when determining this. Your goblin enemy may be able to withstand three normal hits, but a flaming sword may be able to kill him in one stroke.

All the notes about displaying player health apply to the enemy's health as well. Refer to Level 10 rather than make me retype it all here.

I Love Designing Enemies

Enemies offer you a chance to really flex your creative muscle as a designer. It's fun to come up with horrible monsters and evil villains. Personally, I find adversaries to be the most interesting characters in a story. And not just the "big bad" bosses. Look at all the great cannon fodder found in movies and comics: Imperial stormtroopers, orcs, Cobra troopers, death eaters, AIM scientists, parademons, Nazi soldiers, those henchmen in James Bond films that flip through the air whenever a grenade explodes.

But I'm proud to report that no one comes up with more creative cannon fodder than video game designers. In games, **anything** can be an enemy! An angry pickle! An irate toaster! Whatever the heck a goomba is! A whole glorious world of psychopathic possibilities is yours for the choosing . . . but rather than overwhelm you with a huge list,[10] I've created—tada!—

---

[10] Besides, that's what books like the AD&D Monster Manual are for!

The Alphabetical Bestiary of Choices

A is for arachnid, our pois'nous, crawly friend. Beware his webby legs or you'll meet a sticky end.

Battlemechs, huge and metal, with cannons all a-blazin'. Stand beneath their feet, and you'll go squish just like a raisin.

C is for criminals, quite the cowardly lot. Better catch them quickly, or you're likely to be shot.

D is for the dinosaur that's chewing on my rear. Who said genetic engineering was such a good idea?

Evil creepy children, blank eyes stare so sadly. They're easy to dispose of ('cept when guarded by Big Daddy).

Flying devils bedevil you while climbing a wall. Give 'em a whack, knock 'em back, before they make you fall.

I hate those **G**hosts who chase me merely out of habit. But they'll run the other way if I eat a power pellet.

Henchmen, mercs, and soldiers: they'll kill you for a buck. My advice? Shoot them first. If they shoot back, duck.

Irradiated Insects! It's my house they invade. Someone know where I can find a 10-foot can of Raid?

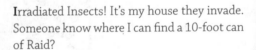

Do not shoot a **J**ungle Beast; treat with kindness instead. Even when it steals your gal, throwing barrels at your head.

Killer Plants may look pretty, but do not stop to smell. Shooting thorns and whipping weeds will send you straight to hell.

A **L**ich is just a skel'ton that has a fancy name. You should place a score or more of these into your game.

M is for mutant freaks, scarred by radiation. Their drippy flesh could use a little bit of lotion.

Red **N**injas vanish from sight, throwing stars at you. If they do any other attacks, make sure to tint them blue.

Orcs, the standard foe of any knight or wizard. Can be fought by the score in any game by Blizzard.

P is for the pirates who sail the seven seas, in ships laden with treasure and crews full of disease.

Dragon, spider, alien: whichever type of fiend; they're always harder to defeat when they are called "the **Q**ueen."

Robots are a paradox—they're s'posed to make life better. But when they're in video games, they always make me deader.

Spaceships, as an enemy, come in many fla-vors. Try *Galaxian*, *Sinistar*, or plain ol' *Space Invaders*.

T is for treasure chest; their mimics should be banned. First you're reaching for the gold, but then you lose your hand.

Darn those **U**nholy cultists! Their demons are a blight. They're crazy, but without these guys, there'd be no one to fight.

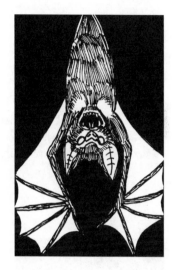

Vampire bats are all a-twitter, flying rather quickly. Trying to draw a bead on them is making me feel sickly.

Werewolves have fearsome claws, sharp and ready to maul. But rendering all that hair makes games slow to a crawl.

Xenomorphs are nothing but an intergalactic pest! They eat your brains, infest your ship, and burst right through your chest.

Behold these enemies of **Y**ore! Gorgons and animal-men. (Lead designer's been watching Harryhausen films again.)

Zombies are the final foe, so with your gun, take aim. They'd be so much scarier if not in every game.

If you don't want to use any of those traditional enemies, don't sweat it. Come up with your own foes! Here's how:

- **Start with your theme.** Brainstorm the types of enemies based on your game's environment. For example, an ice world can have killer snowmen, yetis, disgruntled skaters, snowball-throwing wizards, and penguins with machine guns.

- **... or start with your story.** Who is the main enemy in your story? For example, in an original trilogy *Star Wars* game, I would expect to be fighting stormtroopers no matter what planet I am on. Other villains can appear, but players should be constantly reminded of their arch-nemesis.

- **Come up with a way to tie the two of them together.** What's the one visual or behavioral cue that will differentiate your enemy from the others in your game? Or from other games? Within your game, you can create groups of enemies based on shapes, color, physical attributes, weapons, or uniforms.

- **Be economical with your enemies.** Re-use models, animations, and textures wherever possible to get the most bang for your production buck. When creating similar enemies with different behaviors and attacks, make them look different at a glance. I call this design mentality **"Red Ninja/Blue Ninja"** because a red ninja enemy may be set to hop and throw shuriken, whereas a blue ninja may use dash attacks with sai. Sub-Zero and Scorpion, two of the most famous characters from the *Mortal Kombat* series, were originally just reskinned versions of each other.[11]

- **Decide whether the enemy belongs in your world.** You wouldn't expect to find a cybernetic death-mecha in a *Super Mario* game; that world is too whimsical for such "serious" enemies. Conversely, a goomba would be seriously out of place in a realistic *Medal of Honor* style title.

- **Make your enemy look like an enemy.** Glowing red eyes, demonic horns, fangs, clawed hands, spikes, skull ornamentation, ragged capes, fearsome masks and helmets that obscure faces. Sure, this is stereotypical imagery, but if your players see characters in the world with any of these visual traits, they're going to shoot first and ask questions later. Stereotypes are stereotypes for a reason: they're easy for viewers to understand. Don't be afraid to use them to your advantage.

- **. . . or go against expectation and type.** You can go against type and juxtapose your enemies' visual with their behavior. How about a cute bunny that turns into a slavering killer? Or a hulking troll that will burst into tears when attacked? The more personality you can add to make your enemies feel and look unique, the better.[12]

I Hate You to Pieces

When introducing your boss to players, do it in a memorable fashion. Who can forget Darth Vader's entrance in *Star Wars*? Make sure players get a good look at the villain, that they understand "this is the bad guy" they will eventually fight. You always want to give your main villain[13] a "Joker moment," when the bad guy executes a henchman or some other NPC to show what a truly bad guy (or girl or he-she-demon) he is. This can happen within the game or a cutscene.

---

[11] Of course, in the case of Sub-Zero and Scorpion, it would be "blue ninja, yellow ninja," which doesn't quite have the same zing.

[12] Just remember not to violate the triangle of weirdness.

[13] If other enemies besides just the main villain can have this "being bad" moment, that's even better.

Have other characters talk about how bad the boss is before you introduce him. Or give the players information in collectable form like audio clips or data files or letters to warn them about the enemy. This works when dropping hints to players on how to defeat the enemy or boss. Arm them with knowledge along with the firepower. Anticipation of fighting the boss will be greater if players know the fight is coming.

When I was working on a game based on the movie *Demolition Man,* the designers were presented with an interesting challenge. Simon, the movie's bad guy, didn't fight the hero until the very end of the game. But the designers knew that Simon had to be a recurring villain in the game, so they came up with a clever solution.

At the start of every level, Simon would run out onto the screen, shake his fist at players, and then run off. The effect on players was electric. They'd shake their fists back and say, "Oooh! That darn Simon! I'm a-gonna git him!" and then proceed to blast their way through a half hour of gameplay. By the time these players reached the next level, they were probably so heady from all the killin', they forgot why they were there until Simon would run out again, shake his fist, and re-energize the players. This taught me a **very important thing:**

MAKE THE PLAYERS HATE THEIR ENEMY

How? Simple. Make sure your boss does bad things! This is why villains are always killing off their own henchmen—so that they have someone to kill if they can't kill the main characters! Have the enemy take something the player needs or cares about. Kill the hero's parents, kidnap the princess girlfriend, burn down the quaint village—you get the idea. Whatever your enemy does, make sure it impacts the gameplay as well as the story. Make the parent the blacksmith that gives the hero that magic sword. Does the girlfriend heal the hero whenever he visits her hut? Not anymore! The enemy just kidnapped her! And now that the village has burned to the ground, where is the player going to store all the collectables he's found? Japanese RPGs do this right: they kill off the player's girlfriend, who happens to be your best party member. Are those tears I see? Are they being shed for a lost love or because you can no longer heal every other turn?

When it comes time to design your boss fights, you don't have to kill the boss at the end of each battle. In fact, it's better if you don't. This way, you give the player someone to fight later in the game. Because your player will have "history" with this bad guy, he will hate him even more! If you kill off your enemy in the first act, who is left for the player to fight? Unmotivated, your hero loses the will to live, starts drinking, and moves in with his parents.[14]

Pathetic.

And more importantly, not fun.

Taunts are a great way to get the player mad at an enemy, but you have to be careful not to overuse them. To paraphrase Spider-Man, "With great power comes dialogue-the-player-is-going-to-tire-of-hearing-over-and-over-again." Taunt the player physically as well as verbally. You can even build these taunts into your enemy's attack moves. For example, in *Maximo: Ghosts to Glory,* there is a sword-wielding skeleton that, every time he successfully hits the player, does a little flourish with his sword, like a gunslinger spinning his guns before he holsters them. This flourish was created to give the player an opportunity to strike back and wipe the grin off that cocky little so-and-so's face.

---

[14] Oh right, his parents are dead! Now you've turned your hero into a homeless person. Are you happy with yourself?

Simple animations like idles and taunts go a long way toward making an enemy feel smarter than he actually is and provide lots of character. Has the player retreated too far for the enemy to attack? Have the enemy berate the player or make "come here" gestures. Did the player successfully elude the enemy with stealth? The player should shrug his shoulders and mutter that he must have been seeing things. Some games have guard enemies taking smoking breaks or falling asleep at their post to make them easier pickings for the hero. But keep in mind you don't want every one of your enemies to act this way; otherwise, you've just thwarted the uniqueness you were trying to achieve.

One last thing about enemies: sometimes you should let the bad guys win.

I don't mean killing off players to give your enemies a victory, but you shouldn't baby your players either.[15] Let the enemy get in a hit (or a cheap shot) once in a while. Give the enemy a temporary invulnerable attack state. Force the player to run away or at least block an attack. Have your enemies outnumber the player several times over. Let them sweat it out as to whether they'll survive the encounter. The player should feel as though he is actually in danger from the enemies. Bad guys aren't going to feel very threatening if the player doesn't have to struggle to defeat them. And the players' victory is going to feel hollow if the enemies don't provide a challenge.

---

[15] I talk more about difficulty in Level 13, so hold your horses.

Non-Enemy Enemies

As mentioned at the start of this chapter, not every game has physical enemies that are to be overcome with hot lead and cold steel. There are plenty of ways to push and punish your players without resorting to fighting sentient beings:

- **Gremlin**—This character looks like an enemy but doesn't directly engage the player. Instead, a gremlin will disrupt the game by undoing the player's progress. For example, *SimCity* features a Godzilla-like monster that stomps through the player's city, leaving destruction in his wake.

- **Tormentor**—This enemy challenges and taunts the player throughout the course of the game but never directly confronts or attacks him. The alien overlord of *Space Fury* and *Portal's* sentient computer GLaDOS are examples of tormentor enemies. In the case of *Portal*, the player can "defeat" GLaDOS by tearing her apart, but it is implied that—SPOILER ALERT!—she is "still alive" at the end of the game.

- **Time**—"Time pressure makes people think something is a lot more complicated than it really is."[16] Found primarily in skill-based games like driving/racing and puzzle games, a ticking clock is a great way to unnerve the player, creating pressure without using an enemy. Some games will allow the player to extend or slow the clock for temporary relief. If the player doesn't achieve the objective or finish the task within the allotted time, the player either loses a life or the scenario is reset. Time can also be used as an endgame, where the player has to escape a base before it blows up.

- **Human competitor**—Player versus player, competitive or cooperative—regardless of the gameplay mode, I find the best and worst thing about multiplayer games is . . . the other players.[17] Your friends (and complete strangers) will always find new ways to torture, torment, and humiliate you during a game. As a designer, never underestimate the power of one-upmanship and revenge. Just give the players the tools they need to act on these and sit back and watch the fun unfold. As the old saying goes, keep your friends close and your enemies closer because sometimes they are the same person.

---

[16] A succinct quote from Portal designer Kim Swift from GDC 08: Portal Creators on Writing, Multiplayer and Government Interrogation Techniques, Chris Faylor, Shacknews.com (http://www.shacknews.com/featuredarticle.x?id=784).

[17] I am reminded of Jean-Paul Sartre's famous quote: "Hell is other people." Because Sartre died in 1980, we'll never know whether he would have appreciated a good death match.

How to Create the World's Greatest Boss Battle

Video game BOSS (n): a large and/or challenging enemy that blocks a player's progression and acts as the climax/ending to the game's environment, level, or world.

At first glance, a **boss battle** may appear to be an encounter with a very, very, very large enemy with too much health. But this is an underestimation. Bosses are very complex creatures with many separate working parts that should be thoughtfully designed.

Just as with enemies, boss characters are fun to create. But before you start designing your boss, you must first make sure that you have completely defined the player's move-and-attack set. When that's set, you can design a boss fight in three different ways:

- **Learned moves**—The boss encounter is designed around the players' existing set of moves. You don't have to teach the players anything new, and they feel as though they've mastered those skills when they defeat the boss. The *Mario* titles design their bosses this way.

- **New abilities**—The boss encounter is designed around players gaining a new weapon or new move. The players' learning curve is part of the boss round's difficulty. You find this in many of the bosses in the *Legend of Zelda* series.

- **Combination**—You can try to use both methods in one boss fight, but why complicate things for players? Don't be so mean.

Who's the Boss?

Boss design is just like enemy design: form should follow function. Knowing the boss's movement and attacks will determine the boss's appearance: if he can shoot, give your boss a gun (or a magic spell or a rocket launcher or a large nose to sneeze out nose goblins); and if he can defend himself, give him a shield (or a force field or protective cowling or a missile-deflecting karate move). In a nutshell, if the boss can use it, he should have it.

Next, consider how the boss relates to the hero. No, I don't mean in a "Darth Vader is your father" way, but rather what the boss represents. The James Bond movies of the 1960s and 1970s had a really good formula for bad guys. There were technically three "boss types" that Bond had to defeat.

physical   mental   global

The first villain was the arch henchman: the **physical adversary.** A muscle-bound goon would beat the tar out of Bond until he turned the tables with one of his spy gadgets or a deftly executed judo move to throw the goon into a pool of piranhas. Physical adversaries in the Bond films are the classic henchmen like Jaws, Tee Hee, and OddJob. In video games, these characters are monstrously large, freakishly hideous, and very heavily armed.

The second villain type is the mastermind: the **mental adversary.** Bond fought these villains at the film's climax. Usually, mastermind intelligence leaves the hero at a disadvantage and against overwhelming odds. In video games, this is when the boss gets into his robotic suit to blast away at the hero or forces the player to solve an environmental puzzle that, when solved, brings the cackling villain to his knees.

Even though the mastermind has been defeated, there is still one more "villain" to defeat: the **global threat.** This isn't a person so much as a threat to the hero's world. This can be the timer on Goldfinger's nuclear bomb, Hugo Drax's deadly spore bombs, or SPECTRE's space-capsule-eating rocket.

Here are some questions to consider when designing bosses:

- **What makes the boss a worthy adversary?** Most bosses have the upper hand on players in size, strength, firepower, and defenses. Make sure players know they are in trouble even before the fight begins.

- **What does the boss represent to the hero?** In many games and movies, the villain is merely an obstacle to the hero gaining true love (rescuing the princess) or a threat to peace. But don't be content with those tropes. Villains can represent the inner demons of the hero. In *Return of the Jedi*, Luke Skywalker must reject the dark side and become like his father in order to defeat the Emperor (or at least motivate daddy to toss him down a shaft).

- **What does the hero gain by defeating the villain?** It shouldn't be treasure, weapons, or power. In most movies and games, the hero is content to merely save the world and restore the status quo. But in the classic "Hero's Journey" story structure, the hero returns from his adventure with knowledge. For example, in *Indiana Jones and the Temple of Doom*, Indy finds out that fortune and glory aren't the only important things in life.

- **What is the boss's motivation and goal?** Give your boss a more compelling motivation than "he's evil." I find "the seven deadly sins of man" (lust, gluttony, greed, sloth, wrath, envy, and pride) to be a great starting point for villainous motivations. The Riddler wants to prove that he's smarter than everyone. Voldemort wanted to regain his corporeal form and power. Sinistar is just hungry. Whatever the villain's motivations and goals, they have to come in conflict with the hero's own. The boss is the primary obstacle to the hero's success. Only after the villain is defeated can the hero truly achieve his goal.

- **What's the boss's job?** In video games, most bosses are guardians: the guardian of a magic weapon, of a captured princess, of progression. But by keeping it at just this, you are doing a disservice to your villain. Give your boss a motivation for doing what he does.

- **Is your game based on a licensed property?** Remember that these boss fights are the highlight of the fans' play experience. If you aren't a fan of the property yourself, research it enough to find out what the players would want to do. It's safe to say that *Star Wars* fans will find a lightsaber fight against Darth Vader a lot more thrilling than shooting down his advanced TIE fighter.

Congratulations! You've done a great job giving your boss a believable motivation, clear goals, and an intriguing backstory. He looks menacing and has awesome attacks and behaviors. But the most common way to make a boss look bad and dangerous is to make him **huge**.

Size Matters

A bigger boss means a badder boss . . . and bigger camera problems. You can start to solve this issue by always focusing the camera on the boss. Because the boss should completely command the player's attention, you should try to keep the boss within camera view (unless the player does something stupid like turn his back on the boss). Avoid placing your camera:

- **Too high**—The high angle de-emphasizes drama and the scale of the boss.

- **Too low**—The foreshortening that happens makes it hard to gauge the distance to the boss and see incoming attacks. It can also cause clipping issues if the camera drops through level geometry.

too high!

too low!

Use elevation in the level and with the boss to help rectify some of this issue. Allow the player to reach the boss by climbing geometry to higher elevations. Or you can bring the boss down to the player's level just in time for the player to give the enemy a good smack to the face. One thing you want to avoid is **crotch whacking.** This is when the player is just tall enough to reach the crotch of the huge boss.

A big boss means big attacks. Why be content with the boss throwing rocks when you can have him throw cars? Why not buildings? Or entire city blocks? The more dramatic your attacks, the

more memorable they are. Take inspiration from games with bombastic bosses like *Contra* and *God of War 3*. Regardless of how spectacular the attacks are, you will need to give the player an opportunity to fight back. The player needs to work out when it is safe to attack. The player needs to memorize the boss **attack patterns.** Patterns are at the heart of every traditional boss fight and are created when several attacks and behaviors are strung together into a predictable sequence. Here's a simple example to show how patterns can be created:

fig. 1.   fig. 2   fig. 3.   fig. 4.

Let's say the player is fighting a giant mech armed with a laser cannon. The cannon's laser sight sweeps the arena three times (fig. 1). Once the sight has acquired a target (the player), the cannon will fire a stream of laser blasts—first to the right, then to the left, and then in the middle of the arena. The mech's cannon then transforms into a larger weapon. This new form charges up for a second (fig. 2) and then fires a single thick beam that sweeps the ground of the arena and can be avoided only by jumping or ducking behind cover (fig. 3). When the attack is over, the mech's chest cowling pops open and vents steam (fig. 4). After a couple of seconds, the cowling snaps back closed in a burst of electricity, and the mech retransforms its cannon back into its original configuration. The attacks cycle until there is a break in the pattern initiated by the player, such as the player taking damage, dying, or successfully attacking the boss.

This example shows the components of a boss fight: the primary attack, the invulnerable attack, the vulnerable state, and opportunities.

The **primary attack,** the laser blasts, create **movement patterns** for the player to memorize and follow (left, right, center). As long as the player knows that sequence, he'll be able to avoid taking damage.

Movement patterns should be easy to remember, but you should feel free to change the order of events to add some variety. Random movement patterns can be used, but I have found that many players find them difficult to determine and get frustrated if they don't "luck" into a favorable pattern.

The **invulnerable attack,** the charged cannon shot, is a dramatic, large-scale attack that forces the player to take avoiding action. As the player cannot hurt the boss during this attack, the player must act defensively, breaking up the play pattern.

The **vulnerable state,** the mech's chest cowling opening up, reveals the boss's weak spot to the player and is vulnerable to the player's attacks. This should be the chance the player has to inflict the most damage on the boss. The boss's weak spot should be visually designed to be obvious to the player: make it flash or glow, or highlight it in some manner. It should stick out like a sore thumb. You can prolong a vulnerable state by stunning or incapacitating the boss. It becomes very clear to the player that he has a chance to attack without the fear of being attacked in return. Make sure you end the vulnerable state with an attack/event of some sort (in this case the electric burst), which pushes the player away from the boss and informs the player that his chance to attack the boss is over.

Opportunities, like the cannon changing form, are chances the player has to attack. The window of opportunity is usually shorter than the one given by the vulnerable state. Taunts work well for this too. Just don't overuse any vocal cues or the player will get tired of hearing them over and over again.

I like to think of boss battles as a dance between the enemy and the player. Alternate between offensive and defensive moves for both the boss and player. Get more mileage out of your boss attacks and moves by changing the timing, speed, and range; just make sure these changes escalate. Most bosses start out pretty easy and get harder as they go. This is why many bosses have several rounds of patterns: the boss gets madder, and the threats ramp up until the ultimate climax when the boss is defeated.

Even as your boss is trying to kill the player, make sure to do all you can to keep the fight going. Provide plenty of opportunities for the player to regain health or power during the fight. Tools like **dynamic difficulty** will programmatically determine what the player needs to succeed. You can apply dynamic difficulty to enemy AI, reaction times—in fact, just about anything. Delivering the right power-up exactly when the player needs it makes the boss fight feel exciting and dramatic.

I also think the last boss battle of the game should be the easiest. Why? Because I want the player to end the game on a high note and feel like a triumphant hero. He's already done the hard part—playing through the entire game.

When the player gives the boss his comeuppance, use animations, sound cues, and visual effects to show that the player is damaging him. A robotic enemy can shoot off sparks; a fleshy foe can spray out spurts of blood or ichor. Other bosses will limp or crawl as they are close to death. Work with your artist to build your boss to have parts get chopped off or use several models that show increasingly damaged states. No matter how your boss goes, remember this **very important thing:**

LET THE PLAYER ADMINISTER THE *COUP DE GRÂCE*

The last strike of the fight *needs* to be delivered by the player. It's very important psychologically for the player to feel that he has won. This is the climax of the encounter. Don't rob your player of his victory with a cutscene or a canned animation. Once the boss is dead, let the player savor the moment with celebratory text, music, or effects.

Sometimes, due to story or licensing needs, your enemy will escape at the end of a boss fight. As the enemy escapes, do it with style. Having an enemy escape to fight another day shows the player that he is a worthy adversary and another encounter is coming. But even if the boss escapes, you still need to make the end of the fight satisfying. You need the **false kill.** You must first knock the boss to his knees before he gets up and runs away. Hold camera on that defeated boss for a moment. Let him curse the player's good luck (because it's never skill that defeats a bad guy, right?). Make sure it's clear to the player that he's won the fight.

When the enemy is defeated or killed, what happens to the enemy? Does he vanish in a puff of smoke or pop like soap bubbles? Does he dramatically clutch his heart and die an agonizing death? Does he explode? How is treasure delivered to the player after the enemy is defeated?[18]

---

[18] Looks like Level 13 has its work cut out for it!

Determine how the enemy model is removed from the world. Does he fade away, leaving only weapon pickups where his body once was? Does he dissolve into a pile of goo that then melts away? Or does the body stay on-screen as a gory reminder of your combat? Remember, what happens to your enemy affects your ESRB rating.

One more thing: sometimes a player is going to die. When he does, make sure he returns to a safe respawn point. The boss shouldn't attack until the player is ready to fight. Consider keeping the boss's game state upon the player respawn. This means picking up the fight where the player left it rather than restarting the entire boss fight sequence from the beginning.

Location, Location, Location

Where a boss fight takes place is just as important as the design of the fight itself. The level is an extension of the boss fight . . . and sometimes, the level IS the boss fight.

The basic boss fight takes place either in a circular arena or a linear screen-wide walkway. This allows the camera to stay focused on the boss, who generally inhabits the center or back of the room with occasional trips to the side and outer edges. For more dynamic boss fights, add elevation to the arena. *Devil May Cry* had an interesting fight in which the player kept alternating between fighting the boss high up on the walls of a castle and down low in the castle's courtyard.

Think about the boss in relationship to the environment. How will a boss use the level for movement or attacks? Having dynamic elements like collapsing statues or walls or break-away floors can keep things exciting and surprising as the environment gets wrecked by the boss (and the player) over the course of the battle. Bust that joint up! Just be aware that if the player has to replay the boss fight, seeing the event happen again and again may get a little stale.

Designing boss arenas with dynamic level elements is the best of both worlds. The arena contains dynamic objects and elements that will react to a certain boss attack or action. These can be breakable windows, smashable floorboards, crushable computer consoles, and so on. This way, no matter what order the boss interacts with these elements during the battle, interesting things will happen. It creates a different experience every time.

A **scrolling battle,** where the player and boss fight their way through several locations, makes for a dynamic boss fight. First determine the method of player locomotion during the fight. Are the player and boss fighting on foot (chasing each other?), on top of vehicles (like the moving train in *Uncharted 2: Among Thieves* or hopping from car to car as in *Wet*), or while piloting vehicles? (Maybe they *are* vehicles!) Just be careful because scrolling boss fights require as much work if not more than a full level.

Another variation is the **puzzle boss:** a boss that is actually invulnerable and cannot be defeated by a direct assault by the player. Instead of fighting, the player has to survive the boss's attacks long enough to use objects in the level that will defeat it. Spidey can't actually hurt the Rhino boss in *Spider-Man 2* (Activision, 2004), but if Spidey can trick the Rhino into smashing into electrified machinery, he can defeat him. The most obvious (and hilarious) example of a puzzle boss is in *You Have To Burn The Rope* (http://www.youhavetoburntherope.net) where the Grinning Colossus can only be defeated by . . . well, I'll let you guess how to beat this one.[19]

---

[19] Spoiler alert: you have to burn the rope.

Why Not to Create the World's Greatest Boss Battle

Some designers believe that boss fights are too "old school"—that they grind game progression to a halt; that the time and effort to create bosses with their non-reusable artwork, hard-coded behaviors, and unique animations just isn't worth the production cost. Boss fights create a skill gateway; whenever someone has told me that he quit playing a game, the reason was usually that a boss was too hard.

An alternative to these problems can be found in turning the boss fight on its head. Instead of making it about a big *creature*, make it about big *drama*. Make the fight personal to the player and more about pivotal moments in the story.

My friend, designer Paul Guirao (*Dead to Rights*, *Afro Samurai*), created what I thought was the best boss fight design I had ever heard. Early in the game, the player learns an arm-wrestling mechanic. At the climax of the game, the hero is knocked to the ground by the villain, who attempts to plunge a dagger into the hero's eye! The player has to use that arm-wrestling mechanic to force the dagger away and eventually turn it on the villain himself.

Paul's design really opened my eyes (groan) to what a boss fight could be. It sounded awesome and dramatic and very different from anything else I had seen in games. It wasn't just another big stompy boss. What I really liked about it was that it

- **Emphasized drama over scale**—It didn't need a rocket-firing colossus rampaging through a city to be exciting.

- **Used intimacy to create urgency**—Because the camera view was to be very tight (only the faces of the two characters, their hands, and the dagger were to be shown), the impending danger was heightened to a degree not seen in most video games.

- **Better utilized existing assets**—All the assets for the fight—the hero, the villain, the dagger, the arm-wrestling HUD meter—were used in other parts of the game. Nothing new had to be created to make this boss fight playable.

- **Told the story with a boss fight, not cutscenes**—Video games are **interactive** entertainment, so playing the story is always better than watching it.

SPOILER ALERT!

Years later, as I played the ending of *Call of Duty: Modern Warfare 2*, I was reminded of Paul's knife-fight design. In *CoD:MW2*, the player character is stabbed by the game's villain. As the bad guy attempts to murder your partner, the player has to (painfully) pull the knife from his own chest and hurl it into the bad guy's eye (all occurring in very dramatic slow-motion).

Had the designers at Infinity Ward heard of Paul's knife-fight design idea? Or was it just a good idea for a boss fight whose time had finally come? All I know is that it was as awesome and dramatic as Paul's boss fight idea had sounded to me all those years ago.

Level 11's Universal Truths and Clever Ideas

- Form follows function.
- Design your enemies to complement and contrast with each other.
- Carefully balance the enemies' strength, speed, and size.
- Fighting enemies is supposed to be fun.
- Enemies are meant to be fought, not avoided.
- Not every enemy attack has to do damage.
- You always want the player to hate the enemy.
- Use dynamic difficulty to give the player some help.
- Watch out for camera issues when creating a large-scale boss.
- Where the boss fight takes place is just as important as who the player is fighting.
- The player has to give the boss the killing blow.
- There are other types of enemies besides big stompy monsters.
- Emphasize drama over scale.

Level 12
The Nuts and Bolts of Mechanics

If you find a path with no obstacles, it probably doesn't lead anywhere.
—Author unknown

THERE'S NOTHING WORSE than an empty level you just walk through,[1] so you need to start throwing things in the player's way. Good things, bad things, things that make the player cry with pleasure and weep with sadness. You need **mechanics.** Lucky for you, there are four types of these beauties: **mechanics, hazards, props,** and **puzzles.**

The Mechanics of Mechanics

Before you dig in, be aware that "mechanics" is another term that suffers from MDS: multiple definition syndrome. Board game designers say mechanics are the gameplay systems used to play a game. These are things like turns, action points, resource management, bidding, and even rolling the die.

Video game mechanics are objects that create gameplay when the player interacts with them. They can be jumped on, activated with a button press, or pushed around. Combine them with interesting level layouts and enemies. Some of the more common video game mechanics include

- Moving platforms
- Opening/closing doors
- Pushable blocks
- Switches and levers
- Cranks
- Slippery floors
- Conveyor belts

Platforms are a beloved mechanic of action game designers. They come in a wide variety of styles and flavors that can be used to bedevil and delight players. Here's a suitable-for-framing chart that I've devised to help you identify platforms in the wild. Be careful; some of them bite!

---

[1] Because WALKING IS NOT GAMEPLAY!

PLATFORM PRIMER

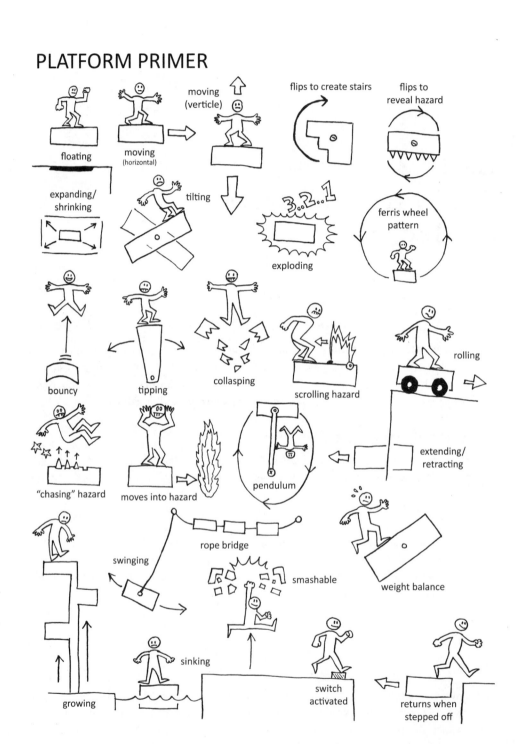

You would think that something like a **door** would be easy to design; after all, everyone has used doors in the real world, right? But doors open their own set of issues. Think about how the player is meant to open a door. Normally? Carefully? Aggressively? Remember, the character's personality comes into play when you're thinking about this. Kratos kicks open doors. "Soap" MacTavish uses explosives to blow open doors. Jill Valentine opens doors very slowly and carefully. Does a player have to pick the lock before entering?

Be mindful of which way your door opens. Does it open in? Does it rise up like a portcullis? Does it lower down? Does it swing out? All these opening actions can lead to different gameplay scenarios. You can turn opening a door into gameplay. Some multiplayer games have players work together to crank open a door simultaneously. *Mappy* (Namco, 1983) used doors to whack and temporally stun enemies. A portcullis in an action game might lower back down after raised, requiring the player to dash under it before it drops down. Even a simple door in a survival horror game can be closed in the face of an enemy to buy the player the time to reload or escape.

Despite their benefits, doors can bring their own problems. Quickly opening doors can clip into the player or cause the player to get knocked back. Make sure your player doesn't get caught on doors and doorway geometry. This problem may seem insignificant, but after getting caught up in hundreds of doorways, your player will get mad. That's the reason so many games make opening doors a canned animation sequence. The early *Resident Evil* games designed their level loading to correspond with the player opening a door. This design not only masked the loading of the level section but also built tension as the door slowly swung open.

Make sure you know the answers to these questions and then keep the method of entry consistent throughout your entire game.

You can use doors as level gating mechanisms. You might not be ready let the player enter the next room or level. He might have to find the right key, solve the right puzzle, complete the right quest, or earn more XP. A closed door doesn't need to look like a door. It can be a magic mirror, a mystic portal, a pool of water, a wall of vines, a force field, debris, or a guard blocking the player's way.

Some doors are just not meant to be opened. Locked doors are perfect for getting players to find another route through a level, but just make sure it's super clear why they can't get through. Your locked door can look as if it's made out of unbreakable metal, it can have a huge lock on it that the player doesn't have the key for, or it can be blocked with debris that the player can't move. Whatever the choice, the appearance needs to be obvious so that you avoid frustrating the players. Locked doors are often (some say too often) used to introduce this common gameplay scenario: the quest to find the key.[2]

Switches and **levers** are more old standbys in video games. Some designers love using them; others avoid them like the plague. I admit that nothing makes my eyes roll faster than seeing a lever sitting in the middle of a room. It's something that screams "video game" to me. However, a lever can be a very useful gameplay mechanic. If you do use switches and levers, keep them visually simple. Now I know that one of the great pleasures in designing video games is creating fantastical things, but if you want your players to be able to identify these items in your world it helps to keep things grounded in reality.

Whatever you end up doing with your switches and levers, make sure that

- You include a visual clue. Consider placing a visual effect like a glow or an icon on your switch or lever. Since levers are often shown as slender poles, the player might have a hard time seeing them.

- The player sees the effect of activating the switch or pulling the lever. That means using a camera cut or a voice or sound effect to indicate what has happened.

---

[2] I talk more about keys in Level 13.

- The switch or button changes appearance to show that it is in a new state. Have it change color, position, or shape. If you use a one-way switch (one that operates only once), play a nice meaty sound effect to indicate that it's permanently changed its state. If it's a resetting switch, play a "timer" sound effect to indicate that that switch is going to revert back to its original state. You can even display a timer graphic so players know how much time they have left.

Cranks are like levers and switches that take time for the player to activate. Some cranks are operated by pressing a button and holding it, whereas others require furious button mashing to open. One common gameplay scenario is to have the player operate a crank to open a door and then have to run back to the door before it closes. Some games turn rotating a crank into a rhythm game where the player has to sync button presses with the animation of the character on-screen. You can even turn a crank into a combat puzzle like the ones in *Devil May Cry*. If turning a crank takes *X* seconds to activate, spawn enemies to attack the player as he is turning it. If the enemies hit the player, he'll be knocked off the crank, which will unwind the crank's progress. The player will have to alternate between fighting enemies and turning the crank.

Need a little more help coming up with mechanics? I just happen to have a list in Bonus Level 7.

Holy Death Trap!

A **hazard** is a mechanic's nasty little brother who will slip an M-80 into your underpants when you aren't looking. Hazards look like mechanics, often act like mechanics, but will kill a player just for snoring too loud. Hazards may also resemble enemies, but the key difference is intelligence and/or mobility. All hazards have predictable patterns and limited movement and usually aren't very smart. They are things like

- Spiky pits
- Smashing blocks
- Blasting flames
- Exploding barrels
- Laser-guided missile launching turrets

When you are designing hazards, the first rule is to make sure that they look dangerous. That means spiky, flamey, frosty, sparky, poison-y. Slap a big death's head on it if you have to.

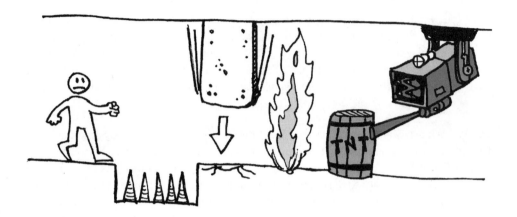

When creating your mechanics, take inspiration from the theme of your level. Create things that look as though they belong in the level. For example, in the dungeon level of *Maximo: Ghosts to Glory*, we had

- Grabbing prisoner hands that pop out from grates

- A suit of armor wielding a chopping axe

- Spinning, spiked iron maidens

- A toxic sewer filled with floating coffin platforms

Get inspiration from dangerous-looking things in the real world: from spiny cacti to razor wire. Use shape, color, sound effects, and particle effects—anything to make it clear to players that they WILL get hurt if they touch or collide with this hazard. Don't make the player have to play a guessing game to what your intention is. Use visual shortcuts and stereotypes—

they can be used as a great shorthand tip to the player. To demonstrate this point, here is a great example of what I DON'T mean.

I was designing a hazard and took the design to the artist who was going to be modeling it. I suggested that the hazard be colored red, as many cultures associate the color red with danger. The artist said, "That's too predictable. I think it should have yellow and black stripes." I was intrigued (I was thinking of the yellow and black hazard edging found on loading docks), so I asked her why. She replied, "Because bees have black and yellow stripes, and everyone knows that bees are dangerous."

Epilogue no. 1: The hazard ended up red.

That story reminds of another story. A designer and I were reviewing level designs. A particular level featured a ship that would sail away as the player started the level. The player had to run to catch up with the ship; otherwise, he would literally miss the boat. I told the designer that I thought that the player would stop and look around to get his bearings when he started a level. If the player took the time to do that, he would literally miss the boat. What would happen to the player if that happened? The designer said, "Oh, we can just drop a big rock on the player's head, so he'll die and have to start the level over again."

Epilogue no. 2: We didn't make that level. Since then, I made this **very important thing** my motto:

NO DROPPING ROCKS ON THE PLAYER'S HEAD[3]

Instant death hazards just suck. They are cheap and mean-spirited. If the player dies because of a hazard, it should be because he didn't pay attention or get the timing right. Make the player realize it was his fault he died, not because the designer decided he needed to die. Death is never a good way to educate the player. It just makes the player frustrated and sad.

What I Learned from Making Kids Cry

Whenever I meet gamers who played *Maximo: Ghosts to Glory* they will often tell me that they never finished the game because it was just too hard. And you know what? It is. It demanded players make pixel-perfect jumps and be combat ready the minute they landed in front of an enemy. It has a needlessly cruel save system. It's been called one of the most difficult PS2 games of all time[4]. It's a difficult game. And after making that game and reading the reviews, I learned my most important lesson as a game designer: The difference between difficulty and challenge.

---

[3] I mean that figuratively as well as literally.

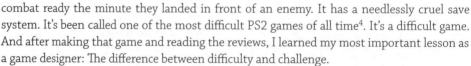
[4] www.ign.com/articles/2005/04/27/the-top-10-most-challenging-ps2-games-of-all-time

Difficulty = Promotes pain and loss

Challenge = Promotes skill and improvement

A difficult game does whatever it can to punish the player. A challenging game confronts the player with obstacles that can be overcome with skill and knowledge. I believe a challenging game is much more rewarding than a difficult one.

Some gamers absolutely love difficult games. The list of ridiculously difficult games could fill this entire chapter: *Demon's Souls* series, the *Ninja Gaiden* series, *Contra*, *Ikaruga*, *Shinobi*, *Devil May Cry 3*, the *Ghosts 'n Goblins* series, *Super Meat Boy*, *Battletoads*. I admit, it is quite an accomplishment to finish a difficult game, but those who do are in the minority. If you want players to play your game to completion, your game needs to be challenging, not difficult.

When I first started designing video games, I would refer to the balance between challenge and difficulty as the **"fun curve."** There is a point in the game at which things have ceased to be challenging and drop straight into difficult and frustrating. The goal was to never "go over the fun curve." Years later, I learned there was an actual psychological theory about the fun curve called **"flow."** I get to flow in a moment.

My key to keep players from "going over the fun curve" is to create **ramping gameplay.** A designer must build one gameplay system upon the last, teaching players a new move and how to master it against mechanics and enemies. These gameplay elements are combined and gently intensify as the game progresses. But I'm getting ahead of myself. If we are going to talk about the timepiece, we are going to have to examine the clockworks first.

Time to Die

When I think of clocks, I think of time. When I think of time, I think of **timing puzzles.** Timing puzzles are mechanics that move. They are perfect for creating tense moments when a player has to wait for the right time to dash through whirling blades or smashing pylons.[5] They cause anticipation for the player as he waits for the right moment to jump to a moving platform. A timing puzzle should have the following:

1. The hazard must have a discernible movement pattern. The pattern can be back and forth, up and down, zigzag, circular, or figure eight: just as long as players can track the hazard's movement and determine when to act.

2. The hazard must have predictable timing. Random timing is unfair to players, who need to understand the pattern to be successful.

---

[5] To this day, I still get tense thinking about those spinning paddles in the Spectre chamber of *Dragon's Lair*, a scenario that may be the first video game timing puzzle.

3. The window of opportunity must be tight, but not impossible. Allow leeway for players at the start and close of the window's opening.

4. Use "tells" in the world to give players clues to where it is safe to stand and where they will be hurt or killed. Bloodstains, grooves in the floor, lighting and shadows, sound effects, particle effects, geometry, decorative elements—players notice these things and will learn to use them as markers for success.

wait for it...   wait for it...   ...go for it!

Props are mechanics that have eaten a big Thanksgiving dinner; they don't move unless someone asks them to get off the couch and do the dishes. Designers and artists can place these items into the level to make it feel more like a real place. Sometimes props act as barricades or obstacles for the player to avoid, jump over, or take cover behind:

- Desks and chairs
- Parked cars
- Barricades
- Statues and gravestones
- Refrigerators
- Fences and walls
- Coffins and alters

- Fire hydrants
- Mailboxes
- Filing cabinets and tool boxes
- Computer consoles
- Tables, wardrobes, and dressers
- Crates
- Potted plants and water coolers

Thinking up props can be an entertaining exercise in free association and brainstorming. Start with the predictable items that you would find in your level and go from there. Here's an exercise: come up with as many items and props as you can for the following level themes:

- **Easy**—The street of a Wild West town

- **Medium**—A supervillain's lair

- **Hard**—Chinese clothing factory

Pro tip: If you find your brainstorming ideas getting silly or obnoxious, you know you've reached a good place to stop. Let your ideas settle overnight or for a day or two before starting again. Or take a research break and look for more inspiration in books, games, movies, or the interwebs.

Don't be satisfied with merely thinking up items to decorate your world; allow your players to interact with them. Start with natural reactions. If you shoot a water cooler, it should explode in a watery splash. Let players knock over light items or shove around heavy ones. Let players closely examine interesting statues, objects on bookshelves, or paintings.

You can shoot or smash props to access new areas or yield treasure. In the LEGO games (like *LEGO Star Wars* and *LEGO Batman*), you can pretty much destroy anything—all yielding studs, the game's version of money. Nothing is more satisfying than busting up junk to get tons of treasure, but try not to overdo it because it can turn your carefully designed level into an empty room full of rubble.

Crates are breakable items that yield goodies and double as platforms, but they're also overused clichés that have become a joke within the gaming industry—visually boring and, frankly, a lazy fallback for designers and artists who don't want to burn the brainpower to think up more interesting breakable objects.

START TO CRATE TIME: 00:00:05

Now, that's just pathetic.

Gaming website *Old Man Murray6* created a review system called **start to crate** that gauges the time it takes a player to encounter a crate in a game. While the article is meant to be satire, I find it to be a good gauge to determine just how creative your game is. Rather than reinvent the wheel . . . er, crate, you can use this list of 50 breakable objects other than a crate to populate your game:

Barrel, treasure chest, vase, urn, trash can, mailbox, newspaper stand, baby carriage, metal drum, cargo container, cardboard box, cage, lantern, lamp post, filing cabinet, fish tank, toy box, keg, hay bale, pile of skulls, dog house, bird house, Tiki idol, statue, fortune-telling machine, church donation box, suggestion box, ATM, hollow tree stump, attaché case, safe, suitcase, TV monitor, fuel tank, refrigerator, oven, breadbox, bureau, wardrobe, parked car, coffin, arcade machine, soda machine, fire hydrant, vending machine, oxygen canister, filled shopping cart, one-armed bandit, copy machine, and toilet.

There. You never have to have a crate in your game again. You're welcome.

There is one more type of mechanic, which is the rarest one of all. It's the mechanic that's "just for fun." This can be the player piano that plinks out a tune as you approach it or the toilet that flushes if you interact with it. Don't be afraid to include these just-for-fun props in your own game.

The Music of Mechanics

In the great chili pot that is video game design, hazards are the beans. Just like beans, they act as filler when you don't have enough meat to go around and . . . they help the designer make "music."[7] The goal of good level design is to help players achieve what psychologist Mihály Csíkszentmihályi[8] calls **flow.** (I told you we'd get back to it.)

Csíkszentmihályi's theory proposes that there is a point between boredom and difficulty. A place where players become so engrossed that they become energized, focused, and unaware of time. But in order to create flow, you need to know how to orchestrate these elements together.

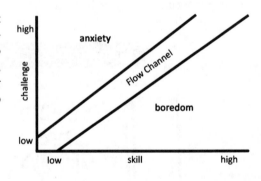

---

[6] www.oldmanmurray.com/features/39.html

[7] Yes, I went there.

[8] Pronounced "cheek sent me high-ee."

Reaching the state of flow feels like making music; it's the rhythm of a great level. A natural rhythm of the player's movement and actions—or flow—starts to emerge as he traverses the level.[9]

To me, game element placement is orchestrated like the instruments in Sergei Prokofiev's *Peter and the Wolf*. In this famous musical piece, each character (Peter, a duck, a cat, a bird, and the wolf) is represented by a different musical instrument. The piece starts out with Peter (represented by strings) walking through the forest. This musical theme gives the impression of movement, just as the player is learning how to do the basics in a game: walking, driving, or manipulating the game character.

Then Peter is joined by the bird, which adds a higher register flute to the music. The two themes intertwine, adding excitement to the music—just as treasure and collectables keep the player excited and motivated to continue playing. The duck (represented by an oboe) joins in, and the music speeds up and gets more complex, similar to the addition of complex player actions and level mechanics to your design. When the lower register cat (a clarinet) comes in, the music picks up as the cat chases the bird, adding a little conflict to the piece—much like hazards in a level.

After all the characters are together, the wolf's dangerous-sounding theme comes in; this echoes the arrival of enemy characters in a game. The music in *Peter and the Wolf* intensifies as the wolf eats the duck, is attacked by the bird, and threatens and battles the heroes until they are rescued by the crashing arrival of hunters. (Represented by drums.)

Let's take a look at how to introduce and orchestrate gameplay elements the same way that *Peter and the Wolf* adds instruments.

---

[9] The ancient Greeks proved there was a correlation between music and mathematics; that each higher octave is twice the frequency of the one below it. The same concept can be applied from a mathematical perspective, where the gameplay elements and mechanics are combined to create a formula of successful gameplay. For example, the PlayStation game *Vib Ribbon* (SCE, 1999) uses musical beats from any music CD to generate gameplay mechanics and hazards.

1. Start your player character moving through the world with simple movement challenges: walking, jumping, and collecting goodies.

2. Start with one mechanic. Repeat it a couple of times so the player understands how it works.

3. Add a second mechanic, and let the player learn that one too. Then combine the first one with the second.

4. Make things exciting with a hazard. Let the player get used to doing the things he would normally do in the game (traversal, collection, interaction with mechanics) but now with the hazard being part of the equation.

5. Now come the enemies! Give the player a chance to learn how to fight them.

6. Combine the enemies with the hazards for more excitement.

7. Finally, just as the player is getting used to all these game elements, toss one of them on its head just to keep the player on his toes!

If you create enemies and hazards to complement each other,[10] they'll end up being versatile tools when populating your level. Think about what order you want players to do the activities and set up the scenario for the players to figure out. Here are a few examples of how to combine enemies and hazards to make life more difficult for your players.

- The player has to jump over the hazardous pit with an enemy waiting on the other side. Place the enemy far enough away so he doesn't engage the player until he safely lands after the jump. To make this scenario more intense, make sure the pit has a timing element: the pit opens and closes, a pendulum swings back and forth, fire shoots up, a block slides down, and so on.

---

[10] This is easy because form always follows function, right?

- Here's an enemy that throws or shoots a projectile through the path of a moving hazard. Design the timing so that it passes through when the opening appears. The solution is for the player to dispatch the enemy (with his own projectile) before running through the moving hazard. Or the player can use the moving obstacle as cover to get in closer to the enemy.

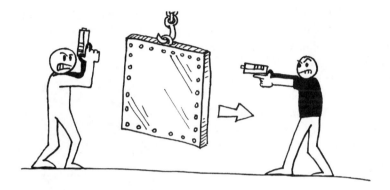

- The whirling saw blade in this chamber will cut the player in half if he collides with it, which makes fighting these multiple enemies a challenge; the player has to dance between combat and avoiding the hazard. However, the blade should also kill the enemies, which makes the player feel clever when he lures them to their death by saw blade. Give the player plenty of opportunities to turn the death traps against their makers. It's all about the villains getting their comeuppance!

Fire pit, moving obstacle, and whirling blade—there are many more combinations you can do with just these three mechanics. As these examples show, you really need only a few mechanics and enemy types to make a rich play experience. A well-designed game uses a handful of mechanics. The key is how you combine them. Play any game by developers Treasure (*Gunstar Heroes, Dynamite Heady, Ikaruga*) or Naughty Dog (*Crash Bandicoot, Uncharted*) to see some great examples. Or you can just read the next section.

Chip Off the Old Block

I believe that the best mechanics are also the ones that are the most flexible. By changing a mechanic's context and use you can create an entirely new challenge. Let's look at a mechanic

that can be found in many action and adventure games—the pushable block. While this mechanic is often maligned for being slow, unrealistic, or boring, the pushable block mechanic continues to be used by designers because it's flexible. Let's follow our hero through the dungeon to see different ways we can use a pushable block for gameplay.

Welcome to the dungeon! Unfortunately, our hero's path is blocked by a large stone block. But if we push it aside, we can enter.

Now our hero has to get up to that ledge. No problem. We just push a block to create a platform that he can jump up onto.

Ah, the old switch gate. If our hero stands on the switch, the gate will open, but when he steps off, the gate closes. What to do? I know! Let's drag that block on top of the switch, its weight will keep the gate open!

What's this? A vent shooting a jet of fire? Let's have our hero push the block over it. Now the fire is blocked and our hero can progress without getting roasted.

Curious. These pushable blocks have letters on them. It must be a puzzle! Nobody said we would have to think in this game! By pushing these blocks into the proper sequence, our hero can E-X-I-T the room!

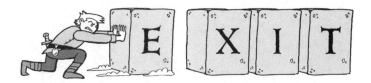

Who put a pit of acid in our way? That's a dirty trick! Fortunately, our hero can push a block into the pit and use it as a stepping stone.

This monster is looking for us! But the monster can't see our hero when he's standing behind the block. Maybe if he alternates between pushing and hiding, he can escape being captured!

That skeleton archer is making life difficult for our hero. But if he pushes the block and uses it for cover, he can survive to reach the far end of the room.

Oh no! How is our hero going to get past that Cyclops sentry? Pushing that block off the ledge onto to his head ought to do the trick!

That's a lot of flexibility for just one pushable block! And we haven't even explored pulling the block! Be mindful that it is possible for players to get bored with mechanics if they are repeated too often, so think about the context in which they are used. A good mechanic is like a baseball pitcher. You need to rotate them in and out of your game to keep them fresh and effective.

A Nice Little Calm Spot

Now that you've gotten past the hazards with your life, it's time to talk about a friendlier mechanic: **checkpoints.** Checkpoints are predesignated locations within the level where players can save their progress; take a break; or reassess their choices of equipment, route, and so on. They can be invisible to the players or visible. You will want to determine which method is better for your own game.

On one hand, visible checkpoints offer players a target in the level, provide a sense of security when they are activated, and can be an opportunity for an exciting or fun animation. The players feel a sense of accomplishment every time they reach and activate one.

On the other hand, visible checkpoints can look "gamey" and sometimes require explanation on how they can be activated.

Invisible checkpoints don't break the players' immersion while playing the game. However, because they are invisible, players may not be sure when they are activating a checkpoint or where they will respawn upon death. This can be frustrating for players as they wonder how far back in the level they will end up.

No matter which style checkpoint you use, here are a few rules of thumb to remember:

- Always face the checkpoint in the direction you want players to travel in. Otherwise, they'll get turned around or have to reorient themselves or the camera upon respawn.

- Never place a checkpoint next to a hazard or in the detection zone of an enemy. It's totally cheap to take damage when you (re)appear in a level.

- Players should respawn on the ground, not in mid-air. Don't make the player wait for the character to land from a drop. Also, avoid long respawn animations for the same reason.

- Place the checkpoint on flat, even ground to avoid any collision problems upon respawn.

- Make sure your game's saved data is retained whenever a checkpoint is activated. Don't make players go into another menu just to save the game.

Riddle Me This

Puzzle mechanics can be tricky; not just because they can be difficult to design or because they often require unique assets to create. It's just that puzzles are tricky to classify. Here's one definition I've found:

A puzzle is fun and has a right answer.
                                    —Scott Kim

While Mr. Kim has designed waaaay more puzzles than I ever will,[11] this definition doesn't feel quite right to me. What bothers me is the use of the word "fun." Fun is completely subjective, like the words "funny" and "sexy." What I think is fun may not be fun for you. And frankly, I don't find many puzzles in video games to be fun. For me, there's nothing worse than a puzzle whose solution I just can't fathom. At least with a difficult boss monster, you can brute force your way through to victory. You just can't do that with a puzzle. So, with apologies to Mr. Kim, I have created my own definition:

A puzzle is a challenge that has a right answer.
                                    —Scott Rogers

The difference is the word "challenge." That's a puzzle's job (and the entire game's job for that matter!): to challenge players. And the challenge the puzzle offers players is "solve me."

Players first need to know what reward is offered for solving the puzzle. It can be to open a door, create a picture, or translate a message. Just make sure players know what they need to do first. I always think this **very important thing** applies:

SHOW 'EM THE DOOR AND *THEN* SEND 'EM AFTER THE KEY[12]

When creating the puzzle, keep the puzzle's pieces simple and modular. You need only a few pieces to create many combinations. Work with as few pieces as possible to prevent players

---

[11] Go to http://www.scottkim.com for loads of puzzley goodness, including free games!

[12] It doesn't have to be a door. And it doesn't have to be a key. I'm speaking metaphorically here.

from getting confused. Make it simple for players to manipulate the puzzle pieces when rotating or flipping them. Make sure that when a puzzle piece is adjusted or changed, players can see that it's been adjusted and a clear way to return it to its original position. Many times it's easy to lose track of any progress. Keep the pieces uniform unless irregularity is part of the puzzle. Uniformity and consistency will keep it easy for players to understand how the elements fit together. Let them concentrate on the puzzle, not the manipulation of the pieces. When players interact with a puzzle piece, a simple button press should show a result. It may not automatically lead to the solution, but they should get the idea that doing the action in a different way will eventually get them there.

When I'm confronted with a puzzle in a game, I "check the puzzle" against every ability I have, every item I'm carrying, and every object in the room. This is the biggest pitfall of puzzle games; they end up being boring permutation fests. Think about what the piece *is* and its relationship to the other pieces as well as to the entire puzzle. If the relationship of the puzzle pieces isn't clear, it's easy to get stumped. And another thing, don't use cultural references (which could be confusing to a foreign audience) or make the player have to use the piece in a bizarre or absurd way to solve the puzzle.

For example, *Resident Evil 2* had a puzzle in which the player needed to open a door in a police station. The puzzle required placing chess pieces into a control panel. Whaaaat? First of all, since when do you find chess pieces in a police station, let alone ones that operate a control panel? Now if it had been . . . I don't know . . . the ID cards of dead police officers found throughout the station, the puzzle would have made more sense. What I'm getting at is: tie the puzzle into the game's story or setting, and it won't seem so senseless or random to the players.

Players should have all the tools nearby that they need to solve the puzzle. I like to place puzzle pieces no further than two rooms away from the puzzle's solution. It's not fair to make players run all over the level, let alone the game world, wondering what works to solve the puzzle and what doesn't.

The layout of the puzzle is as much a clue as the pieces. For example, if you present a chess board-style layout, players can visualize movement and patterns using the board as a guide before they tackle the problem. If the puzzle pieces are moved in a certain way, players should be able to visualize the consequences of moving the pieces. Just like with timing puzzles, movement and layout will help players see pattern that will help them reach their goal.

Puzzles in video games are essentially gating mechanisms. If you have lots of puzzles, make sure there are multiple paths of progression. Eventually, players will have to come back to the puzzle that stumped them to solve it. Give the players time to figure out the solution of a stumper while giving them another puzzle to solve in the meantime.

Tell players whether they are close to finding the solution . . . or not. Remember that kid's game where you are searching for a hidden item and another player says "you're hot" or "you're cold" depending on how close you are? Essentially, that's what the game designer needs to do for the players. Make your hints relevant to the puzzle. Ask yourself, "What would I want to know at this point?" Remind players what their goal is. Use camera cuts to show cause and effects that happen during the puzzle. Use voice and sound effects to give positive reinforcement. There are really only four ways to solve a puzzle: reason, knowledge, skill, or plain ol' dumb luck. The best puzzles allow players to use all four of these ways in some capacity to solve a puzzle. Granted, you don't want players to stumble onto the solution, but if that's what it takes, then stumped players should at least be able to do that.

You need to give players the "Ah-ha!" moment. It's the moment when they realize how the puzzle fits together and what the solution is. They may still need to complete the puzzle, but that part should happen quickly; by that point, it's just a matter of getting the grunt work done.

However, if players don't get that "Ah-ha!" moment and fail to solve the puzzle, don't make it a big deal. Find a way for the puzzle to be solved regardless of the players. Give them hints or even the answer if you have to. Of course, getting the solution without solving the puzzle should cost players something—a bonus or cash, as with the diminishing rewards in the *Professor Layton* games. If players need a hint, just charge them a fine and then let them skip ahead. Don't make them keep guessing wrong answers and then punish them for their mistake. And don't make the punishment something so severe as losing a life. Progression is a right, not a reward.

While I have found that players are generally smarter than you might think when it comes to solving puzzles, you should not give your puzzles cryptic or nonsensical solutions. The most infamous adventure game puzzle was in *Gabriel Knight 3: Blood of the Sacred, Blood of the Damned*. The player had to disguise himself as a non-player character to gain entry into a location. To create his disguise, the player had to stick tape over a hole in a fence that a black cat passed through. The cat's back would rub against the tape and hair would stick to the tape, which the player would then use to create a mustache for his disguise. However, the character the player was disguising himself as DIDN'T EVEN HAVE A MUSTACHE! My **very important motto** for creating puzzles has since become

NO CAT MUSTACHES

In other words, don't be so darn clever that players never figure out the puzzle. If you have created a Rube Goldberg-style[13] solution to your puzzle, you've overthought things and you need to simplify your puzzle. The conflict for players shouldn't be "game designer versus player" but "player versus puzzle." So check your ego at the door and do what's right for the players and the game.

Puzzle Me That

Of course, up to now, I've been talking about the kinds of puzzles that you find in story-based games, but there are so many more types of puzzles. The puzzle genre is the broadest in video games, and these games vary widely in content and gameplay. Let's look at some of the different types of puzzle games:

- **Logic puzzles** are often found in adventure games like the classic games from LucasArts and Sierra. They rely on players finding inventory items and then combining them to solve the puzzle. Make sure the relationship between the items and the solution makes sense (no cat mustaches!) and make it easy for players to combine and test items as they seek the solution.

- In **match three puzzles** like the *Bejeweled* series or *Dungeon Raid* series, players match three or more icons (or jewels or pirate skulls or quilted teddy bears) for points. Match three expert Jasper Juul splits these "breaker" games into four design foundations:

---

[13] Rube Goldberg was a newspaper cartoonist who drew very complex and amusing contraptions to do very simple things. The famous board game *Mouse Trap* is unofficially based on his cartoons.

manipulation, match criteria, obligatory matches, and time. Each of these factors can greatly impact how the game is played and affect the game's difficulty. Match three games offer short play sessions, which has made them popular on mobile devices. This extremely flexible genre is a good match (ugh) with other game genres such as RPGs, word games, and even horror.

- **Math puzzles** challenge players with arithmetic, subtraction, multiplication, division, spatial geometry, and number ordering. If you are going to have math puzzles in your game, it doesn't hurt to disguise them. You can put learning into a game, but the minute players catch on that they're learning, they won't want to play anymore. Give them something else (that would be gameplay!) to concentrate on as they learn.

- **Rigid body physics puzzles** like *Angry Birds* or *No, Human* simulate real-world interactions between objects and environments to create challenges for players. Weight, density, momentum, force, velocity, and kinetic energy become design tools to create challenges. They can be based on balancing stacks of items, engineering stable structures, launching aerodynamic craft, and just smashing up stuff!

- **Liquid physics puzzles** like *Where's My Water* or *Engimo* simulate fluid dynamics from streams of water to giant waves. Don't forget water has momentum, viscosity, force, drag, and buoyancy that affect your sea-worthy game elements.

- When creating **trivia** and **knowledge puzzles,** don't assume everyone knows what you do. Keep your questions short and clear. Do your research and determine what kinds of questions your audience would have fun answering. Players should feel smart for knowing the answers. Make sure you have a wide range of difficulty from simple to obscure, but mostly simple. Write **lots** of questions. Knowledge games cease to be fun the minute you have answered all the questions. There are many different ways players can answer a question. Which one is right for your game?

  - **Multiple choice**—Give players a range of choices—at least three. Create "close answers" that are similar to the answer but could be easily confused with the real answer. Change things up occasionally by asking "Which of these is not true?" style questions.

  - **Find the object/image**—Players must hunt for the answer among a variety of images or objects. Don't make the hunt be pixel perfect. Instead, allow a little space around the item so players can eventually spot and select the answer. Play with image orientation, color, and size to keep your players hunting.

  - **Fill in the answer**—This type of response requires keyboard or writing tablet input. Make sure your word parser is flexible enough to allow for misspellings, synonyms, colloquialisms, and regional terms. *Scribblenauts* has 22,802 words in its vocabulary! If your puzzle's vocabulary is smaller than that, consider letting players learn what words are available so they don't waste time guessing ones that aren't available.

- **Traditional puzzle** games like *Sudoku* and crossword puzzles offer simple challenges. Simplicity is the key here. Make sure your puzzle has only one solution. Allow players to make notes or try out different solutions before committing to the final answer. Add prompts and helpful hints to players. It's better to help players along than let them get frustrated and quit playing the game. Create multiple levels of challenge for all levels of players.

- **Visual puzzles,** especially hidden object games like the *Nick Chase* series or *Criminal Case,* rely on the players' observation skills. As in match three games, you'll find visual puzzle games come in a variety of genres, including mystery, horror, and romance. This may be thanks to the popularity of hidden object games with female gamers. Here are a few pointers for designing hidden object games:

  - People search for visual patterns like shapes, sizes, and colors. By adjusting these, you can hide your objects easily.

  - Fool around with player expectations by using non-stereotypical visuals for your items.

  - Hide objects in plain sight. The most overlooked image is the one right in front of players.

  - Direction and rotation make a big difference in how an object is recognized. Turn an object 45 or 180 degrees to throw off your players.

- **Word puzzles** like *Scrabble, Words with Friends,* and *Letz* focus on spelling. When creating word puzzles, be careful about using slang and colloquialisms. Word games should be visually uncomplicated. Design your interface with clarity in mind. Be careful not to use an illegible font for your letters. Really think about how you can present your word game in a more interesting way like *Typing of the Dead* did.

Whew! I've just barely scratched the surface on puzzle games. It doesn't matter which puzzle genre you design. Just make sure you keep the gameplay fair, the objectives simple, and the logic sound.

Minigames and Microgames

A **minigame** is a simple game created to provide variety, represent activities, and add value to a product. Many minigames are based on or are variations of classic arcade and classic home console games.

A **microgame** is a minigame that takes only seconds to play. Half of the challenge of microgames is learning how to play them within the short time allotted. The *WarioWare* titles are compilations of microgames.

Minigames offer many advantages to game developers. They are quick to create and test, they are easy to play, and they can be used as metaphors for complex player activities. I truly believe ANY activity can be represented by a minigame. Observe:

- Lockpicking—*The Elder Scrolls IV: Oblivion* (2K, 2006)

- Hacking electronics—*Batman: Arkham* series (WBI, 2009)

- Portrait painting—*SpongeBob Atlantis SquarePantis* (THQ, 2008)

- Tagging walls—*The Warriors* (Rockstar, 2005)

- Cooking dinner—*Cooking Mama* (Majesco, 2006)

- Serving dinner—*Diner Dash* (Playfirst, 2003)

- Picking a nose—*WarioWare* (Nintendo, 2004)

Any activity.

When designing a minigame, make sure to

- Keep the controls simple. Minigames, by their nature, imply easy-to-learn gameplay.

- Keep the gameplay sessions short—no longer than 2 to 3 minutes. Some microgames can last only a few seconds.

- Ramp the difficulty gently. Minigames are meant to provide variety, not torture players.

- Add something new with each level. Even a different piece of background art, sound effect, or song keeps the game from getting stale or repetitive.

- Design the minigame's controls using one button, touch control, or a very simple control scheme.

- Allow for player customization if possible. The web-based minigame *Upgrade Complete* (Kongregate, 2009) allows players to upgrade EVERYTHING, including the player's ship, the background graphics, and even the copyright screen!

- Make the victory condition clear to players. How does your minigame end? Does it have an end? Some games can be played "forever"—or at least until the kill screen appears.

Minigames don't even need to be segregated from the core game. The platformer/puzzle game *Henry Hatsworth in the Puzzling Adventure* (EA Games, 2009) and the RPG/puzzle game *Puzzle Quest* (D3, 2007) combine two styles of gameplay: platforming and puzzle. If you do this in your own game, just make sure you allow time for players to make a "brain shift" between the two gaming styles. Give them a second to reorient themselves with a "ready" screen or pause in the action.

And finally, when you've run out of all other creative ideas of minigames and puzzles, you can always resort to Whack-A-Mole.

Seriously, please don't. I consider Whack-A-Mole the last stop on the designer's creativity train. And here's why:

- It relies solely on the player's reaction time, which requires no thought or decision making from the player.

- It's random, which doesn't let the player utilize strategy.

- It's very repetitive. There's no variety to the gameplay other than possibly the speed of the popping moles.

- It requires almost no input from the player other than a single motion, button press, or click.

- It is an "endless game"—there is no end unless the designer dictates it. Usually, the player stops because he's tired of playing it.

I know you can design something more engaging than that! Let's move on to something more exciting: power-ups!

Level 12's Universal Truths and Clever Ideas

- Design mechanics, hazards, and props that work with enemies and complement each other.

- Good game design is like music: it has a rhythm that players can feel.

- Reuse mechanics to create new challenges.

- Games should be challenging, not overly difficult.

- No rocks on the player character's head: be fair when punishing your player.

- Be creative: don't resort to worn-out clichés like crates and Whack-A-Mole unless you have to.

- No cat mustaches: don't make puzzles so cryptic that players can't use logic, knowledge, or skill to solve them.

- A puzzle is a challenge that has a right answer.

- Show them the door and *then* send them after the key.

- Give players opportunities to catch their breath by providing plenty of checkpoints.

- Keep puzzle games simple and fair.

- Keep minigames and microgames simple and short.

Level 13
Now You're Playing with Power

POWER-UPS can be found in every genre of gaming, from driving to puzzle games to action-adventure games to shooters. They are dropped by defeated enemies, hidden in treasure chests, and sometimes just lying all over the place in the middle of the road.

A well-designed power-up is concentrated action. A player only has to touch it to become energized to move at lightning speeds, blow up the world, and return from the dead! The great thing about a power-up is its effects are **immediate:** who wouldn't want to immediately gain awesome power?! The only downside is that its effects are usually **temporary,** so use that power wisely.

Powering Up

A designer should be wise when creating power-ups and should ask the following questions:

- What does the power-up do?

- What does it look like? How will it (or its effects) visually stand out in the world? Does it glow or strobe? Rotate or bounce?

- Can power-ups be combined, or can the player have only one active at a time? Can the player retrieve power-ups that are unused or discarded?

- How does it affect the player's movement? Rate of speed? Number or type of attacks? Health or status?

- How are its effects communicated to the player visually? Aurally?

- What is the player's trade-off for using the power-up? Some reduce speed or mobility or the types of moves the player can do while under the influence of the power-up.

- If the power-up ability is temporary, what cues will let the player know it is about to expire? Is there a HUD element? A visual cue? A sound cue? A music cue? Does it last until the player loses a life?

Consider how the player will be collecting the collectable or power-up:

- Does the player have to walk over it to collect it?

- Does the player have to reach out and actively choose to pick it up?

- Some power-ups are automatically drawn toward the player when she gets a certain distance from them. If so, how close does the player have to be, how quickly does this happen, and so on?

- Is the power-up or collectable activated when the player gets into its proximity?

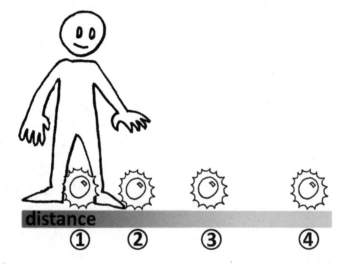

Knowing how close the player needs to get will help you determine the effects of the power-up after it's collected.

Power-ups can be divided into four categories: **defensive, offensive, movement,** and **game changers.**

Defensive power-ups help boost the player's ability to survive damage and continue progress in the game. The most common defensive power-ups include

- **Health-up**—This power-up refills the player's health meter. It can be a partial or full refill. If you have different power-ups that heal different amounts, make sure the power-ups look different from one another.

- **Ability recharge**—This power-up is like a health-up, but it recharges an ability meter rather than the player's health.

- **Extra life**—When the player collects this power-up, she gains one more life/restart that will allow her to continue the game after she loses all her health.

- **Invulnerability**—This power-up makes the player resistant to all damage from an enemy's attack. An invulnerable player might be open to effects from hazards that use physics and geometry (for example, falling off a cliff edge); otherwise, problems can arise with collision detection.

- **Invincibility**—With this power-up, as with invulnerability, the player cannot be hurt when hit by an enemy or his attack, but she can also automatically destroy most enemies by colliding with them, as seen in *Metroid*'s screw attack and *Mario Kart*'s super star. Many games don't allow this kind of ability to work on bosses, or if they do, they cause only minor damage.

- **Protective**—This type of power-up includes temporary forcefields, physical shields, or auras that protect the player from enemy projectiles, fire, or poisonous floors. Protective power-ups may or may not have their own "health meter" or timer to show

how much protection remains. Protective defenses are different from invulnerability and invincibility because the player usually can improve, modify, and extend them.

- **Indirect attack**—Commonly found in fast-moving car combat and kart-racing games, this power-up lets the player "fire and forget" smokescreens, oil slicks, and black bombs with fuses on top, causing havoc to those unlucky enemies and players behind him.

- **Smart bomb**—This power-up provides a clear-the-game screen when things get too tough or the player needs a moment to breathe during all the action.

Offensive power-ups improve or modify attacks, allowing players to defeat enemies faster, more efficiently, or more spectacularly.

- **Ammo boost**—This power-up fully restocks the player's ammunition. Most ammo boosts pertain to a specific weapon in the player's inventory.

- **Buffs**—These power-ups increase the player's skills and abilities for a short period of time. Awesome flame effects are optional.

we're boned.

- **Multi-weapon**—This power-up improves the player's current weapon without fundamentally changing it. *Contra's* spread attack fires five projectiles in a fan-shaped configuration, while heat-seeking rockets will home in on enemies.

- **Weapon upgrade/swap**—This power-up increases the strength, speed, and damage of the player's attack or can change her weapon to an entirely new one (sometimes more powerful, sometimes as powerful but with differing capabilities that may be more suitable—and hence more useful—in a particular situation). New visuals usually accompany the change. For example, *Ghosts 'N Goblins* lets the player change from lance to dagger to torch. The size and effect should at least change if not improve in spectacular-ness as the weapon upgrades.

- **Damage modifiers**—Flame! Poison! Ice! Electricity! These power-ups improve the player's base damage, usually accompanied with a dynamic visual.

- **Direction**—This power-up allows the player to change or augment the direction of his attack. It is most commonly found in shooters, allowing the player to shoot behind as well as above and below him. The change in direction can also be applied to the projectile, as in the case of enemy-seeking missiles.

- **Companion**—When the player picks up this power-up, a small object appears next to the character that can provide an additional attack or shielding function. The companion may or may not have hit points. Many last until the character is destroyed or for a specific duration of time. *Galaga* (Namco, 1981) added the novel twist that a captured ship became your companion. You lost a life, but you gained double shot ability.

Movement power-ups allow the player to improve an existing movement or add some new ones. For example, in *New Super Mario Bros. Wii (Nintendo, 2009)*, the players may fly through large parts of the level using the propeller helmet. This power-up allows player to fly through levels and over hazards as well as avoid bad guys altogether. Be particularly careful to account for these power-ups when designing player metrics:

- **Speed change**—Nitro boosts and other power-ups allow the player to move at incredible speeds. As a trade-off, the player usually has less control of the vehicle or character because of the faster reaction time needed.

told ya.

- **Access**—The player gains access to locations normally unreachable via an ability bestowed by this power-up. The access methods are as varied as flying, helicoptering, gliding, and swimming. For example, think of Mario's bee suit in *Super Mario Galaxy*.

- **Size change**—Depending on the game, changing size can allow a whole suite of abilities, least of which is being able to get into tiny holes. In *Super Mario Bros.*, the super mushroom not only increases the player's size, but also allows the player to take one extra hit and to break bricks to access new locations. The mini mushroom in *New Super Mario Bros.* causes Mario to shrink, allowing the player to leap great distances.

Game changers alter the dynamics of the gameplay and the player's interaction with the game in a significant manner:

- **Change state**—This power-up changes the play dynamics in the game. For example, in *Pac-Man*, the player flees from the enemy ghosts. When he eats a power pellet, the ghosts become vulnerable and the player can become the aggressor.

- **Score/treasure modifier**—Whether it's a *Crazy Taxi* fare multiplier or *Rock Band's* star power, the value of any points/treasure collected by the player is increased for a short period of time when using this power-up.

- **Magnetic**—This power-up draws treasure items toward the player, relieving her of the risk of entering dangerous territory or having to "clean up" treasure and collectables after combat.

- **Invisibility/disguise**—When using this power-up, the player is rendered temporarily undetectable by enemies and hazards, allowing him to safely avoid potentially deadly combat and enter locations barred by annoyingly alert guards.

- **Comedy power-up**—This power-up exists solely to surprise and amuse the player. *MDK*'s "Earthworm Jim" power-up drops a cow onto enemies' heads.

Most power-ups are content to sit still and wait patiently to be consumed by the player, whereas others have a keen sense of self-preservation. Power-ups have been known to move upon spawning out of their hiding place, like the super mushrooms in *Super Mario Bros.* Still others will run and hide when they spot the player, like the "cowardly power-up" in *MDK*. Give your player a chance to catch these **mobile power-ups.** Do not make them move faster than the player or make them resistant to the lure of a magnetic power-up.

Power-ups can be designed to work conditionally. In *Maximo: Ghosts to Glory*, we had an armor power-up that worked only when the player had collected the full set of armor. Another one required a special ability to activate. As long as the conditions for gaining these special powers are clear to the player, there's no reason why you can't add this technique to your design arsenal.

Not all power-ups are delicious and useful. Very evil game designers in their secret lair high in the Alps have created **anti-power-ups.** Like a chocolate truffle stuffed with dog poo, these sinister collectables look like regular, nice power-ups, but they hold a deadly surprise. Poisonous power-ups can sap health, slow movement, drain experience, or even turn the player into a zombie, complete with backward control schemes. While they are fun, they are fun only once or twice. I suggest using anti-power-ups judiciously and with caution.

"Love Thy Player"

Pureiya aishi nasai

Once upon a time, a Japanese game director[1] told me this should be the motto of all game designers. I agree with him, although I have a different way of saying it:

The game designer should be the gentle hand on the rear of the player, pushing him ever upward.[2]

The designer can use many systems to enable players during the game, and we've already talked about some of them in other levels: checkpoints, hoists and teeters, aim assist, ramping difficulty. But there are others that are worth discussing: dynamic difficulty balancing, difficulty level adjustment, rubberbanding, game length, and autosave.

Thanks!

■ **Dynamic difficulty balancing** (or **DDB**) is a way to adjust the challenge and rewards based on performance. For example, if the player dies too often fighting an enemy, the enemy's health is reduced slightly or the enemy doesn't attack as often. If the player is low on health and opens a treasure chest, a health-up will pop out. But if the player isn't low on health when opening the chest, he will be rewarded with treasure instead. The goal of DDB is to give players what they need when they need it to propel them along to success.

---

[1] A different Japanese game director from the "fisherman" from Level 4, btw.

[2] Not as concise, but much more pronounceable.

- **Difficulty level adjustment** gives a player the option to shift the game down to a lower difficulty setting if too many parameters, such as multiple player deaths, are detected. The player can be given the option to decline, or the adjustment may happen automatically. Personally, I don't recommend the latter because some players find it insulting.

- **Rubberbanding** is primarily found in racing games, but it can be used any time the player who is behind needs to be given an advantage to level the playing field. That advantage should be proportional to how far behind the player is. Rubberbanding does not need to be limited to physical distance. Both *NBA Jam* and *NFL Blitz* provide advantages to the player by tweaking the opponent's AI or speed. Rubberbanding is a great solution to help the player when he most needs it.

- The **game's length** is actually a good tool for adjusting difficulty. Take, for example, a battle arena. If the player fights bad guys for about three to five minutes, with sufficient health and a modicum of skill, he should be able to survive just fine. However, make that player fight for a half hour, and player fatigue and attrition start to set in. Odds are the player won't survive the encounter because he'll get exhausted . . . or at least bored.

Trust your feelings, Luke. After you play a level a thousand times,[3] you will know when your level gets boring. That said, you must be very, very careful because you can develop what I call **designer blinders.** Designer blinders occur when you've played your game so many times that you will require a much more difficult level to feel challenged than the consumers, who will play it only a few times. It is a very common problem within game development, which I have seen happen many, many times. I talk about how to solve this problem later in Level 18. In the meantime, consolidate your level. Kill the boring parts. Death to boring! Don't be afraid to cut elements if it will make your game better.

---

[3] Honestly, you will play a level a thousand times (at least) between setting it up; populating it; testing the mechanics, hazards, and combat; placing the collectibles and readjusting them; and then finally officially play testing it.

- **Autosaving** occurs when the game periodically records and saves game data automatically. This way, the player can concentrate on playing the game rather than micromanaging the game's save files. Autosave is helpful when the game crashes [4] or if the player forgets to save the game at a critical part and then dies. Many games autosave whenever loading a new area.

Seriously. "Love Thy Player."

For every positive example of player difficulty, there is at least one negative one. Here's a story illustrating what I **don't** mean about how to design player difficulty: I was reviewing an enemy encounter with a creative director. I told him that I thought the encounter wasn't bad, but it could stand to be a little more challenging. He agreed and his instructions to me were, "The player has to die six times before he can progress." I thought, "I'm sorry, Mr. Creative Director, I know you are my boss and all, but you are an idiot." But I didn't say it because I wanted to keep my job.

What I *did do* was not design the encounter so the player had to die three times to progress. And neither should you. Player death should **never** be a yardstick for game design. "Rewarding" the player with damage or death is negative reinforcement.

In *Maximo*, one of the enemies was a treasure chest mimic—a fun enemy that, when "opened" up, snapped and attacked the player like a dog. But it had an unfortunate side effect. I saw players actually cringe before opening a chest because they expected it to be a mimic. While it was fun for the designer to watch the player get tricked, it was not fun for the player. This defeats the point of the game: to have fun. Your players will hate you for it and stop playing the game. This is bad because the ultimate goal of any game designer should be to keep the player playing. If I ever create this kind of enemy again, I will give some clues to the players so they can spot this enemy and make preparations for it. A clue can be as simple as a color change or wobbling pots with an enemy inside like in *Legend of Zelda: Spirit Tracks*.

---

[4] But your game isn't going to crash, is it?

The way I see it, if players can play through and finish the entire game, they will be happy. They will be happy enough to tell others how much they liked your game, and they will be happy enough to buy your next game. It's a win–win for all parties involved.

More Wealth Than You Can Imagine!

I don't know, I can imagine quite a bit.
—Han Solo

Game designers have many very powerful tools to keep players playing. Mystery, delight, pride, and power we've already talked about, but now we come to the two most powerful of these tools: greed and reward.

Greed will get players to do interesting things. They will grind their way through the grindiest MMOs to get that stronger sword, that unique hat, gain that next level. They will jump onto the smallest platform festooned with the deadliest traps just to grab that one additional coin. They will fight the biggest, meanest enemies just to find out what comes next in the story. Or to score that achievement. The following **very important thing** rings true:

NEVER UNDERESTIMATE THE GREED OF THE PLAYERS

But . . . instead of using the players' greed for evil—luring players to their death to prove that you, the game designer, are cleverer than the players—use their greed for good instead:

- Use the promise of treasure and items to motivate players to fight enemies.

- Give the players a personal and customizable space to show off their trophies and rewards. When they start seeing some of the "shelves" filling up, they'll want to "catch them all."

- Exploit the "me too" factor. Keeping up with the Joneses is a powerful urge for players, especially in the multiplayer space. I was once playing *World of Warcraft* and minding my own business when I saw another player ride by on a mechanical chicken mount. All of a sudden, my player agenda went from "get to the next level" to "MUST OWN ROBOT CHICKEN!"

- Create "guidelines" when placing treasure and hidden objects. Sharp players will pick up on these guidelines, and their observations will be rewarded. For example, in *Maximo: Ghosts to Glory*, buried treasure chests were placed next to trees. If there weren't trees in the level, they were hidden next to similar vertical architectural elements like pillars or gravestones.

- Like the dots in *Pac-Man World* or rings in any *Sonic the Hedgehog* game, you can string collectables through the level to guide players where to go next.

- The designers of *Half-Life* (Valve, 1998) have an interesting method of introducing a new weapon or item to players. First, players hear about the new item from another character. Second, the players see the item in the possession of another character. Third, the players see the item being used by another character, and finally, the players obtain and use the new item for themselves. By the time the new item is in the players' hands, not only have they learned what it looks like, what it is, and what it does, but they want it for themselves.

Like greed, **rewards** are a powerful player motivator. A reward is what players are ultimately working toward. After all, you can't have a game without a victory condition, and you should never have a victory without a reward:

- Expose players to what rewards are available early in the game. This way, they have a laundry list of things "to do" throughout the game and what they will get for achieving them.

- Reward players as soon as possible, reward often, and provide some variety and surprise to the rewards. For example, In *Maximo vs. Army of Zin*, sometimes players would get money as a reward for defeating an enemy, but other times they would get a power-up. Players were never quite sure what they would get, which kept things interesting.

- A win condition needs to show evidence of success. There's no such thing as enough fanfare. Be dramatic, exciting, and even a little goofy. Or a lot goofy! Set off fireworks, do exciting camera pans around the player, have the player character jump in the air excitedly, play cheering crowds and slot-machine sound effects. Use visual effects and particles, lots and lots of particles! The more, the better! You want players to feel as though they are the victors of World War III, the scorer of the winning run at a baseball game, and a lottery winner all at the same time.

- Whatever the reward is, make it matter to the players. Award players something that gives them the edge on the next level and is the solution to a problem that plagued them on the last. The best reward is the one players don't realize they need until they get it.

In video games, rewards come in many shapes and sizes: **scoring, achievements, treasure, loot, power-ups, souvenirs, bonus materials, praise, surprise,** and **progression.**

High Score

Back in the prehistoric era of video games,[5] the players' only reward was a **high score.** Scoring is a useful system to showcase the players' success in a very simple way: a number and three little letters. It's a little hard to describe to someone these days why seeing your three initials displayed on an arcade game screen was so exciting, but it was a little like writing your name in wet cement: something the whole world can see to show that YOU were the master of the game—at least until the game's power was turned off for the night and the scoreboard reset. [6] Many gamers thrive on competition, even when it's against themselves, and love having the bragging rights that come with getting a high score. But is scoring in gaming still relevant?

That was the question many game developers asked themselves in the late 1990s. As the arcade scene was dying and most gaming had moved to PCs and home consoles, scoring represented the old school. Scoring was regarded as a remnant of game designs whose sole intent was to keep players dropping quarters into the slot. Scoring soon became regarded as a meaningless number compared to collecting 100% of the game's secrets and finishing the game's story. A simple numeric score just wasn't as sexy or cinematic as a full-blown ending cutscene. Scoring in gaming was almost as dead as the dodo.

Almost.

In the early 2000s, scoring started to matter again with the rising popularity of browser games like *Bejeweled* (Popcap, 2001) and *Feeding Frenzy* (Popcap, 2004). When **leaderboards** were introduced to Xbox Live (and later to the PlayStation Network), scoring was back up and running. Now players can share their scores and stats on the PlayStation Network, Game Center, Steam, Google Play, and Window's Game Explorer. Developers have attempted to get into the act by creating their own tracking programs such as UbiSoft's Uplay and EA's Origin.

---

[5] Back in those days, the only video games we had to play with were two rocks connected by vines to one bigger rock. Now get off my lawn, you darned kids!

[6] This is why it was always better when you got the high score at a 7-11 store. Those places NEVER closed!

Achievements

Achievements are high scores with personality. Debuting with *Halo 2* on the Xbox 360, achievements motivate players to show off their in-game skills and brag about their accomplishments. Doing a task *X* number of times, completing game goals like defeating bosses, collecting one specific item (or all of them), or just finishing the game are all valid achievements.

Achievements are great fun for the developer to create—as much as they are for players to collect. You can give your achievements clever names and fun icons. Usually published before the game's release, achievement lists act as a play "to-do" list. Achievements are a great way for the designer to point out to players the gameplay concepts that they otherwise may not think of attempting. Achievements can be awarded for anything the developer desires. Here are a few of my favorites:

- **Easiest achievement ever**—Press Start to play (*The Simpsons*).
- **Not bulletproof**—Die on an easy level (*50 Cent: Bulletproof*).
- **Street cleaner**—Hide five dead bodies in bales of hay (*Assassin's Creed 2*).
- **Be polite**—Provide an enemy with a freezecam shot of you doffing your hat (*Team Fortress 2*).
- **Six degrees of Schafer**—Play with or against any player who has this achievement (which means that at least one player in the chain has played the game with creator Tim Schafer; *Brütal Legend*).
- **You've wasted your life**—Be idle for 5 minutes (*Saw*).
- **Losing his mind**—Decapitate a captain with a shield (*Conan*).
- **Wheeeeeee!**—Slide 330 feet continuously through blood (*Fairy Tale Fights*).
- **Skidmark**—Give 50 wedgies (*Bully: Scholarship edition*).
- **I feel so funky**—Get slimed by a charging ghost (*Ghostbusters*).
- **Jawa juicer**—Crush five Jawas by using the grinder in the garbage processing room (*The Force Unleashed: Ultimate Sith Edition*).
- **The cake**—You found the cake, yummy! (*X-Men Origins: Wolverine*).

Money! Money! Money!

Who doesn't love getting **treasure?** The way the coins jingle merrily when they pop out of a treasure chest. The way they glitter and sparkle on the ground after spilling out of a headless enemy. The way they spin in place, luring you to jump through a flaming hoop of death and over a pit of punji sticks . . .

Yeah, collecting treasure is great and all, but what are you going to spend it on? To make treasure mean anything, you need an **economic system.** When designing treasure items for your game, create them in escalating values—1, 5, 10, 50, 100 . . . . You get the idea. But don't spread your values too far apart either. The last thing you want is the virtual equivalent of pennies—treasure that no one wants to pick up.

One of the things I love about video games is that I am far richer than I am in real life. Players feel great when they are flush with cash. The benefit of having wads of dough is that players have lots of choices when shopping—but to do that, you have to make sure there are plenty of items for the players to buy. It's always fun to give players choices between two really good things. Not only do they have the delicious agony over what to buy, but it gives them something to look forward to buying the next time they go shopping. Stock your stores with a variety of things and find ways to rotate the stock to keep the selection from getting stale. Next, determine the price your items will be. Start by classifying your treasure, loot, and other buyable items by their rarity: common, uncommon, rare, and unique. Then apply a price to each of the items. Think about what items you want available to the players from the beginning of the game. Always have some items that can be bought quickly and others that lie tantalizingly out of reach. If I only had a few more coins!

Once you've created a preliminary economy (don't worry about setting it in stone, prices will change over the course of production as you figure out what players will want or need), think about placing treasure in the world. If you want players to be able to afford $300 worth of items, make sure there is at least $300 worth of treasure in the level. You will have to answer the question, "Does treasure regenerate?" If it does, be aware that players can "mine" levels for treasure, which can completely screw up your economy. On the other hand, replaying a level without any treasure to act as a motivator isn't as much fun for players. You may want the players to replay a level multiple times so they can collect enough money to buy what they need. A shortage of funds encourages replay . . . or exploration off the beaten path. If you expose players to all the items they could buy at the beginning of the game (via an "ability tree" like in *Dante's Inferno*), the players can start to plan how they are going to spend their money once they earn it. Sometimes players might have to buy cheaper and necessary gear like ammo or health-ups to be able to progress. Give them options as to how and what they upgrade.

Use color to clarify your treasure's value like the old standbys copper, silver, and gold. Or use different shapes like coins, bags, and gems. Don't get too diverse or crazy; otherwise, players will mistake treasure items for power-ups.

Does your treasure have encumbrance, meaning there is a limit to what players can carry? If so, then how are they going to carry it? Many RPGs and MMOs have a limit to encumbrance, forcing players to find other storage solutions such as magical bags of holding or a bank. Whatever the solution, make sure that players don't have to shuttle cash from their storage to the store. Just have it come out of the players' accounts to avoid all the hassle.

Your treasure doesn't even have to be money. Treasure can be bolts as in *Ratchet and Clank*, studs as in the *LEGO* games, souls as in the *God of War* series, even trash, such as the bottle caps in *Fallout*. It doesn't matter what it looks like, as long as it's sparkly and makes a satisfying cha-ching! sound effect when you collect it!

Speaking of all that treasure, where are your players going to spend it? Most RPGs have friendly (and not so friendly) stores that sell all manner of adventuring goods. *Borderlands* and *BioShock* use vending machines. Make your store specific to the game you're making. A racing game could have a garage where players can buy car upgrades and customizations.

A sports game could have a sporting goods shop. Adding a store is just one more way to add character and theme to your game.

Hey, maybe that slightly creepy guy in the trenchcoat over there in the alley has the magic sword we're looking for? Let's go talk to him.

Who's there? Come in, come in. I have everything the daring hero needs to survive. Take a look around and don't be afraid to ask for help:

- **Offense**—Need a new sword? Lusting after that more powerful gun? How about a nice magic missile spell? It was owned by a little old witch who only used it on Sundays.

- **Defense**—Armor, shields, helmets, forcefield generators: I've got everything that can repel a blade or deflect a laser beam.

- **Repairs**—Swung that sword a little too hard, did ya? Well, it will only cost you a few coins to get it swing-worthy again.

- **Replenishable resources**—Ammunition, health potions, batteries, gasoline; we'll get you back up and running again!

- **Skills**—Want to learn a whirlwind sword attack? Or how to add +2 to your accuracy skill? How about a nice set that grants a lock-picking ability? All ya need is some cash . . .

- **Access**—I've got keys, treasure maps, and even a statue that looks like it may fit into a hole. I'll bet it opens a secret door somewhere.

- **Vanity**—That hat looks very stylish on ya. So does that new costume—much better than your old one, if I do say so myself.

- **Whimsy**—Oh, I absolutely think your hair would look better pink, sir. And yes, Ma'am, a mustache is just the thing ya need.

- **Information**—For just a few coins, I can tell you where the King is handing out jobs for adventurers such as yourself.

- **Saves**—Only the cruelest of designers would charge someone to keep playing . . . . That will be $100 gold, good sir. Thanks and come again!

Let's get out of this place; it's horribly overpriced, especially because you can find most of this stuff lying around the levels.

Loot is all the great stuff you can buy, but it's FREE! Well, if you consider navigating through the temple of eternal pain and defeating the goblin army free. The difference between loot you buy and loot you find is you should always find much better loot on your adventure. Loot can be part of an upgrade system. Make it part of your story like *The Legend of Zelda's* famous "It's dangerous to go alone, take this . . . " moment. Progression in the game can be marked by getting a new weapon or piece of equipment. Save the best weapons, the strongest armor, and the shootiest guns for loot. Let players earn their keep by solving puzzles, surviving hazards, and defeating bosses. And remember this **very important thing:**

THE BEST REWARDS ARE HARD WON

Souvenirs

Souvenirs are physical (well, virtual) reminders of the players' adventures during the game. Souvenirs can be displayed back at the players' base or castle or spaceship or condo. Give players a special place to show them off, like Lara Croft's trophy room in *Tomb Raider Anniversary* (Eidos, 2006) or a nice shelf with proper lighting. They can be animated interactive exhibits like those found in *LEGO Indiana Jones: The Original Adventures* (LucasArts, 2008) or virtual museums like the one in *Uncharted 2: Among Thieves*. No matter which style you choose, use a tight camera or viewer to let players get a good look at 'em and a label to remind them where they found the souvenir.

Not all souvenirs should be kept on a shelf, however. Turning souvenirs into useful game items gives those items more meaning. Defeat the Lich King in *World of Warcraft* and take his sword. *Mega Man* takes the powers of the Robot Masters as he defeats them. Instead of awarding a dragon skin rug, why not give the player a pair of dragon skin boots? That way, as long as the player wears the boots, everyone

Sweet boots!   Level 70 Red!

will know who slew the red dragon. Make sure to give the souvenir items special properties too. Those red dragon boots may allow players resistance to fire attacks or let them walk over hot coals or on lava. It may even give them a special flaming kick attack. Make it special and the players will want to get to the next encounter to see what they can win.

Bonus Section about Bonus Features

The biggest problem with **bonus features** is the production team usually creates them at the last minute. Design them early, but they should be one of the last things you create. This way, you can judge just what constitutes a "bonus" to the players by comparing it to the rest of the game's content. Bonus materials may include

- **Costume changes**—Costume changes help add a little variety—and humor—to your bonus features. The Starkiller from *Star Wars: The Force Unleashed* can wear costumes from the game's other levels. Kratos in *God of War* can unlock a business suit or chef's costume.

- **Alternative models**—Create a new look for your hero or villains! In *Uncharted 2: Among Thieves,* players can unlock a fat version of the hero, while in *Batman: Arkham Asylum,* players can turn all the enemies into skeletons.

- **Alternative modes**—Ah, big head mode. You are so easy to code and yet you get so many laughs. Is it any wonder why we love you? Silly modes run the gamut from changing an enemy's exploding body parts into birthday presents to turning all the cars in a game pink. You are limited only by your imagination and how much time you have left in your production schedule.

I'm not sure why this is hilarious.

- **Downloadable content (DLC)** —Usually downloaded via console networks like Xbox Live Arcade, PlayStation Network, or WiiWare, downloadable content can take many forms, including many of those bonuses included on this list. DLC offers a way for games to live beyond their average play life with additional weapons, gameplay modes, achievements, character models, and new levels.

- **New levels**—The most time-consuming of all bonus materials to make, new levels (and game content) have become a popular type of DLC. Many console games have introduced "season passes": the customers buy the pass when the game is released so that they can gain access to new levels that are released later. *BioShock Infinite, Assassin's Creed III,* and *Batman: Arkham Origins* are just a few of the games that offer season passes to expand the play experience with new levels and stories. By scheduling these passes as additional material that is released after the game has shipped, the development team can put more time, effort, and polish into the levels, thus keeping up the quality of the material.

- **Music**—Want to listen to the game's music without playing the game? Simple. Create an audio player to allow players to hear the music. Or you can just let them insert the game disc into a CD player.

- **Commentary**—An audio track of the team may talk about the game's development. Starting with *Half-Life 2: Lost Coast*, developer Valve has made interactive in-game commentary one of its standard bonus features.

- **"Making of" video**—Another bonus feature is a documentary-style featurette (or feature) that explores the game's creation. These videos are very time-consuming to make; however, they can be a great way to spotlight your hard-working team.

- **Model viewers**—Players can view the 3-D models and assets in the game. Allow the players camera control to pan around, rotate, and zoom in and out on your models to show them off in the best possible light. This feature is particularly good in games like RTSs, where the characters are normally viewed from a more distant camera angle.

- **Art viewers**—These viewers are the most common of bonus features: just scan your preproduction art and voilà! You're done! OK, lazy, you can do better than that. Don't be content to just show a slideshow of your team's art. Set the images to music or commentary from the artists. Show off environments, props, maps, and design materials that will make the players appreciate all the hard work you've put into your games. Make sure the players have control over the pace of the presentation. Don't make them wait around for the next piece of art to appear. How about a magnifier so they can zoom in closely to examine the art? (You can even hide a reward within the art for the players to find!)

- **Promotional materials**—Promo materials are more commonly found in sequels because the assets are usually created late in the game's production process. If included with long-standing franchises, they can be particularly interesting for nostalgia purposes.

- **Trailers**—Movie trailers (especially relevant if the game is a movie tie-in), previews of other games, a sneak peak at a sequel. Just don't make watching them mandatory: allow players the option to skip them.

- **Minigames**—Although some whole games are collections of minigames,[7] don't forget to include them in bigger games too. They provide players a chance to take a break from the protracted grind of a longer adventure without ever having to "leave the disc." Give your minigame a place to live, such as an arcade. Minigames are moderately easy to make: just identify some of your game's most fun gameplay and recontextualize it. In *God of War*, we did just that—everything in the "Challenge of the Gods" was already in the game code; it just gave players a different set of victory conditions. Some minigames give rewards that can be used back in the main game's economy system. Sometimes they are promotional tools, as seen in the case of the iPhone game *Mass Effect Galaxy*, which gives players a reward in *Mass Effect 2* for completing it.

---

[7] For examples, just check out most of the games on the Wii.

- **Multiplayer modes**—While describing multiplayer gameplay could take up an entire chapter,[8] there are still other modes that aren't directly related to gameplay. Asset trading, chat functions, spectator modes, friends, and rival rosters that allow you to check your friends' game stats—these additional modes will give your game value. Remember to keep their interfaces intuitive and user-friendly.

- **Alternative endings**—Will the player turn out good or evil? Save the world or get blown up? Get the girl or get the boy? Many RPG, adventure, action, and survival horror games offer multiple endings to their stories. For example, the *Mass Effect* series offers different endings depending on the sex of the player character and the relationships built with the other NPCs over the course of the game. Multiple endings are a great way to get players to replay the game, as long as they know there are multiple endings to be seen. I've found that it's no longer enough to just have a few different endings based on the decisions made at a few key moments in the game. The struggle between good and evil is much more interesting if they are evenly matched. Build systems and opportunities for the players to "course correct" toward one outcome or another. Make the outcome be the players' choice, rather than one decided by the game.

- **Cheats**—Cheats are usually reserved for use by the development team during production. Cheat modes can be enabled to give players unlimited resources like health, ammo, lives, or just plain ol' invulnerability. I suggest that you don't enable cheats until players have played through the game once; otherwise, they are CHEATING!!! . . . themselves out of experiencing the game the way it was meant to be played. Some games go as far as to encourage "proper" play: cheats might not get the "good" ending of a game, or they might be marked out as a cheater, as in *GTA*. In *Team Fortress 2*, anyone who didn't use a cheat received a special wearable angel's halo called "the cheater's lament."

How to Win at Losing

As an industry, we are really, really good about making players feel really, really bad. We kill player characters at the drop of a hat, force them into near impossible situations, and then mock them when they fail. We'll steal from them in a heartbeat, and we'll mess with their minds any chance we can get. What we're not very good at doing is offering **praise.** And as an industry, we wonder why players complain about games. What we need to do is make players feel like

---

the best people in the world instead. The best example I've seen of giving players praise is in *Zak and Wiki: The Quest for Barbaros' Treasure* (Capcom, 2007). Whenever players do something correctly, the following happens:

- A "success" musical sting plays.

- The hero does a funny reaction or victory animation.

- There is a particle effect coming off the hero.

- Wiki, the player's monkey sidekick, congratulates players (in text form) on how good they just did; Wiki also has his own musical sting and particle effect.

Not only does all the preceding play out whenever players complete a puzzle, but also

- A burst of special effects tints the screen yellow with streaking stars.

- A success musical tune plays, longer than the sting.

- A "look at me!" animation from the hero displays the puzzle piece or item they've just won.

- The name of the item the players have just won is shown.

Eight things to support praising players in the forms of character animation, visual effects, music, and text for solving one puzzle! Fantastic! This game made me feel as if I was the smartest player in the world, and as a result, I wanted to keep playing! Just remember that you can have too much of a good thing. Praise ceases to be meaningful if you receive it for doing nothing or performing insignificant acts.

See how often you can stroke players' egos during the course of the game. NPCs in *Fable* either recoil in horror or compliment the hero, depending on what alignment he is, which is exactly what players wants to hear, especially because they've spent so much time cultivating their goodness or evil.

There are other rewards than just treasure. I'm talking about **surprise** and fun. At Disneyland, Pirate's Lair is a pirate-themed playground. Guests at Pirate's Lair can interact with several items, including a bilge pump and a turn wheel. As you turn the wheel, a rope on a pulley starts to pull up a treasure chest from underwater. In a video game, once the treasure chest is revealed, players would get their treasure and go on their way.

However, if you keep cranking the wheel and raising the chest, you reveal a clinging skeleton who is trying to keep the chest for himself. The skeleton serves no purpose other than to get a laugh out of viewers. There's no reason why video games can't have little moments like this. Some game developers do similar things, such as Marvel Comics creator Stan Lee appearing in *Marvel Ultimate Alliance 2*, *Ape Escape*'s monkeys in *Metal Gear Solid 3*'s jungle level, or *Braid*'s homage to Mario's World 1-1.

Some will argue that **progression** isn't much of a reward and that players shouldn't be rewarded for merely finishing the game. After all, isn't the point to finish it? There are a lot of things competing for your players' free time. What can be done to keep them engaged? You only need a great story, intriguing level design, ridiculously cool boss battles, and awesome upgrades. Easy, right? But what if more than one player at a time wants to play? Well, that's why we're moving on to Level 14!

Level 13's Universal Truths and Clever Ideas

- Create power-ups that are compatible and complementary to the players' actions and attacks.
- Love thy players! Give them the tools to succeed like DDB and rubberbanding.
- If you think something in your game is too difficult or boring, it is. Get rid of it.
- Never underestimate the greed of the players, and use it to prompt interesting scenarios and challenges.
- Plan out your economy for the entire game. Price items according to when you want the players to earn them.
- Provide enough money for the players so they have choices when shopping.
- Have a variety of cool things to buy. Make the players have to choose between (at least) two really good things so that they come back for more.
- Determine whether scoring is right for your game; then reward players when high scores or achievements are obtained.
- Don't forget bonus materials and DLC. Remember that it takes time to make this content, so don't leave it until the end of your production.
- Some rewards are just for fun.

14
Multiplayer—The More the Merrier

THE FIRST TRUE multiplayer game I remember playing was *Gauntlet* (Atari, 1985); up to four people were able to play together. Because of the arcade cabinet's configuration, what I remember most from playing *Gauntlet* (other than "elf needs food badly") is that my friends and I would push and jostle each other as we played the game. Even though *Gauntlet* is a cooperative game, we sure didn't play it that way. We were always trying to grab the health or be the first to activate the "smart bomb" potion.

The jostling continued through the years with *Teenage Mutant Ninja Turtles* (Konami, 1989) and *Captain America and the Avengers* (Data East, 1991). When *Doom* (id Software, 1993) reared its ugly demon head, the jostling became virtual via our local area network (LAN) connection. And by jostling, I mean blasting each other with plasma rifles during death matches. Multiplayer jostling has since evolved even further:

- **Head-to-head**—Two or more players compete against each other in real time on the same game system. Most sports, action, and some FPS games allow for head-to-head play.

- **Network/peer-to-peer**—Two or more people play with and against each other in real time on machines connected via the Internet on a wide area network (WAN) that can be created by the developer or the player. Games can also be played on a wireless network using a Nintendo 3DS or mobile device.

- **Client/server**—These computer systems are big and fast enough to handle multiple users at one time. Some **massively multiplayer online** games (**MMOs**) and **massively multiplayer online role-playing games** (**MMORPGs**) use client/servers to handle the enormous amount of traffic. The **server** is the computer running the game simulation code. **Clients** are computers that connect to the server, send input from users, and display the game world to them. A system may include game servers that run the simulation, account servers that deal with player login, and database servers to store persistent game information.

- **Ad hoc WiFi**—This connection allows players to play device-to-device without cables or a network. It is common in mobile gaming devices, but it suffers from not being able to transfer large amounts of data and players must keep in close proximity during play.

After you decide how your players are going to connect, you have to determine what they are going to play. Three broadly different styles of play are found in multiplayer games:

- In **competitive** games, players have the same objective but work against each other—often fighting to the "death" to complete an objective first or achieve the highest score. (Or maybe it's just fun to fight each other!)

- **Cooperative** games give players the same objective while (in theory) working together to achieve it. After playing *Gauntlet* with my stupid friends, I realized even a cooperative game can easily dissolve into a competitive one.

- **Conjugate** gameplay has players sharing the same gameplay space but not the same goals. With the rise of MMOs and MMORPGs, conjugate gameplay has become increasingly frequent as dozens, if not hundreds, of players dash around the game world at the same time, each with his own agenda and motivation.

So just what are these motivations? Well, I'm glad you asked; otherwise, I wouldn't have had anything to write about for the next few pages. Look at all these game modes found in multiplayer games—some unique to the genre. You can easily combine these modes to create conjugate gameplay scenarios:

- **Death match/free-for-all**—It's every man for himself as players battle each other for high scores or jockey for the best weapon. Usually, players all start on common ground at the beginning of a death match and gain (or lose) equipment that gives them an edge over the course of the game.

- **Team death match**—This mode has teams of players killing each other for dominance. It can even have competitive goals, where players on the same team can compete for the highest score.

- **Fighting**—Two or more fighters enter; only one leaves! It's often connection speeds, not flying fists that cause problems with fighting games. If the connection is slow in a game where split-second moves make a huge difference, that "lag" can cause gameplay to suffer. Make sure your programmer teammates are aware of predictive code solutions such as Tony Cannon's GGPO netcode.

- **Survival**—Usually, the goal of survival game mode is to defeat all the enemies or survive getting from point A to B. Players of the *Left 4 Dead* series watch each other's backs in combat as well as help each other heal when in danger.

- **Area/territory control**—The player has to travel to and protect/defend a certain location from AI enemies or human players. The excitement comes from the tug-of-war struggle of attacking, retreating, and retaking an objective as players attempt to "move the line" closer to the final area. An area control map game can last hours given the right two teams.

- **Defend/king of the hill**—This type of gameplay is much like area/territory control, but one team of players is given a certain location, which needs to be defended for a designated period of time.

- **Capture the flag**—This game mode has one player become a target of the other players, either by possessing an object (like a flag or *Halo*'s oddball skull) or being designated as "it" by the game code. The player who is "it" is sometimes handicapped while being "it." This mode can be played both competitively and cooperatively with other teammates protecting the player.

- **Race/driving**—Racing modes have players competing for position or time. Often that competition can get nasty if players are given the means to mess with the other players during the race (such as *Mario Kart*'s power-ups). For combat races, you can use a regressive system where the player in front is the most vulnerable to attack from the other players who are coming up from behind. *Burnout Paradise* (EA, 2008) introduced the "Easy Drive" mode where multiple drivers can participate in events and socialize as they drive.[1]

---

[1] I wonder if this will lead to virtual cell-phone laws?

- **Team objective**—The players are given an objective, usually one that can be achieved only by working together. Games like *Defense of the Ancients* (IceFrog, 2005) and *Spaceteam* (Henry Smith, 2012) require "all hands on deck" in order to win the game.

- **Asynchronous**—Players play against each other, but not at the same time. Players can either take turns as with *Words with Friends*, *Skulls of the Shogun*, and *Draw Something*, or they can play simultaneously without interacting with the other player as in *Demon's Souls*, *Frozen Synapse*, or *Real Racing 3*.

- **Gambling**—In games of chance, players play competitively or in combination to achieve the highest score (or at least beat the odds.) Avoid progressive systems where the rich get richer, and the poor get poorer.

- **Reflex**—How fast is your trigger finger? Quiz and puzzle games often have players see who's faster to determine victory, or at least give them an opportunity to use their . . .

- **Knowledge**—There's nothing like proving you're smarter than the guy sitting next to you on the sofa. This genre has consistently maintained its presence in video games such as the *You Don't Know Jack*, *Buzz!*, and the *Scene It?* series as well as adaptations of TV game shows including *Who Wants to Be a Millionaire* and the *Price Is Right*.

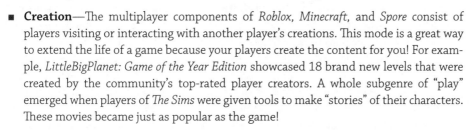

- **Creation**—The multiplayer components of *Roblox*, *Minecraft*, and *Spore* consist of players visiting or interacting with another player's creations. This mode is a great way to extend the life of a game because your players create the content for you! For example, *LittleBigPlanet: Game of the Year Edition* showcased 18 brand new levels that were created by the community's top-rated player creators. A whole subgenre of "play" emerged when players of *The Sims* were given tools to make "stories" of their characters. These movies became just as popular as the game!

- **Virtual life**—PlayStation's *Home*, *Second Life* (Linden Research Group, 2003), and *Animal Crossing* (Nintendo, 2001) are just a few of the games in which players can customize their virtual worlds and interact with other online occupants. What started as text-only chatrooms have become the reality described in Neil Stephenson's visionary book *Snow Crash*. (Now where's my samurai sword code?)

One more important question to ask yourself is: how dependent on multiplayer is my game going to be? For example, some games are multiplayer-only—*League of Legends* (Riot Games, 2009), *MAG: Massive Action Game* (SCEA, 2010), *Titanfall* (Bungie, 2014)—and can't be played as a single-player experience. Knowing the answer to this at the start of the design process will impact the rest of your design.

How Many Is the Right Number?

You may be wondering how many players multiplayer systems should support. Take, for example, a melee-based fighting game like *Street Fighter*. If this type of game had more than two players, there would be all types of problems. Players would bunch up as they fought, making it hard to see individual players. Collision detection would be problematic, and it would all just devolve into mob warfare rather than a contest of skills that makes a good fighting game. On the other hand, an MMORPG like *World of Warcraft* would feel empty if it allowed only a few hundred players to roam around at the same time. So, how many players should there be? Let's look at the numbers:

- Fighting game (*Street Fighter*) = 2 players
- Fighting game (*Power Stone*) = 4 players
- Social games (*Uno*) = 4 players
- Action platformers (*LittleBigPlanet*) = 4 players
- Driving (*Burnout Paradise*) = 8 players
- FPS (*Call of Duty: Modern Warfare 2*) = 16 players
- FPS (*MAG*) = 64, 128, or 256 players (depending on game mode)
- MMORPG (*World of Warcraft*) = roughly 4,000 to 5,000 players *per server*

As you can see, there is a HUGE difference between the numbers of players. Think about the interactions you want the players to have. Smaller game screens such as mobile devices can't handle more than one player—which means WiFi or online solutions—and even the largest TV screen can get too crowded if there are too many players playing on one screen at once. Will the characters run into each other as they play? Sometimes the number *makes* the gameplay as with the *Super Smash Bros* series; other times it will just cause collision issues. How quickly will players move around the playfield, die, and respawn? These values can often be used to help determine player count as well. Finally, you should always "stress test" your game to see how many players it can handle before it breaks.

MMORPGS, or Hell Is Other People

The MMORPG genre has evolved rapidly to have its own set of tropes and methods of play, some of which hardly qualify as "playing" at all. Becoming familiar with these tropes and including them in your own design will not only fill out your game but also keep you competitive:

- **Buffing**—Spell casting affects not only the caster, but also the entire party. This method of play allows players to assume certain roles during gameplay. For example, if a cleric is able to prepare a healing buff (via hotkey), as players take damage, he can restore them fully to allow them to continue fighting.

- **Character customization**—A huge appeal of any MMO is being able to assume the role of another character and to get lost in that fantasy life. The level of player character customization can range from preset character templates to making characters fully customizable down to sex, eye color, and nose length. Within the game, further encourage customization and let the players buy or win clothing, weapons, armor, gear, and mounts that fit the personality and class of the characters they are playing.

I made it myself!

- **Chatting**—A text or voice chat system in your game is expected these days. Players will use MMOs as a social gathering place as much as a place to play your game.

- **Crafting**—Players combine harvested, found, or bought items to create new gear and weapons. Players first need to find "recipes" and "components" for creating items to be able to craft objects. As with the ability to customize characters, let the players craft items into unique creations. The time needed to create an item depends on the power of the item or weapon. Sometimes players can craft in workshop locations or pay in virtual or real money to reduce crafting time. Create a separate screen for crafting so the players can focus on the activity. You can use skill-based minigames to successfully initiate the crafting process. Some games allow for "trial and error" style crafting, with players running the risk of destroying components if they fail in their attempt. Just don't allow players to destroy a hard-to-get or expensive crafting item. It's not fair to punish the players twice!

- **Economy**—Many MMO games thrive on an economy system. Players win treasures that allow them to customize characters; buy better weapons and gear, housing, and mounts; and even buy their own castles! (Or space stations, secret HQs, and so on.) Balance earning and buying. Make it worthwhile for players to go through the effort. Let players store loot and items in personal safes or public banks. Many MMOs have developed an economy that spills over into the real world, where players buy in-game money with real-world cash. I talk more about how to integrate this into your design in the monetization section.

How about you *don't* kill eight of us and we'll buy you those boots instead?

- **Grinding**—As players level up their characters, the rate of their progress slows down. Slow down the rate of progress too much, and players will experience "grind." Grinding is often used to artificially extend the length of gameplay, but it can also get frustrating for players who feel they are wasting their time. Keith Burgun, designer of *100 Rouges,* has this to say: "Grinding is a low-risk activity that the player can do repeatedly for real gain. In any game that has grinding, grinding is the optimal move. It becomes not 'what is the best move' for the player but 'how much can I bore myself for my own gain?'"[2]

  Here are a few suggestions on how to reduce the impact of grinding in your own design:

  - If content is too similar, things will feel repetitive. Add variety.

  - Players grind because they feel they can't progress due to a lack of power, abilities, or money. Make game difficulty ramp smoothly rather than steeply.

  - Give players more freedom. Don't make them always follow designer-defined objectives.

  - Offer more rewards. Grinding is often done in response to monetization. If players have alternative rewards to shoot for, the repetitive activity won't feel so grindy.

  - Make grinding its own reward. Offer achievements or special status for doing the most of an activity.

  - Reduce! Make your game or your victory conditions shorter. Just concentrate on the "good stuff." Remember, if it seems too long or boring, it is!

- **Instanced dungeons**—To make MMO gaming a unique experience, dungeons can be instanced. This means content such as enemies and loot or even the level map are randomly generated to provide a different experience each time it is played. These dungeons exist "outside" the game world, allowing for several groups of players to be in the same albeit alternate versions of the dungeon at the same time. That way, players don't have to wait for the dungeon to "restock" between player interactions.

---

[2] www.cheatcc.com/extra/pokemonshowedmehowgrindingcanbeagoodthing.html

- **Item collection**—Item collection is a huge motivating factor in MMORPGs. Players create items that improve combat and other in-game abilities—especially tedious ones like crafting, mining, or harvesting. Most items fall along a rarity scheme: common, uncommon, rare, and unique. Special items can be gained only by defeating specific creatures (getting these items is known as "drops"), and seasonal items are available only at certain times of the year or by attending specific world events.

- **Open world structure**—Most MMOs feature sandbox worlds where players can (presumably) go anywhere and do anything. However, that is merely an illusion you will need to maintain for players. In reality, you will need to build the world in the way you want players to play the game. **Gating mechanisms,** such as level or gear requirements, will prevent players from  traveling to places they aren't ready for. Some games allow players to wander into higher-level sections, but the humiliation they receive at the hands of the enemies will usually force them to retreat until they've reached the necessary level to tackle the area's foes.

- **Player versus player (PvP)**—Players love to see how strong their characters are by killing other player characters. However, not everyone wants to run the risk of being randomly killed while playing. As a precaution, many MMOs have dedicated PvP servers. Another alternative is that your world has PvP combat restricted to certain locations.

- **Griefing**—When one player harasses another player by constantly killing him, that behavior is called griefing. You can create systems to penalize players for bad behavior or segregate them into friendly fire servers. Make sure your policies are clear to the players, and a warning/zero tolerance system helps keep the peace.

■ **Guilds**—Players are social animals and, as a result, they form groups. Players will form parties of characters, called guilds, to explore, socialize, and run raids. As a designer, you will want to create in-game meeting places for guilds to socialize. While it requires a lot of work, you also may want to design tools to promote guilds within your game world. Useful guild tools include communication tools, stat tracking, calendars for running raids, and guild asset customization.

■ **Player housing**—Everyone likes to play house. Give your players a personal space to show off their achievements, display their souvenirs, or just "park" their player character safely between game sessions. Having a home base will make players feel much more connected and "at home" in the game world, which will make it become a place they want to return to again and again.

■ **Raids**—When players team up to defeat difficult game scenarios, such as storming a castle or battling a particularly fearsome enemy, they are leading raids. Players who assemble and lead a raid need to be one part strategist, one part manager, and one part social director. As a designer, you should create scenarios that can be overcome by a variety of party configurations, and even allow for the players' creative thinking or just plain dumb luck. Creating and cultivating the legends of these raid targets will let players know that they have to marshal their forces to defeat them. Design systems that make it easy for players to share the loot after the raid is over based on each player's performance.

■ **Spawn camping**—This is a practice by players who wait for an enemy or player to appear at a spawn point to kill that player. You can combat this bad habit in your level design by creating multiple spawn points, making camping locations risky to stay at for extended periods of time, or by making spawn camping locations easy to see.

- **Trading/auctions**—Because players often end up with lots of identical loot, or with items that their character class can't use, trading and auctions are good solutions to help players clear out inventory. Make sure your players can easily trade items without ripping each other off. Create locations in your game world to promote trading. Some games have auction houses, where regular auctions are held and players can bid on items using in-game treasure.

Designing Multiplayer Levels

Now that I've overwhelmed you with a ton of information about multiplayer design, let's look at one of the most commonly found elements of multiplayer gaming—levels.

Did you read Level 9 already? The one about designing levels? Good, because most of that information is still valid when it comes to making a multiplayer level. But there are some important differences. Here's some advice for the three stages of making a multiplayer map—planning, mapping and building.

Planning Your Level

Keep these questions in mind as far as planning:

- **What is the gameplay?** The type of gameplay will dictate the design of your level. For example, a "king of the hill" level is going to have a central location where the teams will clash over who controls the hill, while a capture the flag is going to be broken into three zones—team one's base, team two's base, and a no-man's land where the gameplay emphasis is going to be on players racing back and forth between bases.

- **What's the story?** Why are the players fighting in this place? Knowing the story will help you design the level objects that tell the story. For example, you could tell the story of a battle in a war-torn village by using overrun barricades, a building with its wall blown out, and an abandoned tank.

- **What's the theme?** The theme should not dominate the map. Don't sacrifice good gameplay areas just because they don't fit into your theme. There's nothing wrong with combining themes (remember the Mexican Pizza?). Multiplayer levels don't always have to make sense; they just have to be fun.

- **What makes your map memorable?** One of the hardest things for a new player to do during a multiplayer match is to learn the level while trying to keep alive. Memorable geometry and level objects helps a player orient himself when he spawns in. When he sees the object he will say to himself, "Ah-ha! I know where I am."

- **Design for all types.** Many multiplayer games have different player roles and you need to take all of these different play styles into account. Make sure you create interesting spaces that allows each player type to do what they do best.

Mapping Your Level

Here are a few pointers on mapping:

- **Keep your map simple.** It's easier for players to understand how to get around on a simple map. Use simple shapes like squares, figure eights, and circles for paths and open spaces. Simple maps make it easier to guide your player and highlight the objective, and are easy to modify if something needs to be changed.

- **Mirror your map.** Take your map design, copy it, reverse it, and paste it! Not only does it save on production time, but the players can explore their own territory and have a good idea how to get around when they enter the enemy's base.

- **Use walls.** Use walls to funnel the player towards the objective. Narrow spaces like tunnels and bridges can be used to point the player in the right direction and create stand-off scenarios.

- **Set up defensible areas.** Players should have a good idea of where they are going to fight before they get there. Show defensible areas to players as they approach it; for example, a team might have to "hold a platform" during a control point game. This way the players can scope out where the fight is going to be and plan their strategy accordingly.

- **Include a no man's land.** A "no man's land" is where the most danger and action take place—otherwise cover loses its significance. Make players risk exposure to attack if they want to pass through no man's land. Some games will offer alternative paths around or under a no man's land—however, if the other team catches on, the fighting will move to these pathways!

- **Make good use of spawn points.** The player should always have an opportunity to see another player coming but shouldn't be able to use that opportunity to ruin the fun. Give the player a chance to get out of the spawn point alive. Make it too dangerous for an enemy player to "spawn camp" in front of a team's base by making the space wide open or too hard to enter. Many games use gates that prevent enemies from entering so the player can get onto the battlefield without getting killed.

- **Make sure players can find their way around.** Use big and small level objects to help with orientation. You want to help players orient locally as well as globally. Using a weenie like a big castle will help the player know where they are when they first enter the level, but a castle becomes almost useless as an orientation tool once the player is fighting in the castle's hallways and dungeons.

- **Provide alternate routes of approach.** Can the player sneak through tunnels, rocket jump onto rooftops, swim through water, or use a zipline to get across the map? Letting the player use these alternative routes lets them feel smart and sneaky and makes game play unpredictable.

Building Your Level

Pay attention to these items for building:

- **Check collision**—When creating your gray box level, make sure there are no places where a player can get "snagged" on to the level's geometry. Be especially careful of stairs, corners, and ledges. Watch out for "seams" where the player can fall between the collision and drop out of the world!

- **Play test**—After you have your level built in gray box, play it as often as you can with as many different players as possible. Use **heat maps**—code that indicates where players go and what they do during a play session—to determine where players fight, hide, and die. Use that data to modify your map. Your goal is to create a play space in which the player will want to play everywhere, not just congregate in one place.

- **Textures**—Use clearly different textures on floors and walls so players can see the path of the floor. Be careful of textures that tessellate or look visually cluttered. Use light colored textures to create a path for the player to follow.

- **Color**—Color is another way players can quickly determine what level they are in. They will associate a dominant color scheme with each level—even if subconsciously. You can use color theory to help set the mood—green feels dank, red feels dangerous, blue feels stealthy.

- **Lighting**—Use lighting to point out objectives and passageways. Players love to hide in shadows, so create lots of shadowy overhangs, doorways, and tunnels for to them to lurk in. Use the lighting of the time of day to further set the mood of your level. Just changing the lighting from day to night can give a totally different feel to your level.

- **Sound**—Use background noise to help the player get into the mood. Unless you want to put your players on edge, avoid using sounds that the player can mistake for another player—like rustling trees that can be mistaken for enemy movement or explosions in the distance that can be mistaken for enemy gunfire.

The Dirty Half Dozen

The best way to learn how to make a FPS multiplayer map is to play one. Here's a few classics you should check out. Hopefully they will inspire you to make your own great multiplayer level:

- **Blood Gulch**—*Halo* (remade as Coagulation in *Halo 2*, Valhalla in *Halo 3*, and *Forge World* in Halo: Reach)
- **2Fort**—*Team Fortress Classic* (remade in *Team Fortress 2*)
- **Wake Island**—*Battlefield 1942*
- **de_Dust**—*Counter-Strike* (remade in every *Counter-Strike* game)
- **Rust**—*Modern Warfare 2*
- **Overgrown**—*Call of Duty 4*

Level 14's Universal Truths and Clever Ideas

- Design multiplayer systems into your game from the start.
- Offer your players a variety of game modes and objectives.
- The right number of players is whatever is right for your gameplay.
- Allow players to customize their characters, their objects, their world.
- New play patterns will emerge when players are given the tools to create.
- Determine what level you want players to negatively interact with other players (like PvP).
- Players will always do the last thing you expect, but sometimes that's OK.
- A multiplayer level should not be designed like a single-player level.

Level 15
Everybody Wins: Monetization

"The main thing about money, Bud, is that it makes you do things you don't want to do."
—That guy in the movie "Wall Street" who wasn't Gordon Gecko

SINCE THE RELEASE of the first edition of *Level Up!* one design system has become increasingly important to the gaming industry: **monetization.** What is monetization? It's a series of strategies employed by the developer to try to get players to pay additional money past the player's initial purchase.

Game developers have always been happy to separate the player from their money. It's been with us since the dawn of gaming: if you wanted to keep playing, you kept paying (until you got so good at playing you could make a quarter last for hours if not days![1]). Today is no different. Take a look at some of the traditional ways developers could earn a little more cash:

- **Pay-to-play:** Early arcade players fed quarters for additional lives. While pay-to-play faded during the early years of consoles and the decline of arcades, it came back in vogue when players could make financial transactions online. Starting with games on PCs, pay-to-play became increasingly popular with the rise in social gaming, where players could keep playing as long as they had paid for the energy to do so.

---

[1] The longest single-credit arcade game record is currently held by Ed Heemskerk who played one continuous game of *Q-Bert* for 68.5 hours!

- **In-game advertising:** Starting with Pepsi and Canon billboards in *Pole Position* (Namco, 1982), developers have been happy to sell space to advertisers. When free-to-play games appeared on computers, so did advertising—in the form of annoying pop-up ads. When pop-up ads started to clutter up mobile device games, the developers came up with a new trick: an offer to remove the offending ads for a fee!

- **Virtual goods:** The earliest virtual goods were sold to players of multi-user dungeons who realized that it was sometimes cheaper to pay for an item than to earn it. With the success of *World of Warcraft's* virtual economy, the eyes of developers were opened to the possibilities—and profitability—of virtual goods. Virtual game sales in some games were so profitable that the developers were able to offer their core games for free. How much can virtual goods set you back? Anywhere from 49 cents for a (discounted) weapon in *Team Fortress 2* to a virtual planet in *Entropia Universe* that will only set you back $6 million.

- **Downloadable content (DLC):** DLC allows players to extend their gaming experience past the initial purchase. Early downloadable content took the form of promotional codes but soon developers learned that players wanted everything associated with the game, and started charging for it. Costumes and skins, new weapons and vehicles, levels and gameplay modes, brand new storylines . . . every type of content was fair game in this new marketplace.

Some designers (and many publishers) feel that a monetization system is necessary for a game to be competitive in today's market. Other game designers feel that monetization systems ruin a gaming experience and run screaming from them. You've heard about the success stories: *Candy Crush Saga, Bike Race Free, Simpsons Tapped Out, CSR Racing* . . . . How hard could it be to monetize a game? Just add some hats, charge the player for energy, sell them some boosts, and voila! They'll be sending you money by the truckload, right?

But I've also seen games cancelled due to monetization systems that were poorly thought through, as in the case of Supercell's 2012 *Battle Buddies*—a shooter where you had to buy your guns! Or even worse, look at developer MikenGreg. Despite achieving 200,000 downloads with their game *Gasketball,* the developers ended up homeless and had to borrow money to survive. The cause? A poor monetization plan.

If these examples have taught me anything, it is that monetization systems require a lot of work to create, demand a lot of attention to get right, and can ruin a game experience if applied too heavily or lightly. Sounds scary, but not to worry; we will navigate these tricky waters together. Let's start with a couple of questions you should consider when approaching these systems:

- How important is the system to your game? For example, some games lean heavily on monetization and won't let the player progress without it. Other games will make it optional, letting the player choose when to spend money . . . if at all. Making this decision at the start of the design process will impact the rest of your design.

- How dependent on the system is your game? *Batman: Arkham Origins* (DC Entertainment, 2013) is a free-to-play download—which allows players to watch a motion comic—but won't start the game unless players pay its 99-cent unlock fee.

Give monetization systems lots of attention early in the design process. Don't leave them to the last minute. You can exploit some aspects of these systems to your benefit in all aspects of your entire design. For example, the Card Hunter's Club in *Card Hunter* (Blue Manchu, 2013) allows paid members to gain a third treasure upon the successful completion of a level.

Now that you've asked the big questions, let's consider what kind of business model you are going to follow to make your money. You have plenty of models to choose from:

- **Trial**—A free version is severely limited in scope—it's usually just a few levels—just enough to give players a taste of the game in the hopes that they buy the "premium" version.

- **Freemium**—Freemium is the best-known monetization model. This unlimited trial or "velvet rope" model lets players play without paying. While the players can play most of the game, key features are missing. At a certain point, players can pay for a "premium" version of the game.

  The freemium model has been in the running ever since Nexon made a splash with its freemium game *KartRider* in 2005, but it really gained steam with *FarmVille* (Zynga, 2009), where players could pay to speed up game processes that required friends—recruited from the players' Facebook lists—or time to complete. Why wait when you can pay to build your farmhouse immediately? When *FarmVille* gained 50 million players and $100 million in profits,[2] the industry took notice and monetization became the new model.

---

[2] http://tech.fortune.cnn.com/2009/10/26/farmville-gamemaker-zynga-sees-dollar-signs/

- **Free-to-play (F2P)**—These games are free to download, but if players want to avoid grinding or to progress faster, they can pay for more currency, power, or time. *Smurf Village, Simpsons Tapped Out,* and Zynga's *–Ville* series all follow this model.

- **Downloadable content (DLC)**—The game offers content that improves or enhances the experience. Players can still advance in the game, but they just might not look as cool doing it. DLCs can be vanity items like *Team Fortress 2*'s hats or *LittleBigPlanet*'s costumes or full-blown play experiences like *Grand Theft Auto IV's Ballad of Gay Tony* or *Borderland 2's Zombie Island of Dr. Ned.*

- **Season pass DLC**—Most commonly found in more traditional console games, the "season pass" offers a bundle of content ranging from new episodes to weapons to vanity items offered as a reduced cost package deal. Season passes are increasingly offered on the first day of a game's release, ensuring that players will have plenty to play after they finish the core game.

- **Membership**—Membership grants players benefits not available to regular players. Players gain access to special treasure, costumes, minigames, or other experiences. Often, these experiences are shown to non-member players to entice them to join. Memberships often offer to remove annoying ads that interrupt or obscure gameplay.

- **Premium**—The full version of the game is often sold at a "premium" price. Even when players pay full price, the game can still sell them DLC, memberships, and other in-game purchases.

- **Subscription**—Subscriptions ask for a regular payment—usually month-to-month. The challenge to the subscription model is to make sure you continue to add content so players feel as though they are paying for something worthwhile. *World of Warcraft* is one of the largest subscription games.

Cashing In

So you've convinced your players to pay. But just what are you giving players for their money? Here are some things your players might want to pay for:

- **Chance**—If players have an opportunity to improve their chances of success, they will pay. A chance might take the form of an item that increases stats or a single-use boost that temporarily changes the game's conditions.

- **Customization**—Whether it's decorating their virtual house or wearing a virtual hat, players love to express their identity through customization.

- **Convenience**—Today's players have less time to play games. And as they say, time is money. So instead of waiting for that pumpkin to grow or for a character to do a chore, why not just pay to speed things up? Some games give players the option to have friends help (what a hassle!) or pay to do it themselves. Make sure the benefits are clear and what you are offering is too good to pass up!

- **Exclusivity**—Rare items and experiences are prized by many players. Appeal to their vanity and status by creating limited or expensive items. Then other players will see these items and want to buy them too!

- **Progress**—Stuck on a level? Want to keep playing? Why not pay to progress! Economist Ramin Shokrizade lists two different gates to progression: "soft gates" and "hard gates." Players eventually can pass soft gates by grinding. However, they can pay to accelerate the process. With hard gates, the players have no choice but to pay. A common technique is to make players pay to pass a hard gate only to find a more expensive hard gate lies beyond. Because players already paid to pass one hard gate, why *not* spend for the next one, right?

Money Is the Root of Something Something

There's a shady side to monetization. Companies want players to play for years, not months, and monetization can keep them coming back because the more the players pay, the more invested in the game they feel. These consistently spending players, known as "whales," are the targets of **coercive monetization**—techniques designed to get players to spend even when they don't want to:

- **Currency obfuscation**—There should be a difference between your in-game currency, which is earned by the player, and premium currency, which is used to buy content using real money. For example, *Puzzle and Dragons* (GungHo Online, 2012) uses coins as its in-game currency and magic stones (or eggs) as its premium currency. Players defeat monsters to earn coins to pay for items in games and use real money to pay for stones to buy premium (including more coins!). Simple right? Even more confusing are the rates of exchange: 1600 Microsoft points costs $19.99. So how much is each point worth? And if games cost 1200 points, what can you spend your remaining 400 points on? Anything? I'm going to have to buy more points to afford something! See? If you keep prices just confusing enough, buyers won't be exactly sure how much they are spending.

- **Bundling**—Bundling makes items more appealing and makes players feel as if they're getting a deal. For example, the antlers hat in *TF2* costs $7.49, but if I buy the Smissmas 2012 bundle, for $14.97, I also get the Wreath and the Reindeeracorn—an additional $23.00 value—even though I wasn't planning on buying them in the first place! A common pricing trick is to list the "actual" cost and then list the bundling price below it so players can see the discount they are receiving. Hmmm. How much do virtual goods cost anyway?

- **Ramping**—Ramp the game's difficulty to the point where players *need* to buy boosts to progress. *Candy Crush Saga* (King, 2013) has an extremely sharp difficulty spike that forces the players to buy if they want to succeed.

- **Fun pain**—While at Zynga, Roger Dickey promoted a concept called "fun pain" to help with monetization. He said you need to provide both fun and pain to the players. For example, in *FarmVille*, the constant clicking players do to perform tasks is a "painful" action—requiring time and effort but eventually yielding the "fun" result for players. He warned that too much clicking would drive players away too! Designing fun pain is a delicate balancing act![3]

- **Reward removal**—Another popular trick is to threaten to remove rewards unless players pay. Placing a big ol' timer (only three days left!) forces players to decide—to buy or not to buy? (That is the question!) It's easier to get players to make digital payments during the heat of the game rather than before or after when they have time to think about exactly how much money that bushel of Smurfberries cost. Another trick is to give players so many rewards that they can't hold them all and so they must pay for more space! Sneaky!

As you can see, there are downsides to all these models. Players feel as if they are being taken advantage of when the game doesn't let them progress without paying. They are constantly being asked to pay for extras they don't want or need. They have to pay for access to the full game experience even after paying for the product. These situations can create bad feelings toward the game and the publisher. As a result, monetization and free-to-play have become quite controversial within the gaming community. Some developers have become rich using monetization techniques, whereas others feel that these techniques are taking advantage of the players. However, capitalism isn't all bad. There are many ethical ways to monetize:

- **Provide alternative ways to earn.** Let players realize there are multiple paths to reach their goal. Paying will provide the quick path, but they can play longer to reach the same results.

- **Warn players that your game costs money to play.** Let players know what they're getting themselves into from the start. Sometimes you can turn around players' opinions if they are really enjoying your game and feel it "deserves" to be supported.

---

[3] See Roger Dickey on how to monetize games: http://vimeo.com/32161327#.

- **If they pay, provide discounts.** Use bundling, early player adapters, and membership to give your players benefits and save them some money. They're more likely to spend if they feel that they're saving money.

- **Let the players back out of the pay option.** Don't lock players into paying. Let them back out if they get cold feet or make a mistake. They will be much more likely to spend in the future if they know they aren't going to regret doing so now.

People can lose their head when it comes to money, so it's always best to treat others the way you'd want to be treated. If you think your monetization method is taking advantage of your players, perhaps it's time to rethink that plan. Your players will appreciate it in the long run.

Level 15's Universal Truths and Clever Ideas

- Decide how dependent your game will be on monetization.
- Design monetization systems into your game from the start.
- Don't ignore the power of coercive monetization.
- Design ethical monetization systems.

Level 16
Some Notes on Music[1]

WHEN THE IMAGINEERS were creating the *Star Wars Star Tours* attraction at Disneyland, they initially intended the experience to be "realistic." The audience would hear only the sound of the Starspeeder 3000 and the pilot's dialogue. However, when they tested the attraction, something didn't feel right. Without the classic theme by John Williams, the attraction just didn't seem like "Star Wars," so the music was added in.

Music brings a lot to any entertainment experience, be it a theme park attraction, movie, or video game. But it also requires a lot of work and coordination between many members of a team, which contributes to the reason music and sound are usually left until late in production. This is a mistake. Sound and music can bring so much to a game that leaving it until to the last minute means missing out on some great design opportunities.

---

[1] Get it? Notes?

Music and sound in gaming have come a long way in a short time. Back in the 1970s and 1980s, arcade and console programmers had only electronic beeps and boops to play with. Even with those limitations, game creators were able to create some simple but memorable musical themes (or even just jingles) for games like *Pac-Man*, *Donkey Kong*, and *The Legend of Zelda*. Sound advances happened with almost every system; voice synthesizing and MIDI format audio meant that music became more lush. However, game creators were limited because sound and music files took up a good amount of memory on cartridges.

The big jump in game music came with CD media games. Starting with Red Book audio (Red Book being the set of standards for CD audio), music in games began to sound just like any other recorded music, and it was possible to store more of it on the CD. As games moved onto DVD media, the biggest problem with sound and music—storage space—was no longer an insurmountable issue. Nowadays modern PC and console games use streaming sound (compressed into MP3s, Ogg Vorbis, or console-specific formats and decompressed as needed by the sound chip). Emphasis shifted from the programmatic issues with music and sound to what to do with it creatively.

The first question you need to ask yourself when thinking about music design is, "What kind of music do I want?" There are really two answers to this question: licensed or original.

Licensed music is previously recorded music that can be "licensed" for use in a game for a fee. While music publishers own the rights to the recorded music, companies that work on behalf of the publishers, including the American Society of Composers, Authors and Publishers (ASCAP) and Third Element, negotiate licensing deals. Game publishers usually handle the job of obtaining the rights to music licenses and negotiating deals.

Because video games currently don't generate royalties once published, game publishers will negotiate **one-time buy-out fees** for music licenses lasting over a period of seven years to "life of product." Licensing fees can range from $2,500 to more than $30,000 a song. The more popular and prestigious a song is, the higher the licensing fee. I don't want to think how much the licensing fees were for *The Beatles: Rock Band* (EA, 2009).

If the song you want for your game is too expensive for your budget, don't fret; there are still plenty of options. You can license a less-expensive cover version of a song—this was done in the first *Guitar Hero* (Activision, 2005). Or you can find a similar

How the heck do you draw a picture of licensed game music?

sounding but less expensive song at a music library. In fact, libraries are great if your game calls for a wide variety of musical styles or requires incidental music, like that heard on a radio or in the background of a bar scene.

Your other option is to use **original music.** Original music is a composition that is created specifically for your game. Unless you can compose, perform, and record your own music, I suggest hiring a music director to work with your team.[2] Not only will she create the music, but she can also handle the resources required for performing, recording, and preparing the music for your game. Even though that's a lot of work, a game designer still has plenty of prep work to do before even getting to that stage.

I Know It When I Hear It

I find it helps to be able to talk to a music director in his own language, even if you can't write music, play an instrument, or carry a tune. You just have to know what you like and have an opinion about it! Provide examples of what you want for your composer: try to cut out as much of the guesswork as possible. For *Maximo: Ghosts to Glory,* I gave the composer a mix tape of music from movie soundtracks and songs I thought would be appropriate for the game's levels. While they say that "a little knowledge is a dangerous thing," I have found it useful to develop a musical vocabulary so you are speaking the composer's language. Doing this will make it that much easier to request changes when you know what to listen for and what it's called.

Here are a few **musical terms** that I have found useful to know:

- **Accent**—Emphasis placed on a beat to make it louder or longer. As in "please place more accent on the drums."

- **Beat**—The "pulse" of the music. Music is measured in beats. Music can have fast beats or slow beats.

- **Chord**—Three or more tones played at the same time to create a harmony.

- **Instrument**—An object that produces music. Synthesized music replicates the sounds instruments make. The choice of instrument can greatly change the theme and mood of a piece.

---

[2] That is, if you don't already have a music director working on your team.

- **Mood**—The "feel" or theme of a musical piece. The mood of a musical piece can be based on emotion (fear, excitement), action (sneaky, combat), or even location (tropical, Russian). Mood is created by instruments and changes in tempo and beat.

- **Octave**—This is the interval between one musical pitch and another with half or double its frequency. One octave up has twice the pitch; one octave down has half the pitch. You will likely be telling the composer to bring something "up an octave" or "down an octave" to make it sound higher or lower pitched.

- **Pitch**—The highness or lowness of a tone. A tone's pitch can be adjusted either higher (to sound like the Chipmunks) or lower (to sound demonic). A tone's frequency is adjusted to add variety into game sounds without creating new sounds. For example, a sword clanging on metal can have its frequency changed so the player doesn't have to hear the same sound over and over.

- **Rhythm**—The controlled movement of music in time. Ravel's *Bolero* builds in rhythm to a frantic conclusion.

- **Tempo**—The rate of speed of the music, which can range from very very slow to very very very fast. There's even a specific tempo for walking speed called *andante*!

- **Theme**—The "heart" of the musical composition. Usually, a composer will come up with the theme first and then "flesh it out" to fit the length required. For example, John Williams created the *Raiders of the Lost Ark March* when Steven Spielberg couldn't decide between which of two themes he liked better . . . so he had Williams combine them!

- **Tone**—The sound or characteristic of a particular voice or instrument.

- **Upbeat**—The last beat of a measure, but can also refer to making the music sound happier, friendlier, or faster.

- **Volume**—The softness or loudness of the music.

Music with Style

Now that you can communicate with your music director, you need to consider the genre of your game. What style of music do you want for your game? A traditional route would be to use the style of music generally associated with that genre. Say you're making a sci-fi game. Do you want orchestral music like John William's score from *Star Wars* or something like Vangelis's synthesized music from *Blade Runner*, or do you want to go old school with 1950s' theremin[3] music in the style of the original *The Day the Earth Stood Still*? Feel free to go in

---

[3] You ever hear that strange "weee-ooooo-oooooo" music in a 1950's sci-fi film? Odds are it was created using a theremin—an electronic instrument that is played without using any physical contact. You can hear a theremin here: www.youtube.com/watch?v=JzRb1OVpat0.

another creative direction: how would a sci-fi game feel with a hip-hop soundtrack? Or a trance soundtrack? Or polka?

Creating a **temporary soundtrack** for your game will cut down on the guesswork for your composer and give him clear examples of what you want. Finding music is incredibly simple compared to the past, when we had to scour our CD collections or go into "the field" with microphone and recorders to get samples from the real world. But with the advent of iTunes, YouTube, Spotify, Pandora, and other music-finding websites, assembling tracks is a breeze: put in a couple of keywords and you'll get hundreds, if not thousands, of results. You can have your team's programmer insert this temp music into your game during production, but keep in mind there is always a danger that your team will really start to like (or hate) the temp tracks and complain if they are changed! Also, **make absolutely sure** you don't leave any music in your game that you don't have a license for. You may have to pay big money to use it or scrap all that work!

And the Beat Goes On. . .

Next, prepare a list of your musical needs. To determine this, figure out how many levels/ environments/chapters/race tracks/unique encounters your game has. Each one of these levels will require **background music**—literally, music that plays in the background as a kind of audio backdrop for gameplay.

Traditionally, background music is themed toward the level. Spooky music on the haunted house level, medieval music for the castle level, jungle drums for the jungle level—you get the idea.

Background music tracks usually run for a few minutes and loop over again to save space in memory and composition time. Work with your music director to make sure the transition between the beginning and the end of the song sounds correct and isn't marred by silence or an awkward change in tempo.

The next question to ask is whether you want—or more realistically, you can afford—to have background music on every level. You may have to reuse tracks throughout the game. For example, in *Maximo vs. Army of Zin,* we had two songs created for each world and alternated between them so players wouldn't have to hear the same song twice in a row.

Instead of having a straightforward song-per-level system, you may want to work with your sound programmer and music director to create a **dynamic score** instead. In this method of scoring a game, music is broken up into themes that play when a certain situation arises. For example, dynamic music can kick in during combat to make a fight feel more exciting and fast paced. The main theme music will come back in once the fight is won.

Dynamic scoring is similar to the music convention **leitmotif,** in which a specific character or scenario has a specific musical theme associated with it. One of the most commonly known leitmotifs is from the *Star Wars* films. Darth Vader, Luke Skywalker, Yoda, and the Princess Leia/Han Solo romance all have unique themes that play whenever the characters are on-screen. If more than one is on screen, it's up to your composer to switch between them without sounding too jarring.

Hey! Sweet theme music!

The most commonly encountered dynamic score themes include

- **Mystery**—The player has entered a new and mysterious locale. A little bit of mysterious music can help set the mood.

- **Warning**—Sinister or menacing music plays whenever the player is entering a hazardous area or about to encounter enemies. This type of theme can be found in many horror games.

- **Combat**—Exciting music plays whenever the player is engaged in combat.

- **Chase/fast movement**—Chased by dinosaurs? Pursuing villains? Giant boulder hot on your heels? A fast-paced chase theme will make the action feel even more exciting.

- **Victory**—Be sure to sonically reward your players, even if it's a "sting" (a very short piece of music) to let players know when a fight is over and they are victorious or to celebrate a successfully accomplished event in the game. *The Legend of Zelda* games have some great examples of rewarding players with music.

- **Walking**—While most games play "walking" music, I believe that if you play slow music, the player is going to move slowly. But if you make the music's beat faster than the player can walk, it will motivate the player to move faster. In other words, remember this **very important thing:**

ALWAYS MAKE THE MUSIC MORE EXCITING THAN THE ACTION ON-SCREEN

Don't forget to budget in music for your title screen, pause/options/save screen, game-over screen, any bonus or minigames your games may have. Your opening theme is very important: it's the first piece of music players hear and sets the stage for the rest of the game. I suggest using your best piece of music for the start screen to really get players excited about playing your game.

Environmental effects are the music of the world around us. Locations have their own special background sounds; a graveyard at night sounds very different from a city during lunch hour. Sometimes music can just be too overbearing or feel wrong for certain environments or games. Combining environmental effects with a dynamic score to punctuate action can be very effective. In *Maximo: Ghosts to Glory*, the hub levels were designed to have environmental effects to help players get into the mood of the locations while the gameplay levels had more traditional background music.

When is a sound not a sound? When it's **silence.** Silence has a powerful effect on the listener. Often sound is used judiciously to indicate that something special is happening to the player or the world. It can be used to indicate great speed (when the music drops off as the player engages the boost in *Burnout*), intense action moments (as in "reflex time" in *F.E.A.R.*), suspense, or even a character's failed attempt at humor.[4]

Sounds Like a Game to Me

Next, assemble a list of sound effects. Develop your sound effect lists as you develop the move sets of your characters and enemies. Start by cataloging the basic sound effects for your main character:

- **Movement**—Start with the sounds for walking and running on specific surfaces like stone, gravel, and metal, and splashing through water to make your character feel grounded in the world. Jumping, landing, rolling, and sliding all need sounds too to let players know they've pulled off the moves.

- **Attacks**—Making swings and kicks "swoosh" will make them sound more dynamic. Make unique attacks sound distinct, like Pac-Man's "eating a ghost" or Mario's jump/ stomp.

---

[4] Usually accompanied with the sound of crickets—so I guess it isn't silent after all.

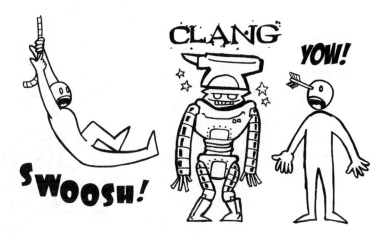

- **Impacts**—A nice meaty "whack" will make a punch or kick feel more powerful. Weapons, spells, and explosions all need dynamic and loud sounds to make players know they've hit something or someone. Don't forget object reaction effects like breaking wood, shattering glass, and clanging metal.

- **Weapons**—Guns bang, swords clang, and laser blasters "pew pew!" The bigger the weapon, the bigger the sound effect. Your weapons should sound as unique as they look; for example, the iconic hum of a light saber matches its distinctive visual.

- **Hit reactions**—"Oomph!" "Ow!" and "Aarrgh!" may sound funny while you are recording them, but they are some of the most important sounds in the game. Whenever players get hit, they need to know it and the sound will clue them in.

- **Vocal cues**—Need to communicate with the players? Use your character. Having your hero say "What's this?" when he spots treasure or "That's better!" after being healed will not only let players know what's been accomplished or is possible, but provide a chance to add some character to your character. Don't forget effort cues, such as grunts of exertion when pushing moveable blocks and pulling stubborn levers.

- **Death**—Nothing says "you're dead" better than a good blood-curdling scream. Make sure you account for all the horrible ways to go, from a groan when getting slain to the gurgle of death by drowning to a long scream when plummeting off a cliff.

- **Success**—Use sound effects to indicate success to your players. Play a "sting" to let players know they've won and don't forget to have your character celebrate vocally with a "woo-hoo!" or "yeah!"

For temporary sound effects, I suggest buying CD libraries from sound-effect providers like *Sound Ideas*[5] or *Hollywood Edge*[6]. Their libraries have sounds for things you can't even believe anyone would ever need—cougars sneezing or the hum of a nuclear reactor. They even have sound effects from some of the most popular Hollywood movies and TV shows. Even if you don't have a dedicated sound effects designer on staff, sound effects are useful tools to have around the studio. Be prepared to spend many hours trying to find "the right" sound effect.

You can also find many sound effects online for free (though, of course, you should always check for copyright and so on—better to be sure than on the end of a lawsuit later). However, even with all these great resources online, sometimes you just can't find the effect you need. This is the reason I turn to sound editing tools like *Sound Forge*[7] or *Vegas*[8]. With these programs, I can quickly and easily mix together two or more sounds to get an idea across to a sound effects designer.

Decide whether you want your sound effects to be realistic or cartoony. This choice will generally be set by the theme of your game, but sometimes there are exceptions. Realistic sounds make the world feel grounded in reality, but sometimes the sounds can be too subdued. Cartoony sound effects are exaggerated and great for "video game-y" things like extra lives and treasure collection, but sometimes they are a little too "on the nose" and they risk taking the player out of the game's world.

---

[5] www.sound-ideas.com/

[6] www.hollywoodedge.com/

[7] www.sonycreativesoftware.com/soundforgesoftware

[8] www.sonycreativesoftware.com/vegaspro/audioproduction

Make sure your sound designer is using sound to its greatest potential. Make sounds go "up" in pitch and tempo to make something sound positive, like collecting an extra life or completing a task. Make sound effects go "down" to reinforce negative and failure situations.

Sometimes your sound designer will have to "sweeten" a sound effect because the real-world version just doesn't sound right. For example, I have found that breaking bones never sound right; they sound more like dry twigs cracking. Instead, my team "sweetened" the effect with the sound of a bowling ball cracking into pins.

When you are creating attack and reaction sound effects for your characters, work with your animators to determine **timing.** You want to make sure your sound effect doesn't last longer or end before the animation does. After you determine the animation's timing, create the sound effect to fit. Make sure your sound programmer knows what frame of animation the sound effect is supposed to play on.

Sounds can be used to give the player a warning or clue to something else in the game. The whistle of a falling bombshell can give the player enough of a chance to dive for cover. A crackle of electricity or ominous thrum of magical power will give the player pause when approaching a protected doorway. A player can search for an item like a lost pocket watch or misplaced cell phone by following the sound of its ticking or ringing.

Be careful not to have too many sounds playing at once. To prevent sound effects from creating cacophony, you will have to prioritize them. Your sound programmer can help you designate sounds into three categories: **local, distant,** and **priority.**

- **Local sound effects** play when the player is close to the source of the sound effect. This may be a babbling brook, a ticking clock, a ringing phone, the hum of machinery, or the growls of an enemy. As the player gets further from the source, these sound effects fade away.

- **Distant sound effects** are sounds that the player can hear even if she is far from the sound's source. These include explosions, a wolf's howl, approaching vehicle engines, or the ominous thrum of a tower o' doom.

- **Priority sound effects** are sounds that will always play regardless of where the player is. These are sounds that provide the player gameplay feedback, including loss of health; collection of treasures/goodies; score or combo increase; power-up or countdown timer; successful enemy hit; death; world interaction such as landing, collision, or weapon impacts; and footsteps/swim strokes/wing flaps.

Priority   **Local**   **Distant**

When naming files for production, give your music and sound cues descriptive but short names so your teammates don't have to guess what they are. For example, music for level 2 of your game may be called Lv2Song.wav, and the sound file for a variation on a robot enemy's blaster shot may be roblast2.wav.

Sound not only is effective for communicating what is going on in the game, but also can be used for gameplay. Whole genres of games are centered around music and sound, from *Dance Dance Revolution* (Konami, 1998) to *Band Hero* (Activision, 2009) to *Papa Sangre II* (Playground Publishing B.V., 2013). When creating sound-based and music-based gameplay, don't rely completely on the sound. Create visuals to echo the music and sound. You can never provide too many clues for the players, and you get the benefit of creating gameplay that can be played by impaired players.

- **Short-term memory games** like *Simon* (Milton Bradley, 1978) require players to memorize and repeat a short piece of music. It helps to have a visual component to the gameplay, not only to help players remember which notes to play but also to accommodate deaf (and tone deaf) players.

- **Rhythm games** like *PaRappa the Rapper* (SCE, 1996) *Taiko: Drum Master* (Namco, 2004), *Rhythm Heaven* (Nintendo, 2008), the *Guitar Hero* series, and the *Tap Tap* series require players to keep the beat in time to the music. Many of these games require or come with specific peripherals resembling instruments from guitars to maracas. When designing rhythm games, make sure you account for player fatigue. This is doubly true for games that use motion controllers or dance pads. You don't want to give your players a heart attack! Provide mandatory breaks between songs and levels so players can catch their breath and keep playing.

- **Pitch games** have players sing in order to match a song's pitch. These games require a microphone to play, as seen in the *SingStar* or *Karaoke Revolution* series of games.

- **Music creation games** blur the lines between music creation tool and game. *Electroplankton* (Nintendo, 2005) and *Fluid* (SCEI, 1998) feature charming player characters and dynamic on-screen activity; however, their end goals are not to win but to create and enjoy.

Other music games defy classification. *Vib-Ribbon* (SCE, 1999) creates platform-esque gameplay based on whatever CD players insert, creating different play experiences with every game. *Rez* (Sega, 2001) is a classic rail shooter with the added layer of players creating complex electronic music with each enemy they destroy. *Battle of the Bands* (THQ, 2008) is a rhythm game in which players play a musical tug-of-war (from disco to country, for example) as they launch attacks at each other.

As you can see, there are plenty of ways to use music and sound in gameplay. Don't neglect them; they're an important tool for a designer to use.

Level 16's Universal Truths and Clever Ideas

- Determine sound needs early in production. Don't wait until the last minute.
- Learn how to "speak musician" to communicate your desires to the composer.
- Communicate important game actions to players using sound effects and vocal cues.
- Don't use music and sound effects you don't have the rights to use.
- Use music to move the game's action.
- Use leitmotifs to help tell your story.
- Determine proximity and timing of sound and music to make it feel more realistic and interactive.
- Silence can be as powerful as music.
- Use music and sound effects as gameplay (but make sure you have accompanying visuals for sound-impaired players).

Level 17
Cutscenes, or No One's Gonna Watch 'Em Anyway

A CUTSCENE IS an animated or live-action sequence used to advance the story; create spectacle; provide atmosphere, dialogue, and character development; and reveal clues that players would otherwise miss during gameplay. Players often have no control over the game while a cutscene plays.

I find cutscenes to be a double-edged sword. On one hand, they usually look fantastic, allowing your game world and characters to be shown in a way that may not be reproducible in the game engine. On the other hand, however, there is a history of many cutscenes being too long, not necessary to the story, or a downright chore to watch. Many players will skip through cutscenes (if the game gives them the option to do this!) to "get to the game." To avoid this, you should first ask yourself this **very important thing:**

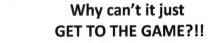

Why can't it just
GET TO THE GAME?!!

CAN THE ACTION BE DONE WITH GAMEPLAY?

Since cutscenes are very expensive to make, it's best to use them judiciously. I say "cutscenes are best saved for kissing and blowing things up" for these reasons:

- You can create more emotion in a cutscene because you have direct control over all of the elements.

- Collisions in games just don't look as good as they do in a pre-rendered movie. Two characters kissing (or holding hands or whatever) just looks a lot less awkward.

- It's often better to take the control away from the player so they can get swept up in the story or blown away by the spectacle.

- Explosions look awesome when they are pre-rendered.

A Cut Above

Just as there are many ways to make movies, there are many ways to make cutscenes: full-motion video, animations, flash-animated sequences, prerendered cutscenes, puppet shows, and scripted events.

- **Full motion video** (or **FMV**) cutscenes were popular when video games were first being published on CD media. Titles like *Wing Commander III: Heart of the Tiger* (Origin, 1994), *Command and Conquer* (EA, 1995), and *The Horde* (Crystal Dynamics, 1994) employed live-action cutscenes featuring Hollywood actors and production values. An outside production company usually produces FMVs because they require all the resources of a motion picture production.

  During the mid-1990s, FMVs became so popular that several systems dedicated to playing **interactive movies** were produced. Early game systems like the 3DO Interactive Multiplayer, PlayStation, Philips CD-I, and Sega Mega CD (as well as PCs) specialized in games with extensive or playable FMV sequences, such as *Night Trap* (Sega, 1992), *Sewer Shark* (Sony Imagesoft, 1992), *Phantasmagoria* (Sierra Online, 1995), and *Psychic Detective* (EA, 1995). Even though DVD media can easily handle the file size of the videos, FMVs have become less popular with game developers these days. They're usually deemed too expensive to produce for something the game's audience may not watch.

- **Animated cutscenes** or **full-motion animations (FMAs)** offer a stylistic alternative to FMVs. A cell-animated or stop-motion-animated cutscene is converted into a video format that the game's engine can play, and it is then shown during the game's title and story sequences. Players have no control over the game during these sequences. Due to the involved production, generally long shooting time, and cost, animated cutscenes are scarce in video games. However, there have been many gorgeous examples of animated cutscenes, such as the *Neverhood* titles (Dreamworks Interactive, 1996), *The Curse of Monkey Island* (LucasArts, 1997), and the *Professor Layton* series (Nintendo, 2007).

- **Flash-animated sequences** are created in Adobe Flash, which, due to the use of still images and simple movement, lends the animation a distinctive visual style that often resembles graphic novels. *Batman: Arkham Origins Blackgate* (WB, 2013) and the *Sly Cooper* series use this method for storytelling.

- **Pre-rendered cutscenes** are created using high-resolution versions of the game's character models and environments, with cinematic cameras to create dynamic and dramatic choreography, imagery, and storytelling. Players have no control over the game during these sequences. With enough money, time, and manpower, these pre-rendered cutscenes can look spectacular. Check out any Blizzard title, Final Fantasy series game, or Namco fighting game to see what I mean.[1]

- **In-game cinematics** or **"puppet shows"** use in-game assets such as characters and environments to create cutscenes. They are called puppet shows because the characters in early versions of these cutscenes moved unnaturally, giving an impression of marionettes. Visually, they are only distinguished from gameplay by the use of a cinematic camera. Puppet shows can be noninteractive or allow players limited character and camera movement (such as looking around with the main character's head) as seen in *Assassin's Creed* (Ubisoft, 2007) and the *Call of Duty: Modern Warfare* series.

- **Scripted events** are similar to puppet shows where in-game assets are used to create animated sequences, but here players are allowed limited to full interaction with the game during the sequence. Since their inclusion in games such as *Half-Life* (Valve, 1998), *The Operative: No One Lives Forever* (Fox Interactive, 2000), and the *Medal of Honor* series, scripted events have become the preferred method to convey story without upsetting the pace of gameplay. They are quite common in FPS and action games, but if these events are not properly choreographed, players run the risk of missing or not seeing the event. They can also get repetitive if players have to experience them repeatedly due to dying before the event's objectives can be completed.[2] Here are a few ways to make sure your players are watching your scripted event:

  - Have your events activate only when the player character is actually looking at or facing the scripted event.

---

[1] During the production of *Tekken 3*, I remember the game's Japanese producer proudly telling me that the game's spectacular cinematics were the work of just two animators. He then told me that both of them ended up in the hospital due to exhaustion.

[2] This often leads to the "Groundhog Day" phenomenon, where players feel as if they are caught in a time loop having to live out the same sequence of events over and over again.

- Build your level geometry to "frame the scene" so players get a clear view of the action.

- Move the camera around the environment to give players an idea of its layout and space.

- If you have a mobile camera, be sure to start your event from the player's POV or position. This is particularly important for cutscenes that use the in-game camera to show events like geometry changing position or when giving hints about puzzle elements or revealing enemies. You should use the camera to always show a clear cause and effect, such as "pull this lever and that door opens."

The good news is that you can now determine which type of storytelling device is best for your cutscene. The bad news is that you now have to write it.

How to Write a Screenplay in Eight Easy Steps

Because there are so many books on screenwriting, I'm not going to even attempt to go into the detail that they do. If you're interested in reading an in-depth analysis on screenwriting, I suggest the following books:[3]

- *Screenplay: The Foundations of Screenwriting* by Syd Field (Dell, 1984)

- *Story: Substance, Structure, Style and the Principles of Screenwriting* by Robert McKee (It Books, 1997)

- *Screenwriting 434: The Industry's Premier Teacher Reveals the Secrets of the Successful Screenplay* by Lew Hunter (Perigee Trade, 2004)

Since you are reading this book and not one of those, here is a quick-and-dirty guide to teach you how to write your screenplay like a professional, to be used by storyboard artists, animators, or voice actors:

Step 1—Outline your story. If you don't know the beginning, middle, and end of your story, you won't know what the heck you're writing. But you already learned how to do this back in Level 3, right?

Step 2—Break down your story scene by scene to determine which characters are in each scene and what locations they take place in. This information is going to be important for staging as well as asset-creation purposes. You may not be able to have

---

[3] Do me a favor and read them AFTER you've finished this one, OK?

10,000 Orcish warriors charging over a hill in a puppet show cutscene. You may want to play around with the order of your cutscenes. Maybe you want to start with a flashback because there is more action in a later scene than in your first scene. For example, in *SpongeBob SquarePants: Atlantis SquarePantis* (THQ, 2007), we started the game at the end of the story because it was the scene with the most action, and we wanted the game to start with a high-action scene. I find it better to start with a bang to grab the viewers' attention.

Step 3—Determine which scenes of your story are going to be cutscenes versus being told through gameplay. I prefer to tell as much of the story as possible through gameplay because this is what players will be doing the most—playing the game.

Don't make players watch something they should doing. It's always better to have the players do than watch. . . . Wait a second; that's a **very important thing.** Let me try that again:

IT'S ALWAYS BETTER TO HAVE THE PLAYERS *DO* THAN *WATCH*

Step 4—Write your scenes and dialogue. Determine what needs to happen and what needs to be said. Try to communicate your scenes with action as much as (if not more than) with words. Write to entertain. It doesn't hurt to be funny either. What you do need to be is brief. As Shakespeare once said, "brevity is the soul of wit." Or in other words, **keep it short.** Don't bore with a lot of yapping or technobabble.[4] Try to get your point across in as few words as possible. I used to treat writing dialogue like a game of "Name That Tune." "George, I can write that dialogue in 12 lines." "Oh yeah, well, I can write that in eight lines or less." "Write. That. Dialogue!"

Step 5—Write your script in the official screenplay format. If you are going to be a writing professional (hey, you're writing a video game, so guess what? You *are* a writing professional), you'd better learn to do it the way the pros do. Every other entertainment professional uses this format, so there's no reason to reinvent the wheel. Here's a simple style guide:

```
SCENE #. INT./EXT. (choose one) — LOCATION — TIME OF DAY
CAMERA ANGLE
Describe the setting, introduce CHARACTERS in ALL CAPS,
  highlight
  any ACTION in ALL CAPS too.
CHARACTER'S NAME
(actor's direction goes in parenthesis)
Dialogue is written here. Keep it brief.
```

---

[4] Yes, *Metal Gear Solid* series, I'm still looking at you.

That's pretty much the basics of screenwriting format! Plenty of screenwriting formatting programs like *Final Draft* or *Movie Magic Screenwriter* are available if you want to save time pressing the Tab key on your keyboard.

Step 6—Read your dialogue. Dialogue often sounds great "in your head" when you've written it down, but sounds strange or clunky when it's read aloud. Expect to rewrite (and rewrite and rewrite) your dialogue.

Step 7—Let it simmer for a day or two. Often you will get new ideas or think of better ways to write scenes or snappier dialogue. Have others read it and give you their feedback. Try not to hover too much over them as they do it.

Step 8—Prepare your script for voice actors using a spreadsheet program like Microsoft Excel. "Break out" the characters' dialogue line by line because this is the way voice actors read and record their dialogue. Having the actors' lines isolated will make it easier for them and you to get through what they need to read without having to page through a lengthy script. Make sure to retain scene numbers on your spreadsheet. Remember to give each line of dialogue a file name so the sound engineer has something to name each sound file when cutting up the session tracks. This will be the same file your programmer uses to put the track into the game. Here's an example:

Cold Steele VO Script: Jake Steele dialogue (Actor TBD)

File Name	Dialogue	Notes
Opening_01_01	Those terrorists have hidden from us for too long, Montoya.	Opening cinematic
Opening_01_02	Well, they're about to get a taste of COLD STEEL.	Place emphasis on "cold steel"
Opening_01_03	Saddle up, amigo. We're going hunting.	
Opening_01_04	Heh. You can say that again.	
Opening_01_05	Montoya! Nooooo!	Montoya is killed by terrorist
Cutscene_01_01	Just because you've got me trussed up like a Thanksgiving turkey doesn't mean you've won, Von Slaughter.	
Cutscene_01_02	I wouldn't give you the map even if I did have it. . . Ungh!	Jake is slapped by Von Slaughter at end of line
Cutscene_01_03	Go ahead, sucker. Do your worst.	Hurt but not defeated
Jake_Climb_01	Unnnh!	Climbs mountain
Jake_Climb_02	Umphf! Umphf!	Alternative climbing take
Jake_Collect_01	Come to papa.	Collects pick-up or cash
Jake_Collect_02	This will come in useful.	Collects pick-up or cash
Jake_Collect_03	Heh heh.	Collects pick-up or cash

File Name	Dialogue	Notes
Jake_Health_01	Oh yeah, that's the stuff.	Drinks health tonic
Jake_Health_02	That was a good one.	Drinks health tonic
Jake_Yell_01	Yaaaaah!!	Jake's charge move
Jake_Yell_02	Here I come, suckers!	Alt charge move
Jake_Victory_01	Take that, sucker!	
Jake_Victory_02	Ha ha! That's how we did it in the old days!	
Jake_Hit_01	Ow!	
Jake_Hit_02	Oomph!	
Jake_Hit_03	Aarrgh!	
Jake_Death_01	Yaaaaaaaah!	Jake falls off cliff
Jake_Death_02	Ung! Ooooh!	Jake is shot and drops to his knees
Jake_Death_03	Not again! Uhhhhh!	Alternative death take
Jake_Death_04	YAAAAAAAAAAAAAAAAAAAA!	Burned to death

As you may have noticed from this example, VO (which stands for **voice over,** btw; and **btw** stands for **by the way,** btw) scripts have a lot of "YAAAAAAAAAAAAAAA!" and "Oomph!" and "Unngh!" in them. Voice actors read these lines literally, so write this dialogue the way you want it to sound. There's a big difference between "Arg!" and "Aaaargh!" to voice actors. One's a pirate, and the other is a death rattle.

If you're not sure how to spell a grunt, hit reaction, or death cry, I suggest reading comic books. They're filled with all sorts of onomatopoeic[5] words like "POW!" "CRASH!" and "AIIEEE!"

ARG! VS. ARGHH!!

---

[5] That's a fancy way of saying "It's spelled like it sounds."

Finding Your Voice

Now that you've written your script and broken it out, you might find it helpful to record a **temp track,** like I do. This is a track of moderately talented amateur actors and team members—such as you—reading the lines for the purposes of determining audio file size and length. All you need to record a temp track is your script, a willing actor, a decent microphone, computer software that can record audio, and a quiet place that doesn't echo to record. Try to do your best to read each line the way you will eventually want it performed by a professional voice actor. However, it's a bad idea to animate a character's lip sync to a temp track: the actor's performance will end up very different than that of the temp actor. You should use temp track audio only for timing and blocking purposes.

Speaking of **voice actors,** while *you* could play the part of Jake Steele, international terrorist hunter, you really should hire a professional actor for the final game. I've had the privilege of working with dozens of VO actors over the years and, believe me, there is a HUGE difference in the performance you get from an actor versus an amateur. You want the best for your game, right? So hire an actor. (Or two. Or three. Or a dozen.) But before you can hire an actor, you're going to need to hire a **voice director.**

Voice directors will help you cast your game's characters based on the character descriptions you give them. Make sure you're accurate with what you send and don't be vague. If necessary, give your voice director the name of an existing actor you imagine would be perfect for the role. Who knows, you may even be able to get that person for the part![6] The voice director will book the studio time and help you get the best rate. He or she also will help you schedule your time to get the most recording time with your actors. The voice director will direct the actors during the voice-over sessions and work with the sound technicians to get the best quality results.

As you get ready for the voice-over session, send the script to the voice director. It doesn't have to be the final draft, but make sure you let the voice director know that you will be bringing changes to the script with you. On the day of the voice session, be sure to bring the following with you:

- Extra physical copies of the script.

- A highlighter, for calling out lines to the actors in the script during the session.

- A ballpoint pen or pencil, to make notes and to keep track of changes to the script. (Trust me, there will be changes.)

---

[6] This happened to game developer Tim Schafer, who thought he could never get Jack Black to play the lead in *Brütal Legend*.

- Images of the characters the actors are playing. Bring whatever you can to give each actor an idea of what his or her character looks like. In many cases, VO actors will play several parts in your game (the voice actors union allows an actor to portray up to three characters in one game), so even if it's "drooling alien no. 2," bring an image to help the actor bring that character to life (and send that image ahead of time to the voice director as well to aid in casting).

- A book or handheld game. "Hurry up and wait" is the motto of the entertainment industry. There is always plenty of downtime as actors and sound technicians prepare for the session. Keep out of their way, but don't wander off too far.

- Provide beverages and snacks. Voice sessions can last all day if not all week. According to the voice actor's union, you need to provide a meal for your talent if your session lasts a whole day. Even though all you're doing is sitting and listening to actors all day, it can still be exhausting!

If you aren't the game writer/designer, make sure your writer/designer is on hand when it's time for the voice-over recording session too. Very often, there will need to be script rewrites, and the actors and voice director don't always know the context of the line. You may need something very specific for your game: don't leave it up to someone else. Not that there's any problem with improvisation—giving actors free rein to create great additions and alternate takes on your script will give you plenty of material to work with, and the actors enjoy doing it too—and if they enjoy working with you, they will want to work with you again in the future.

And finally, **have fun!** Remember, you are getting paid to sit in a room listening to actors say lines that you have written! It doesn't get much better than that!

Check. Check 1. Sibilance! Sibilance!
Is this thing on?

Level 17's Universal Truths and Clever Ideas

- Your cutscenes should fit the style, budget, and schedule of your game.
- Learn and write your script in the standard screenwriting format.
- Start off your game with a bang to draw audiences in.
- It's better to have the players do than watch: tell your story using gameplay.
- Allow the players to skip cutscenes and don't make them watch these scenes over and over again.
- Keep your cutscenes short to save players' time and your money.
- Use cutscenes for kissing and explosions. Save your cutscenes for big spectacular moments and intimate ones. Do everything else in gameplay.
- Professional actors make a big difference. Use them whenever possible.
- Break out your actors' material when preparing for voice acting sessions.

Level 18
And Now the Hard Part

IF YOU FOLLOWED the instructions in this book, you are now the proud creator of a great game idea and a corresponding game design document. You have everything you need to make an actual video game, right? Wrong! Your work is just beginning. Before you actually **make** the game, you *might* have to find someone to **publish** your game.

Now I say "might" because since the first edition of *Level Up!* came out, the video game industry has radically changed. We'll talk about how it's changed in a moment, but if you want to make a game you will need money. And to convince someone to give you money, you are going to need a **pitch.**

A pitch is a streamlined, easily digestible version of your game design document. It contains everything that's great and original about your game without all the "twiddley bits."[1]

Because most pitches are presented to groups in boardrooms, I highly recommend using PowerPoint or Keynote or some other presentation software to create your pitch document. To help, I have included an outline of what you should include in a pitch presentation in Bonus Level 10. The basics of this document are these:

- Title screen with logo

- Company profile

- High concept

- Who your game is for

---

[1] "Twiddley bits" is game industry lingo for all the details you've worked really hard on but other people don't really need to hear about when you are telling them about your game. These bits are important to making the game but not to selling it to a publisher.

- Why anyone should care about your game

- What your game is about

- How your game will be awesome/what makes it different

When creating a pitch presentation, remember the basics of making presentation slides: choose a font that you can read easily, don't put too much information on one page, and recall that everyone loves pictures. In fact, I once saw a great pitch that was nothing but pictures. But make sure you use a few of them. Don't let your audience stare at the same image for too long. Remember that just like gamers, an audience likes variety.

No One Cares About Your Stupid Little World

Putting together a good pitch presentation is like putting together an artist's portfolio: you want to show off your best work but not include too many pieces and overwhelm your audience.

This was a story pitch I once sat through. The minute the writer started telling us the intricate machinations of his fantasy world, I tuned him out. It was just too much information to process at once. While worlds are fun to create and inventing a world's details is important to making a world feel real, realize that nobody else cares about your world and those details at this stage. I didn't care who the Nebulons were or what the significance of a Galactic Imperium was. I just wanted to know how the game played. Don't overburden your readers with story details. Keep it simple, and more importantly, keep those details to yourself . . . for now.

In the year thirty-two forty-five, the Zorgan Hegemony has encroached the Nebulon Armada at the Azimuth cluster, causing the political balance of the galactic imperium to shift for the first time in over a millennium...

Here are a few more rules of thumb when pitching:

- **Pitch to the right people.** You need to consider to whom you are selling your idea. Too many times, coming out of a pitch presentation, I've heard, "That was a great pitch, but we'd never publish that type of game." This is sad, because if the developer had taken a little time to do some research about the publisher, that situation never would have happened. You don't want to waste your time (not to mention the publisher's). Some publishers publish only certain genres of games. Don't pitch a family game to a publisher that specializes in hardcore action games. That said, many publishers do publish a wide range of titles, and their company objectives may change. Timing is everything. There are many stories of someone pitching a certain type of game exactly when a publisher was looking to publish that type of game. You never know!

- **Pitch in a controlled environment.** You can never be sure where a pitch presentation is going to take place, but you want to pitch your game in a location where the audience's attention is on you and your presentation. Do what you can to have control over where the meeting takes place. Work with whomever you are pitching at to present in the right environment. For example, pitching a game on the show floor of E3 is much harder than in a private meeting room.

- **Be prepared.** Just as with any other type of performance, you need to practice. Practice giving your pitch in front of your peers. Invite them to give you feedback on content as well as your performance. Don't be afraid to access your inner actor. You will be telling the story and the narrative of your game to the publisher, so you want to get the publisher's team as excited about your game as you are excited to make it. If someone on your team is better suited to speak in front of a group, have that person give the presentation instead—with your supervision, of course. You still should be present at the pitch to help answer questions and fill in details. You want your game to shine in the best possible light, and you have only one chance to impress. Make sure your computer is compatible with any type of setup, and always bring backup data on a flash drive or disc. I have seen presentations stop cold because the sound wasn't working correctly. Bring plenty of copies of documents. Knowing how many to bring is a little harder to predict because the number of attendees can be unpredictable. Here's another situation to consider: would you still be able to make your pitch if the power went out? So, as the Boy Scouts say, be prepared.

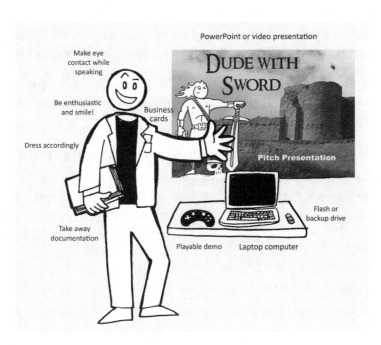

- **Know your project inside and out (and then some).** Even though your game hasn't even been made yet, you should know everything you can about it. Publishers will ask questions to try to poke holes in your design. It's not that they're malicious; they're just looking for topics that may cause trouble after the game starts production. Be able to talk about your game in depth, but remember not to go on and on. You don't want to drown your audience in details unless they ask for them. If you don't know an answer to a question, it helps to say, "I'd like to hear your thoughts on that."

- **Keep the focus.** Production teams sometimes bring in several pitch ideas in an attempt to find out what the publisher is interested in. I'm not sure I agree with that strategy. Having more pitches means that (a) the meeting will go on longer, (b) less time will be spent on each game presentation, and (c) you may not get consensus on which idea is the best. There will always be one idea that stands out from the others, so why muddy the waters? I say let the attendees concentrate on that one idea. You may have to revisit the publisher to pitch another game idea. If you do present several ideas at a pitch meeting, make sure that all the presentations are at the same level of quality.

- **Maybe you need a team.** If you are pitching more than one game idea, you might want to take a page from Double Fine. The team came in with three ideas, but rather than one person pitching every game, three different people pitched the different games. As an audience member, I appreciated that because I was able to put a different face to each game, and each person's presentation style was different, which made each pitch its own unique experience.

- **Pitch to represent.** Even if you don't have a great game pitch or truly original idea, but you have a great piece of technology or a prototype gameplay mechanic, it may not hurt to present it to a publisher. Sometimes a publisher has a license but hasn't picked a studio to develop it into a game. Sometimes timing and good luck play just as much a part of the pitch process as having a great game idea and strong presentation. In my many years working at a publisher and hearing scores of video game pitches, I have developed the "pitch equation":

GAME DEMO > GAME DESIGN DOCUMENT > PRESENTATION > PITCH

Game demos are a lot of work. If not planned for properly, they take time away from the production of the main game. They can really disrupt the flow of your production and can lead to crunch time: long hours trying to get content into your game. However, demos show you are serious about making your game and allow potential publishers a chance to get their hands on code, which sometimes is the best way to sell your game.

Who's Paying?

When the game industry started out, developers programmed games in their garages.[2] These young game creators soon formed companies like Atari, Activision, and Sierra, and eventually sold their games around the world.[3] As gaming took off, many of these developers evolved into publishers, manufacturing their own games, gaming consoles and eventually hiring other development teams to create games for them.

Since the mid-80s, as consoles became the dominant system for playing video games, the publishers gained more control over what games were made. During this time, you could still create and distribute your game without a publisher . . . but only if it was on a computer, not a console. While there were some digital distributors like Stardock, it was mainly publishers who controlled major releases, as they were the ones who could afford to invest the capital necessary to develop console games. When Internet-enabled consoles became the norm, publishers started to offer downloadable content as add-ons to their retail games. In 2002, Microsoft and the Valve Corporation started digitally distributing games through the Xbox Live and Steam platforms, changing the way players purchased games. Sony, Nintendo, Origin and other digital distributors soon followed suit.

While mobile gaming has been available since the early 2000s, the real game changer came in 2008 when Apple launched the App store. Developers leapt on board and after a few early successes,[4] the new gaming gold rush was off and running. Since then things have cooled down, but the success of digital distribution has opened up many new markets for game developers:

- **App stores:** Apple's App Store. Google Play. Android Market. Amazon's Kindle store. All these publishers of downloadable games offer appealing alternatives to their console counterparts. Overall, it is cheaper for a game developer to submit a game to these app stores. They take a smaller cut of the profits and have less restrictive submission guidelines than their console publisher counterparts. However you are competing with hundreds of thousands of titles in an already over-saturated market. How do you stand out from the crowd? Simply be awesome.

- **Digital distributors:** Digital distribution platforms such as Valve's Steam, Microsoft's Xbox Live, Sony's PlayStation Store, and Nintendo's Wii shop traditionally were the

---

[2] Richard Garriott (*Ultima* series), William Anderson (*Disney's Aladdin, Cool Spot*) and Danielle Bunten Burry (*M.U.L.E., The Seven Cities of Gold*) all got their start by creating games at home and selling them packaged in plastic baggies to local computer stores. These homebrew efforts launched the careers of many early game creators.

[3] Or they were existing companies like Nintendo, Namco, Sega, and Konami who got into the video game business.

[4] *Trism* (Demiforce, 2007) earned $250,000 in the first two months of release and was one of the App store's earliest success stories.

homes to PC versions of big-budget games. But since Valve started its Project Greenlight program and Xbox Live Indie Games, new developers have a shot of getting their games onto platforms that have an installed base of millions of users.

- **Crowd funding:** Launched in 2009, Kickstarter created a platform where game developers (and inventors and artists) could get their projects funded by the donations of individual contributors. Soon other crowd-funding sites like Indiegogo and GoFundMe cropped up, giving developers new ways to earn capital. While funding isn't guaranteed, successes like *Broken Age* (Double Fine, 2014), which earned $3.45 million from over 87,000 backers within a month, and *Wasteland 2* (inXile, 2014), which earned $2.93 million, make crowd funding an appealing option.

- **Web hosting:** Online sites like Kongragate, Newgrounds, Addicting Games, Adult Swim Games, and Pop Cap host free-to-play games created by all levels of developers, from amateurs to experienced game creators. These web-hosted sites are great for gaining an audience or launching your game onto another platform. Many popular games like *Bejeweled*, *Plants vs. Zombies*, *Robot Unicorn Attack*, and *Peggle* got their start as web games.

- **Social media:** The good news is that Facebook offers full developer support for game creators. The bad news is, your game will be competing against established developers like Zynga, King, and Pretty Simple as well as traditional publishers like Ubisoft and Disney Interactive.

- **Traditional publishers:** These are the EAs, the Sony Computer Entertainment, the Nintendos, the Activisions. Sure, you could walk in off the street with a great game demo, but unless you have an agent or manage to get a meeting with a business developer, chances of success are slim. Usually publishers like to work with established talent or their own development teams. However, if you do get a meeting, you will need a killer demo and/or pitch presentation.

Video Games Is a Haaaard Business

Making video games may sound like fun and games, but it is a lot of hard work. It takes lots of effort and hours to design and create a game. And even after all that hard work, a game that may seem to be a "sure hit" may get poor reviews or mediocre sales. There are plenty of examples of well-made and fun games that received great reviews and still did badly sales-wise. Sometimes the publisher may not be able to finance the promotion of the game to the level you feel it deserves. Sales projections may be set at levels that the game just can't reach. It's not all the publisher's fault though. Sometimes team members may not put their best work into the game; family and health issues may distract them from their jobs. God forbid, your lead designer or a key team member gets sick or dies during production.

When Reality Gets in the Way

Remember this **very important thing:**

VIDEO GAMES ARE MADE BY PEOPLE

These things happen, so you want to give your game a fighting chance to be the best possible. Most games that go badly are the result of bad planning. Here's a list for troubleshooting your game during production:

- Don't overpromise content and bite off more than the team can chew.

- Plan ahead. Prepare for team illnesses and vacation. Prepare for hardware failure, brown-outs, or other technical issues.

- Try to lock down design and content as soon as possible. Constantly changing content in the pursuit of perfection will eventually wear down your team and may even kill your game.

- Players will always find ways to break your game, so make sure to play the game the way they would. Don't just play the game the way it's "meant to be played." Do unusual things and bang on the game until it breaks. Then fix it and keep working.

- If you are creating an international version of your games, make sure you account for sensitive cultural differences. For example, Titan Studios, the creators of *Fat Princess* (SCE, 2009), had to redesign the cartoony four-fingered game characters to have five fingers for the game's release in Japan.[5]

- Beware of **designer blinders,** the phenomenon that happens when you are too close to your game. It results in game creators thinking their game is too easy or half-baked elements are "good enough." Here are eight ways to take off your designer blinders:

  - Imagine you are the "first player." This can be tough to do, but try to imagine what it would be like for someone playing your game for the first time. Are you giving players all the feedback they need to play and understand what's going on? Are you giving them enough excitement and fun?

  - Look at your game with the "10,000-foot view," an objective look at everything in your game. Use tools like beat charts and outlines to identify weak spots in your design.

---

[5] There are at least three explanations to why the four-fingered visual is considered taboo in Japan. Yubitsume is the practice performed by members of the Yakuza—the cutting off at the knuckle of the pinkie finger as atonement. The resulting mutilated hand has the appearance of having four fingers. The number four, pronounced Shi, also means death. It's an unlucky number—much like 13 is in Western cultures. The Burakumin are a social class that is still met with discrimination. The four-fingered sign was used to designate Burakumin (because they often worked with four-legged animals) and became a derogatory gesture. Modern Buraku activist groups have sued over the use of the four-fingered sign in Japanese media.

- Try to break the game. Do things you wouldn't normally do. Often designers get so used to playing a game the way it is supposed to be played that they forget that players might play their game another way. Put yourself in someone else's shoes.

- Compare your game to other games. Does your game make you feel the same way other games do? If not, what is it about that other game that you like that yours doesn't have?

- Tell your game's story. As you play the game, you are creating the game's narrative—the order of events as players play the game. Does this narrative match with how you want the players to play the game?

- Iterate on your game design in all stages of production. This one is super important, so I'm going to write it in all caps to make sure you don't miss it: ITERATE ON YOUR GAME DESIGN. ITERATE. ITERATE. ITERATE! What does this mean? It means you need to polish your game by playing it over and over and over and over and over and finding problems and fixing those problems and then finding new problems and fixing those problems and the more you play, the more problems you will find that need to be fixed. But that's okay, because in the end, you will have a better game than you started with.

- Get feedback. There are three types of testers: (1) those associated with the project, like teammates, (2) friends and people friendly to the project, and (3) people who have nothing to do with the project. You want feedback from all three groups, especially the last one. These people will give you the most honest feedback on your game. But don't get mad at them when they tell you something you might not like to hear. Many times, they are right. If people feel strongly enough about something to complain about it, there is usually a legitimate reason they are complaining and you should address it.

- Use a focus group. These are people who are picked to play your game for a particular reason: they like action games or play games a certain amount of time a week, or they might be of a particular age or sex. They are often paid to play your game and give their opinions. There are a few things to be careful of. Sometimes one person in the group will become the "alpha"; that means this person's opinions carry more weight than the rest of the group and he can steer the group's opinions. Other group members might not be brave enough to voice their own opinions, even though that's why they're there! Make sure everyone gets asked questions. Another problem with focus groups is if the group members are being paid for their opinion, they might feel as though they need to say something nice about your game. You want honesty, not flattery. Lastly, just because you are paying people for their opinions, that doesn't mean they're right. Take all focus group feedback with a grain of salt.

- If something doesn't work, throw it out. Don't be precious with your ideas. They're a dime a dozen. But when you do throw something out, have a backup plan in mind. Don't make throwing away work a habit. It's better to plan things out to anticipate problems than to waste work. Wasting work means wasting time. Wasting time means wasting money. Both time and money are limited resources for a developer. It's better to be getting rid of good ideas; that means you have too many good ideas! You can always use them on the sequel.[6]

Cutting content happens in every game. But the more you cut during preproduction, the less you will have to cut during production. Make sure you are cutting content for the right reasons. Don't cut or change content that connects and has an impact on multiple game systems; otherwise, you will be asking for trouble.

Emergent, Vertical, or Horizontal?

I don't want to go too much into game production (that subject could fill an entirely different book), but you should consider how to go about building your game before you start making it. Having a solid plan of attack will avoid a lot of problems in the long run.

Some game designers employ a design concept called **emergent gameplay**—gameplay that will "just happen" if the player is given a set of gameplay tools and a chance to play with them. However, a problem arises when designers use the concept of emergent gameplay as an excuse to under-design gameplay, hoping that the player will "find the fun."

---

[6] S.I.F.S.—"save it for the sequel"—was a popular saying at many of the studios where I worked.

I say "emergent, eschmergent!" I think of game design this way. A game design can go in many different directions. A game designer should be like a gymnast on one of those pommel horses at the Olympics. You can move up. You can move down. You can move sideways. You can move diagonally. As a game designer, you should move your "design vision" in as many directions as you can. Make believe you are playing the game every way it can be played. Play with all the combinations of elements in your game. Predict what every element in the game will do when it comes in contact with another. Sounds like an impossible task, doesn't it? Well, it can be, but problems in design arise when the designer hasn't explored the width, depth, and breadth of the game. And when things happen that haven't been accounted for, the designer calls it emergent gameplay. But I say there's no such thing as accidental design. If you, as a designer, are relying on "emergent" gameplay for fun, you're praying for success, not planning for it. Knowing how all the gameplay elements work with each other is part of the design process. If you take the time to plan and think about how the elements relate to each other, the outcomes of those relationships can be predicted. Granted, unusual relationships can emerge from bugs and other inconsistencies, but you should never plan your game design around those!

Some teams create a **vertical slice** that acts as a demo to be shown to publishers and a template for the rest of the game. A vertical slice is a level or sequence of your game that has been designed, built, and polished to the highest level of playability possible. When creating a vertical slice you need to start off with a grey box level but instead of stopping there, you continue to develop the level until it has the highest quality of controls, camera, visuals, gameplay, code, effects, and audio that the final version of the game will have. Usually, the target is 80% of final game quality.

Although experienced teams can create vertical slices in as little as a matter of months, it is a very time-consuming process that can lead to **crunch time**—long working hours that can be very stressful to the team as they rush to create, insert, and test content into the game. In fact, any poorly planned production plan will lead to crunch time, whether you are making a vertical slice or diving right into making the entire game.

May I have another vertical slice, please?

I have seen many young game designers think that doing crunch time is a noble thing—that working long hours and late nights means that you really care about the game. You're making a game, not saving the world, so don't sacrifice your health, your sanity, and your life to make it. Crunch time is often caused by bad planning, but it can be caused by other things. Here are nine ways to help you avoid crunch time:

- **Schedule.** Creating a schedule of all the work required to make the game will help you determine how much time it will take to make a game. You know what tool will help you determine what work there is? That's right, your game design document.

- **Do the hard stuff first.** Often people are scared to do the hard stuff. This might be a tricky camera system, a complex collision system, or a complicated design. However, doing the hard stuff is the point where you run into trouble. If you tackle the hard stuff early on, you can do the things you know you are good at later in production. Don't put off the hard stuff!

- **Allow for revisions.** Your GDD will help the team determine what work there is to do, which is why it's important to keep it up to date. You wouldn't want anyone to work on anything you don't need, right?

- **Make up your mind.** If you keep changing your mind, you won't know what to make. One game I worked on changed an enemy character ten times. That's a lot of wasted time and effort. Make a decision and stick with it.

- **Communicate.** You'd think that a team of people working toward a common goal would want to talk to each other. However, that's not always the case. Egos, differences in opinion, thoughtlessness, and even fear of doing the wrong thing can get in the way of everyone making a great game. Don't be afraid to communicate with your team and let them know you are willing to talk and, more importantly, listen to them too.

- **Don't put off meetings.** Sure, they can be long and sometimes boring, but don't put them off. Show up on time and set a time limit. Keep your meetings centered on just a few topics to avoid distractions. Try to keep the meetings on topic and make sure they don't turn into meandering stories, shouting matches, or long debates. Provide snacks to keep people's energy up and offer pens and paper so they can track their ideas.

- **Expect delays.** Life happens. People get sick, take vacations, and have events in their life. Life is going to get in the way of making your game. Just roll with the punches and keep moving forward.

- **Plan for learning.** It takes time for someone to learn something new. An artist might have to learn a new plug-in; a programmer might need to learn a new way to write code. As a designer, you should always be learning new tools and new ways to make your game better.

- **Plan for mistakes.** Humans make mistakes. It's going to happen. You might overwrite a document file you had been working on for days (it's happened to me), you might give an artist the wrong image to model (it's also happened to me), or you might edit the wrong file and check it back in (I'll give you three guesses if it's happened to me). Let your team-mates know you made a mistake. Don't try to hide it. Just do your best to avoid mistakes, use version control and other failsafes, and try to recover from the mistake as quickly as you can.

A **horizontal layer** is another alternative to game production. The team members bring "up" all elements of the game, from beginning to end, at the same time in **gray box** form. When your team are creating gray box levels, geometry is roughly built and character animation assets are mostly placeholders. Details such as texturing, effects, and sound are generally absent at this point. After all game assets have been play tested and approved, the team can move on to the next step of "prettying up" and polishing the game even further.

It may not look like much now, but you've got to imagine it with stone walls, the skull torches, the spike-filled pit and the goblin henchmen...

The hardest thing about presenting gray box gameplay to other team members (and publishers and marketing partners and so on) is that it requires them to **use their imagination.** Don't laugh! Even in a creative industry such as making games, that ability is rarer than you'd think. The trick is not to let these people get the wrong idea about your game. Make sure there is concept art on hand to help communicate these visuals before they are in the game. What's great about this type of iteration is it gives the team a chance to play around with the game and discover what's great about it. If bouncing off enemies' heads turns out to be more fun than punching them, it's not too late to adjust the design to compensate for the gameplay.

What to Do for an Encore?

If your game reviews well or sells well, or if your publisher can afford to pay you a second time around, you may get to make a sequel. Publishers like sequels. Now that I have worked for both a developer and a publisher, I think I have a good perspective on sequels. Just like in Hollywood, sequels are safe(r) bets—proven intellectual property (IP) that doesn't need to be explained to the audience: "If you loved the first one, you'll love the second!"

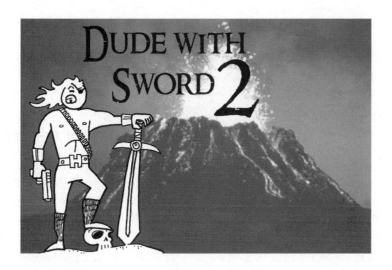

It's easy to understand why a safe bet is appealing to a publisher, but it's not without its problems. Sequels often seem to represent a missed opportunity. Some teams just "phone in" or rush to make their sequel, creating retreads of the last game. Sequels should be treated as an opportunity to get it right. The first time you make a game, you are limited by several factors: you have to build a team, build an engine, figure out just what the heck this character and the gameplay are going to be. Get the whole thing to work and actually be fun. Then you hope that the audience is going to like and buy it. After you've finished that, you've licked the hard part—especially if you've sold well enough to warrant a sequel. You should start your preproduction with the driving desire to make the game perfect.[7]

For example, after finishing the first *Maximo* game, I went to my producer with a list of 40 things I thought were broken and needed to be fixed in the sequel (to my delight, I was able to get 39 of those requests fulfilled!). Although the first game sold better, I still think the second one is a better game. We wouldn't have had the opportunity to make that better game if we didn't have a chance to make a sequel.

Besides, if there were no sequels, there would be no *Super Mario World, Legend of Zelda: The Ocarina of Time, Angry Birds Star Wars, LEGO Batman,* or *Grand Theft Auto trilogy* . . . you get the idea. Here is some advice on making a video game sequel:

- Use the "spine" of the original game as a basis of your gameplay design for the sequel. Take everything that was good in the first game and improve on it. Take everything

---

[7] OK, odds are you will never obtain perfection, but it's not a bad goal to shoot for. Then again, it didn't help *Duke Nukem Forever*, did it?

that was bad and throw it away. This advice seems like common sense, but it's not all that common—things like lousy camera, control, and gameplay mechanics are "justified" by teams because they were in the first game. Just because they were in the first game doesn't mean they were that good. Don't be afraid to cut out the bad bits. If it's better than the original, no one will complain.

- Don't let the players down. They expect all the good things from the first game to be in the sequel, and you shouldn't disappoint. For example, if your audience loved the wall-running mechanic in your first game, then by all means, keep wall running in the sequel. Don't make the players have to re-earn or, worse, rebuy things that they could get free in the first game. In *Maximo vs. Army of Zin*, players started with all the major moves from the first game and earned brand new ones in the second. It only made sense that Maximo would have known how to do all the things he learned in the first game!

- Name it something other than "*GameName 2*." Names are really important to a game. Giving your sequels titles that are exciting, mysterious, or cool will further your game's fiction rather than reduce your games to a numbered outing.

- Always introduce something new. This may seem to be pandering to marketing, but make sure there are five new things in your game for the back of the box, preferably new gameplay concepts to bring something fresh. Also, try to introduce at least one new hero and villain to the franchise. Remind the players that this is a new experience, not just a rehash.

- . . . But don't make it too new. In *Maximo vs. Army of Zin*, we didn't realize that the players wanted to fight more supernatural enemies. We had them battling clockwork creatures instead. The fans were unhappy because we had deviated away from what they liked in the first title. My friend, project manager George Collins, recommends that every sequel should be "30/70": 30% new material and ideas and 70% based on the original game. It's not a bad formula to follow.

- If you get a chance to make several sequels, you have an opportunity to create more change. Don't let your franchise get stale. Why not try doing something wildly different? This, of course, requires buy-in from your publisher and marketing department, so it can be tricky to pull off. I've worked on franchises that were in their 5th, 8th, or even 16th incarnation and sometimes a completely new direction is what it needed to shake things up. Give it a try; it worked for both the *Grand Theft Auto* and *Team Fortress* franchises![8]

---

[8] Just be aware that it also may not work. Nothing is ever guaranteed.

Level 18's Universal Truths and Clever Ideas

- Demo > GDD > pitch presentation > pitch outline.
- Cater your pitch to the right audience.
- Be prepared for any technical problem.
- Know your game completely to answer any questions your audience might have.
- Practice your pitch in front of an audience.
- Video games are made by people: schedule in "people issues," both good and bad.
- Remove designer blinders any way you can.
- Build games using either horizontal layer- or vertical slice-style production. Pick one and go!
- If something doesn't work in your game, throw it out, but try to plan ahead to avoid this issue.
- Avoid crunch time with responsible design goals and detailed production planning.
- Don't rely on emergent gameplay to make your game fun. All good design is preplanned.
- Use the 30/70 rule when creating sequels: repeat all the stuff that was great in the first game, but throw out everything that didn't work.
- Don't let legacy keep your sequel down. Take a hard look at what can be improved from the first game.
- Don't let the players down.

Continue?

Time to Level Up!

So, let's see . . . . You've thought up some game design ideas, you've written some game design documents, you've made some chili, and you've pitched your game.

Congratulations! You've leveled up!

And just as in games, you're just getting started. Now it's time for you to learn firsthand that making video games is the best job in the world. Do me a favor: as you make your own games and move forward with your game design career, keep this book in your backpack. I hope it will come in helpful the next time you get stuck on a problem, or maybe it will provide a little inspiration from time to time.

Finally, always remember these very important things:

- **You're only human.** You're going to make mistakes. You are going to experience doubt. You are going to run out of ideas (temporarily). When those things happen, don't be too hard on yourself. Take a break. You're making video games, not performing heart surgery. No one is going to die if you don't get it done today. Your health and your sanity come first.

- **Always be fair and generous.** Give credit where credit is due. Let people know when they're doing a good job or when you're having fun working with them. Try mentioning one thing you like about their work before going over the list of things that need fixing. It never hurts to be a thoughtful and decent person. This is a very small industry, and word gets around very fast when you don't play nicely with others.

- **Keep learning.** The world is filled with so many wonderful things, who know what will inspire you to make a game? Read a book, take a class, and talk to another human being. Keep your mind open to new things and good ideas will come!

- **Always keep playing games—even the bad ones.** Never let someone else play the game for you. You need to put your hands on the controller to understand how a game feels and plays and why it is good or bad.

- **Do what you love for a living.** If you don't get up in the morning looking forward to what you will do during the day, you shouldn't be doing it. Follow your passion. Remember that not many people get to make video games for a living, so enjoy every minute of it.

- **Give something back whenever you can.** Answer a fan's letter, mentor a younger coworker, teach a class, give a lecture or lead a discussion group, write a blog about making games, or even write a book. You never know where giving something back will lead you, but it always ends up someplace good.

It did for me.

You're still here?
The book's over!
Go design your own video game!

Bonus Level 1
The One-Sheet Sample

THE DOCUMENTS SHOWN on the following two pages are examples of one-sheet templates used for creating a concept overview. The one-sheet template is a very important document. Its purpose is not just for the team and managers to "be on the same page" with the project's priorities and objectives, but as a tool to pass on to management, marketing, sales, and licensors to get them excited about your game when you aren't there to do the job yourself.

Ultimately, the style in which you create the one-sheet doesn't matter as much as the information in it. The first example is a text-only version, whereas the second adds images. No matter what format you use for your one sheet, the key is to keep it short and informative.

Reiterate the points on the one-sheet every time you talk about your game. You'll know when the concept eventually sinks in to your teammates when you propose a new design feature and they reply, "That doesn't fit in with what it says on the one-sheet," and they're right. Don't be insulted; consider it a victory! (We designers need to take them where we can!)

Bedbug: Rooftop Rumble (game title) concept overview

iOS/Android/Kindle (game platform)
Target Age: 8-up (target audience)
(Rating goes here – note no rating is necessary since ESRB doesn't rate "mobile" games)

Game Summary: Bedbug, the leaping lawman, protects the citizens of Silicon City from the forces of evil. Unbeknownst to him, **Player One**, the couch jockey of crime, has "leveled up" Bedbug's arch-villains with video game technology, turning them into super-powerhouses! Can Bedbug run fast enough, punch hard enough and jump high enough to defeat his vilest villains? Only **you** can decide!

(Include a beginning, middle and end of the game story. Keep it short and sweet.)

Game Outline: As Bedbug, the player runs and jumps across the rooftops of Silicon City, earning points for punching out criminals and rescuing citizens. Collect enough points to execute super-moves or earn the assistance from favorite Bedbug characters like Captain Superior, Blue Tiger or Elvira. The player can purchase and stock their utility belt with power-up items that aid them in their fight against crime. Using Bedbug's jumpin' boots, players can launch themselves into the air to avoiding hazards and break height and distance records. Watch out! Super-villain bosses will attempt to stop the leaping lawman, forcing the player to change tactics to survive.

(Don't go into great detail, but give an indication of the gameplay genre, the player's objectives and gameplay elements.)

USP: (Unique Selling Points)

- Superhero jumper meets superhero endless runner
- Stock your utility belt with gadgets like gas pellets and the bug-bite zapper
- Over 50 gadgets and power-ups pack a super-powered punch
- Summon heroes like the Vampire Bat and Battle Girl to come to your aid
- Battle Bedbug's fearsome foes like Grave Robber, Scrapper and the Boogeyman
- Compete with and against your friends in "Duo Duel" mode

(Use USPs to highlight cool and unique features – gameplay style, game modes, single or multiplayer, technology innovations, cool features. Don't use more than 5-7 of these.)

Similar competitive products:
Punch Quest, Knightmare Tower, Rayman Jungle Run
(Choose competitive products that are successful, recent or very well known – preferably all three.)

MAXIMO VS The ARMY of ZIN

A Single Player Combat / Action Game!

The Sequel to Maximo: Ghosts to Glory

A Compelling Story. A mystery that unfolds thru cinematic and puppet story sequences

Excitement! Fun! Heroic!

The Second Saga Begins....
Eight months have passed since Ghosts to Glory and Maximo and Grim have searched in vain for Sophia.... Their search is suddenly interrupted when they encounter a maiden menaced by a strange "clockwork" monster....

Maximo's appearance reflects his status!

TEEN (Violence) Rated

MAXIMO:

- **More Heroic** - Maximo has to save others not just his own skin!
- **More attack moves!** Cool Combat Motions & combos, simple to command!
- **Get Stronger!** - Build up your character with the new experience system to gain effective and powerful abilities, armor and new weapons!
- **Responsive movement and combat feel** - Satisfying to play controls
- **Customize your character** with unique boxers and abilities!

Maximo's character image:
- He's Brave, Heroic and Impulsive!
- He's a man of action! Physical in nature.
- Will always do the right thing even if it's to his disadvantage.

Maximo's telling character traits:
- He is always holding a sword
- He fights even in his underwear
- He has Death as a companion

THE ARMY OF ZIN

Unique, marketable and Very Cool

- **Created by the famous artist Susumu Matsushita**
- **Enemy Variety** - Different size, shape, movement and method of attack and defeat.

FUN TO PLAY AND EASY TO GET INTO!

The Zin Legend....
500 years ago the Army of Zin attacked! The forces of man rallied and in a great and terrible battle the Zin were defeated and placed in the Great Vault. There they tick away the centuries waiting to freed so they can march once more.

Innocent and not so innocent characters for Maximo to interact with and rescue!

Collect Death Coins to play as DEATH!

Grim finally shows his true nature as the reaper, an invulnerable and unstoppable floating force!!

Unexpected game play situations, enemies and story twists!

Keep collecting Koins to buy unique items!

Jump over obstacles and beat the crap out of stuff with style!

The Besieged village:
This once peaceful village is bombarded into ruin by the army of Zin. Maximo must search out the mysterious Gearmaster who lives in the dark forest.

Cool dark atmospheric stylized creepy environments!

The Haunted Forest:
Maximo must brave the horrors of the haunted forest where even the trees don't want him to leave alive.
Maximo learns about the Zin from Tinker, the cute and intelligent Gearmaster, before being abducted by Lord Bane.

Hazardous obstacle courses and physical puzzles!

The Crystal Mountains:
Maximo will have to cross teetering bridges and crumbling paths to reach Castle Hawkmoor and the great Vault. Maximo duels with his old rival, the Baron, to gain access to the Great vault.

Active environments that move and change as you smash stuff!

The Dead Sea:
The Dead Sea has been sucked dry by the Zin Fortress and the mysteries of the deep uncovered. Maximo must battle his way to the Soul crusher.

The Zin Fortress:
Maximo must survive the grinding gears to rescue Tinker, destroy the soul crusher and the soul stones that power the Army of Zin.

Bonus Level 2
The Ten-Page Design
Document Sample

UNLIKE THE ONE-PAGER, which should be kept to one page, the ten-pager is more like a set of guidelines than a strict policy.[1] It's more of a "ten-pointer" than a ten-pager, but as a general rule you should dedicate a page per topic.

What's important is that you include all the broad strokes of information and the document is accessible and exciting to read. The goal is to use this document as the foundation for both your GDD and the slides of your pitch.

---

[1] Kind of like the pirate's code.

Page 1: Cover Page

Include a graphic if possible, a title (preferably a logo) and your contact information, target platform, target audience, target rating, and expected shipping date.

Design by Scott Rogers

Date

For IOS, Android and Kindle

Ages: 8 – Up

Ship Date: TBD

Bedbug: Rooftop Rumble   Name and Contact Info   Date

Page 2: Story/Game Summary

Outline the story (beginning, middle, and ending . . . or at least a cliffhanger) mentioning the setting, the characters, and the conflict. Give a brief description of the gameplay and some of the cool things the player can do in the game.

Game Story Summary: Bedbug, the leaping lawman, protects the citizens of Silicon City from the forces of evil. Unbeknownst to him, **Player One**, the couch jockey of crime, has "leveled up" Bedbug's arch-villains using his holographic video game technology; turning the bad guys into a super-powerhouses! Can Bedbug run fast enough, punch hard enough and jump high enough in this endless runner/jumper?

Game Flow Outline: Bedbug: Rooftop Rumble is a side-scrolling endless runner/jumper that finds Bedbug, the single-father superhero dashing across the rooftops of Silicon City. Using Bedbug's jumpin' boots, the player can launch themselves into the air to avoiding hazards and break height and distance records. The player punches out criminals and rescues citizens to earn Pow! points. Earn enough Pow! to execute super-moves or earn the assistance from favorite Bedbug characters like Captain Superior, Blue Tiger or Elvira. Watch out! Super-villain bosses will attempt to stop the leaping lawman, forcing the player to change tactics if they hope to survive. Players can defeat bosses and earn (or purchase) Bug Bytes to restock their utility belt with power-up items that aid them in their never-ending fight against crime! Players can try to improve their high scores and post them to Game Center. Or compete against friends in "Duo Duel" mode.

Bedbug: Rooftop Rumble   Name and Contact Info   Date

Page 3: Character(s) and Controls

Who does the player control? What is his/her/its story? What can the player do that is unique or special to this game? Does the player play as more than one character? How does the player do these things with a controller or a finger (in the case of touch-controls)? Show a control map if applicable. Obviously, this page is very nosy and needs to know the answers!

CHARACTER: As a child, **Buddy Sprang** wanted to be a superhero when he grew up but a tragic accident resulted in an injury that confined him to leg braces and crutches. Turning to computer programming and the internet, Buddy created a search engine he sold for millions. Using his newly earned fortune, he built jumpin' boots that allow him to not only walk but jump as high as a building and kick hard enough to dent steel and shatter concrete. He spends his days taking care of his daughter, Elvira and nights as **Bedbug**; striking terror into the hearts of criminals who fear the Bedbug's bite!

CONTROLS: Bedbug: Rooftop Rumble use the following touch-controls to play:

- Bedbug **runs** constantly, requiring no player input, but Bedbug will slow down if he takes damage or runs into an enemy or obstacle.
- **Tap** the left hand side of the screen to **uppercut**. This allows Bedbug to jump over obstacles and leap high into the air. Upgrade his Jumpin' Boots for higher jumps.
- **Tap** the right hand side of the screen to **punch**. Punch enemies to defeat them and collect Pow!
- **Tap** both the left and right hand side simultaneously to **block**.
- **Tap** on a utility belt pouch to use an equipped **gadget**. Players can equip up to four utility belt gadget during one game session. Each gadget is a one-time use power-up.
- Bedbug automatically collects Bug-Bytes and Super-Helper power-ups. Players can spend Bug-Bytes for gadgets and upgrades. Super-Helpers are one-shot advantages to help Bedbug – from summoning the destructive power of Captain Superior and the flashing claws of Blue Tiger to the healing aid of his daughter Elvira.

Bedbug: Rooftop Rumble   Name and Contact Info   Date

Page 4: Gameplay Overview

What game genre is your game? (If you need help, refer to the handy list of gameplay genres in Bonus Level 5.) What is the primary action of the player? What awesome things is your player doing? The gameplay overview should give the reader a brief idea of the flow of the game. Break the information about gameplay into bullet points if conveying info that way is easier.

GAMEPLAY: Bedbug: Rooftop Rumble is an endless runner, where the player automatically runs from left to right over the rooftops of Silicon City. Along the rooftops, he will find criminals to fight, innocent victims to rescue, Bug-Byte chips to collect and super-villain bosses that bar his way. But the action doesn't restrict itself to the horizontal plane! Bedbug uses his Jumpin' Boots to launch himself up the sides of buildings, dodging hazards and enemies as he goes.

All of the controls in Bedbug: Rooftop Rumble are optimized for touch screen play. A simple tap can make Bedbug punch, jump, and block or use one of the gadgets from his utility belt.

As Bedbug defeats bad guys – from muggers and bank robbers to costumed criminals – the player will earn Pow! Once a player has collected enough Pow!, the player will be attacked by one of Bedbug's super-villains. Unfortunately for our hero, all of the baddies have receive high-tech upgrades from Player One, turning them into holographic versions of famous video game enemies. Bedbug will have to keep on his toes and the player will have to change tactics with each boss encounter if they want to survive.

But Bedbug isn't without his tricks. Players can either collect Bug-Byte chips or spend real money to buy gadgets for Bedbug's utility belt. Flash pellets temporarily stun enemies. Bug-bite zapper causes more damage. Snacks can restore health. The player can also collect Super-Helper power-ups that summon help from Bedbug's family and fellow superheroes – from the Blue Tiger's spectral claw attack that clears the screen of enemies to a simple hug from Elvira that restores all of the player's health.

The levels in Bedbug: Rooftop Rumble are programmatically generated – changing up enemy placement, mechanics, hazards and background art to keep things fresh for the player. The player can try to beat their best time (and display it in Game Center and at Google Play Games) or fulfill the requirements of over 50 achievements to earn more Bug-Bytes.

DUO DUEL MODE: Players can compete against each other in Duo Duel mode: an asynchronous game mode where players take turns "ghosting" each other's moves for points. Think of it as a game of H-O-R-S-E with far more punching, jumping and super-villains!

Bedbug: Rooftop Rumble   Name and Contact Info   Date

Page 5: Gameplay Overview (continued)

Sometimes your game is so awesome, you need a second page to describe all of the goodness!

GAME WORLD: It's bad enough that the rooftops of Silicon City is a dangerous place filled with hazards like sparking electrical wires, swinging crane arms and treacherous drops but it's also a haven for ruthless criminals who prey on the innocent. Fortunately for the citizen of Silicon City, Bedbug patrols these rooftops.

Leaping from building to building, the leaping lawman helps those in need and battles crime no matter where it shows up – whether on the urban sprawl of downtown to the smoky rooftops of Little India to the gleaming spires of the Cassandra Building.

When play shifts to vertical leaping sections, the player will jump past hazards like dropping plant pots, flocks of pigeons and open windows – some hiding criminals while others show amusing vignettes of city life and cameos from Bedbug supporting characters.

As the player's run continues, the locations will randomly change to prevent the scenery from getting boring – shifting in color and lighting to indicate to the player that they are making progress.

| Bedbug: Rooftop Rumble | Name and Contact Info | Date |

Page 6: Gameplay Experience

Here's where you talk about the overall feel of the game. What is it like to play it? What emotions or moods are you trying to convey? How is the game's story going to be told? (Cutscenes? Movies? Text boxes?) When do they appear? (In between levels? At the beginning and end of the game?)

GAME EXPERIENCE: After the Bedbug Games logo, the player is taken to the start screen. The player will have three options: Shop, Play and Duo Duel. Shop allows the player to buy Bug Bytes, power upgrades and gadgets for the utility belt. Duo Duel starts the two-player competitive mode. Play starts the game.

A short cut scene shows Player One in his lair vowing revenge on Bedbug. The camera pulls back to reveal he is speaking to all of Bedbug's greatest foes. Then Player One presses a button on his gamer glove which shoots out a beam of energy and imbues the villains with a mysterious power. Cut to Bedbug running along the rooftops – this is where gameplay begins.

The world and characters of **Bedbug: Rooftop Rumble** isn't grim like *Batman: Arkham Origins*, but it isn't a parody like the *Middle Manager of Justice*. The overall feel of the game and its world is of a classic American comic book from the 70's and 80's. The stakes are high, the danger is real even if it's from super-villains wearing holographic armor based on classic video game characters. That's not to say there isn't room for humor in the game. The reaction of an enemy getting defeated by an attack or super-move could be look or sound funny, as long as it doesn't descend into the realm of silliness.

The music in **Bedbug: Rooftop Rumble** should be up-tempo and heroic – either orchestral or rock. It should be something you never get tired of hearing even after the 100th time a player attempts to break their distance record.

Bedbug: Rooftop Rumble   Name and Contact Info   Date

Page 7: Mechanics and Modes

Break down some of the cool gameplay mechanics and play modes. Is there a multiplayer mode? Are there mini or micro games? Let us know!

GAME MECHANICS: These are some of the hazards, purchasable gadgets and collectable items available to the player.

HAZARDS: The rooftops can be a dangerous place for even a superhero! In addition to enemies and super-villains, here are some of the hazards that our hero faces:

Sparking neon signs	Collapsing walkways	Falling flower pots
Smoking chimney tops	Whirling air conditioners	Flocks of dangerous pigeons

GADGETS: Fortunately, Bedbug's utility belt is packed full of gadgets including:

- Steel gauntlets – does double damage to enemies
- Smoke pellets –
- Flash bomb - temporarily stuns criminal enemies
- Bug-bite taser - zap baddies and earn double the Pow!
- Boot Boosters – gives Bedbug a longer and higher jump
- Jamming device – reduces projectile accuracy by 50%
- Nighty-night gas pellets - knock out an entire screen of enemies
- Kevlar body suit – provides 25% protection from melee damage
- Nomex body suit – provides 25% protection from projectile damage
- Snacks – replenish 25% health
- Tech magnet – makes bug bytes easier to collect

SUPER-HELP: At random intervals, Bedbug can collect Super-Help Icons. Super-Help icons instantly summon Bedbug's family and allies

Captain Superior: The leader of the Super Battalion upstages Bedbug again by zooming in and attacking enemies before Bedbug even gets near them. Be sure to collect the resulting Pow! or you might lose it!

Blue Tiger: This mystical member of the Super Battalion unleashes the power of his spectral tiger gem, creating a flurry of claw attacks that does major damage to all enemies on screen.

Vampire Bat: The late-night avenger unleashes his flock of bats that collects all Pow! and Bug Bytes pickups for a short period of time.

Battle Girl: This princess of patriotism uses her mystical spirit shield to protect Bedbug temporarily from any damage.

Mistress Mind: The mistress of mind-control mesmerizes all enemies on screen, stunning them and leaving them easy targets for Bedbug to mop up!

Elvira: Bedbug's daughter arrives for a big hug – that replenishes all of the player's health.

Bedbug: Rooftop Rumble   Name and Contact Info   Date

Page 8: Enemies and Bosses

While it doesn't hurt to weave descriptions of enemies into the other pages like story and gameplay, sometimes you need to call attention to a particularly gnarly enemy or boss character. What makes your enemies unique? If applicable, what kinds of boss characters does the player face? How does the player defeat them? What does the player earn for defeating them?

If you have no enemies in your game, you obviously don't need this page. Instead, you can use this page to describe the game's conflict. How will players be challenged and how will they overcome it?

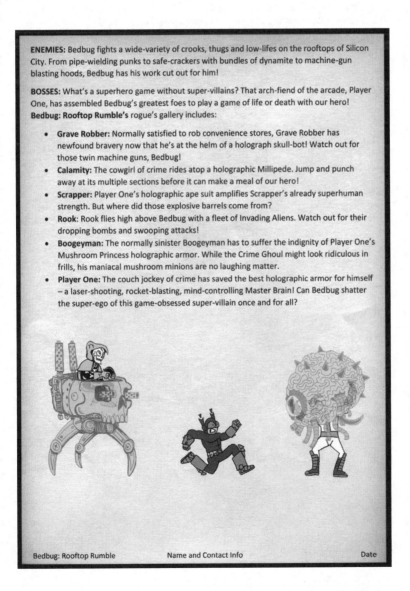

ENEMIES: Bedbug fights a wide-variety of crooks, thugs and low-lifes on the rooftops of Silicon City. From pipe-wielding punks to safe-crackers with bundles of dynamite to machine-gun blasting hoods, Bedbug has his work cut out for him!

BOSSES: What's a superhero game without super-villains? That arch-fiend of the arcade, Player One, has assembled Bedbug's greatest foes to play a game of life or death with our hero! **Bedbug: Rooftop Rumble's** rogue's gallery includes:

- **Grave Robber:** Normally satisfied to rob convenience stores, Grave Robber has newfound bravery now that he's at the helm of a holograph skull-bot! Watch out for those twin machine guns, Bedbug!
- **Calamity:** The cowgirl of crime rides atop a holographic Millipede. Jump and punch away at its multiple sections before it can make a meal of our hero!
- **Scrapper:** Player One's holographic ape suit amplifies Scrapper's already superhuman strength. But where did those explosive barrels come from?
- **Rook:** Rook flies high above Bedbug with a fleet of Invading Aliens. Watch out for their dropping bombs and swooping attacks!
- **Boogeyman:** The normally sinister Boogeyman has to suffer the indignity of Player One's Mushroom Princess holographic armor. While the Crime Ghoul might look ridiculous in frills, his maniacal mushroom minions are no laughing matter.
- **Player One:** The couch jockey of crime has saved the best holographic armor for himself – a laser-shooting, rocket-blasting, mind-controlling Master Brain! Can Bedbug shatter the super-ego of this game-obsessed super-villain once and for all?

Bedbug: Rooftop Rumble   Name and Contact Info   Date

Page 9: Bonus Material, and Downloadable Content

What extra cool stuff can the player earn or unlock? Can they purchase additional content? How will the game live beyond its initial release? What incentive is there for the player to play again?

BONUS MATERIALS: Players that download **Bedbug: Rooftop Rumble** will also get a digital copy of Bedbug #1. This exciting 32 page comic features the origin of Bedbug, three additional Bedbug adventures, four who's who guides to Bedbug's greatest allies and enemies and never-seen before artwork.

ACHIEVEMENTS: Each game, **Bedbug: Rooftop Rumble** players can attempt to earn three achievements. New achievements replace older ones when collected. There are over 30 achievements that will challenge the player's skills, endurance and patience!

- **Crime Smasher:** Defeat 100 criminals
- **Combo Artist:** Get a 100 hit combo
- **Punching Bag:** Get knocked out 100 times
- **Block Master:** Block 200 attacks
- **Friends for Life:** Collect all six Super-Help icons in a single game
- **Blow Back:** Deflect a dynamite bundle back into its thrower
- **Pow! Procurer:** Didn't miss collecting a single Pow! during a game
- **Fully Loaded:** Purchase all utility belt gadgets

Bedbug: Rooftop Rumble   Name and Contact Info   Date

Page 10: Monetization

Does your game have an economy? How will the game make additional money? Is there additional material for the player to buy?

MONETIZATION PLAN: While **Bedbug: Rooftop Rumble** will be a paid game ($1.99) Players will still be able to make in-game purchases. There are no hard gates within the game, rather the player will be able to collect and spend two currencies in the game: **Pow!** and **Bug Bytes.**

POW!: Players earn Pow! every time they defeat an enemy. The bigger the baddy, the more Pow! is rewarded. Players must collect Pow! by tapping on it or collect it with a power-up, gadget or Super-Help ability. Earn enough Pow! to unlock Boss Fights and new gadgets.

BUG BYTES: Bug Bytes are small microchips that are collected throughout the game. Players can also earn Bug Bytes by defeating bosses. Use Bug Bytes to purchase gadgets, one-shot boost power-ups and special costumes. Players can visit the in-game shop to purchase packages of Bug Bytes (at .99, 4.99. 9.99 and 19.99 increments) or a one-time purchase Bug-Bite Zapper ($1.99) to double the Pow! yielded from defeating a bad guy.

| Bedbug: Rooftop Rumble | Name and Contact Info | Date |

To sum things up, you want the content in the ten-pager to act as a starting point—for both you and the reader. It should provide a framework for your GDD outline, so you aren't starting from a blank page. It should excite readers enough to want to learn more about your game. And that's where the GDD comes in—filling in all those details.

Bonus Level 3

Game Design Document Template

THE FOLLOWING PAGES provide a template for creating a *game design document*, or GDD. This template skewed toward an action, adventure, platform, RPG, or shooter-style game. However, you can adapt most of the elements listed in the template for any style of game. I just wanted to give you a starting point. If your game is a driving game, then obviously you are going to describe the vehicles and how they handle rather than a character and his/her moves.

Don't feel as though you have to fill in every detail of information while creating the GDD, but it is better to have areas of the design roughed out than not to have them at all. I tell the developers I work with that listing "TBD" is better than nothing at all. You are trying to get an idea of the scope of the work involved. You can always come back to it later.

Remember that a GDD is a living thing: everything in it is liquid and might change due to anything from technology limitations to production time realities.

In the end, this template should be a guide to help you get started, but what matters most is that your team understands what the game is about and how they are going to make it. If you need to draw pictures to get your teammates to understand the gameplay, then do so. If listing everything in bullet points helps them understand the game play, then do that instead.

COVER

(Insert evocative cover image here)

YOUR GAME'S TITLE

Document version number (keep this current!)

Written by (your team name here)

Point of contact (producer or lead designer with phone number)

Date of publishing

Version number

Footer should always have:

Copyright Company Date   *Page number*   *Current date*

GDD Outline

Table of contents—Remember to keep this current.

Revision history—Update this information with publishing dates and track which author updated the material.

Game goals—Why should the audience/readers care about your game? Aim for five "back of the box" goals.

- **Game's "high concept"**—Provide a brief description of your game. Make sure to mention the game's genre.

- **Who, What, How?**

    - **Who**—Tell who this game is for. What ages? What ESRB rating?

    - **What**—Provide a game summary. What is this game about? Include a concise description of the gameplay.

    - **How**—Explain how this game will be awesome. Mention "back of the box" items like new/novel mechanics or gameplay features.

- Explain what platform this game is for. Will it feature multiplayer capability? Does it have any technical requirements?

- Provide short descriptions of gameplay types (stealth, battle arena, driving, flying, and so on) in the game.

Story overview—Remember to keep this description short and frame it in the context of the gameplay. Include the setup (how does the player start the game?). List all locations and how they relate to the narrative (how does the player get from one location to the next?). Don't forget the finale (What is the ending? What is the player expected to be/have done by the end of the game?).

- How are you communicating the story? Movies? Cutscenes? In-game?

Licensor points and concerns—List all goals of the licensor and how they will be addressed.

Game controls—Provide an overview of the controls. List specific moves the player will be doing, but don't go into detail on the actual moves . . . yet.

- Show an image of a controller, touchscreen, or keyboard with corresponding control mapping.

Technological requirements—Keep this information brief because many of these features will be included in the game's technical design document (TDD).

- What tools will this game use?

- How are camera, physics, bosses, and so on going to be done? Implemented by programmer? By designer? Hard-coded? Scripted?

- What design tools will this game use? List level creation and scripting tools used.

- What are the proposed tools for cheats? Include controls for level, invulnerability, camera, and other gameplay-related cheats.

- For PC games, include a section covering the target specs of the computer needed to run the game. This would list things like the amount of RAM, minimum CPU speed, minimum graphical abilities, required peripherals, and so on.

Front end of the game—Indicate what credit screens will be shown when the game is first turned on, including the following:

- Publisher

- Studio logo

- Licensors

- Third-party software manufacturers

- Legal screen

Attract mode description (if applicable)—Give a description of what in-game material will be shown if the game is left idle on the start screen.

Title/start screen—What is the first impression of the actual game? Include the following:

- An image of the title/start screen and any associated animation and graphics.

- A list of what selection options are available to the player.

- Save/load file—Describe how a game file is saved and loaded and naming conventions for the player.

- Player options—Include image, sound and music, and player interface details. Include details on connecting links to options:

    - Video, audio, music, and subtitle settings; contrast tool; and alternate control settings (airplane controls, feedback on/off, and so on)

Game flowchart—Show how all the screens from "title/start screen" to "game over" connect with each other.

Loading screen—Explain what the player sees when the game is loading. What images or information is presented?

Game camera(s)—Call out any specific camera types.

- What kind of camera is used? (First person, third person, forced scroll, locked camera, and so on.)

- What is the logic system for the camera? Include the following:

  - Game-specific situations requiring unique cameras

  - Camera troubleshooting guide with examples of what the camera will do when encountering problems

HUD system—Describe and/or illustrate how information will be presented on-screen to the player. Include images of all associated imagery such as health/status, power/fuel, money, timers, maps, plings, speedometer, lives/continues, targeting, and special view like "predator vision" or bullet-time.

Player character(s)—Provide information about the player character (if applicable) including images, names, and relationships to other characters in the game.

Player metrics—List and detail the player character and provide metrics pertaining to movement, combat, context-sensitive moves (such as QTEs), health, player death, and idles.

Player skills—List the player's skills and provide a list or "tech tree" of the player's upgrades.

Player inventory tools (equipment, spells, buffs, and so on)—List all tools and inventory items—things the player will use and how to use them. Describe or illustrate the Inventory screen and how the player will access items.

Combat—Describe and/or illustrate all combat moves and reactions including combo moves; different weapon types (melee and ranged); weapon tech tree; ranges; how the player equips, reloads, and changes weapons; lock-ons; and targeting systems.

Power-ups/state modifiers—List power-ups and state modifiers. Show images and list what their effect and duration are.

Health (if applicable)—Describe how health is tracked on HUD and how players can lose and replenish health. Describe how players can tell when health is low.

- **Alternate states**—Describe any alternate states (stunned, poisoned, turned into a baby, etc.) the player can get into and how it might affect controls.

- **Lives (if applicable)**—Explain how lives are earned or lost and what happens when the player runs out.

- **Death (if applicable)**—Describe what happens when death occurs. List situations requiring unique animations (fire, drowning, and so on). What happens when the game is over? What does the game-over screen look like? Is there a penalty for dying?

- **Checkpoint system**—Describe the in-game checkpoint system. How does the auto-save system work?

Scoring (if applicable)—Assign point values to actions and explain what happens when players reach them. How do players earn bonuses in the game (like chaining or combos)?

- **Leaderboard setup**—What does it look like? What stats are being tracked?

- **Achievements**—What achievements are available and how are they earned? List them and provide images for badges if applicable.

Rewards and economy—Describe the game's monetary system including how money is earned, spent, and saved (if applicable). List purchasable items and cost. Describe how the shopping interface works.

Collectibles/object sets—Provide a list of all items in the game, where they can be found, and what they do. Provide images.

Vehicles—What vehicles are used? Provide visuals. How does a vehicle interact with the world, enemies, objects, and so on? How does it control? Does it require a different camera system? How does the player enter or exit the vehicle? What abilities does the vehicle have?

Game progression outline—Provide an overview of all game levels. Insert a beat chart here. Show how gameplay and story intertwines. Indicate introduction of major elements such as enemies, bosses, rewards, items, puzzles, or twists to the story.

World overview/level select/navigation screen—Provide images and a control scheme showing how the player will navigate. List locations and where they lead to. Provide sound and music requirements.

Universal game mechanics—List mechanics that will be found throughout the game. Always include images of each mechanic. List each platform, portal, breakable, hazard, interactable object, and puzzle element and how the player interacts with them.

Game levels—List each of the levels mentioned in the world overview including name, short description, major gameplay, enemies, and items found in the level. Describe how the level relates to the story if applicable. Include a list of time of day, color guide, and music needs.

General enemy rules—List behavior types (patroller, flyer, and so on) and how the behavior type AI operates. Describe spawn and defeat parameters. List reward rules.

Level-specific enemies—Provide an image and description of the enemy and where it appears in the game. List all movement and attack patterns and ways the player can defeat the enemy. Describe any combination attacks or encounters between different types of enemies. Describe what happens when the enemy is defeated and what the player gets for doing so.

Bosses—Provide an image and description of each boss and its environment. Describe the encounter and what it will be like to play it. List all movement, attack patterns, and ways the player can defeat the boss. Describe what happens when the boss is defeated and what the player gets for doing so.

NPCs—List characters in the game. Provide descriptions, images, and where they appear. List what function they serve in the overall context of the game. List what rewards or items they are associated with.

Minigames—List the types of minigames and provide illustrations showing each game type. Describe how to play and use control schemes. List what original and repurposed game elements the minigames require. List what levels the games are found on and what rewards they yield.

Monetization—Describe how monetization will work over the course of the game. Show the interface for purchasing content. List purchasable items and estimated cost.

Downloadable content—List the DLC. Give estimated time frame for content release.

Cutscenes—List the cutscenes. Provide a short outline of each cutscene and where each one is presented.

Music and SFX—List all music needs. Describe the tone or feeling of each piece. List on what level the music is needed, and don't forget the title, pause, and option screens as well as end credits.

Other screens—Describe this unlockable content accessed from the title screen. Make sure to include image, sound and music, and player interface details. Possible screens include

- **Credits**—Include names, job titles, a team photo, or images of the studio at work.

- **Bonus material**—Include images of screens. Explain how the player will interact with the interface and activate this material (unlockable, Easter eggs, and so on).

  - List all alternate costumes or weapons, cheats, art galleries, video players, and special features such as commentary, interviews, deleted material, documentaries, and gag reels.

Appendix(es)—This is the place where long lists go, including player animation, enemy animation, sound effects, music, cutscene scripts, in-game text, and VO scripts.

Bonus Level 4
The Medium-Sized List of Story Genres

STORY GENRES ARE categories of fiction based on subject matter. There are so many of story genres, I find it helps to have a list to keep track of them all.

- Adventure: period piece/swashbuckler/pirate
- Adventure: pulp/"two-fisted" action/explorer/treasure-hunter
- Adventure: survival/disaster
- Adventure: young adult
- Blaxplotation/grindhouse
- Caper/heist/thief
- Cartoon/anthropomorphic
- Comedy: romantic/misunderstanding
- Comedy: screwball/slapstick
- Crime drama/police
- Documentary/showbiz
- Educational
- Erotic
- Espionage
- Family drama

- Fantasy: fairytale/alternate world
- Fantasy: mythology (Greek, Japanese, Chinese, Norse, and so on)
- Fantasy: swords and sorcery
- Fantasy: whimsical
- Film noir/crime-drama/hard-boiled detective
- Game show
- Historical
- Historical: alternate
- Historical: mythological
- Historical: warfare
- Horror: B-movie/giant monster
- Horror: gothic (ghost, vampire, werewolf, Frankenstein)
- Horror: sci-fi
- Horror: slasher

- Horror: zombie/end of the world
- Martial arts/ninja
- Medical drama
- Mobster/gangster
- Musical
- Music/rock 'n' roll
- Mystery
- Nurture/tamagotchi
- Political
- Romance drama/gothic
- School/teen drama
- Sci-fi: cyberpunk
- Sci-fi: invasion
- Sci-fi: Japanese/Sentai/giant robot
- Sci-fi: psychic
- Sci-fi: realistic/NASA
- Sci-fi: retro (1930s)
- Sci-fi: space opera
- Sci-fi: steampunk
- Sci-fi: time travel/parallel universe
- Sci-fi: undersea
- Sports: fantasy/sci-fi
- Sports: individual (boxing, wrestling, skateboarding, snowboarding, skiing)
- Sports: Olympic
- Sports: racing
- Sports: team (American football, soccer, hockey, baseball, basketball, and so on)
- Superhero
- Western/spaghetti western

Bonus Level 5
Game Genres

WELL HELLO THERE. Did you wander over here from Level 1? In case you are missed it, a **genre** is used to describe a category of something but a **game genre** is used to describe the type of gameplay. There are so many of them, I decided to put together a list of them for you.

Ever since the dawn of gaming, video games have been wildly diverse. Consider that the first three video games in existence were a sports game (*Tennis for Two*), a puzzle game (*Noughts and Crosses*), and a head-to-head shooter (*Space War*)! Diversity has been what makes gaming so great, and over the years, games have splintered off into many different genres and subgenres. In the following descriptions, italicized games are examples of the genre.

- **Action**—These games require hand-eye coordination to play. The action genre has several subgenres:

  - **Action-adventure**—This combination of genres features an emphasis on combat, item collection and usage, puzzle solving, and long-term story-related goals. *Legend of Zelda* series, *Uncharted* series, *Batman Arkham* series.

  - **Action-arcade**—These games are presented in the style of early arcade games with an emphasis on "twitch" gameplay, scoring, and short play time. *Kaboom*, *FantaVision*, *Nidhogg*.

  - **Beat 'em up/hack 'n' slash**—In these games, also called **brawlers**, players battle against wave after wave of enemies, increasing in difficulty. *Double Dragon*, *God Hand*, *Castle Crashers*, *Scott Pilgrim vs. the World*.

  - **Endless Runner**—In these games, the player character constantly runs (or flies or swims or rockets) through a "never-ending" environment. To stop is to die! *Canabalt*, *Jet Pack Joyride*, *Temple Run* series.

- **Fighting**—In these games, two or more opponents battle in arena settings. Fighting games are distinguished from other action games by the depth of their player controls. *Street Fighter* series, *Soul Calibur* series, *Mortal Kombat* series.

- **Maze**—In these games, players navigate a maze environment while collecting items and power-ups and avoiding enemies. *Pac-Man* series, *Mappy*, *Go Marble*.

- **Platformer**—Platformer games usually feature a mascot character jumping (or swinging or bouncing) their way through an obstacle course-like environment that often includes platforms of some sort. Shooting and fighting may also be involved. There might be a pirate ship. At one time, the platformer was the most popular subgenre in gaming. Nintendo's Mario titles (*Super Mario World*, *Mario 64*, and *Super Mario Galaxy*), *Sly Cooper* series, *LittleBigPlanet* series, *Super Meat Boy* series.

- **Sandbox**—Also called "open world" games, these are action games with non-linear gameplay that takes place in very large game world. Sandbox games offer a variety of activities from driving to puzzle solving to shooting and melee combat. *Grand Theft Auto* series, *Saint's Row* series, *Lego Marvel Super Heroes*, *Elder Scroll IV: Oblivion*, *Red Dead Redemption*.

- **Stealth**—These action games put an emphasis on avoiding enemies rather than directly fighting them. *Metal Gear* series, *Thief: The Dark Project*, *Sneak Beat Bandit*.

- **Adventure**—Adventure games focus on puzzle solving, plus item collection and inventory management. Adventure games can be solely text-based, such as *Colossal Cave*, *The Hitchhiker's Guide to the Universe*, *A Mind Forever Voyaging* or *Varicella*, or can utilize graphics such as *Adventure*, the *King's Quest*, *Leisure Suit Larry* series, *The Wolf among Us*.

  - **Graphical adventure**—This subgenre has players uncover clues, solve puzzles, and navigate their character from screen to screen. *Myst* series, *Monkey Island* series, the *Sam and Max* series, *The Walking Dead: Season One*.

  - **Role-playing game (RPG)**—This subgenre is based on pen and paper role-playing games like *Dungeons and Dragons* and *GURPS*. Players choose a character class and enhance their "stats" by earning experience undertaking quests, defeating enemies and finding treasure. Characters can either play as generic character classes like a Fighter, Magic-User or Thief or as fictional characters. *Star Wars: Knights of the Old Republic* and the *Mass Effect* series, the *Elder Scrolls* series, *Freedom Force*, *Card Hunter*.

- **Japanese role-playing game (JRPG)**—JRPGs first appeared on Nintendo's Famicom system but have such a distinct feel from traditional RPGs that they have evolved to become a genre of their own. Players manage a team of characters and increase their "stats" through combat, exploration, and treasure finding. A greater emphasis is placed on interpersonal relationships and story than found in traditional RPGs. *Pokémon* series, *Final Fantasy* series, *Kingdom Hearts* series, *Ni No Kuni*.

- **Massively multiplayer online role-playing game (MMORPG)**—This type of RPG can support hundreds of players together in one environment. MMORPGs are known for player versus player gameplay, repetitive gameplay or "grinding," and group battles or "raids." *World of Warcraft*, *DC Universe Online*, *EVE Online*.

- **Survival/horror**—In these games, players attempt to survive a horror or survival scenario with limited resources, such as sparse ammunition. *Resident Evil* series, *Silent Hill* series, *Amnesia: The Dark Descent*, *Ao Oni*, *The Last of Us*.

- **Augmented reality**—AR games use peripheral devices like cameras and global positioning systems (GPSs) to blur the "real world" with virtual gameplay. *Majestic*, *ARDefender*, *Star Wars Falcon Gunner*, *Zombies, Run!*, *Parallel Kingdom*.

- **Educational**—In these games, the primary intention is to educate players while entertaining them. Also known as **edutainment** games. Educational games are often aimed toward a younger audience. *Carmen Sandiego* series, *Math Blaster* series, *Typing of the Dead*, *Wolf Quest* series, *Bot Colony*.

  - **Activity**—These educational games have some game content but primarily focus on non-game activities such as dress-up, coloring, and reading. *JumpStart* series, *Reader Rabbit* series, *Magic School Bus* series.

  - **Brain training**—These games are scientifically designed to improve the players' mental facilities using memorization and reaction time or to help users work through psychological issues such as post-traumatic stress disorder. *Brain Age*, *Big Brain Academy* series, *T2 Virtual PTSD Experience*, *Nevermind*.

- **Life simulation**—This genre is similar to the management genre but revolves around building and nurturing relationships with artificial life forms. *The Sims* and *Princess Maker* titles are both life simulators.

  - **Pet simulation**—Pet simulations became popular with the Tamagotchi digital pet pocket games. Pet simulators (or **virtual pets**) revolve around nurturing animals through feeding and relationships. *EyePet*, *Rat Realm*, *NintenDogs*, *NeoPets*, *Hatch*, *Tomogotchi L.i.f.e*.

- **Minigame**—A minigame can be any genre, but is only played for a limited time. Minigames are used to provide variety to other game genres such as the asteroid shooter in *Dead Space* or the card matching game in *Super Mario Bros. 3*. They are often a stand-in for an activity such as the hacking minigame in *Bioshock* or the lock picking minigame in *Fallout 3*. There are even compilations of mini games such as *Mario Party*, *Ape Escape: Pumped & Primed*, *Sonic Shuffle*, and *Big League Sports*.

  - **Microgame**—A super-short (usually seconds) mini game where half of the challenge to the player is learning how to play the game before it is over! *WarioWare* series, *Dumb Ways to Die*, *Frobisher Says*!

- **Party**—Party games are specifically designed for multiple players and are based on competitive play. More often than not, gameplay is presented in the minigame format. *Mario Party*, *Start the Party*, *Spin the Bottle: Bumpie's Party*.

- **Puzzle**—Puzzle games are based on logic, observation, and pattern completion. They can utilize slow, methodical piece placement or use quick hand-eye coordination. *Tetris*.

  - **Hidden object**—Players attempt to find a list of objects among visual clutter. One of the few games that uses the romance story genre. *Samantha Swift* series, *Jewel Quest Mysteries* series, *Mystery Case Files* series, *Mushroom Age*, *Angelica Weaver: Catch Me When You Can*.

  - **Drawing**—Players draw images or sometimes just lines to create gameplay. In many cases, the players even draw the game's mechanics. *Draw to Life* series, *Line Rider* series, *Draw This!*, *Pixel Press*, *Let's Draw!*

  - **Match Three**—Players match three (or more) icons to gain points (or cash or whatever). Gameplay can either be timed, have a limited number of moves, or be open-ended. Recently, the match three gameplay has been used as a "stand-in" mechanic for combat and minigames in other game genres. *Dr. Robotnik's Mean Bean Machine*, *Bejeweled* series, *Peggle* series, *PuzzleQuest* series, *10,000,000*, *Zuma's Revenge*, *Candy Crush*.

  - **Math puzzle**—Sometimes players do math problems; other times numbers are used to guide the gameplay. Either way, players are doing math whether or not they realize it. *Addicus*, *Super 7*, *Math Gems*, *Brain Age Express: Math*, *Sudoku 2 Pro*.

  - **Physics games**—These titles use physics such as gravity, trajectory, and fluid dynamics to create gameplay. *The Incredible Machine*, *Angry Birds*, *Where's My Water*, *Cut the Rope*, *Labyrinth*, *World of Goo*.

  - **Word Puzzle**—Players use words and letters as part of the gameplay. Sometimes the point is to spell words for points; other times wordplay is used to activate other gameplay mechanics. *Letz*, *Scribblenauts* series, *Words with Friends*, *SpellTower*, *Puzzlejuice*.

- **Rhythm**—In these games, players try to match a rhythm or beat to score points. *Parappa the Rapper*, *Tap Tap* series, *Elite Beat Agents* series.

  - **Music simulation**—In this type of rhythm game, the emphasis is on playing a musical instrument. These games often require special peripherals to play. *Guitar Hero* series, *Samba De Amigo* series, *Donkey Konga* series.

  - **Dance simulation**—In this type of rhythm game, players have to match a beat by moving their body. These games always utilize a special peripheral such as a pad or a camera to capture to the players' movements. *Dance, Dance Revolution* series, *Just Dance* series, *Dance Central* series.

  - **Singing simulation**—In this type of rhythm game, players have to match the melody of a song using their voice. These games always utilize a microphone peripheral. *SingStar* series, *Rock Band* series.

- **Serious games**—Serious games are designed for some reason other than entertainment.

  - **Advergames**—These games were created to advertise a product or company. This genre has been around since the Atari 2600 days and has been used for everything from fast food to pet food (kinda the same thing, I guess). *Chuck Wagon, Kool-Aid Man, Cool Spot, Chex Quest, America's Army, Sneak King, You Vs. Cat.*

  - **Art games**—These games have very light mechanics, emphasizing visuals and storytelling over gameplay. *The Cat and the Coup, Journey, Little Inferno, Papa Sangre* series, *Type:Rider.*

  - **Social message games**—These games educate players about social injustice with the intention of changing the players' perspective. *A Force More Powerful, Disaffected!, Darfor Is Dying, Food Force.*

  - **Training**—These games are designed to train players in the fundamentals of vehicle or systems operation. *Harpoon, Microsoft Flight Simulator, SimPort.*

  - **Productivity games**—In these games, players do activities in the real world and use the game to track their progress. *Epic Win, HabitRPG, CARROT.*

  - **Purpose games**—These games were designed to reach a result such as solving a genetic sequence (*Phylo*) or cataloging an art collection (*Artigo*). *Foldit, Google Image Labeler, EteRNA.*

- **Shooter**—These games focus primarily on firing projectiles at enemies. While fast-paced and "twitch" oriented, like action games, this genre has evolved to include several subgenres that are distinguished by their camera view.

  - **First person shooter**—These shooter games are seen from the player's perspective. The tighter camera view is more limiting but more personal than in a third person shooter. *Quake, Halo* series, *Half Life* series, *Team Fortress* series, *Medal of Honor* series, *Call of Duty* series.

- **Shoot 'em up**—Shoot 'em ups (or shmups for short) are arcade-style shooters in which players shoot large quantities of enemies while avoiding hazards. The player's avatar in a shmup is usually a vehicle (such as a spaceship) rather than a character. These games can be presented from several different camera angles. *Space Invaders, Robotron 2084,* the *Contra* series, *Ikaruga, The Touhou Project.*

- **Third person shooter (TPS)**—In these shooter games, the camera is placed further behind the player, allowing for a partial or full view of the player's character and surroundings. Despite the wider view, the emphasis on gameplay remains on shooting. The *Star Wars Battlefront* series, *Gears of War* series, *Bulletstorm, Dead Space 2 and 3.*

- **Simulation**—This genre focuses on creating and managing a world designed, if not created, by the player. Often other gameplay styles can be created and played within these meta-worlds. Many scholars call this genre **"toys,"** as these games often do not have victory goals other than the personal satisfaction of the world's creator.

- **Construction simulation**—Players can exercise their creativity through building their own world by harvesting resources. These world-building games often have a social aspect. *Minecraft, Lego Universe, Roblox.*

- **Management simulation**—This subgenre has players expand a property, business, or location based (somewhat) on reality. Predesigned buildings and environments evolve as the player-created world grows. *SimCity, Harvest Moon* series, *Game Dev Story.*

- **Social simulation**—Often found as a browser or mobile game, this subgenre has players building locations that can be visited by other players. The other players can have an effect on the player's world—often helping the player with tasks. *Farmville, Smurf Village, The Simpsons: Tapped Out.*

- **Sports**—These games are based on athletic competitions, whether they are traditional or extreme. It is common to see annual versions of these titles.

  - **Traditional sports**—Based on team sports like baseball, football, hockey, soccer, and basketball, these games try to accurately represent the "real-world" game, down to licensing real-world teams and players' likenesses. These games range in play complexity from arcade-style controls to true simulations in which players can choose from a variety of moves and plays. *Madden* series, *FIFA* series, *Major League Baseball 2K* series.

  - **Multi sports**—These games offer a variety of real-world sporting events in one title. They often offer shorter play experiences, feeling much like a collection of sports-themed minigames. *Track and Field, Mario and Sonic at the Olympic Games* series, *Justin Smith's Realistic Summer Games.*

- **Extreme sports**—Based on individual sports such as skiing, snowboarding, skate boarding, and surfing, these games don't always try to accurately represent the sport. They rely more on arcade-style controls and action. They often feature celebrity athletes as the player's guide through the game. *Skitchin'*, *Tony Hawk* series, *Shaun White Snowboarding*.

- **Sports management**—Rather than directly playing the sport in these games, players manage players or teams. *FIFA Manager* series, *NFL Head Coach* series.

- **Strategy**—From chess to *Sid Meir's Civilization*, thinking and planning are the hallmarks of strategy games. They take place in both historical and fictitious settings.

  - **Real time strategy (RTS)**—Similar to turn-based games, these faster-paced games focus on the "four X's": expansion, exploration, exploitation, and extermination. RTS has become the dominant strategy subgenre. *Command and Conquer* series, *WarCraft*, *StarCraft* series, *Dawn of War* series.

  - **Turn-based**—The slower pace of these games allows players time to think, providing more opportunity for strategy to be employed. *X-Com* series, *Advance Wars* series.

  - **Tower defense**—In these games, players create automated projectile shooting "towers" that keep enemies from reaching a destination. Games are often played from a third-person perspective so players can keep track of the "creeps" advancing in from multiple directions. *Defense Grid: The Awakening*, *Plants vs. Zombies* series, *Orcs Must Die* series, *Kingdom Rush: Frontiers*.

  - **Multiplayer online battle arena (MOBA)**—Also called DOTA-style gameplay—named after *Defense of the Ancients*, the first MOBA game—this genre of game pits two teams of players in a tug-of-war struggle of territory control. Players respawn after defeat while upgrading their characters over the course of the battle. *League of Legends*, *Heroes of Newerth*, *Infinite Crisis*.

- **Traditional games**—These games first appeared in another physical form.

  - **Board games**—This genre simulates board games played on a tabletop. Typically the code is used to perform "mundane" tasks such as rolling die, managing money or resources, or acting as an opponent. Often these games can be played by multiple players. *Scrabble*, *Monopoly*, *Settlers of Catan*, *Small World*, *Talisman*.

  - **Card games**—These games simulate traditional and thematic card games. *Solitaire*, *Uno*, *WarStorm*, *Magic the Gathering*, *Dominion*, *Dead Man's Draw*, *Yu-Gi-Oh*.

  - **Casino games**—These are any games you'd find at a casino: poker, slots, roulette, craps, bingo, even betting on sporting events. *Hoyle CasinoGames*, *Hollywood Spins*, *Big Fish Casino*, *SportsCasino*, *World Championship Poker* series.

- **Miniature games**—These games replicate tabletop miniature games. Often the graphics are meant to invoke the visuals of miniatures. *Heroclix Online, Sid Meir's Ace Patrol series, Space Hulk, Combat Monsters.*

- **Pinball**—These games replicate the physics and the bells and whistles of a pinball table. *Zen Pinball, Pinball Arcade, Pinball HD Collection.*

- **Trivia games**—In these games, players compete to answer trivia questions. *Scene it series, You Don't Know Jack series, Buzz! series.*

- **Vehicle Simulation**—In these games, players simulate piloting/driving a vehicle, from a sports car to a spaceship. Emphasis is placed on making the experience as "real" as possible or on creating an action-based arcade-like experience. There may or may not be stunts involved. *Night Driver, Rush series, Midnight Club series, Wipeout series.*

  - **Racing**—Players race and upgrade vehicles, from motorcycles to hovercrafts. Driving games can be ultra-realistic experiences like the *GTR* series or more action oriented like the *Burnout* series. *Gran Turismo series, the NASCAR Racing series, Wave Race, Grand Prix series.*

  - **Kart racing**—Kart racers are a much more arcade-like experience than their racing counterparts. Cartoony drivers and environments, crazy looking karts and power ups that can be used to improve performance and attack other players are all hallmarks of this sub-genre. *Super Mario Kart series, Sonic Drift series, LittleBigPlanet Karting.*

  - **Flight simulation**—Players pilot aircraft for the pleasure of flying and to learn the basics of flight as in the *Microsoft Flight Simulator* series.

- **Combat flight simulation**—Players battle against AI enemies or other players. Controls can be simple like an arcade game or complex, replicating a true aircraft or fictitious spacecraft. Battle throughout history in the *Red Baron* series, *War Thunder, The Jane's Combat Simulations series, Ace Combat* series or take the fight into outer space in the *Wing Commander* series, *Star Wars: X-wing* series, the *X* series, *Freespace* series.

Bonus Level 6
The Big List of Environments[1]

- Abandoned city
- Air/clouds
- Airplane
- Airport/airship port
- Alien planet
- Alien ship
- Amphitheatre
- Ancient ruins
- Aquarium
- Arcade
- Atlantis
- Bank
- Bar/cantina
- Barren rock (planetoid or moon)
- Battlefield/war zone/no man's land
- Bayou
- Beach
- Biomechanical area (à la *Alien*)
- Boardwalk
- Campsite
- Candy land
- Carnival
- Cartoon world/comic book world
- Casino/Las Vegas/Atlantic City
- Castle
- Cave
- Chemical plant
- Chinatown
- Chinese temple
- Church
- Circus
- City street

---

[1] I must have made half a dozen versions of this list over the years, so it is as much for me as it is for you!

- Cliff city
- Clock tower
- Comic book store
- Concert hall
- Construction site
- Crack house
- Cruise ship
- Cyberspace/computer world (à la *Tron*)
- Deep space
- Desert
- Desert island
- Disco
- Dojo/temple
- Dungeon/catacombs
- Egypt/Egyptian tomb
- Factory
- Fairytale land
- Famous monument
- Farm/ranch
- Fast-food restaurant
- Fire level/world
- Forest
- Fort
- Fort Knox/treasury
- Freeway
- Funeral home
- Futuristic city
- Garden
- Giant-sized world (can be applied to any theme)
- Glacier/ice flow
- Government installation
- Graveyard
- Haunted house
- Heaven/Olympus
- Hospital
- Hotel/inn
- House/apartment
- Ice
- Indian reservation/village/burial ground
- Inside a creature/on top of a giant creature
- Jungle
- Junkyard
- Kitchen
- Laboratory
- Library
- "Little" world (where the player has been shrunken down)
- Mall/marketplace
- Mansion
- Marina/seaport
- Mayan jungle/temple
- Maze/hedge/labyrinth
- Medieval village
- Metropolis/megalopolis/arcology

- Military base/Area 51
- Mines
- Missile silo
- Monastery
- Mountain
- Movie set/TV studio
- Movie theater
- Moving train
- Museum
- New York City
- North pole
- Nuclear reactor
- Ocean park (à la "Sea World")
- Ocean surface
- Office building
- Oil refinery
- Opera house
- Palace
- Park
- Pirate ship/town
- Playground
- Police station
- Post-apocalyptic city
- Prehistoric village/caves
- Prison
- Racetrack
- Restaurant
- River
- Rooftops
- Russian city/military base
- Rustic village
- Savannah/veldt
- School/elementary/college
- Secret lair: superhero/supervillain
- Sewer
- Ship/boat deck/interior
- Sky/clouds
- Skyscraper
- Sock puppet world
- Space station/spaceport
- Sporting arena
- Strip club
- Submarine interior
- Suburbs
- Subway
- Surface of the sun
- Swamp
- Temple
- Theater stage
- Theme park/water park
- Topiary maze/garden
- Toy land
- Toy store
- Train station
- Treehouse/village
- Undersea base/city/grotto

- Underwater
- Underworld/Hell
- Urban city
- Utopia
- Volcano

- Warehouse
- Wild West town
- Zeppelin interior
- Zoo/wild animal preserve

Bonus Level 7

Mechanics and Hazards

- Balance beam
- Blasting flame/wind/cannon timing puzzle
- Breakable object/smashable glass/force shields
- Buildable structures/objects using level objects or inventory puzzle pieces
- Carryable/throwable object
- Catapult that launches player or object
- Cause and effect: operate/move/interact with one item; another one acts in the opposite manner
- Climbable wall surface
- Collapsing floor/platform/staircase
- Collectable items organized as a set
- Conveyer belt
- Crank/pump
- Crank-operated door that drops if motion is not maintained
- Deadly surface/sticky floor/poison gas that slows player movement
- Deadly surface/spikes/thorns/lava/electrified water used to cause damage
- Elevator
- Escort: defend target from incoming attacks/damage
- Exploding object
- Hazard that smashes down or up
- Health/ammo dispenser
- Hidden image/clue in environment/inventory item
- Floor switch/pressure plate
- Forced scroll/moving environment that keeps player moving
- Ladder
- Lighting fixture to control light/darkness effect
- Limited number of moves
- Locked door/treasure chest requiring key
- Lock-picking/hacking mechanic requiring dexterity or puzzle solving

- Money or economy mechanics such as purchasing/bidding/selling/investing
- Multiple choice
- Multiple operations at once: player's concentration/resources are split between multiple mechanics and objectives
- Music/sound pattern recognition/repeat
- Movement accelerator
- Moving platforms: horizontal, vertical, diagonal
- Object that grabs the player, requiring another move to break free
- Opening/closing door/drawbridge
- Pattern repetition/Simon says
- Pendulum/swinging object timing puzzle
- Positioning an object in a particular place/orientation
- Pull lever
- Push/pull block or object
- Remote control for a character/object/mechanism

- Rotating platform
- Shooting arrow/laser/machine gun turret
- Shootable target/moving target
- Sinking/shrinking platforms
- Slippery ice/slide/oil
- Spring/trampoline/jump pad/air gust
- Spinning hazard
- Spotlight/character that player must avoid using timing, cover, or disguise
- Swingable vine/trapeze/chains
- Teleporter
- Timing puzzle: wait for "safe" state to move
- Time bomb
- Timer/race
- Two-stage openable or breakable object
- Water hazard
- Zip line/bungee cord

Bonus Level 8

Enemy Design Template

Enemy name: _____

Enemy image: (Insert concept or inspirational image here.)

Description: (Write a short description of the enemy; what is the enemy's personality and motivation?)

List of required animations including:

- Stand
- Idle
- Taunts
- Attacks (melee)
- Attacks (projectile)
- Hit reactions
- Death animations
- Victory animations

Movement patterns: (Add as many as necessary.)

- **Move 1:** (image and description of enemy's movement)
- **Move 2:** (image and description of enemy's movement)

Attack descriptions: (Add as many as necessary.)

- **Attack 1:** (melee, projectile, special)
- **Attack 2:** (melee, projectile, special)

Enemy is defeated by: (How will the player defeat the enemy?)

Damage description: (How is damage communicated to the player? Does the player require any special visual effects?)

Particle effects: (What visual effects are required for attacks, movement, or damage states?)

Projectiles: (If used, list what projectiles will be needed for attacks.)

HUD elements: (Are any additional HUD elements required for the enemy fight, such as icons for QTEs?)

Sound effects list: (Match the sound effects list with the animation list.)

Voice effects list: (Match the voice effects list with the animation list.)

Special requirements for player character: (Are any special animations, effects, and so on required to communicate to the player what has happened to the character when affected by an enemy's attack or interaction?)

Player reward: (What does the player get, if anything, for defeating the enemy? Experience? Treasure? Random or specific item?)

Bonus Level 9
Boss Design Template

Boss name: _____

Boss image: (Insert concept or inspirational image here.)

Description: (Write a short description of the boss; what is the boss's personality and motivation?)

List of required animations including:

- Stand

- Idle

- Taunts

- Attacks (melee)

- Attacks (projectile)

- Hit reactions

- Death animations

- Victory animations

Movement patterns: (Add as many as necessary.)

- **Move 1:** (image and description of boss's movement)
- **Move 2:** (image and description of boss's movement)

Attack descriptions: (Add as many as necessary.)

- **Attack 1:** (melee, projectile, special)
- **Attack 2:** (melee, projectile, special)

Boss is defeated by: (How will the player defeat the boss? Does the boss have any weak spots or vulnerable states?)

Damage description: (What does the boss's health bar look like? How is damage communicated to the player? Are any special visual effects required?)

Particle effects: (What visual effects are required for attacks, movement, or damage states?)

Projectiles: (If used, list what projectiles will be needed for attacks.)

HUD elements: (Are any additional HUD elements required for the boss fight, such as icons for QTEs?)

Sound effects list: (Match the sound effects list with the animation list.)

Voice effects list: (Match the voice effects list with the animation list.)

Special requirements for player character: (Are any special animations, effects, and so on required to communicate to the player what has happened to the character when affected by a boss's attack or interaction?)

Player reward: (What does the player get, if anything, for defeating the boss? Experience? Treasure? Random or specific item?)

BOSS FIGHT ARENA

Arena image: (Insert image of environment; could be a concept drawing or map.)

Arena description: (Write a short description of the environment and what action takes place there.)

Level elements: (Are any mechanics, hazards, or props needed for the boss fight?)

Boss fight music tracks: (List music tracks here, including notes on any contextual music.)

High-Concept Pitch Presentation

Slide 1: Title Page

Start with a compelling image and logo that sums up your game.

Put the date of presentation on the PowerPoint slide so the people you present to will remember when the meeting took place.

For author credits, use the studio's name. Remember, no one makes a game by himself.

Include contact information with e-mail address and/or phone number.

Slide 2: Developer Profile

Briefly outline who you are, what you've done, and how long you've been doing it. This is a great place to showcase the covers of any games your studio's created.

Obviously, you can skip creating this slide if you are presenting to your peers.

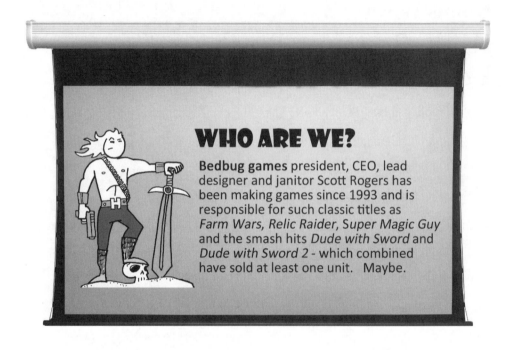

Slide 3: Game Overview

This slide covers the basics of the game. What type of game is it? What is it rated? Who is the audience? How long will it take to play?

Slide 4: Game Story

Who is player character (if applicable)? What is the game's story (if applicable) or genre? What's the conflict? Don't forget a beginning, middle, and end, or at least a cliffhanger that gets the readers/audience interested in knowing the ending. If there is no story, then what is the game's theme?

Slide 5: Game Features

Why should the audience/readers care about your game?

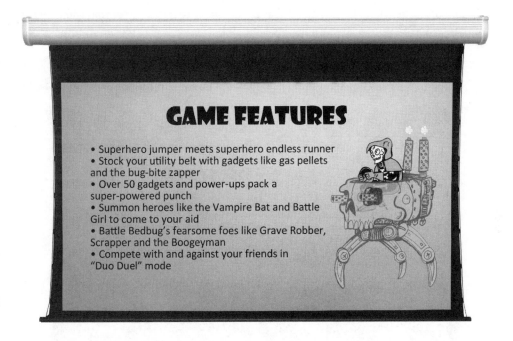

Slide 6: Gameplay Summary

This slide should briefly summarize the gameplay. What is the primary action of gameplay? What is the camera view? How will the play build in challenge during the course of the game? What are the gameplay environments? What are the super-cool features of your game? What are the "hooks" that make this game unique? Mention unique play modes. You may need several slides to cover this topic.

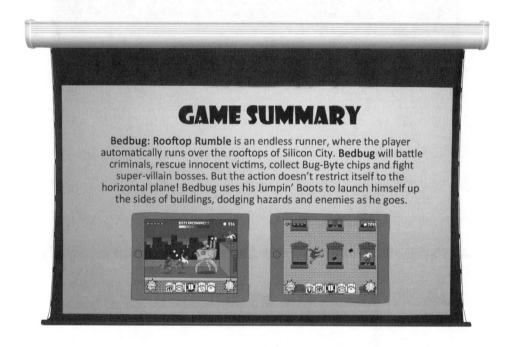

Slide 7: Gameplay Details

Dive into the interesting gameplay details. Your goal here is to describe what is like to play the game. Dedicate specific slides to unique or cool features to highlight how they impact gameplay and add to the experience.

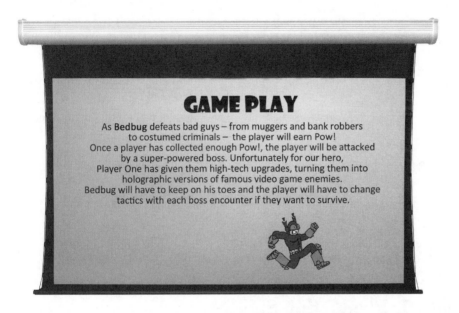

GAME PLAY

As **Bedbug** defeats bad guys – from muggers and bank robbers to costumed criminals – the player will earn Pow! Once a player has collected enough Pow!, the player will be attacked by a super-powered boss. Unfortunately for our hero, Player One has given them high-tech upgrades, turning them into holographic versions of famous video game enemies. Bedbug will have to keep on his toes and the player will have to change tactics with each boss encounter if they want to survive.

GAME PLAY (CONT)

Bedbug isn't without his tricks. Players can either collect Bug-Byte chips or spend real money to buy gadgets for Bedbug's utility belt. Flash pellets temporarily stun enemies. Bug-bite zapper causes more damage. Snacks can restore health. The player can also collect Super-Helper power-ups that summon help from Bedbug's family and fellow superheroes from the **Blue Tiger's** spectral claw attack that clears the screen of enemies to a simple hug from his daughter **Elvira** that restores all of the player's health.

Slide 8: Monetization and Download Strategy

How are you going to extend the life of the game beyond release? What is the monetization model? Give examples of what the player can purchase and how the purchases can impact the game.

Slide 9: Production Specs

Share the production plans here. How large is your development team? How much time will it take to create the game? How much is it going to cost to make the game?

Bonus Level 11

Achievement Unlocked: Exactly Like Making Chili

(FEEDS 6 TO 8)

1 15 oz. Hormel Turkey and Beans chili

1 30 oz. can of black beans

1 28 oz. can of peeled and crushed tomatoes

1 14.5 oz. can of petite crushed tomatoes

¼ cup of extra virgin olive oil

1–2 large green peppers

1 large sweet onion

1 pound ground lean turkey

½ tablespoon of chili powder

½ tablespoon of cumin

½ tablespoon of oregano

½ tablespoon of paprika

½ tablespoon of onion powder

1 teaspoon of cocoa power

1 tablespoon of Lowry's garlic salt

1 tablespoon of lemon juice

cornbread or tortilla chips or corn tortillas (for serving)

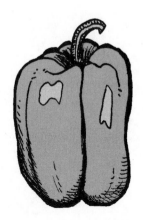

1. Mix together chili powder, cumin, oregano, paprika, onion powder, and cocoa powder in a bowl. This is the chili seasoning mix. Set this aside for later.

2. Open can of black beans. Drain beans of all liquid. Put beans into a crockpot.

3. Open both cans of crushed tomatoes. Add tomatoes into crockpot.

4. Open can of chili. Add that to crockpot and turn the crockpot onto its lowest setting.

5. Slice peppers into strips.

6. Dice onion into pieces.

7. Sauté peppers and onions in a pan using olive oil on high setting. Start with onions and add in peppers. Season with garlic salt and lemon juice. Once pepper/onion mixture has sautéed, add peppers and onions to crockpot (aka slow cooker).

8. Using residual oil from the pan, sauté the turkey. After it has browned, turn down heat to low and add chili spice mixture liberally. Mix. After meat is thoroughly coated, pour off remaining oil and add browned turkey to the crockpot.

9. Cook chili in the crockpot on low for at least 4–6 hours. The longer it simmers, the better it will be.

10. Spoon chili into serving bowls.

11. Chili goes best with cornbread, tortilla chips, or warm corn tortillas on the side. Enjoy!

Index

Acknowledgements: Everything I've Learned About Writing a Second Edition

What I've learned is, just like making games, writing a book is hard work. And it can't be done alone. I couldn't have written the second edition of *Level Up! The Guide to Great Video Game Design* without the help, support, inspiration and love of the following people:

- Brenda Lee Rogers, Evelyn Rogers, Jack Rogers, Noah Stein, David Jaffe, Jeremy Gibson, Jason Weezner, Jackie Kashian, Laddie Ervin, Jeremiah Slackza, Jeff Luke, Andy Ashcraft, Hardy LeBel, Dr. Brett Rogers, Richard Browne, William Anderson, David Siller, Mark Rogers, Eric Williams, George Collins, Scott Frazier, Tommy Tallarico, Joey Kuras, Ian Sedensky, Evan Icenbice, Brian Kaiser, David O'Connor, Jaclyn Rogers, Dr. Christopher Rogers, Patricia Rogers, Anthony Rogers, Aden Goldberg (Number One Fan), the 2008 GDC selection committee, my fellow Imagineers—past and present, Tracy Fullerton and the USC interactive media department, everyone I've had the pleasure working with at Namco, Capcom, Sony, and THQ, Cory Doctorow, my fellow Lair Bears, the editors at John Wiley & Sons: Ellie Scott, Sara Shlaer, Polly Thomas, Juliet Booker, Gareth Haman, Katherine Parrett, Chuck Hutchinson, and most importantly, Chris Webb for making that call back in 2009.

But my biggest thanks go to YOU. If you are a first time reader for this edition, I hope you found this book educational and inspirational. If you already own the first edition, thank you twice! I hope you found the new information worthwhile. Don't forget to try the new chili recipe!

Now go out and design some great games! I can't wait to play them!

About the Author

After discovering that game designers have more fun, **Scott Rogers** embarked on a 20-year (and counting) career as a video game designer, author, educator, and cartoonist.

He has helped design many awesome and successful video games that you might have played, including *Pac-Man World,* the *Maximo* series, *God of War,* the *Drawn to Life* series, and *Darksiders*. In addition to the first edition of this book, Scott wrote *Swipe This! The Guide to Great Touchscreen Game Design* and is the creator of the superhero comic book *Bedbug*. Scott is an adjunct professor for USC's prestigious School of Interactive Media and when he's not doing all that other stuff, he creates happiness for guests around the world as a Principal Imagineer for Walt Disney Imagineering.

Scott lives just outside Los Angeles with his wife, two game-obsessed children, and more action figures, comic books, and games than he has time to play with.

Why not visit him on-line at http://www.mrbossdesign.com or follow him on Twitter at @mightybedbug.